Shaw Shadows

The Florida Bernard Shaw Series

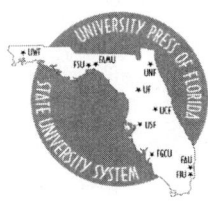

Florida A&M University, Tallahassee
Florida Atlantic University, Boca Raton
Florida Gulf Coast University, Ft. Myers
Florida International University, Miami
Florida State University, Tallahassee
University of Central Florida, Orlando
University of Florida, Gainesville
University of North Florida, Jacksonville
University of South Florida, Tampa
University of West Florida, Pensacola

Shaw
Shadows

Rereading the Texts of Bernard Shaw

Peter Gahan

University Press of Florida
Gainesville
Tallahassee
Tampa
Boca Raton
Pensacola
Orlando
Miami
Jacksonville
Ft. Myers

Copyright 2004 by Peter Gahan
Printed in the United States of America on recycled, acid-free paper
All rights reserved

09 08 07 06 05 04   6 5 4 3 2 1

A record of cataloging-in-publication data is available from the Library of Congress.
ISBN 0-8130-2769-1

The University Press of Florida is the scholarly publishing agency for the State University System of Florida, comprising Florida A&M University, Florida Atlantic University, Florida Gulf Coast University, Florida International University, Florida State University, University of Central Florida, University of Florida, University of North Florida, University of South Florida, and University of West Florida.

University Press of Florida
15 Northwest 15th Street
Gainesville, FL 32611-2079
http://www.upf.com

To John and Mary Gahan

THESEUS: *The best in this kind are but shadows; and the worst are no worse, if imagination amend them.*

William Shakespeare, *A Midsummer Night's Dream*, V.i

The old formula of two trestles, four boards and a passion still holds, and will hold until we grow out of playgoing altogether, provided the passion be passionate enough; for the best in this sort are but shadows, and the worst no worse if imagination mend them.

Bernard Shaw, "Wanted: A New Sort of Theater for an Old Sort of Play" (1923)

Man that is born of a woman is of a few days, and full of trouble. He cometh forth like a flower, and is cut down: he fleeth also as a shadow, and continueth not.

Job (14:1)

Take from the activity of mankind that part of it which consists in the pursuit of illusions, and you take out the world's mainspring. Do not suppose either, that the pursuit of illusions is the vain pursuit of nothing: on the contrary, there can no more be an illusion without a reality than a shadow without an object.

Bernard Shaw, "The Illusions of Socialism" (1896)

Contents

Foreword by R. F. Dietrich xi
Preface xiii
Acknowledgments xix
List of Abbreviations xxiii

I. Reading Shaw

1. Reading Writing: Going Behind the Scenes of the Text 3
2. The Critic: The Writer's Shadow 38
3. Authorial Identity: Promethean Strategies of a Pantomime Ostrich 59
4. The Spoken/Written Subject: The Machine in the Ghost 91

II. Reading the Plays

5. A Writing Machine (*Man of Destiny, How He Lied, Village Wooing*) 135
6. The Playwright and the Critics (*The Philanderer, Fanny's First Play*) 157
7. Mystery and Ritual: Theater and Textuality (*Candida, Getting Married*) 189
8. The Image and the Word (*Back to Methuselah*) 228

Post Scriptum 264

Notes 269
Bibliography 291
Index 309

Foreword

About once a decade a book comes along in Shaw Studies that tackles the whole subject of Shaw in such a fresh and comprehensive way that it invites the epithet "seminal," for it clearly intends to generate discussion to the end of significantly shifting critical perspectives. Peter Gahan's *Shaw Shadows* has a chance, I think, of being such a seminal work.

It's partly that Shaw is overdue for this sort of comprehensive application of poststructuralist critical theory, precedents being few and more limited in their scope. The mystery is that it has taken so long for this to happen, for Shaw was trying out poststructuralist moves long before Derrida, and you'd think the theorists would have noticed by now. The mystery can be accounted for, in part, by the fact that Shaw's typically strategic, polemical, overstated lingo, aimed at Victorian-Edwardian-Georgian audiences accustomed to logocentric speech and writing, often gave no clue to poststructuralist intimations or sometimes even suggested the opposite. Note how often Shaw began sentences with "The truth is . . ." as though Truth really was Something Incarnate for him. But attention to what follows in each case makes it clear that he was well aware that "the truth" he spoke of was for that sentence and that moment, subject to the contingencies of both language and life. So he has to be "translated." Trained in philosophy at Trinity University in Dublin and widely read in critical theory, Peter Gahan expertly provides that translation, explaining the process as he goes while keeping the jargon to a minimum.

Gahan helps us see that Shaw's view of the world was as radically different as he said it was, part of which was in his understanding that, as his Don Juan says, words can be turned inside out like a glove at will, and one of the most fascinating aspects of his works is how they reveal his constant struggle with the constraining language of his day to express his difference and to turn the glove of logocentric language inside out. His difficulty, Gahan points out, was similar to that attendant upon Derrida's acknowledgment that deconstruction needs a Platonic metaphysics to work upon, which sometimes leads to confusion because of the constant juxtaposing of a language and its antidote, as one can't do without the other. Shaw's linguistic predicament was even greater. He played off against the same essentialist and absolutist Platonism Derrida did, but had to make do with a language that often disguised the fact or even misled.

And of course while this was partly just the fault of an inherent inadequacy in the language inherited, this was also due to Shaw's insistence on involving himself in the politics of the day and writing polemically on behalf of causes, for this suggests commitment to a closed system. Political language, like religious language, is notoriously the vehicle of the closed mind, at the mercy of prepackaged language. But while Shaw thought that there were indeed times when one needed to close the mind in order to act, he more customarily worked to open the idealist mind of the Western world to possibilities and potentials as well as problematics. Clear examples are provided in that very model of self-deconstruction, "The Illusions of Socialism," and in the dismantling of "Ibsenism" as a program in *The Quintessence of Ibsenism*. Shaw said that "the quintessence of Ibsenism is that there is no quintessence," which was later echoed in "The golden rule is that there are no golden rules" of *The Revolutionist's Handbook*, either one of which could be used as the motto for poststructuralism. On the other hand, as one by one Shaw settled the hash of all the "isms" of his day, he perhaps also showed us a way to be knowing enough about the futility of "isms" without succumbing to futility itself. That is, Shaw thought it was okay to be a socialist (or whatever), if one went in with eyes wide open.

About half of Gahan's book engages the matter of Shaw's poststructuralist pioneering in a general, philosophical way; the other half devotes itself to critical readings of mostly "marginalized" works that reveal, in their self-reflexivity, the writer's awareness of the subjectivity of human experience in general and the writer's in particular, and the need for openness in living life and writing about it. Gahan's reminder that "poststructuralism often finds peripheral writings more symptomatic than major or better-known works" applies well to Shaw. It's the potboilers and minor pieces and generally ignored pieces that tell the story. And Peter Gahan has put it all together in a very convincing demonstration of Shaw's continuing relevance.

R. F. Dietrich
October 15, 2003

Preface

Shaw Shadows is about reading the writing of Bernard Shaw. The book offers one approach, without being prescriptive, to reading or rereading Shaw, to reading the different types of writing and plays of Bernard Shaw, referred to here as the Shaw text, and which may also include texts with Shaw as their subject. The following paraphrase from Stephen Jenkins's introduction to *Fritz Lang: The Image and the Look* offers a preliminary statement of this approach (only substituting, where appropriate, Shaw and his context as playwright): What is signified here by the name [Shaw]? While it is obviously not biography, neither is it [Shaw] the structure named after him, since this implies such a structure exists, as something to be grasped. [Shaw] here is a space where a multiplicity of discourses intersect, an unstable, shifting configuration of discourses produced by the interaction of a specific group of [plays and disparate writings with the signature "Shaw," as well as biographical and critical texts associated with the name Shaw] with particular, historically and socially locatable ways of reading/viewing those [writings](Jenkins, *Fritz Lang*, 7).

This book seeks to supplement this mutable, shifting space called Shaw, where discourses and texts intersect and where different shadows are cast by different lights, with the introduction of the discourse of poststructuralism.[1] The use of shadows in this study becomes clearer in chapter 1, but here it may suggest both how his texts can be read as his shadows, Shaw shadows, and how what we call Shaw (itself a SHAdoW of the word shadow) can be read as a continually shifting shadow or series of shadows cast by his texts. This preface, therefore, offers a few markers for the journey ahead.

This book is structurally divided into two parts of four chapters each (eight in all), primarily to distinguish the literary criticism of selected critically neglected plays in part 2 from the general discussion of approaches to Shaw's writing in part 1. Because of the predominance of the dramatic writing within the Shaw text after 1900, the plays deserve a part to themselves. However, the poststructuralist theoretical background—primarily elaborated in part 1—informs both parts, with the themes raised in part 1 reappearing in the discussions of the plays in part 2. Indeed, each chapter reflects its equivalent in the other part. Thus the book adopts a simple shadow patterning with each part a shadow of the other, and each chapter a shadow of the respective chapter in the other part. Part 1 outlines a more philosophical approach to reading different types of Shaw's writing against a theoretical background of poststructuralism in terms of language, meaning, textuality, writing, and subjectivity. Poststructuralism, which extended the critique of reason initiated by Kant in the eighteenth century, is taken here selectively to mean certain key texts of Jacques Lacan, Roland Barthes, Jacques Derrida, and a few others.

Although the book does not seek to engage in the controversy of critical theory, the challenge is to show Shaw to be a suitable candidate for such theoretical consideration. It does not propose that Derrida and others are right and their critics wrong; but neither does it acquiesce to the proposition that poststructuralism has become irrelevant following the possibly premature declaration of "the end of history." Rather the argument presented here stresses what is common between Shaw and these writers in respect of their critiques of modern discourses of knowledge, as well as in their understanding of subjectivity. Thus a consideration (rather than an inquiry) of poststructuralism is presented as a useful (insofar as it facilitates an understanding of certain problems encountered in earlier readings of Shaw), but by no means sole or correct way, of (re)reading Shaw, whose writings from the essays of the 1890s onward offer a consistent critique of rationalism.

A major problem in reading Shaw has been how to come to a theoretical understanding of his philosophy of the Life Force and Creative Evolution. Rather than as a system or structure confined to the discourses of biology and religion that have been the subject of previous inquiries, the Shaw text is resituated here as a problematic of writing, language, and meaning. This approach may contribute to reappraising the still underappreciated parable of Creative Evolution, the five-part play-cycle *Back to Methuselah* (1921), which Shaw himself referred to as his *magnum opus*.[2] However, a difficulty for any poststructuralist reading of Shaw is the implicit—and sometimes explicit—Platonism (or even neo-Platonism) in both *Methuselah* and the Life Force play, *Man and Superman* (1903).[3] This study suggests that such Platonism coexists alongside the critical iconoclasm so characteristic of the Shaw text, much as deconstruction, according to Derrida himself, has to take place as a discourse within a language of Platonic metaphysics. A related difficulty is Shaw's demand for a discourse of metaphysics that appears antithetical to poststructuralism's antagonism to any metaphysics associated with the Western tradition of Plato's Logos. But unlike Plato and like Derrida, Shaw does not subscribe to the metaphysics of truth. Shaw's metaphysics resulted from a specific vision, informed by the limitations of language and reason, of what it is to be human ("human, all too human," as Nietzsche said, not without a touch of irony). Shaw never ascribed to abstract reason (feelings produce thinking, not the reverse, he declared) nor to essentialist notions of the human—a large part of his writing is a critique of so-called liberal humanism. The humanism of the Shaw text is much closer to, say, Heidegger's existential inquiry into *Dasein* in *Being and Time*—human existence as derived from a phenomenology or hermeneutics of historically existing selves.

These questions are broached in chapter 1 as a general introduction to aspects of poststructuralism with their possible relevance to Shaw and enlarged upon in the shadow chapters 4 and 8, the final chapters in parts 1 and 2, respectively. Chapter 2 considers Shaw's critical writing as the drama of the creation of the subjectivity of the critic and its relation to his writing in general, and chapter 3 examines the implications of authorial subjectivity in the context of his autobiographical writing. In the light of Shaw's powerful critique of modern science as writing, especially biology, chapter 4 follows threads from that discourse to connect thematically a chain of disparate texts starting from *The Infidel Half Century* (the preface to *Methuselah*), through Freud's *Beyond the Pleasure Principle* to key texts of Lacan and Derrida, in order to show that a poststructuralist understanding of language and writing in relation to the Shaw text can rework the old Cartesian problem of dualism and the even older conflict between materialism and metaphysics. Although part 1 is not specifically concerned with the play-texts, certain aspects of plays are discussed: textuality and intertextuality in *Man and Superman* in chapter 1, and threads of autobiography in his Irish play, *John Bull's Other Island* (1904), which is perhaps the most critically ignored of the major plays, in chapter 3.

Chapter 5, like chapter 1, serves an introductory purpose, in this case to part 2's consideration of dramatic texts. It discusses three short plays, in which the thematic of writing and language plays a major role: *The Man of Destiny* (1895), *How He Lied to Her Husband* (1904), and *Village Wooing*

(1933). Chapter 6 examines two works as shadows of chapter 2 and its subject of critical writing: the critically neglected second play, *The Philanderer* (1893), which foregrounds the theme of criticism in a theatrical context, and *Fanny's First Play* (1911) with its frame play as a satire of contemporary critics. Chapter 7, shadowing the autobiographical concerns of chapter 3, takes as its subject two plays that powerfully figure his subjectivity as playwright in self-reflexively theatrical and textual terms of mythology and ritual: *Candida* (1894)—one of the most commented upon—and *Getting Married* (1908)—one of the least commented upon in the canon. Finally, chapter 8, transposing the biological, psychological, and grammatological concerns of chapter 4 to that of dramatic poetry, concentrates on Shaw's flexible understanding of imagination in the play-cycle *Back to Methuselah*, in particular the relation between Image and Word corresponding to Lacan's distinction between the Imaginary and the Symbolic.[4] These play-texts, for the most part underrepresented in Shaw criticism up to now, are discussed here for reasons both practical (a desire not to retread previous criticism) and theoretical (poststructuralism often finds peripheral writings more symptomatic than major or better-known works). Even so, this study cannot extend its reach to a much needed reappraisal of the extraordinary group of late plays Shaw wrote between finishing *Back to Methuselah* in 1921—when he was already in his mid-sixties—and the early 1940s, but for which it may nevertheless supply some groundwork.

Is Shaw more susceptible to this theoretical treatment than, say, such Edwardian contemporaries as Rudyard Kipling, Thomas Hardy, John Galsworthy, Joseph Conrad, or H. G. Wells? The question, of course, begs another as to why some twentieth-century writers like James Joyce, Antonin Artaud, Bertolt Brecht, and Samuel Beckett might seem more suitable as cases for poststructuralist consideration than others. Of course, while any writing is susceptible to a poststructuralist reading, a discussion of the novels of Wells, for example, in the context of poststructuralism may be difficult to imagine. This study proposes that the Shaw text is a rare open text that may be read as both very much of its time and place and out of it. The writer-critic Shaw and the artist-writer Shaw are almost always writing together, each a shadow of the other, which results in an insistent critique of the times to ensure the Shaw text never exemplifies a writing of either logocentric or ideological subjectivity. And its equally insistent refusal to be confined to a single way of viewing or interpreting the world or reality allows it to emerge beyond its own time more strongly than others.

Three related points might be quickly made. First, perhaps because of a self-declared didacticism and his well-advertised political activities, the strength of that quality in Shaw that Keats deemed necessary in a poet—"negative capability"—has generally gone unappreciated outside a tradition of fine Shaw scholarship. Shaw's most revealing statement on himself as a writer in a letter to Frank Harris of June 20, 1930, describes this as a negation of subjectivity: "I understand everything and everyone, and am nobody and nothing" (*Letters 4*, 189). An exemplary, sensitive, sympathetic, and generous intelligence in respect of people and their predicaments, an understanding that subjectivity only arises in language and in relation to others (intersubjectivity, as Lacan—borrowing from Hegel—calls it), is a required quality in a playwright and can be read both in his drama and in his writing in general. Second, in a letter to Wells Shaw distinguished between their methods of writing: "Classical literature is made up nine-tenths of allusions" (*Shaw-Wells*, 117). Shaw claimed that his writing exemplified this reliance on allusion, whereas Wells's did not. This allusiveness between texts (whether conscious or not), this writing as rewriting, is called intertextuality in poststructuralism—a quality that not only distinguishes the Shaw text from those of contemporaries like Wells but also associates his writing more with modernists like Joyce. Indeed Black's *Shaw and Joyce: The Last Word in Stolentelling* has suggested that Shaw served as a model or paradigm for Joyce in this respect. *Shaw Shadows*, chapter 7 especially, attempts to trace various strands of this all-pervasive intertextuality in the Shaw text. Finally, Shaw knowingly questions any understanding of subjectivity as a coherent unity, quite unlike that in the writing of his contemporaries. That subjectivity, language, reading, and writing are mutable if interdependent constitutes a major thematic of poststructuralism, a point reiterated throughout this book, and this may explain how this study on Bernard Shaw becomes a space where literary criticism intersects with theory and philosophy.

The modernity of the Shaw text is stressed as a counterpoise to (rather than a denial of) the sometimes argued view of Shaw as the last of the great Victorians. That the powerful radical force of the Shaw text on intellectual cultural discourse, so obvious to his contemporaries, has diminished might be accounted for by a certain cultural amnesia during the fifty years after his death and the more than one hundred since he became a public participant in that discourse. This book is written in the hope of jogging the collective memory, for those who forget history condemn us all to repeat it. The ideology of the present age seems to have reverted to that of the late nineteenth-century Western imperial powers, which, as Shaw never tired of reminding us, ended in the catastrophe of World War I and the consequent World War II. No body of writing deconstructed that ideology as effectively as the Shaw text, while at the same time laying a textual foundation for the social reconstruction of Western society that lasted for about thirty-five years after 1945. In retrospect, that period seems to have been a Golden Age.

Shaw, the Socrates-Aristophanes or Rousseau-Voltaire of his era, lamented in old age that he was "stuck all over with labels like a tourist's trunk" (*Prefaces*, 908). *Shaw Shadows* now proposes to paste the label of poststructuralism onto the Shaw trunk, with a qualification restricting its validity to this particular journey. Thereafter it becomes one among many old labels; it does not substitute for the others. To *identify* the Shaw text with poststructuralism or to contend that it offers the only possible basis for a reading, a poststructuralist would argue, would be a severe case of logocentrism requiring urgent deconstruction. Shaw, a hater of all -isms, would have agreed. Given that understanding, we can embark on our voyage with our newly labeled old trunk, Shaw.

Acknowledgments

I would like to thank particularly those who have read this work, or parts of it (even parts that may have fallen by the wayside), in manuscript. These include Richard Dietrich, to whom I express gratitude for his general prodding to undertake the manuscript and his subsequent encouragement and patience while it was being delivered, Sidney Albert, Joanne Carrol, Olga Cox, John O'Flynn, Jean Reynolds, and most of all, Sibylle Ferner, who has read the several drafts many times and has helped refine its syntax and punctuation into some sort of orthographic orthodoxy. I would also like to express my thanks to the various editors of the SHAW journal, which has published my articles, two of which have formed the basis for chapters in this book, and to the Penn State University Press for their permission to republish them here in their modified form. These include the late Fred Crawford, and again I would like to record with thanks his persistent and enthusiastic encouragement in publishing my first two articles, Gale Larson, Milton Wolf, and Michel Pharand. Gratitude is also owed to the Bernard Shaw International Summer School, organized by Frank Brennan of the Dublin Institute of Technology, held three times in the 1990s, which offered me the occasion in several papers to develop some of the ideas expressed in this volume, as well as to the Shaw Seminar organized by Marquette University, Milwaukee, in 2001. Other Shaw scholars throughout the years have been invariably friendly and helpful and these include, in addition to the above mentioned, A. K. Bhatt, T. F. Evans, Charles Berst, John Bertolini, Nicholas Greene, Michael Holroyd, Dan H. Laurence, Margery Morgan, the late John O'Donovan, Sally Peters, Éibhear Walshe, John Wardrop, and anonymous readers of both this manuscript and other articles. To Colin Wilson's plea for a rereading of Shaw in the last page of his book, *The Outsider* (1956), I duly acknowledge this study as one such attempt. Last in this context but not least, I would like to thank the producers, directors, and actors who have staged some of the wonderful productions of Shaw plays I have seen over the years in Dublin (including such legends there as Siobhán McKenna, Cyril Cusack, Christopher Casson, Micheál Mac Liamóir, and Hilton Edwards), London, Niagara-on-the-Lake, New York, Milwaukee, and southern California. I single out one—John Schlesinger's 1975 production of *Heartbreak House* at the National Theatre in the Old Vic—because it demonstrated for the first time to a somewhat younger incarnation of the present writer the full power of a Shaw play in the theater. I can still hear the extraordinary *crescendo* of the wail from the late Colin Blakely as Captain Shotover toward the end of Act I. I have never heard that wail—and this should be a lesson to producers to take note of Shaw's stage directions—in the many subsequent productions I have seen since, although the text specifies that Shotover raise "*a strange wail in the darkness*" (*Plays*, 774).

As stated in the text itself, the strand of Shaw scholarship to which this study stands most indebted includes the work of Eric Bentley, Martin Meisel, Margery Morgan, and John Bertolini. Especially must I acknowledge Morgan's *The Shavian Playground*, the first critical study to open up for this reader the textual complexities in Shaw's writing. I am also indebted to the critical works of Elsie Adams, Charles Berst, Martha Black, Charles Carpenter, Louis Crompton, Richard Dietrich, Bernard Dukore, Daniel Leary, Margot Peters, Sally Peters, Valli Rao, Arnold Silver, Maurice Valency, Barbara Bellow Watson, Rodelle Weintraub, Jonathan Wisenthal, and especially to the gargantuan editorial and other labors of Dan H. Laurence and Stanley Weintraub. I also acknowledge having read with profit other and more recent works on Shaw.

In disparate non-Shaw areas, I should acknowledge the work of scholars whose high standard of writing offered models I could only aspire to. These include Noel Bürch's study of Japanese cinema, *To the Distant Observer*, Carole Fabricant's study of Jonathan Swift, *Swift's Landscape*, Christian Metz's Lacanian study of cinema, *The Imaginary Signifier*, and the Irish cultural journal, *The Crane Bag*, edited by Mark Patrick Hederman and Richard Kearney. I also thank Rik Loose of the Centre for Psychoanalytic Studies at LSB/DBS College, Dublin, and Felicity Casserly of the Institute of Psychoanalytical Psychotherapy, Dublin, both of whom invited me to deliver courses on psychoanalysis and cinema, which allowed me to explore strands of poststructuralism before embarking on this work. For prompting my initial interest in poststructuralism generally I thank Malachy Higgins of the Dublin Institute of Technology.

I also express my gratitude to the translators of and commentators on the writings of the French poststructuralists, who are duly cited in the text, as well as to the writers themselves.

At the University Press of Florida, I gratefully acknowledge the ready guidance and professional efficiency of my editors, Amy Gorelick, Lisa Jerry, and Susan Albury.

Needless to write, to none of the above-mentioned writers should the views expressed in this work be attributed, for which this writer assumes all due responsibility.

For permission to quote from the works of Bernard Shaw, I would like to thank The Society of Authors, on behalf of the Bernard Shaw Estate. To the University of Chicago Press and to Routledge and Kegan Paul, I acknowledge with gratitude their permission to quote from Jacques Derrida's *Writing and Difference*, translated by Alan Bass, © 1978 by The University of Chicago.

Finally, I thank my parents, family, and friends for all their support and encouragement. And I remember with gratitude the late Muriel Gahan, an indefatigable Irish world-betterer in the mold of both her kinswoman Charlotte Shaw and Bernard Shaw, who quoted to me at an impressionable age the line from *Back to Methuselah*: "Imagination is the beginning of creation." It was the seed from which this study grew.

Abbreviations

All citations are noted parenthetically in the main body of the text. In the case of Shaw's works, his name is omitted; all other references include the name, short form of the title, and page numbers. Full information on all works cited is found in the bibliography.

The following are the most common abbreviations for works by Shaw used in the text.

Agitations	*Agitations: Letters to the Press (1875–1950)*
Autobiography 1	Shaw: *An Autobiography 1856–1898*
Autobiography 2	Shaw: *An Autobiography 1898–1950*
Books 1	*Bernard Shaw's Book Reviews—in The Pall Mall Gazette 1885–1888*
Books 2	*Bernard Shaw's Book Reviews: Vol. 2 1884–1950*
Diaries 1	*Bernard Shaw: The Diaries 1885–1897, Volume 1*
Diaries 2	*Bernard Shaw: The Diaries 1885–1897, Volume 2.*
Drama 1	*Bernard Shaw: The Drama Observed Vol. I 1880–1895.*
Drama 2	*Bernard Shaw: The Drama Observed Volume II 1895–1897.*
Drama 3	*Bernard Shaw: The Drama Observed Volume III 1897–1911.*
Drama 4	*Bernard Shaw: The Drama Observed Volume IV 1911–1950.*
Letters 1	*Collected Letters: 1874–1897.*
Letters 2	*Collected Letters: 1898–1910.*
Letters 3	*Collected Letters: 1911–1925 Vol. 3.*
Letters 4	*Collected Letters: 1926–1950 Vol. 4.*
Music 1	*Shaw's Music: Complete Musical Criticism Vol. 1 1876–1890.*
Music 2	*Shaw's Music: Complete Musical Criticism Vol. 2 1890–1893.*

Music 3	*Shaw's Music: Complete Musical Criticism Vol. 3 1893–1950.*
Non-Dramatic	*Selected Non-Dramatic Writings of Bernard Shaw* (1965).
Plays	*The Complete Plays of Bernard Shaw* (1965).
Plays 1–7	*Collected Plays with Their Prefaces* (7 volumes) (1970–1974).
Pleasant	*Plays Pleasant and Unpleasant* (1898).
Prefaces	*The Complete Prefaces of Bernard Shaw* (1965).
Shaw-Trebitsch	*Bernard Shaw's Letters to Siegfried Trebitsch.*
Shaw-Gregory	*Shaw, Lady Gregory and the Abbey: Correspondence.*
Shaw-Wells	*Bernard Shaw and H. G. Wells: Correspondence.*
SHAW 1–24	*SHAW: The Annual of Bernard Shaw Studies,* Volumes One to Twenty-Four.

PART I

Reading Shaw

The ego is an absolutely fundamental form for the constitution of objects. In particular, it perceives what we call, for structural reasons, its fellow being, in the form of the specular other. . . .

So there's the plane of the mirror, the symmetrical world of the egos and of the homogeneous others. We'll have to distinguish another level, which we call the wall of language. . . .

We would have no reason to think [that authentically intersubjective relations exist without] . . . the characterizing feature of intersubjectivity [which is] that the subject can lie to us. . . We in fact address. . . those we do not know, true Others, true subjects.

They are on the other side of the wall of language, there where in principle I never reach them. . . I always have to aim at true subjects, and I have to be content with shadows.

Jacques Lacan from *Seminar II* (1954–1955)

1 Reading Writing

Going Behind the Scenes of the Text

> *Nothing is more significant than the statement that "all the world's a stage." The whole world is ruled by theatrical illusion. . . . The great critics are those who penetrate, and understand the illusion: the great men are those who, as dramatists planning the development of nations, or as actors carrying out the drama, are behind the scenes of the world. . . . Even the great metaphor itself is inaccurately expressed; for the world is a playhouse, not merely a stage.*
>
> Bernard Shaw in "Toujours Shakespear" (December 5, 1896)

Introduction

Let us begin by remembering that myth of shadows, Plato's metaphor of the cave in *Republic* Book vii, which itself casts a looming shadow over the Western intellectual tradition. Men in Plato's cave are trapped, as if in a cinema, watching shadows of manipulated puppets and models of animals thrown on the cave wall by a fire from behind them. These shadows of simulacra are the source for all their knowledge and thus constitute their reality. Even if they could turn their heads round to try and understand the mechanics of the show, they would not come to a knowledge of true reality as the world of real things lies visible outside the cave, where the source of light is not a fire, but the sun itself. Occasionally someone—Plato's philosopher—escapes to this outside world and then returns to the cave of shadows to tell of his knowledge of this real world outside, but he has the greatest difficulty in trying to explain this reality to those who have never experienced it.

Shadows, reflections, and images are all presented in Plato's myth as metaphors of vision and light for how we apprehend reality. But the metaphor of shadows has been used in other ways to give or enhance a visual illusion of reality in Western representational art. We see depth in three dimensions primarily because of binocular vision, which is impossible to depict in two dimensions. Our perception of reality in a two-dimensional representation results from the scholars of *quattrocento* Renaissance Italy; they conventionalized highly theoretical and mathematical rules of monocular perspective. For instance, the perspective resulting from a system of optics allows us to say that a photograph—a modern mechanical product involving chemical shading, sometimes colored, printed on paper—is real. Likewise a film projecting a series of colored shadows on a theater wall-screen is taken to be real or realistic, as is its fictional narrative. As a conventionalized form of visual representation (leaving aside the aural and narrative elements), perspective mimics the already conventionalized forms of our knowledge of reality, as proposed, say, by Kant for our *a priori* understanding of time and space. The structuralist Marxist Louis Althusser might ascribe such visual representations or illusions of reality to an ideology of realism, particularly as manifest in such a rigidly codified narrative form as the Hollywood film. The poststructuralist psychoanalyst Jacques Lacan might suggest that the relation between reality and representation is problematic, rather than a simple visual correspondence. Reality, as usually understood, he calls the Imaginary and he suggests that our knowledge can be derived only from exploring the by-ways of the Unconscious, the Symbolic, which, he insists, is structured like language. Jacques Derrida might call an uncritical concept of reality logocentric and insist that any concept of reality is derived from representations, particularly from writing, rather than representations as being derived from such a putative reality.

Beyond the monocular perspective that Renaissance intellectuals discovered as a way of representing three-dimensional space in two dimensions lies a supplementary technique for the conventional representation of three-dimensional space: the use of shadows and shading, the techniques of *chiaroscuro* (based on contrasts of light and dark), a concept extending beyond the visual arts to that of Baroque music in the seventeenth and eighteenth centuries, and of *sfumato*, a type of color shading to suggest depth associated with the theoretical and practical studies on the diffusion of light by Leonardo, who avoided the direct depiction of shadows. Shadows and shade, therefore, are not so much mistaken for reality, as in Plato's cave; rather, they supplement the constitution of a conventionalized, albeit highly theorized, illusion of reality.

This study uses the word *shadow* and related visual metaphors of light, such as *reflection* and *image*, as markers to draw attention to their functioning as metaphors in language; for example, consider the common phrases "to think clearly" or "the light of reason." This is not to suggest that a metaphor of shadows may be applied systematically or consistently to a reading of the writing of Bernard Shaw. Here the uncertain ontological status of shadows along with their potency historically as metaphor for the construction of reality underlines this uncertain relation between logic and language, if either is considered independently. Any phrase inflected (or even infected) by metaphors of vision and shadow needs deconstruction, as Derrida would contend, although the language of metaphor and metaphysics cannot be escaped. Shaw's *The Tragedy of an Elderly Gentleman* (the fourth play of the *Back to Methuselah* cycle) critiques the use of metaphor in language, yet the longlivers, who would eschew metaphorical language, cannot escape it. Derrida pointed out that, while some may argue that metaphoricity is made possible by logic, the logic of identity implicit in the verb "to be" (that is, "*a* is *b*"), the reverse might be equally asserted: logic is made possible by the metaphorical attributes of language.

A third resonance of shadows beyond Plato's cave and the conventions of visual representation lies in writing. The title of this study plays on the linguistic coincidence that in the semiphonetic Roman alphabet generally used for writing in English, the word *Shaw* is a shadow of the word *shadow* (this is not the case in a strictly phonetic alphabet, such as proposed famously in Shaw's will). Thus, light and shadow as metaphors for both knowledge and apprehension of an Imaginary reality (as suggested by Jacques Lacan) become shaded by the thematic of language (Lacan's Symbolic) and especially by writing as a human manual activity of inscribing shadows, tracings of black ink marked on white paper, as signs. The ontological, epistemological, and grammatological systems deriving from (or in opposition to) disparate metaphors of light and shade are not homologous. Thus arise troubling relations between different systems of knowing and representing the world: for Plato, between those of appearance and reality; for Bernard Shaw, between Idealism and Realism; for Jacques Lacan, between the Imaginary and the Symbolic (language); for Louis Althusser, between ideology and science (historical materialism); for Roland Barthes, between the image-repertoire and reading; for Jacques Derrida, between logocentrism (the 2,500-year-old tradition of Western metaphysics derived from Plato's metaphor of light and shadow) and grammatology, his proposed new science of writing.

Here these writers offer perspectives useful in considering Bernard

Shaw's writing: Does it pertain to the old metaphysics of Plato's *logos*, or does it open itself (or may even have opened the way) toward a new metaphysics, to those new human sciences associated with the structuralists and poststructuralists that end with the antimetaphysics of Derrida's grammatology? Is the incessant quest for meaning in the Shaw text compatible with poststructuralism? Can an understanding of poststructuralism contribute to an understanding of shadow's shadow, Shaw? This book attempts a reading that extracts meaning by throwing the light of poststructuralism—to resort to a metaphor of light and shade (we cannot escape them)—on the object Shaw. It offers a new reading of Shaw's writing as a series of rereadings of disparate Shaw shadows or texts—in terms of both the history of ideas in part 1 and as some of the less critiqued plays in part 2. To introduce these readings, this chapter offers three procedures: outline a general description of the object Shaw, the status of the Shaw text, and a possible approach to both; discuss aspects of reading and writing, of language and meaning, associated with some poststructuralist writers; and, finally, suggest that the approach of these writers to the problem of subjectivity as fractured, as nonunitary, is compatible with Shaw's own understanding of subjectivity, which thereby facilitates the project of reading Shaw's writing.

Legibility

The problematic addressed here is that of legibility, of how to read the Shaw text. For Shaw, the relation between the writer and the world is literally theatrical. He adopted Shakespeare's metaphor of the world as stage:

> Nothing is more significant than the statement that "all the world's a stage." The whole world *is* ruled by theatrical illusion . . . . The great critics are those who penetrate, and understand the illusion: the great men are those who, as dramatists planning the development of nations, or as actors carrying out the drama, are behind the scenes of the world. . . . Even the great metaphor is inaccurately expressed; for the world is a playhouse, not merely a stage. (*Drama 2*, 714)

The reader needs to go behind the scenes of the text, as it were, in order to engage with it, to inspect what is happening in the rest of the playhouse, rather than simply focus on the subjective illusion of the stage. This problem of legibility is partly one of visibility: to see both what is there and what is not. Different strands must be traced in a text other than those immediately visible or present, and a piece of writing by Shaw can often comprise different writings for different sets of addressees or readers.

Shaw was writing in a popular medium, bourgeois comedy, for both connoisseurs and the general public. Shaw's popularity as a playwright, his eventual success with his bourgeois audience, has actually hindered what might be called a multilectical approach to the Shaw text, where any one text can yield several different readings. The possibility of such a variety of readings might have been expected from his widely reported high intellect, broad range of interests, depth of background knowledge in the subjects he wrote about, as well as his fame as a critic. Puzzling as it seems, the connoisseurs, the literary *cognoscenti*, have generally proven themselves resistant in their reading of the Shaw play-texts, where they see bourgeois comedy and little else. Shaw dramatized this failure of reading by a cultural elite in *Heartbreak House* (1916). Surely the tragedy of that play is that its characters, those very representatives of high culture who could have read in a multilectical way the signs of their own culture's demise, the proverbial writing on the wall leading up to the Great War, failed to do precisely that? That failure still provokes a peculiar *frisson* or *Schadenfreude* in the cultured bourgeois audience of Shaw's theater.

Shaw's wit is universally acknowledged, yet there persists a suspicion that his art and his understanding of it was for the most part superficial. Only *Saint Joan* (for its subject matter) and, possibly, *Heartbreak House* (as a pale and not entirely successful imitation of Chekhov) now seem to suggest the metaphorical depths to Shaw in the general consciousness of more enlightened readers. The case of Shaw is not unique. The Goethe text, within European culture, is similarly ignored, yet no one suggests the cultural irrelevancy of Goethe. Shaw as the *philosophe* of the quotidian, like Voltaire to whom he is often compared, might have become historically irrelevant, but this book contends that there is more to Shaw than an iconoclastic intellectual wit attuned to the foibles of his contemporaries. This study proposes how the Shaw text as a *Weltanschauung* aligns with the writings of French poststructuralists on such subjects as textuality, reading, writing, and subjectivity in either its Imaginary or ideological relations to the world.

The Shaw text is not systematic; it does not provide the basis of a philosophy systematized à la Hegel or Spinoza.[1] Nevertheless, for a text spanning several thousands of pages written over a period of seventy-four years, it can surprise us with its consistency, as Eric Bentley has pointed out: "Everything in Shaw leads to everything else: we have had many vaster and many more scientific thinkers but few whose thinking was at the same time so many-sided and so much of a piece" (Bentley, 29). For example, a neo-Platonic seam (along with others) runs through the Shaw text, which can be traced over a long period of nearly fifty years in a variety of works: *Man and Superman* (1903), *Back to Methuselah* (1921), *The Adventures of the Black Girl in her Search for God* (1931), the dialogue on truth in the preface to *On the Rocks* (1933), the 1941 preface to *The Miraculous Birth of Language* by R. A. Wilson, the 1945 postscript for the Oxford World Classics edition of *Methuselah*. No one source is exactly the same, and their different emphases complement each other.

Especially valuable for such prospecting are isolated texts in occasional pieces and peripheral works, letters, journalism, lectures, and plays, which can yield nuggets of useful information in the most unlikely of places. Of course, each nugget must be tested for its Shavian gold, and care must be taken to avoid confusion by contradictions in statements taken out of context or by reading too much into isolated statements. But, by and large, Shaw was careful in his use of language, and Keegan's statement in *John Bull's Other Island* that "every joke is an earnest in the womb of time" suggests that the Shaw text yields up its meanings slowly over time and not always in the most obvious ways.

There is no one right way of reading the Shaw text or even a correct plurality of ways. Depending in large part on the mutable subjectivity of the reader, there is simply more than one way. Shaw himself facilitated a certain plurality of readings, but possible readings are not confined to those. Countering the strand of neo-Platonism mentioned above, another consistent strand that runs through the texts is a refusal to propose final meanings for anything, to declare that a truth is *the* truth. Meaning in the Shaw text is ever-present as a possibility in the play of different truths, of separate texts, and of several points of view of competing subjectivities. Shaw would have favored the type of critical reader Barthes called for: the reader creates the text from the work the author provides. Barthes insists, as did Shaw, that meaning rests between the text and the mortal reader, rather than originating from the intentions of a godlike author: "a text is made up of multiple writings, drawn from many cultures and entering into mutual relations of dialogue, parody, contestation, but there is one place where this multiplicity is focused and that place is the reader, not, as was hitherto said, the author" (Barthes, *Image-Music-Text*, 148).

As an instance of this plurality of readings, take the title of one of Shaw's most famous plays: *Man and Superman*. It refers to Friedrich Nietzsche's *Übermensch* (overman) as the latest manifestation of nineteenth-century Voluntarism—a philosophy of the Will, which stems from the writings of, among others, Lamarck, Kant, Goethe, Schopenhauer, Nietzsche, and Bergson. A close reading, however, might suggest that Shaw's text should not necessarily be confined within this strain of European thought. A pun on the word *will* humorously denotes the connection to Voluntarism by making the action of the play spring from the will (a written text signifying death) of a recently deceased father. Yet, while Nietzsche's concepts of the Will to Power and the Übermensch become the Life Force and the Superman respectively in Shaw's play, the title of this self-declared Don Juan play can also generically refer to the two leading characters of his play as "Man and Woman," which was the title of a 1894 book on the physiology and psychology of the two sexes by fellow Fabian Havelock Ellis, written as a Prolegomena to the seven volumes of his famous *Studies in the Psychology of Sex*.[2] Thus the allusiveness of the second term in Shaw's title may extend beyond Nietzsche's Übermensch to include Woman, reinforced by the Epistle Dedicatory's suggestion of another literary source, the medieval morality play *Everyman*: "every woman is not Ann [Whitefield, the leading female character], but Ann is Everywoman" (*Prefaces*, 161).

A related inflection of meaning arises in relation to the notorious misogyny of Nietzsche, who cautioned men to "never approach a woman without a whip." The feminist socialist democrat Shaw was having some mischievous fun at Nietzsche's expense by proposing to translate Nietzsche's term Übermensch as Woman. Worse from Nietzsche's point of view, Shaw's play displaces the evolutionary burden on to Woman, thus giving her a gender priority antithetical to most European religious and philosophical thought, a priority *both* chronological *and* logical: Woman must bring forth Superman; yet she is Superman. Such a logical conflation runs against the grain of most Western logic and language outside poetic discourse since the time of Plato and Aristotle. But as Shaw explained in the essay "The Illusions of Socialism": "A logical theory, with its assumptions of cause and effect, time and space, and so on, is just . . . a mental handle and nothing else" (*Non-Dramatic*, 411). This conflation of the chronological and the logical provides for a certain complexity in the Shavian text. Eric Bentley describes this "Shavian inclusiveness" in terms of the construction: "both . . . and . . ." (Bentley, xvi, 22), to which we refer back with some frequency in the following pages. As a chronological myth of a linguistic predicament, the superman is not a future ideal, she or he is a present reality: if not as a present given, but an ever-present possibility. The superman *both* is *and* is not. "What is the objection to man as he really is and can become . . . ?" he protested in his fight against idealists in the essay "How to Become a Man of Genius" (*Non-Dramatic*, 345).

The Superman (the antithesis of Man) also alludes to the leading figures in two musical texts adapted from literary texts that have haunted the modern European imagination: the rake as social anarchist in Mozart-Da Ponte's *Don Giovanni*, an adaptation of the old Spanish Don Juan story as well as of Molière's play *Le Festin de Pierre*, and the overreaching intellectual world-bettering scholar in league with the devil in Gounod's *Faust*, whose most famous previous incarnation was Goethe's two-part play.[3] Shaw knew both operas intimately from his childhood: his opera-singing mother and her musical associates rehearsed them in the family home; he painted a mural of Mephistopheles from Gounod's opera in his bedroom in Dalkey; and he taught himself to play the piano by practicing, not scales, but the overture to *Don Giovanni*.[4] In *Don Juan in Hell*, the dream scene from *Man and Superman*, these two antiheroic Supermen of his childhood imagination are brought together in text and on stage for the first time. Shaw thus plays with language and texts, narratives and writing, linguistic and textual devices, to suggest that the title has several quite distinct, yet overlapping meanings. *Man and Superman*'s intertextual credentials enable it to be read as a rewriting of several key texts in European culture including *Faust, Also sprach Zarathustra*, the old Don Juan legend, and *Everyman*. Shaw in a sense marries the latter two texts, with both his play and the Superman as textual products of that marriage. Somewhat nonchalantly, Shaw remarks in the Epistle Dedicatory: "I should make formal acknowledgement to the authors whom I have pillaged in the following pages if I could recollect them all" (*Prefaces*, 161).

Shaw's linguistic theme is reinforced by his subtitle: "A Comedy and A Philosophy," a combination of two distinct types of discourse not usually associated with each other, except, perhaps, in the writings of Nietzsche and Bergson. Courtship leading to marriage, with the accompanying theme of generation, is a staple of classical comedy, and here marriage is not only that of its two leading characters but also of texts and modes of discourse and their generation. Uniquely in Shaw's work, a multiplicity of texts and discourses accompanies the play to comprise the book, *Man and Superman: A Comedy and a Philosophy*. An Epistle Dedicatory to the well-known London drama critic Arthur Bingham Walkley, who Shaw associated with strict Aristotelian notions of drama, especially the so-called art of plot construction so antithetical to Shaw's dramaturgy, serves as a preface. Two types of play include the bourgeois comedy and the detachable dream play; the latter is *both* integral *and* peripheral to the former, while the comedy and philosophy of the subtitle contribute, perhaps, to the dialectic at work in both plays. *The Revolutionist's Handbook and Pocket Companion* is written by John Tanner, M.I.R.C. (Member of the Idle Rich Class), the play's protagonist. Finally, "Maxims for Revolutionists" inspires "aphoristic fireworks" à la La Rochefoucauld. As so often in a Shaw play, written texts serve as analogues of the action, and, not surprising, *Man and Superman* has two: Tanner's *Handbook* and Anne's father's will. This multiplicity of texts and types of discourse, as well as an assumption of multiple authorship, readership, and audiences, allows for a multiplicity of readings to be made from this fractured text, which he later likened to a vertiginous whirlpool.[5]

Man and Superman proposes a philosophy of the Life Force in a play about life under the auspices of death, *both* death *and* life, a binary opposition that returns in *Back to Methuselah*. The shadow of death is never far off in *Man and Superman*; both the main play and the dream play, *Don Juan in Hell*, function as postmortems. The dream play, set in one of those peculiarly postmortal places, Hell, is occasioned by Donna Ana's death and becomes a playful textual postmortem on not only Mozart's *Don Giovanni* but also all the other Don Juan, Faust, and Everyman texts he draws on; in addition, he alludes to many other texts and his own character's *Revolutionist's Handbook*. The text provides a stage for a fantastical textual afterlife without proposing a specific secret or truth as to death or life.

The Shaw text is multivalent and polysemous: the writing is capable of many readings and meanings as a result of its differing and deferring strategies (to use Derrida's language). These strategies, readable over several texts or even over the whole Shavian text, center on several aspects of language: meaning and subjectivity; the activities of writing, reading, thinking, speaking; technique and individual writers; readers, critics, and speakers as they intersect with other subjects, other texts, and other types of discourse. The Shaw text, in general, exemplifies such multiplicity, and a reading of some of its various complexities and difficulties—the primary focus of this book—requires a dexterity of interpretation irrespective of the author's intention. As Shaw puts it in the preface to *The Adventures of the Black Girl in her Search for God* (1932): "And now, the story being written, I proceed to speculate on what it means, though I cannot too often repeat that I am as liable as anyone else to err in my interpretation" (*Prefaces*, 645).

The allusive intertextuality suggested by this preliminary consideration of one of Shaw's more famous plays might suggest why a multilectical inquiry into his work generally is now necessary. Shaw remains the paradigm of the writer as a master of different types of writing and discourse: novelist, playwright, leading social and political writer, economist, remarkable music and drama critic, notable public speaker, debater and lecturer, wit, perpetual letter writer, autobiographer, journalist, English prose stylist, preeminent cultural critic, and so on. Yet in some ways the Shaw text has a strangeness appropriate to that of another era, as if written in a different but related language just beyond our grasp. For instance, words like democracy and sexuality, which have become homogenized within present cultural discourse, had not then acquired any notional consensus. When encountered in Shaw's writing, such terms and related locutions may seem questionable or awkward from our point of view, although the resulting linguistic friction may add interest to a reading of how this paradigmatic text functioned and might continue to function within that larger text known as Western culture.

Although the Shaw text may now seem obscured by the shadows of history, it remains a prime textual exhibit for any demonstration of the transition between the Victorian and modern eras. Indeed, the modern world is partly a linguistic product of its grammatological energetics. Bertrand Russell (a friend, but not one with any particular sympathy for the Shavian Weltanschauung) pointed out that Shaw changed the very language we speak in the period from 1885 to 1914: "We all talk in a different way from that in which people talked before Shaw, and even our emotions hardly allow themselves such delicious exhibitions of concealed egoism as were customary in Victorian times. . . . The latter stages of the change perhaps owe most to Freud, but the earlier stages, so far as England is concerned, were brought about by Shaw" (Russell, "George Bernard Shaw," 2–3, as quoted in Carpenter, *Destroying Ideals*, 208).

Freud, in spite of the intellectual battering psychoanalytic psychotherapy has taken in the recent past, still makes headlines. But Shaw in that capacity of the avant-garde breaking down the barricades at the nineteenth-century fin de siècle has to a great degree disappeared from general discourse. Yet precisely by questioning cultural absolutes, by deconstructing the manifestations of logocentrism in his time, Shaw signaled a radical break. One reason an attempt should be made to read the Shaw text in the context of such writers as Barthes, Lacan, and Derrida is because Shaw, the autodidact, developed methods of cultural understanding at variance with those of his own time; later these methods became part of the common cultural language with poststructuralism.

A multilectical approach to the Shaw text might seem antithetical to Shaw's well-advertised didacticism that always implies a primary reading, one designed to lead the bourgeois audience toward a special Shavian political or religious doctrine of socialism or Creative Evolution—a reading that, by demanding precedence over *any* other, would be symptomatic of logocentrism as a discourse of truth. Such an argument, however, could be double-edged: it raises the pertinent relation between Shaw and his particular audience, a problematic for him as for Brecht later.

How does a radical playwright acquire an audience? Shaw was as unsuccessful a playwright at the beginning as he had been a novelist, and as a socialist dramatist he had great difficulty in acquiring his audience. He exacerbated this failure by labeling his first set of plays "Unpleasant" in a deliberately antagonistic move to the audience he hoped to develop. Again like Brecht, his strategy in these *Plays Unpleasant* was to change and radicalize the late Victorian bourgeois (for the most part) audience. He sought both to alienate and implicate his audience in the dramas they were witnessing with the subjects of rack-renting in *Widowers' Houses* (1892), nonromantic promiscuous sexuality in *The Philanderer* (1893, 98), and prostitution in *Mrs Warren's Profession* (1894). He sweetened the bitter pill by labeling the second accompanying set of plays "Pleasant," when published together as *Plays Pleasant and Unpleasant*.

He comically figured his English bourgeois audience as a stereotypical English army officer and his wife in the short play *Great Catherine* (1913), in a cultural confrontation with the eponymous Russian empress, a sometime playwright herself and Enlightenment pupil of Voltaire. Catherine expresses her desire to keep the English officer captive in Russia—not as a lover as her aide suggests, but to put him in her museum—an analogy of Shaw's own wish for his audience: in viewing his play the audience may be so changed that their former selves, the bourgeois identities, would be fit only for a museum. Shaw remained as sympathetic to his audience as Catherine is to the officer. For all his intellectual wit, Shaw never posed as superior to his audience, although he often posed as superior to politicians, scientists, and professionals, in general. Neither did he acquiesce with the views of what is essentially a naive, as opposed to critical, audience that Shavian drama requires.

One further aspect of the complexity of the Shaw text that might easily be missed in reading is its virtuosity or artistry. Mozart's music, which combines complexity of expression with simplicity of means, can suggest how Shaw, as writer, always insisted that in matters of form he owed more to music, to "that extraordinary *literature* of modern music from Bach to Wagner" [my italics] (*Non-Dramatic*, 446), as he put it, than to literature itself. Mozart, indeed, functioned for Shaw as what Barthes calls an "intertext" (Barthes, *Pleasure*, 36)—a text through which all other texts are read:

> For my own part, if I do not care to rhapsodize much about Mozart, it is because I am so violently prepossessed in his favour that I am capable of supplying any possible deficiency in his work by my imagination.... In my small-boyhood I, by good luck, had an opportunity of learning DON GIOVANNI thoroughly and if it were only for the sense of the value of fine workmanship which I gained from it, I should still esteem that lesson the most important part of my education. (*Music 2*, 481–82)

Always keen on downplaying formal and aesthetic concerns, his prefatory note to *Getting Married* (1908) referred negatively to that play's innovative form—a return to the unities of Greek theater: "Its adoption was not, on my part, a deliberate display of virtuosity in form." If we translate the rhetoric, then the denial becomes an acknowledgment that his writing was just that. Shaw was as much a *virtuoso* in his use of language, both spoken and written, as Mozart was of musical language. But can such virtuosity be read? If it can, then it requires a capacity for reading a multiplicity of (sometimes overlapping) meanings in the writing, so that the text unfolding in time operates on different levels. The reader, then, needs to create a score-text, as it were, for any Shavian work in order to read and appreciate it. Shaw positively invites such an endeavor, a practice of reading encouraged by writers like Lévi-Strauss and Barthes, who invoke the model of a music score in their analyses of myth and narrative.[6] A music score can be read both vertically (synchronous—the notes sounded at the same time yielding harmony or dissonance), or horizontally (diachronous—the notes sounded in succession to produce melody).

If the Shaw text does yield different readings simultaneously, then the model of the music score can be applied to it. Shaw himself expressed his frustration at not having a form of notation analogous to a music score for the writing of his play-texts.[7] So the onus is on the critical reader to produce in her reading a putative score-text with extra lines on the stave, beyond those bound up with authorial intentions or textual design. For example, Shaw's use of the multiple meanings of "will" at the beginning of *Man and Superman* becomes part of its score-text, and "reading the will," in several senses, becomes the text of *Man and Superman* as generated by the reader/audience. Further readings and meanings remote from his time, whether generated by recent literary theory or not, may be added to the score-text at either the discretion or the whim of the reader, if it can be put this way without too much strain, *ad lib* rather than *obbligato*.

Reading Writing

The openness of the Shaw text to different readings anticipated poststructuralist concerns in some ways. This section of the chapter outlines overlapping areas of interest between texts of writers from this tradition, sometimes simply called theory, and theoretical concerns within the Shaw text. This discussion was designed for both those who might know something about Shaw but little about poststructuralism and those who do know about theory but know little about Shaw; furthermore, for those who know something about both, it should be suggestive as to how the Shaw text and theory may be brought together.

As there is an overlapping both between structuralism and poststructuralism and between poststructuralism and postmodernism (at best a loose term, introduced by Lyotard's 1979 essay "What is Postmodernism?" and used here in the most general sense to throw doubt on a unitary concept of the subject or of discourse), as well as with other writers who do not easily fit into any category (for example, Paul Ricoeur and Michel Foucault), poststructuralism serves as the theoretical background for this study's reading of the Shaw text.[8] Most of the poststructuralist texts of Jacques Lacan, Roland Barthes, and Jacques Derrida referred to in this text were written, in fact, before 1970.

Marx, Nietzsche, and Freud

Interpretation is a key aspect of the legibility of any text, and poststructuralism offers several varieties of interpretation. Almost all the structuralists and poststructuralists of the 1960s and 1970s looked back to and drew inspiration from the writings of three mold-breaking German-speaking writers from an earlier era: Karl Marx (1818–1885), Friedrich Nietzsche (1844–1900), and Sigmund Freud (1856–1939). In different ways, each proposed a new method of interpretation and each provided a critique of that legacy of the Enlightenment, Western rationalism. Their critiques mirrored Shaw's own powerful critique, written mostly in his essays of the 1890s, and all three writers are to be encountered in the Shaw text. Although he criticized each, his knowledge of them may have allowed him to forge paths similar to those followed by the later generation of French writers, whom they so heavily influenced.[9] Shaw himself acknowledged Marx's decisive impact on his writing in its embryonic stage. Marx was largely responsible for converting Shaw to socialism, and its first artistic consequence, after reading *Das Kapital* in French translation (there was no English version), was his last novel, *An Unsocial Socialist* (1883). Shaw followed this up by writing many political and economic tracts for the Fabian society later in the 1880s and the seminal critical essays of the 1890s, including *The Quintessence of Ibsenism* (1891) and *The Perfect Wagnerite* (1898). Shaw, although a critic of all determinisms, including Marx's Dialectical Materialism and its problematic claim to offer a scientific account of history, accepted Marx's insistence on the importance of economics for any interpretation of history. To the end of his writing life, he retained from Marx his iconoclasm in relation to ideology and what he called the moral force of Marx's analysis in the later parts of *Das Kapital* as a *narrative* of the working of Capital in history. Marx opened Shaw's eyes to the horrors underlying late nineteenth-century capitalist ideology with which he thenceforth undertook to do battle.

Nietzsche, another iconoclast, was younger than Marx, and Shaw had arrived at his point of view independently before he read Nietzsche sometime in the 1890s.[10] Nietzsche's *The Birth of Tragedy, Out of the Spirit of Music* (1872) with its Apollonian-Dionysian distinction, which emphasized Dionysian irrationality underlying the usually emphasized Apollonian rationality of ancient Greek culture, launched the attack on Western metaphysics that Derrida would pick up later with his deconstruction of Platonic logocentrism. Nietzsche's book most probably contributed to Shaw's equation of madness and poetic inspiration in *Candida* and in the theatrical experience of *Major Barbara* (1905), where Undershaft, nicknamed "Dionysos" by Cusins, himself adopts the tragic mask of Dionysus in the eyes of the spectator—the rational form masking the madness of war and poverty (Cusins, of course, adopts Undershaft's name and identity at the end of the play). Although different in regard to such political issues as socialism, democracy, and feminism, both the Nietzsche text and the Shaw text emerged from a similar European intellectual tradition. Shaw, for instance, was familiar with the writing of two of Nietzsche's principal influences: Schopenhauer and Wagner. The section "First Aid to Critics" in the preface to *Major Barbara* (1905) responds to criticism of influence, in part, by Nietzsche, insisting that no "brilliant" or "original" writer can acquire knowledge in an "intellectual void . . . if there be such a thing on the philosophic plane as a matter of course, it is that no individual can make more than a minute contribution to it. In fact, [the critics'] conception of clever persons parthenogenetically bringing forth complete original cosmogonies by dint of sheer 'brilliancy' is part of that ignorant credulity which is the despair of the honest philosopher" (*Prefaces*, 118).

Freud, exactly the same age as Shaw, had no formative influence on his thinking, but both brought into open public discourse subjects hitherto considered unmentionable, especially in the area of personal sexual experience. Shaw's first three plays all raised hitherto unmentionable sexual problems: female sadism in *Widowers' Houses*, open sexuality outside marriage in *The Philanderer*, and incest and prostitution in *Mrs Warren's Profession*. Again, Schopenhauer, whose notion of the Will prefigures the workings of Freud's Unconscious as well as Shaw's Life Force, was a mutual influence, as was Samuel Butler (1835–1902), whose concept of the unconscious influenced *both* Freud and Shaw. As early as the Epistle Dedicatory to *Man and Superman*, Shaw had called for a "genuinely scientific psychology which the world still waits for" (*Prefaces*, 161), and, although he did not believe that Freudian psychoanalysis had achieved it, he saw psychoanalysis as a step in the right direction by opening up areas of inquiry he considered necessary, especially those of sexual behavior and fantasy that had already been broached by his friends Havelock Ellis and Edward Carpenter during and following the 1890s.[11] As he put it in an article in 1916: "I pay serious if disrespectful attention to Freud" (*Books 2*, 328–29).

As Nietzsche, like Shaw, disdained system, Marx and Freud were left to develop what Barthes calls "the two great *épistèmes* of modernity" (Barthes, *Image-Music-Text*, 212), the two revolutionary methods of interpretation: Historical Materialism and psychoanalysis. Both instituted virtual priesthoods to propagate and preserve their doctrines with their own versions of apostolic succession derived from the founder of the practice. Both methods are not only determinist, but, as with Darwin's theory of

Natural Selection, also reductionist in ultimately deriving from a single factor, a final truth, a secret, to reveal all. Shaw was critical of such reductionism, as was Derrida later. Nevertheless, their critiques of the construction of subjectivity, of the rational ego in relation to both ideology and the subconscious, are specifically related to our concerns, as we shall see when we come to their structuralist reinterpreters.

Saussure and Structuralism

Another important figure, almost an exact contemporary of Shaw although there is no evidence that Shaw knew of him despite his interest in linguistics, is the Swiss linguist Ferdinand de Saussure (1857–1913). Structural linguistics, so influential on structuralism and poststructuralism, derived from Saussure's lectures, published posthumously as *Cours de Linguistique Générale* (1915), and as later developed by such writers as Roman Jakobson, Emile Benveniste, and Gérard Genette. Saussure's work was imported into other disciplines as structuralism: anthropology by Claude Lévi-Strauss, psychoanalysis by Lacan, politics by Louis Althusser, and literature by Roland Barthes. Saussure even influenced writers on the periphery of structuralism like Michel Foucault, who refused the structuralist label, and Paul Ricoeur, whose interest was in hermeneutics (the interpretations of texts).

Saussure spoke of two aspects of a sign, what he called the signified (the thing denoted by the sign) and the signifier (the sign of the thing). He suggested that the relation of the signifier to the signified was one of convention that depended, not on identity of signified and signifier, but on *differences* at the levels of both signifieds and signifiers. Structural linguistics, thus, allows the student to understand meaning as a product of the structure of the sign with its conventional or arbitrary relation between differences in both of its two aspects: the signifier and the signified. A tree as tree is marked off by differences from other objects, such as hedges, shrubs, animals, while the word *tree* is marked off by differences in a lexicon from other words. These two systems of differences (called "double articulation" by Lévi-Strauss) are not homologous. Each obeys its own rules, although theorists base both systems on simple binary oppositions.

Anthropologist Lévi-Strauss (b. 1908) applied the lessons of structural linguistics to his own discipline. He found, for example, that structures or conventionalized systems of differences allowed him to understand that the meaning of a mole in a myth may have nothing to do with the animal itself; rather, the meaning of mole derives from its typical behavior of spending much of its time underground. Meaning arises where this behavior is contrasted with, say, that of an eagle, who spends much of its time high in the air. This simple binary opposition (belowground/aboveground) then becomes, for Lévi-Strauss, part of a system or structure of differences including other binary oppositions from a particular myth and its variants. Interpretation of a myth involves analyzing its variant structures of differences over a set of related myths. Structuralism, derived from Saussure and as practiced by Lévi-Strauss, became a main target of Derrida's deconstruction, even if Saussure's emphasis on difference formed the basis of Derrida's own thinking.

Perhaps to compensate for the synchronic emphasis of structuralism (structural relations between the elements of a system at any moment), Lévi-Strauss developed his very useful notion of the conceptual *bricoleur* ("handyman" gives a sense of its meaning in English), the person, and *bricolage*, what the person does. A literary artist like Shaw can be seen as a bricoleur whose skills lie in taking already existing bits and pieces of "whatever" from "wherever" possible, rather than making something new out of nothing. As a writer, the bricoleur constantly reuses and rearranges the letters of the alphabet and uses old texts, words, or concepts. Every language uses new arrangements of old signifiers. Every sentence we utter or write uses old words, learned from other people's use of them, to create new specific meaning. Shaw well understood this in his distinction between "living" and "dead" words and thought in the dialogue between the Elderly Gentleman and Zoo in *Back to Methuselah: Part IV*. Words, like money, must have currency; they must come from a current lexicon. But, when they lose all sense of differentiation, when the signifier is seen as identical with signified, they are liable to become ideological (Shaw's "dead thought"), and the discourse that employs them as signifieds becomes abstract (purely conventionalized) or "dead."

Lacan and Subjectivity

Jacques Lacan (1901–1981) is the major exponent of psychoanalysis among (post)structuralists, and in general terms his "return to Freud," which critiques the ego as a unitary subject, translated the problematic of psychoanalysis from that of interpretation of an ego in terms of behavior to that of analysis of the fissures and gaps created by desire in language. Freud himself had placed much importance on language and on unconscious symbolic structures formed by *condensation* and *displacement* as proposed in *The Interpretation of Dreams*. Lacan reasserted this linguistic emphasis by reinterpreting Freud's key concepts in line with Roman Jakobson's application of the old rhetorical terms "metaphor" and "metonymy" in the field of structural linguistics.

For Lacan the subject is created in, or constituted by, language (every sentence requires a subject). But before language has even been acquired, there occurs what Lacan calls a fundamental misrecognition at "the mirror stage," when the child, who hitherto has had no sense of differentiation, (mis)identifies with her or his mirror *image*, thus splitting the hitherto undifferentiated unity of mother and child. Identifying its nascent subjectivity with this mirror image sets up a "split" or "lack," which differentiates this image from the sense of wholeness the child had in combination with its mother. This process results in misrecognition of identity with inevitable implications for subjectivity when language is acquired. This lack, or gap, between the identification with the mirror image and what Lacan calls "the other" (the undifferentiated unity of mother and child) launches desire on its lifelong journey in the realm of the Imaginary, which, thereafter, is always present and traceable within language (with its need to use an abstract "I"). Lacan's distinction between the Symbolic and the Imaginary—two nonhomologous systems of differences, between which there is no one-to-one translation—features strongly in this study.

As with all structuralists, difference for Lacan provides the basis for all subjectivity and language. He formulated his somewhat controversial concept of the phallus as *the* signifier of the signifying process of difference, the primary concept of difference (the mother of all binary oppositions, to coin a phrase) that makes all signification and language possible. The fact that human beings can either have or not have a penis, which Freud thought all important, allows for the concept of difference and, therefore, for the possibility of all symbolization. However, Lacan stressed that the phallus is a signifier, *the* signifier of difference; it is not a signified, not the penis. The phallus, as differentiation, makes signification and language possible. In realizing that some people have, and others have not, a penis, the child, at what Freud called the Oedipal stage, learns to understand difference.

The child's identification with the many "I"s she or he uses in language is always a partial one, a misidentification, that leaves a gap of desire, which can never be (ful)filled in language. Shaw humorously illustrates why language and its grammar force us to adopt what he calls "misusage" in the preface (1905) to *The Irrational Knot*:

> When I say that I did and felt these things, I mean, of course, that the predecessor whose name I bear did and felt them. The I of to-day is (? am) cool towards Carmen; and Carmen, I regret to say, does not have the slightest interest in him (? me). And now enough of this juggling with past and present Shaws. The grammatical complications of being a first person and several extinct third persons at the same moment are so frightful that I must return to the ordinary *misusage*. (*Prefaces*, 681–82; my italics)

We may note here another striking thematic coincidence between Lacan and Shaw in their similar descriptions of the social or psychological construction of femininity, as opposed to essentialist concepts of "woman" and "womanliness." Gender is as much a construction as subjectivity. "Woman does not exist," wrote Lacan; "A woman is only a man in petticoats," declared Shaw. And earlier, in *The Quintessence of Ibsenism*, in part a feminist tract, Shaw had deconstructed the Victorian ideal of the Womanly Woman.[12]

Barthes and Text

In *Elements of Semiology* (1964), "Introduction to a Structural Analysis of Narratives," *Mythologies* (1957), and other writings Roland Barthes (1915–1980) developed Saussurean structural linguistics as a form of literary theory dealing with narrative, often mirroring what his contemporaries were writing, whether that be Benveniste, Lévi-Strauss, Derrida, or his student, Julia Kristeva (who introduced ideas like intertextuality and *signifiance* into poststructuralism).[13] His later poststructuralist writings are notable for their emphasis on the text, the relation of the reader to the text, and his playing down the authority of the author, most infamously with his phrase "the death of the author." None of this should be new to a reader of Shaw, whose whole project as writer was to promote the relation between text and reader or spectator at the expense of his own author-ity or reputation, the demise of which he encourages with some irony in the preface to *Three Plays for Puritans*: "we must get rid of reputations: they are weeds in the soil of ignorance. If this preface will at all help to get rid of mine, the writing of it will have been well worth the pains" (*Prefaces*, 753).

In relation to the question of how to read the multiple texts that comprise the Shaw text, we might note that for Barthes, as for Derrida, a key word is *play*, which has obvious resonance in relation to reading such a playful playwright as Shaw: "'Playing' must be understood here in all its polysemy: the text itself plays (. . . like a machine with 'play') and the reader plays twice over, playing the Text as one plays a game, . . . also playing the Text in the musical sense of the term" (Barthes, *Image-Music-Text*, 162).

The titles of Barthes's "The Death of the Author" (1968) and *The Pleasure of the Text* (1973) direct us immediately to their relevance. Both Barthes and Derrida are semiotic polemicists, who—given the antipathy they shared with Nietzsche and Shaw to the type of moral binary thinking characteristic of most Western discourse that favors one term of a binary opposition over the other (for example, good over evil, light over dark)—are themselves touched with the Manichean heresy. For Derrida deconstruction is good, metaphysics is bad, or writing is good, speaking is bad. For Barthes the text is good, the work is bad; the reader is good, the author is bad. This possibly unfairly reductive summation conveys the crusading aspect to both writers. For Barthes "the work"—the material book produced by the writer—is "consumed" by the reader. That, of course, has ideological, economic, and political implications not pursued here. But the text as opposed to the work is produced by the reader, not by the author, in a critical act of reading, not as passive consumption. Shaw uses "text" precisely in this sense when referring in a letter to William Archer on August 17, 1890, to his act of critical *reading* that led to the *writing* of *The Quintessence of Ibsenism*: "an eminent socialist critic made [Ibsen's] plays the text for a fierce attack on the idealist section of the English Social Democrats" (*Letters 1*, 257). In Barthes's essay "The Death of the Author," the relation between the reader and the text might parallel the productive act of the scriptor in writing the work, but the scriptor as author is not in a position of divine authority over the reader's text. The author, as Shaw is understood in this book, is a paper-author, a fictional shadow. As Barthes puts it in his essay "From Work to Text": "It is not that the Author may not 'come back' in the Text, in his text, but he then does so as a guest. . . . He becomes, as it were, a paper-author: his life is no longer the origin of his fictions but a fiction contributing to his work" (Barthes, *Image-Music-Text*, 161). Utilizing this concept of the author as a textual shadow, in chapter 3 we *read* Shaw as author in the (con)text of autobiographical writing that constitutes him as a fictional subjectivity.

Beyond this shadowy fiction, Barthes insists that "linguistically, the author is never more than the instance writing, just as *I* is never more than the instance saying *I*: language knows a 'subject,' not a 'person'" (Barthes,

Image-Music-Text, 145). That this is in line with Shaw's own view, he expressed, for instance, in relation to *Heartbreak House*: "I am not an explicable phenomenon; neither is *Heartbreak House*" (Henderson, *Man of the Century*, 626); and in relation to *Saint Joan*: "I have no theory about Joan, and understand her no more than I understand myself" (Sarolea, "Has Mr. Shaw Understood," 182). Both comments underline his cryptic and revealing comment to Frank Harris in a letter of June 20, 1930: "I understand everything and everyone, and am nobody and nothing." Shaw also defended Harris's biographies of both himself and Oscar Wilde against critics who complained that Harris got the facts wrong; Shaw claimed they were missing the point with such criticisms, while—with a certain amount of healthy hypocrisy—correcting and rewriting the factual elements of the Harris biography of himself after Harris died. "Plato and Boswell [were] the dramatists who invented Socrates and Dr Johnson" (*Prefaces*, 162), he wrote in the preface to *Man and Superman*. Shaw was even more radical in writing of autobiography when he insisted: "All autobiographies are lies." And, in case anyone misunderstood, he explained: "I do not mean unconscious, unintentional lies: I mean deliberate lies. No man is bad enough to tell the truth about himself during his lifetime, involving, as it must, the truth about his family and his friends and colleagues. And no man is good enough to tell the truth to posterity in a document which he suppresses until there is nobody left alive to contradict him" (*Non-Dramatic*, 433).

He goes on like Barthes to make himself, his authorial identity or his biography, a product of his *writing*: "As to myself, my goods are all in the book shop window and on the stage: what is communicable has been already communicated in a long life of which, though I cannot say that no day of it has been left without a written line, yet I have perhaps brought it as near to that Roman ideal as is healthily and humanly possible." Thus Barthes explained the implications for biography (life writing) as Shaw might understand it: "The word 'bio-graphy' re-acquires a strong, etymological sense, at the same time as the sincerity of the enunciation . . . becomes a false problem: the *I* which writes the text, it too, is never more than a paper-*I*" (Barthes, *Image-Music-Text*, 161).

Derrida and Writing

In the most surprising ways, Derrida repeats Shaw's own project, and so Derrida's works can be used heuristically: as a guide to reading the Shaw text. Jacques Derrida (b. 1930), frequently cited as a postmodernist, is a poststructuralist best known for what he introduced as deconstruction: this type of critical writing exposes the metaphysical assumptions underlying structuralism and, more generally, those of any text produced within the tradition of Western metaphysics deriving from Plato, which he calls logocentrism. Derrida insists that metaphysics has repressed writing within Western discourse in favor of presence, the spoken word, and Logos (the word, reason, discourse, thought, or idea). However, deconstruction would be nothing without the metaphysics it deconstructs, as Derrida admits, and can take place only within its discourse. Similarly, within the Shaw text there persist two interwoven strands (rather than two different periods, say, of early and late texts): deconstruction in the form of an iconoclastic anti-idealism and a form of Platonism in the teleological philosophy of Creative Evolution. Derrida has a horror of final meanings and teleology in all its guises, but he is interested in a process or play of meaning that is without origin and never final, never centered, never totalized, a process without origin or end, of deferring of differences between signifiers, in which every apparent signified becomes yet another signifier. That process, *différance* (to use the word Derrida coined) or signifiance, is always a form of writing, inscription as marks or traces of differences. And every writing is a suitable text for deconstruction as it can never be read as bearing a final truth.

The problematic associated with the name Derrida, especially his rhetorical assault on Platonism, poses the greatest challenge to considering Shaw as a forerunner of poststructuralism. In Shaw's dialogue on truth between Christ and Pilate in the preface to *On the Rocks*, Jesus at one point says, "thought is the substance of the word" (*Prefaces*, 374). Derrida would see this assigning of substance to thought and in another statement the favoring of the voice ("everyone capable of receiving the truth recognizes it in my voice," *Prefaces*, 372) as major symptoms of Platonic metaphysics or logocentric phonocentrism, where truth depends on a relation of identity between the spoken word as signifier and the thing as signified; therefore, it becomes general evidence of the repression of writing in Western thought. In a later text, the preface to *Farfetched Fables* (1949), Shaw himself humorously offers a deconstructive gloss on this line of thought on thought (Logos): "I cannot call myself the Way and the Life, having only a questionable hypothesis or two to offer. . . . Some thirty years ago I wrote a play called *As Far As Thought Can Reach*. Perhaps I should have called it as far as my thought could reach; but I left this to be taken for granted" (*Prefaces*, 908). Thus, Shaw yet again refers us back to writing as texts, but not as receptacles of truth.

Margery Morgan came close in her study *The Shavian Playground* (1972) to recognizing the nonlogocentric thread running through the Shaw text, although she would not then have used Derrida's term. Signaling the anti-Platonic thread in Shaw's writing, her chapter on the late play *Too True to be Good* (1932) is called: "Farewell to Platonism," and the title of the play, which points to a disjunction between the two Platonic ideas of the truth and the good, is what Derrida would call an aporia (see page 26), and works as deconstruction of metaphysics. In a chapter on *Man and Superman*, Morgan notes the paradox that in Shaw's major attempt at an exposition of his Platonic Life Force philosophy there is "a tendency away from clear organic unity and the self-containment of art. The interrupted plot, the variation of style, the shifting locale, and even the proliferation of ideas represent a struggle away from rationally determined form and order" (Morgan, *Playground*, 118).[14] Its form seems to deconstruct its content. Thus, recognizing that the text is too contradictory to have systematic meaning, she suggests that, maybe, its meaning lies in its music: "the thought... is in fact being forced into patterns and grooves under a rhythmical and musical impulse" (Morgan, *Playground*, 105).

Derrida is particularly useful as a corrective to any unitary reading of the Shaw text that would read one aspect into it exclusively. The Shaw text could be, and has been, read variously as the work of a logical rationalist, or of a religious antimaterialist mystic, or of a dualist who in true Platonic fashion approved spirit over matter. Deconstruction demands that we deconstruct these unitary readings, although their diverse multiplicity is tantamount to a deconstruction in itself. Furthermore, the deconstruction is largely anticipated by Shaw himself or rather is already contained within the Shaw text. In the dialogue on truth when Pilate asks Christ to explain what he means by the phrase: "The word was the beginning," Jesus answers, throwing us back, with some irony perhaps, to *Man and Superman*: "the difference between man and Roman is but a word; but it makes all the difference." He continues by deferring the difference: "the difference between Roman and Jew is only a word." When Pilate retorts, "it is a fact," Jesus replies, "a fact was first a Thought; for a Thought is the substance of the Word" (*Prefaces*, 374). We might translate that into Saussurean terms as "the difference between Roman and Jew is only a sign," "it is a signified," "a signified was first a signifier; for a signifier is the substance of the sign." Although Derrida would certainly have problems attributing substantiality to a signifier, which for him is a trace (with its own peculiar logic of being both an absence of presence and a presence of absence), it does suggest that Shaw sees meaning in language and in writing in terms of the signifier, rather than in the signified, or in the identity of signifier with signified.

Aporia. Aporia is a term of Derrida's, which I referred to in relation to *Too True to be Good*, that is useful in reading the Shaw text. Derrida's translator explains his use of the concept in the Introduction to *Writing and Difference* (1967) as:

> the Greek word for a seemingly insoluble logical difficulty: once a system has been "shaken" by following its totalizing logic to its final consequences, one finds an excess which cannot be construed within the rules of logic, for the excess can only be conceived as neither this nor that, or both at the same time—a departure from all rules of logic. Difference often functions as aporia: it is difference in neither time nor space and makes both possible. (Derrida, *Writing and Difference*, xvi–xvii)

This succinctly gives a basis for Bentley's formulation of "both/and" referred to earlier, which might help us to understand a certain contradictoriness within the Shaw text, noted by practically all commentators. As Wisenthal writes in his Introduction to *Shaw and Ibsen*, "Shaw's attitude towards art (like his attitude to most things) is a complicated subject because of his varying and apparently contradictory utterances on it. That is why it is important not to take any one statement as Shaw's whole view on this or any other subject" (Wisenthal, *Shaw and Ibsen*, 46). Shaw's playing in *Methuselah* with the life/death, life/body, and life/matter dichotomies or binaries exemplifies this.

Metaphor. Derrida's is a true writing of shadows, of traces, rather than of light and substance. For him, the metaphor of darkness and light is: "the founding metaphor of Western philosophy as metaphysics. . . . Metaphor in general, the passage from one existent to another, or from one signified meaning to another . . . anchors discourse in metaphysics, irremediably repressing discourse into its metaphysical state" (Derrida, *Writing and Difference*, 27).

If we want to understand the connections between Derrida's insistence on redressing the priority given to the spoken word and the metaphor of vision over writing in language (or the complicity of the first two in representing the subject-object relation in logocentric terms), the phonological and the photological as opposed to the grammatological, his translator of *Writing and Difference* explains in a note:

> Derrida . . . is specifying several characteristics of metaphysics without demonstrating their interrelatedness. 1. "Heliocentric metaphysics" refers to the philosophical language founded on metaphors of light and dark, e.g., truth as light, error as dark, etc. 2. This language always implies a privileged position of "acoustics," i.e., a privilege accorded to a phonological, spoken model of the *presence* of truth in living, spoken discourse, and a concomitant abasement of the silent work of the "force" of differentiation. This abasement is typically revealed in the philosophical treatment of writing. 3. This system is set in motion by Platonism, whose doctrine of the *eidos* implies both points just mentioned. (Derrida, *Writing and Difference*, 306)

Shaw himself could not have been clearer. In fact, Shaw's clarity, which has been called a "chaos of clear opinions," and Derrida's obscurity, to employ the inevitable metaphors of light and darkness, serve similar functions.[15] They constantly yield difference, and thus différance. In as much as Derrida's practice is the more earnest, paradoxically it might be the more logocentric.

Deconstruction and Logos are, like Shaw's metaphorical Heaven and Hell in *Man and Superman*, two different ways of looking at the same thing or reading the same writing. One irony in the play is that Don Juan, who wishes to be in Heaven, finds himself in Hell precisely because he is such a talker, a compulsive employer of spoken discourse. This point is made right at the end of the main play when, after Tanner's final long speech, Ann encourages him to "Go on talking." "Talking!" exclaims Tanner, accompanied by "universal laughter." Hell is the home of presence, the home of ideals and the spoken word ("talk"), and Don Juan finds himself there, very much as Derrida finds himself writing within a tradition of logocentrism. Like Derrida wanting to escape or elude the linguistic traps of Western metaphysics, Don Juan wants to leave Hell for Heaven, which cannot be described by metaphor:

> DON JUAN. Senor Commander: you know the way to the frontier of hell and heaven. Be good enough to direct me.
>
> THE STATUE. Oh, the frontier is only the difference between two ways of looking at things. Any road will take you across if you really want to get there. (*Plays*, 388)

When he has finally gone off, the Commander gasps: "Whew! How he does talk! They'll never stand it in heaven." Don Juan, unlike his modern-day counterpart in the play, Tanner, is not a writer. His "evolutionary appetite" therefore is expressed in talk and sex, not writing, and so he is stuck in hell.

Force. A key word in the Shaw text (and much nineteenth-century discourse following the invention of the steam engine) is "force." And although little commented on, "force" is also a key word for Derrida. It figures in his seminal essay "Differance": "force itself is never present; it is only a play of differences and quantities" (Derrida, *Speech and Phenomena*, 148). Also the title of his first essay in *Writing and Difference*, "Force and Signification," notes its importance. Derrida's critique of structuralism is of great interest to this study. Structuralism, he points out, utilizes the metaphor of geometry, of spatialization that dispenses with time, with duration: "In the future [structuralism] will be interpreted, perhaps, as a relaxation, if not a lapse, of the attention given to *force*, which is the tension of force itself. *Form* fascinates when one no longer has the force to understand force from within itself. That is, to create. That is why literary criticism is structuralist in every age" (Derrida, *Writing and Difference*, 4).

Derrida quite definitely considers it a lapse, not merely a relaxation on structuralism's part, to neglect force, as the rest of his essay demonstrates. Pertinent here is Derrida's sequential linking of those two key concepts in the Shaw text, "force" and "create," which might be used to deconstruct Derrida's deconstruction as a species of Bergsonian-Shavian voluntarism. For Derrida's critique of structuralism here is similar to Bergson's criticism of time as an abstracted homologous form of spatialization as opposed to intuited "duration." Perhaps with Bergson in mind, Derrida repeats his general critique of binary thinking while acknowledging that his discourse takes place within traditional discourse, or logocentrism:

> Our intention here is not, through the simple motions of balancing, equilibration or overturning, to oppose duration to space, quality to quantity, force to form, the depth of meaning or value to the surface of figures. Quite to the contrary. To counter this simple alternative, to counter the simple choice of one of the terms or one of the series against the other, we maintain that it is necessary to seek new concepts and new models, an economy escaping this system of metaphysical oppositions. This economy would not be an energetics of pure, shapeless force. The differences examined *simultaneously* would be differences of site and differences of force.... The force of the work, the force of genius, the force, too, of that which engenders

in general is precisely that which resists geometrical metaphorization and is the proper object of literary criticism. (Derrida, *Writing and Difference*, 19–20)

Derrida's differences of force (the force that "engenders in general") can also be said to operate in the Shaw text. And while Derrida would be wary of Shaw's and Bergson's teleological tendencies, neither Shaw's Life Force nor Bergson's *Élan vital* were put forward as totalizing concepts, as metaphysical names that would shift the emphasis from signifier to signified. Rather they sought to put them "under erasure," as Derrida's use of Heidegger's terminology would have it. Compare Derrida's above account of force in writing to Shaw's famous remark about style in writing from the Epistle Dedicatory to *Man and Superman*: "effectiveness of assertion is the Alpha and Omega of style. He who has nothing to assert has no style and can have none: he who has something to assert will go as far in power of style as its momentousness and his conviction will carry him. Disprove his assertion after it is made, yet its style remains. Darwin has no more destroyed the style of Job nor of Handel than Martin Luther destroyed the style of Giotto" (*Prefaces*, 165–66).

That "effectiveness of assertion" means "force of assertion" Shaw explains in a gloss on this text written ten years later; again, he links style in literature to the music of Händel, in a piece for French publication by his French translator, Augustin Hamon: "It was from Handel that I learned that style consists in force of assertion" (*Music 3*, 639). Shaw is writing in the context of efficacy in literature and art, of writing and of texts:

> My contempt for *belles lettres*, and for amateurs who become the heroes of the fanciers of literary virtuosity, is not founded on any illusion of mine as to the permanence of those forms of thought (call them opinions) by which I strive to communicate my bent to my fellows. To younger men they are already outmoded; for though they have no more lost their logic than an eighteenth century pastel has lost its drawing or its colour, yet, like the pastel, they grow indefinably shabby, and will grow shabbier until they cease to count at all, when my books will either perish, or, if the world is still poor enough to want them, will have to stand, with Bunyan's, by quite amorphous qualities of temper and energy. (*Prefaces*, 165)

Paradoxically, this much-quoted passage of Shaw's is usually interpreted with the emphasis on what is being forcefully asserted (the signified rather than the signifier) instead of what we read into it here, and which is emphasized in the sentence itself: writing as significance (the metonymy of signifiers, the process of the signifier as opposed to the signified). Note the words: "disprove his assertion," "literary virtuosity," no "illusion . . . as to the permanence of . . . forms of thought," "communicate," "logic," "books," "amorphous," "qualities of temper and energy." All these terms are relevant to what Derrida is saying. "Amorphous" is particularly interesting as it indicates that Shaw is aware of the metaphor of spatialization as a property of metaphor, of language, of difference.

Structuralism, in abstracting structure from time, aims to avoid what Derrida calls *telos*. Yet such abstraction is inherently teleological. In a paragraph detailing his critique of structuralism, and crucial to an understanding of what Shaw's Creative Evolution might mean, Derrida writes:

> To *comprehend* the structure of becoming and of force, is to lose meaning by finding it. . . . Hegel demonstrated convincingly that the explication of a phenomenon by a force is a tautology. But in saying this, one must refer to language's peculiar inability to emerge from itself in order to articulate its origin, and not to the *thought* of force. Force is the other of language without which language would not be what it is. (Derrida, *Writing and Difference*, 26)

This is no more than what Shaw was saying about "force" in writing. Force, though known through writing in a language of images of shadow and light that needs to be deconstructed, needs to be understood as the other of language, of writing, but not as its origin.

Play. In "Structure, Sign, and Play" (1966), a later essay in *Writing and Difference*, Derrida elaborates his concept of play in the context of his notion of "the supplement," borrowed, ironically, from Lévi-Strauss's discussion of the concept of *mana*, in his essay "Introduction to the Work of Marcel Mauss" (1950). Lévi-Strauss wrote, "*mana, Wakau, oranda* and other notions of the same type [are] the conscious expression of a semantic function, whose role is to permit symbolic thought to operate in spite of the contradiction, which is proper to it. . . . In the system of symbols constituted by all cosmologies, mana would simply be a zero symbolic value, that is to say, a sign marking the necessity of a symbolic content *supplementary* [Derrida's italics] to that with which the signified is already loaded." He adds in a note: "the function of notions like mana is to be opposed to the absence of signification, without entailing by itself any particular signification." Although critical, Derrida appropriated Lévi-Strauss's concept of "supplementarity" and made it fundamental to his own thought: "The *overabundance* of the signifier, its *supplementary* character, is thus the result of a finitude, that is to say, the result of a lack which must be *supplemented*" (Derrida, *Writing and Difference*, 290).

This goes back to the idea of the earlier essay that structuralism, in trying to escape metaphysics, is still embedded in it, insofar as structure acts as a totalizing concept: "If totalization no longer has any meaning, it is not because the infiniteness of a field cannot be covered by a finite glance or a finite discourse, but because the nature of the field—that is language and a finite language—excludes totalization. This field is in effect that of *play* . . . this movement of play, permitted by the lack or absence of a center or origin, is the movement of supplementarity" (Derrida, *Writing and Difference*, 289).

As a deconstruction of humanism, Derrida draws implications for interpretation in terms of play, with which writers as different as Barthes and Ricoeur are also concerned:

> There are two interpretations of interpretation, of structure, of sign, of play. The one seeks to decipher, dreams of deciphering a truth of an origin which escapes play and the order of the sign. . . . The other, which is no longer turned towards the origin, affirms play and tries to pass beyond man and humanism, the name of man being the name of that being who, throughout the history of metaphysics . . . has dreamed of full presence, the reassuring foundation, the origin and the end of play. (Derrida, *Writing and Difference*, 292)

Shaw raised this opposition between logocentric metaphysical certainty and deconstructive playful uncertainty in *Back to Methuselah: Part I*, where Adam's need for certainty, when faced with the problem of death in Act I, is opposed to Eve's curiosity and belief in dreams in Act II. And Shaw as playwright and as dialectician does not come down on one side or the other, in spite of his obvious sympathy for Eve's position.

Reading Shaw

The names of Lacan, Barthes, and Derrida are used in this text to connote subjectivity, textuality, and writing, respectively, in order to understand Shaw in terms of a textuality that includes writing and reading, language and subjectivity in a process of subject-object relations. The challenge of the Shaw text is how to interpret/translate/read what is written and presented there as a philosophy of the Life Force or Creative Evolution, albeit in several distinct types of discourse (prose, drama, science, religion, and so on), in the framework of a nontotalizing interaction of the human subject with the world. The complexity of the Shaw text derives from its explication, its understanding of the flexibility of subject-object relations within language, in writing and reading, and within the sentence, where neither subject nor object is abstract. In a significant piece of deconstruction that applies the poststructuralist argument against binary thinking, he clearly stated that the world (as a signified) does not exist; it is, rather, an Imaginary in Lacan's sense:

> We are not within a million years, as yet, of being concerned with the meaning of the world. Why do we recognise that philosophy is not a baby's business, although its facial expression so strongly suggests the professional philosopher? Because we know that all its mental energy is absorbed by the struggle to attain ordinary physical consciousness. It is learning to interpret the sensations of its eyes and ears and nose and tongue and finger-tips. It is ridiculously delighted by a silly toy, absurdly terrified by a harmless bogey, because it cannot as yet see these things as they really are. Well, we are all still as much babies in the world of thought as we were in our second year in the world of sense. Men are not real men to us; they are heroes and villains, respectable persons and criminals. Their qualities are virtues and vices; the natural laws that govern them are gods and devils; their destinies are rewards and expiations; their conditions are innocence and guilt—there is no end to the amazing transubstantiations and childish imaginings which delight and terrify us because we have not grown up enough to be capable of genuine natural history. And then people come to you with their heads full of these figments, which they call, if you please, "the world," and ask you what is the meaning of them. The answer is, that they have not even an existence, much less a meaning. (*Non-Dramatic*, 454)

The "common sense" or "scientific" view of the world is just such an abstract relation, which Shaw referred to as "the old-fashioned metaphysics of Bacon and Locke" (*Books* 2, 142) between an abstract subject (for example, a coherent ego or what Derrida calls the punctual simplicity of the classical subject) and an abstract object (for example, a Platonic idea, or material nature, or atoms).[16] This abstract simplistic metaphysical relation

(Imaginary in Lacan's critique or ideological in Althusser's) might be illustrated in simple diagram form as one between two points:

However, with all due deference to Derrida's criticism of Leibniz's penchant (philosopher-mathematician that he was) for illustrating metaphysics by means of a line, and, indeed, of metaphors of punctuality, linearity, and geometry in general, Shaw's position may be better illustrated by adapting the above diagram as a relation between two lines rather than two points thus:

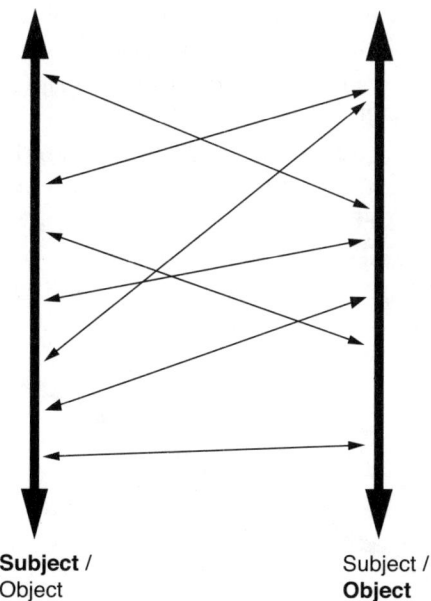

Here the subject, the "I" in the sentence, can take its position for any one sentence at any point along the line of subjectivity. The object can be at any point along the line of objectivity. The subject-object relation, becoming more flexible, can be expressed as one between any point on one line and any point on the other. Where the Shaw text intersects with poststructuralism is in saying that the position of the subject is a variable within a single text or discourse, as it is within a multiplicity of texts or discourses, or within a single dialogue between two subjects. A singular unified individual subject can only be a metaphysical abstraction, a misrecognition, or a "misusage," to use Shaw's word. Rather, the subject-object relation within a sentence may become a site of discourse(s), of a play of many different sets of linguistic relations, of a play of texts.

This diagram can be further adapted in two ways according to Shaw's own prescription. The first mirrors Lacan's contention that the subject is constituted in relation to the other(s), the subject as shadow. In his review of Chesterton's book on him, Shaw writes: "Like all men, I play many parts; and none of them is more or less real than another . . . I am, in short, not only what I can make of myself, which varies greatly from hour to hour and emergency to non-emergency, but what you can see in me" (*Pen Portraits and Reviews*, 82). Thus, as indicated in the diagram above, the above relation can be either direct between two subjects or even reverse, where the subject becomes the object of another's gaze, as in Lacan.

The second option suggests a variant of the diagram above, in which Shaw strikes a decidedly Derridean note in relation to the possibility of truth: "I learnt long ago that though there are several places from which the tourist may enjoy a view of Primrose Hill, none of these can be called *the* view of Primrose Hill. Wherever I have been I have found and fervently uttered *a* true view of it; but as to *the* true view, believe me there is no such thing" (*Music 2*, 664).[17] In this case the diagram might become something like this:

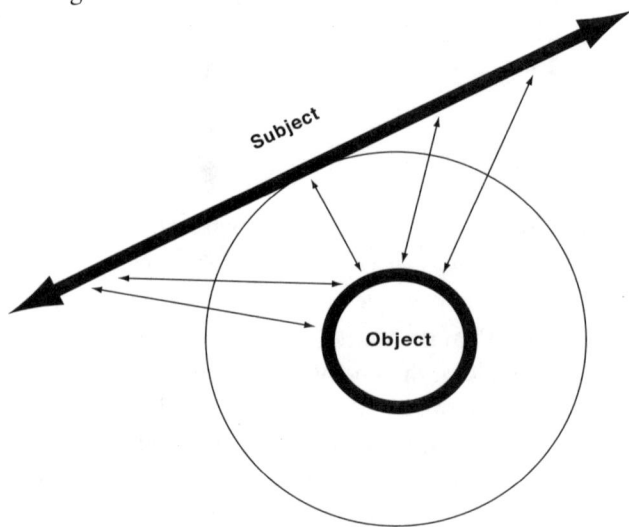

A three-dimensional model would be even better, but, after all, these are only illustrations, visual metaphors to suggest the flexibility of Shaw's writing and his use of language and logic ("Have you been sent here to make your minds flexible?" the longliver asks the shortlivers in *The Tragedy of an Elderly Gentleman*). They cannot explain that understanding of the heterogeneity of spacing and temporality that Shaw shares with both William Blake ("the variation of Time & Space Which vary according as the organs of perception vary," wrote Blake at the end of *Jerusalem*) and Derrida. Shaw himself explained: "when [man] comes to reason deductively, he cannot get on without hypotheses, postulates, definitions and axioms that do not hold good of anything really existent.... the path of a bullet as deduced by a physicist [does] not coincide with reality, because the reality is the result of many more factors than the physicist is able to take into account with his limited power of thinking" (*Non-Dramatic*, 345). And, of course, as a dramatist he was necessarily flexible with different subjective points of view. The Epistle Dedicatory to *Man and Superman* contains his most famous statement on point of view. But what is often overlooked in that statement is its context: the question of the authorship of *The Revolutionist's Handbook*, a text where Shaw conflates himself, Don Juan, and John Tanner:

> In that handbook you will find the politics of the sex question as I conceive Don Juan's descendent to understand them. Not that I disclaim the fullest responsibility for his opinions and for those of all my characters, pleasant and unpleasant. They are all right from their several points of view; and their points of view are, for the dramatic moment, mine also. This may puzzle people who believe that there is such a thing as an absolutely right point of view, usually their own. It may seem to them that nobody who doubts this can be in a state of grace. However that may be, it is certainly true that nobody who agrees with them can possibly be a dramatist or indeed anything else that turns upon a knowledge of mankind. (*Prefaces*, 160)

In view of this multiple flexibility the question arises as to how Shaw can maintain a consistent position on anything, a question often asked of poststructuralists. His answer simply is that, as we can never know everything ("Facts mean nothing by themselves"), we must act on our opinions of the few facts we do "know" (*Shaw-Wells*, 152). As he put it in the preface to *Androcles and the Lion*: "The open mind never acts: when we have done our utmost to arrive at a reasonable conclusion, we still, when we can reason and investigate no more, must close our minds for the moment with a snap, and act dogmatically on our conclusions" (*Prefaces*, 602). His writing, rather than being simply prescriptive, is aimed at provoking informed practical action.

In maintaining that this flexibility of the subject-object relation applies not only to different enunciators but also within a single enunciator as subject, the Shaw text was truly radical in its anticipation of much poststructuralist writing. The second and third diagrams above become particularly useful in reading the Shaw text and in trying to understand its rhetoric when the contradictions within the discourse become too difficult to accommodate on the lines of the first diagram. During his lifetime, for example, Shaw's discourse on politics became unacceptable on several occasions within his own (British) culture: during the Boer War when he offended liberals by adopting an anti-Boer position that coincided with the Imperialist position (to which he was otherwise so opposed); by his scathing attack on militarism and the empires in the face of English jingoism at the beginning of the Great War; and by his support for Soviet communism and his damning criticisms of liberal democracy as practiced by parliamentary governments in the 1920s and 1930s, mixed with praise for the achievements of Mussolini, Hitler, and Stalin. He, the great campaigner against all forms of human cruelty and capital punishment, even infamously argued a case for liquidation in the preface to *On the Rocks*. But once both his subjective position and the object are understood as "moveable feasts," as it were, within his discourse, we are then forced to read the texts critically without either immediately assenting to or rejecting one interpretation out of hand, or aligning them exclusively with a liberal humanism, an antidemocratic fascism, or a doctrinaire communist content, all of which at different points the text contradicts.

Shaw's elaboration of Shakespeare's metaphor of "all the world's a stage" uses the theater itself to understand the subject-object relation, where "even the great metaphor itself is inaccurately expressed; for the world is a playhouse, not merely a stage" (*Drama* 2, 714). This strongly suggests that subjects relate to the world, not in a single relation of subject to object, but *both* individually *and* socially as members of a theater audience. The subject-spectator can choose either to be locked into the theatrical illusion, Lacan's Imaginary, or can equally choose to relate to that experience by reading it as a text, to interpret it critically, to go behind the scenes, to write the drama of the text. The subject can thus come to comprehend where and how it is positioned socially, whether as actor, dramatist, or critic, within the cultural Symbolic playhouse.

This symbolic theater, the Shaw text comprising both the play-texts and the nondramatic writing, becomes what he calls, in "The Author's Apology" (1906) to *Dramatic Opinions*, "a factory of thought," which we might call a factory of textuality, the temple of his religion, whose actors (Shakespeare's "shadows") are "the hierophants of a cult as eternal and sacred as any professed religion in the world" (*Prefaces*, 779). Readers and spectators become adherents to that cult of shadows and illusion, where, by partaking in a communal social rite, dispositions to act and subjective identities may be re-created. Thus, the identity of the reader-spectator is (re)forged in the Shavian theater/factory/temple in a playful transforming encounter between subjective knowledge and experience of the world with the text. Shaw's theater becomes a Symbolic machine where this encounter between the audience-reader and the Lacanian Other ("We in fact address . . . those we do not know, true Others, true subjects . . . I always have to aim at true subjects, and I have to be content with shadows" [Lacan, *Seminar II*, 244]) is represented by the Imaginary of the players on the stage. Producing the diverse texts of the play, readers or audience critically adjust identities in the Symbolic, in Lacan's sense. A refusal "to play," as Barthes would put it, the textuality of the Shaw text condemns the reader to remain locked in an Imaginary, critically unengaged and, as subjects, passively and ideologically constituted.

2 The Critic

The Writer's Shadow

> *The claim of art to our respect must stand or fall with the validity of its pretension to cultivate and refine our senses and faculties until seeing, hearing, feeling, smelling and tasting become highly conscious and critical acts. . . . The worthy artist or craftsman is he . . . [whose products] call the heightened senses and ennobled faculties into pleasurable activity.*
>
> "A Degenerate's View of Nordau," G. Bernard Shaw in *Liberty*, July 27, 1895

Writing and Criticism

Chapter 1 began an approach to the reading of Shaw's writing, and chapter 3 considers how Shaw played with that protean shadow, his own identity as writing subject, the author as a fictional nonfiction within the writing for the delight of his reader. However, Shaw, not content with re-creating his own fluctuating identity in terms of autobiography, also sought to remake the world as object, in his political activities and writing. An attempt to read his critical writing in such essays of the 1890s as "The Quintessence of Ibsenism," "A Degenerate's View of Nordau," and "The Religion of the Pianoforte," as well as in his regular critical writing over the initials G.B.S. or the *nom de plume, Corno di Bassetto*, can provide us with another way of showing how Shaw dealt with the implications of the variables of the subject-object relation in writing, discussed at the end of chapter 1.

There is always a shadowy relation between writing and criticism. Not only is the writer a shadow of the critic, but the critic is also the writer's shadow in as much as the critic is the reader who writes and whose writing reflects both on and of a prior text. Every text is a critique, a deconstruction, of previous texts. As a seeming reflection of this, some preeminent writers like Shaw have been exemplary critics. In Barthes's terms, the critic's text provides a secondary account of the attempted seduction of the reader by the pleasures of the primary text, the fetish object, thus provoking a doubly perverse pleasure. In Derrida's terms the deconstructive supplement, a writing that is both a completion of and an addition to the original text, in its turn prompts a supplement from its reader in an ongoing process of textuality.

The absence of an ostensible author-subject and the presence of a plurality of character-subjects in dramatic writing might have forced Shaw to compensate with the insertion of a colorful subjectivity as dramatic fiction into his critical writing. But writing is not simply a question of employing different possibilities of subjective identity. Nineteenth-century novel writers, like Shaw's favorites George Eliot and Charles Dickens, and Shaw himself, took the phenomenological relation of the individual's apprehension of the world in postmedieval bourgeois society, analogous to the subject-object/predicate structure of the sentence, as their theme. In Shaw's last novel, *An Unsocial Socialist*, this became a specifically Marxist reading of social relations that sought to deconstruct the prevailing liberal model of capitalist economics. The critic as writer, by contrast, takes as his object not the world, but its cultural texts that can all be considered as writing—if, in the larger sense, we can say that all artworks are a type of writing, as Shaw seemed to imply in the Epistle Dedicatory of *Man and Superman*, when he described several English visual artists—Turner, Hogarth, Blake—along with a group of continental writer-artists—Goethe, Schopenhauer, Wagner, and so on—as "writers whose peculiar sense of the world I recognize as more or less akin to my own" (*Prefaces*, 162). Shaw, the failed novelist turned critic, therefore became a writer, not on his world (as a signified), but on the texts (signifiers) that constitute it. He also declared in the Epistle Dedicatory that the world described by artist-philosophers and writers "in books, whether the books be confessed epics or professed gospels, or in codes, or in political orations, or in philosophical systems, is not the main world at all" but rather what he calls "the self-consciousness of certain abnormal people" (*Prefaces*, 157). Thus, the relation of the writer to "the world," insofar as it can be known, becomes a problematic of textuality; the writer as reader becomes a critic.

This chapter shifts the emphasis from a phenomenological relation between the writer and his world to the textual relation between the reader and the writing, the critic and the artwork/text, and the reader and the critic-reader/writer. Shaw, in fact, by insisting on the corporeal subjectivity of the critic in writing, his sensitivity to the pleasures and pain of art, his need to become a "skilled voluptuary," anticipates the importance that Barthes places on "the pleasure of the text." The author of *Plays Pleasant and Unpleasant* may, if titles are anything to consider, have textual concerns in common with the author of *The Pleasure of the Text*. Shaw, then, positioned himself as critic-reader by inserting himself as critic-writer into that textual play of signifiance, into a textuality where cultural and social relations may be either obscured or highlighted, unraveled or traced, by vivifying, as he puts it, the abstractions of the subject and the word *criticism*: "Let us try to vivify our ideas on the subject by getting away from the abstraction 'criticism' to the reality from which it is abstracted: that is, the living, breathing, erring, human, nameable and addressable individual who writes criticism" (*Music 3*, 235–40). By insisting on the critic's body—a corporeality capable of feeling sensuous pleasures, pains, and passions—he comes close to Barthes's understanding of the reader's pleasures of the text. This chapter shows the staging of the deconstructive drama that takes place in Shaw's critical writing through the fictional character of the corporeal critic.

The critic as shadow of the dramatist in Shaw remains as impossible to pin down as any other shadow. His eclecticism renders difficult a consistent reading of both his writing in general (the many different types of discourse in which he intervened) and his critical writing in particular. As a critic, he covered a plurality of specific artistic disciplines (literature, art, music, and drama), but all his writing (like that of Ruskin) embraced larger cultural, economic, and social matters. Shaw could write in one place as a cultural critic-philosopher on the relation of Philistines and Idealists to Ibsenite Realists in society, and in another place specifically as a music critic on the technical implications of Helmholtz's theoretical writing on harmonics in relation to the problem of keyboard temperament in music, or in yet a third place as a theater critic on the importance of Garrick and Talma to the history of acting. Considered separately from his writing in general, Shaw's critical writing, that shadow writing of writing on writing, could be seen as preparation for the play-texts, but it might be better read in a context of the critical texts being imbricated with the dramatic texts, or vice versa. Such imbrication is most evident in his famous conjunction of preface and play, which became his favored method of presenting his texts to the reading public; the preface has a separate significance from what would otherwise be considered the main text while, nevertheless, sharing certain thematic concerns. But this imbrication can also hold between the criticism and the plays, as is the case between his first major critical essay, *The Quintessence of Ibsenism*, and his second play, *The Philanderer*, written two years later. The final part of this chapter briefly discusses the former, while chapter 6 picks up the rewriting of its themes in the latter.

The Subjectivity of the Critic and Humanism

Just as Shaw's socialism was a deconstruction of the orthodoxies of prevailing political and economics texts, so his criticism deconstructed cultural orthodoxies. He championed Wagner and Ibsen, antagonists of everything that used to be called Victorian, and he wrote a book devoted to the work of each of those nineteenth-century titans. Even more outrageous, his criticism deprecated the reputation of his most famous predecessor, the English national literary idol William Shakespeare, which many took to be an attack on the Shakespeare text itself. Indeed, Shaw, the critic as puritan, coined the term "bardolatry" for the literary idolization of the Elizabethan/Jacobean dramatist and poet. And he compounded this insolence by suggesting that he, the author Bernard Shaw, might have been "Better than Shakespear?" as the subheading to a section of the preface to *Three Plays for Puritans* interrogatively puts it. In fact, Shaw was an astute, sympathetic, and close reader of the Shakespeare text, as the large body of his criticism devoted to Shakespeare's plays makes clear. He complained, for instance, that although he had seen many productions of *Hamlet* in the theater, not once had he seen the character of Fortinbras appear on stage.[1] In other words, he had never seen Shakespeare's *Hamlet*, which he knew only through reading the text. His critique of Shakespeare's reputation extended to the theatrical tradition of performing Shakespeare, and the lack of a discernible Weltanschauung in Shakespeare's works—a characteristic of such eminent European writers as Dante, Goethe, and Ibsen.

That Ibsen's writing possessed this characteristic enabled Shaw to distill a social philosophy from the Ibsen text as "the quintessence of Ibsenism" in his book of that name, although Shaw deconstructs his own distillation by "reminding those who may think I have forgotten to reduce Ibsenism to a formula for them, that its quintessence is that there is no formula" (*Non-Dramatic*, 293). In *The Perfect Wagnerite*, Shaw demonstrated not only the presence of a revolutionary social philosophy in *Der*

Ring des Nibelungen but also delighted himself and discomfited Wagnerites by identifying inconsistencies between the philosophy and work. He thus places the perfect *bourgeois* Wagnerite, a reader of both Wagner and Shaw, in a doubly uncomfortable position: first, that reader must acknowledge an underlying revolutionary social philosophy in Wagner's massive work and then admit that it was imperfectly applied by the Bayreuth *Meister*. Shaw, the deconstructive critic, was neither disconcerted by this acknowledgment nor prevented from enjoying the pleasures of the four music-dramas by his exposition of inconsistency on Wagner's part. However, for those who believe in the artistic integrity of Wagner's *Gesamtkunstwerk* (total work of art), hold consistency, coherence, and unity to be indispensable to art, or maintain social theory's irrelevance to art, *The Perfect Wagnerite* necessarily makes for uncomfortable reading.

Shakespeare was concerned more with life's diversities than its unities, as Shaw himself put it, which, paradoxically, might make Shakespeare seem more postmodern than the artist-philosophers mentioned above and, especially, than Shaw himself. Shaw claimed that Shakespeare's failure to read critically the text of his own culture and epoch resulted in a philosophy of unrelated platitudes, in a pessimism that was no philosophy at all; Shaw was fond of quoting the characteristic lines: "As flies are to wanton boys, are we to the gods; they kill us for their sport" (*Prefaces*, 543–44). Yet Shakespeare's undeniable literary preeminence, in spite of the limitations of a text from which no "quintessence" could be distilled (other than this generalized pessimism and the chauvinistic ideology of Elizabethan imperialism), made the Shakespeare text fertile ground for Shavian criticism. It allowed him to consider the text under many different aspects: performance, history, philosophy, textuality, reputation, vocal sound (as in his contention that one of Shakespeare's great strengths as a dramatist was his command of "word music," another term coined by Shaw that has since become indispensable to Shakespearean criticism) in a steady stream of writing that included the plays *The Dark Lady of the Sonnets* (1910), *Cymbeline Refinished* (1937) right up to his last published (puppet) play, *Shakes Vs Shav* of 1949.[2]

Crucially, Shaw's role as critic allowed him to insert himself into the cultural debate, as instanced in his inquiry as to Shaw the dramatist's merits relative to Shakespeare's. Shaw as playwright, like Shakespeare, generally eschewed first-person narrative and narration, although other chapters discuss how he contrived nevertheless to inscribe his authorial subjectivity into his plays. Chapter 6, shadowing this chapter, looks at how his experience precisely as critic in the 1890s is inscribed into both *The Philanderer* and *Fanny's First Play*. As critic, Shaw occupied unabashedly the subjective position, which yields its very idiosyncratic, rather than generic or abstract, singularities and poses. In response to an article by the Irish composer Villiers Stanford, "Some Aspects of Musical Criticism," which pleaded for more considered notices of new musical compositions than the usual rushed overnight reviews, Shaw insisted that criticism is neither objective nor the result of an abstract subjectivity:

> Justice is not the critic's business; and there is no more dishonest and insufferable affectation in criticism than that impersonal, abstract, judicially authoritative air, which, since it is so easy to assume . . . is directly encouraged by the haste Dr Stanford deprecates. . . . just substitute for "the critic" the initials G.B.S. Instantly the realities of the case leap to light; and you see without any argument that the lapse of a few days between the performance and the notice, far from obliterating the writer's partialities and prejudices, his personal likes and dislikes, his bias, his temperament, his local traditions, his nationality—in a word, himself, only enables him to express them the more insidiously when he wishes to conceal their influence. . . . We cannot get away from the critic's tempers, his impatiences, his sorenesses, his friendships, his spite, his enthusiasms (amatory and other), nay his very politics and religion if they are touched by what he criticizes. They are all there hard at work. . . . The critic who cannot interest the public in his real self has mistaken his trade: that is all. (*Music 3*, 237–38)

His "real self," of course, is neither an abstract unified self nor an essential human self, but rather a particular, if disparate, subjectivity inscribed in his writing.[3] Shaw refuses to reduce the signifying process of writing to that of a logocentric "truth," to a series of signifieds, to what something is (rather than what it is not). Neither can the objective be separated from the subjective, so he would praise critics whose opinions he disagreed with for their honesty in both revealing themselves along with their opinions in their reviews. Not at all incidentally, he sought to shift the emphasis in criticism from what is said to how it is said: "I therefore add . . . a further plea for sincerity of expression, not only of the critic's opinion, but of the mood in which that opinion was formed" (*Music 3*, 238).

This insertion of individual subjectivity into critical writing can be considered an aspect of Shaw's humanism that insists on human particularity, but it should not be confused with other (logocentric) humanisms characteristic of the Renaissance humanists who generalized "man" as the measure of all things, or of the Enlightenment philosophes who saw "man" as ennobled by Reason, or of the nineteenth-century apostles of human progress, science, free-trade, and modern liberal imperial parliamentary democracies, who view the European hero as the evolutionary victor in a competitive struggle for survival. Roebuck Ramsden in *Man and Superman*, Tom Broadbent in *John Bull's Other Island*, and the elderly gentleman in *Back to Methuselah: Part IV* are satirical portraits of this latter type. Like the differing ideologies or épistèmes or metanarratives of humanism, which became the object of criticism by Althusser, Foucault, and Lyotard, Shaw's essay "A Degenerate's View of Nordau" critiques the myth of "Man" as "hero of . . . the history of British-American Christianity," who "as Rationalist and Materialist, regard[s] Reason as an eternal principle, independent of and superior to his erring passions" (*Non-Dramatic*, 358–59). No essential, abstract, or ideological humanity can be the measure for Shaw, whose humanism is one of particular human responses to the world in which subjects find themselves enmeshed, individually and socially, and which involves writing and criticism. Thus we need to look at the historical and biographical context of the particular subject as critic, the asserting self, the real if heterogeneous self, inscribed in Shaw's criticism.

The Ruskinite Critic

Ruskin, the epitome of the Victorian art and culture critic, had an immense impact on Shaw as critic. Ruskin, the sometime Oxford Slade Professor of Art, served Shaw, as he did Proust, as a model critic. Shaw had probably first read Ruskin's writing on art during his early years in London, a period of building on knowledge gained during adolescence when he had haunted the National Gallery in Dublin, read Vasari, studied as many art books as possible, and aspired to become a painter in the Michelangelo mold. But Ruskin was more than just an art critic. As a follower of Carlyle, he and Matthew Arnold, whom Shaw did not admire so much, personified the late Victorian phenomenon of cultural critic who wrote on social matters and economics as well as art. In all these capacities Ruskin cast his shadow: over the aspiring young novelist G. Bernard Shaw; over G.B.S. the critic, who began his literary career in London as an art critic before becoming the wittiest and most incisive as well as sympathetic, of cultural critics writing in the last decade of nineteenth-century London; and later, over the writings of Bernard Shaw, dramatist, social prophet, and citizen of the world. As playwright, Shaw found an ideal literary outlet for expanding his Ruskinite critical and political writing in the prefaces to his increasingly read plays. Indeed, Ruskin served also as his model for publishing his own works; his English publisher, Constable, was technically the distributor, not publisher, of his books. Chapter 6 suggests how Ruskin's shadow looms over Shaw's play *Fanny's First Play* as a dramatic discourse on criticism.

Shaw declared in the preface to *Widowers' Houses*: "it is impossible for any fictionist, dramatic or other, to make true pictures of modern society without some knowledge of the economic anatomy of it" (*Prefaces*, 708). Thus, his political writing, his plays, and his criticism are all campaigning writing, informed by the autodidact's mastery of the abstruse discipline of economics in combination with his voraciously accumulated knowledge of the technical and historical aspects of the various art forms with which he dealt. All three types of his writing (political, critical, and creative) sought to encourage in their readers an active engagement with the texts, rather than a passive consumption of the writing, to use Barthes's distinction. All are Shaw shadows, different reflections of the radical avant-garde agitator informed by Ruskin's critical moralism attacking the ramparts of the status quo as socialist, dramatist, and critic. In an age when the slogan "art for art's sake" had some currency, neither the criticism nor the plays (insofar as they were seen as political tracts) were taken as seriously as they might have been. As Shaw himself put it in the preface to *London Music in 1888–1889*: "all the journalists believed that the affair was a huge joke, the point of which was that I knew nothing about music . . . [rather] I was one of the few critics of that time who really knew their business" (*Prefaces*, 853). Such self-confidence, combined with his intellectual background, enabled him to take his place at the end of a line of Victorian critics such as Thomas Carlyle, Matthew Arnold, and John Ruskin, while becoming the paradigm of the twentieth-century critic.

By common consent, Shaw is one of the twentieth century's major dramatists, but that reputation came later. In the 1890s, his literary reputation was based on his recently acquired renown as a readable, witty, and radical critic of several of the arts, a view enhanced, if anything, by his socialism and his sartorial eccentricities. For Shaw this period of regular journalism spent reviewing painting, books, music, and theater lasted thirteen years, from May 1885 to May 1898; the last seven years overlapped with the beginning of his playwrighting years. Going back a little in time may make it easier to trace the strands of his disparate activities during his time as a critic.

His fifth novel, *An Unsocial Socialist*, proved to be his last completed novel. The book shared the same immediate fate as the others; no publisher would take a risk on works of such unconventionality. His failure as a novelist seemed complete. Yet the following year turned out to be Shaw's *annus mirabilis*, although it might not have seemed so at the time. In September 1884, he joined the Fabian Society, the most intellectual and nondoctrinaire of the socialist groups. As a leading member involved in committee work, lecturing, and writing on economics and, later, international politics, he became one of the most active socialists of his generation. Within four years, the failed novelist turned socialist barnstormer had edited, arranged for publication, and written two of the *Fabian Essays* (1889), one of the most influential of all English books on socialism. Ironically, 1884 was also the year that his novels at last began to be published—in serial form in the socialist journal *Today* (one of whose editors was his friend Belfort Bax—socialist, philosopher, and music critic), and in *Our Corner*, edited by his Fabian colleague and close friend Annie Besant. Strictly speaking, 1884 was also the year his playwrighting career began; on August 18 he embarked on a play, called first "The Way to a Woman's Heart" and subsequently "Rheingold," to be coauthored with William Archer, critic, Ibsen translator, and Shaw's friend since the early 1880s.[4] It proved an abortive enterprise. Three years later, only two acts had been completed. On October 6, 1887, Shaw noted in his diary that, when he read the draft to his coauthor, Archer received it "with contempt" (*Letters 1*, 175). The play was abandoned; his career as a dramatist at the first hurdle proved to be even less successful than his novel writing had been. Not until he returned to the discarded manuscript in 1892, to complete what was now called *Widowers' Houses*, did his career as playwright really begin.

During this period of politicking, playwrighting, and philandering, for which he became notorious in socialist circles, Shaw as critic adopted the persona of G.B.S., the fabrication, the textual shadow of the socially and politically contentious personality he had become in London society, which seemed to lend a coherent, if fictional, identity/subjectivity to these disparate activities. Criticism allowed him a median position between trying to re-create the world as a socialist and to re-create himself in writing. As used in his 1896 essay "On Going to Church," that word *re-create* (*Non-Dramatic*, 381, 384, 389) had significant overtones for him. In another major critical essay of the time, "The Religion of the Pianoforte" (1894), he stated that "music alone requires an artistic act on the part of the reader [that is, the piano player], which act, in its perfection, becomes such an act of recreation as Wagner found in Liszt's playing of Beethoven's sonatas" (*Music 3*, 120). While he makes this act of re-creation of the reader as subject specific to music, it could be argued that he demanded as much of the reader/spectator of his plays, and it has been often noted that such moments of self-recreation, of subjective transformation, of conversion form the structural climax of his plays. On March 23, 1895, around the same time he wrote to Janet Achurch: "[Artists] must have either recreation, in the literal sense of that profoundly significant word, or else stimulation. Now recreation is the secret of the religious life—of the old cathedral building. You go in there and pray or meditate, and are profoundly rested and recreated" (*Letters 1*, 504).

Although William Archer had tried and failed to launch him as either a novelist or a playwright, he was more successful in getting Shaw his first regular jobs as critic: as book reviewer on the *Pall Mall Gazette* (1885–1888) and as art critic on *The World* (1886–1889). Later, as Corno di Bassetto in *The Star* from 1889 to 1890, he began the work that earned him enduring fame as music critic. In May 1890, when he started writing for *The World* (after his political journalism became too contentious for that organ and its liberal editor, T. P. O'Connor), he finally adopted the initials G.B.S. for his music criticism that he had sometimes used for his occasional journalism. He resigned from *The World* in August 1894, but he missed the regular income from reviewing and began a three-year stint as drama critic on Frank Harris's *Saturday Review* in January 1895, a year after the noteworthy run of Florence Farr's production of his fourth play, *Arms and the Man*.

Shaw undertook to lecture on Ibsen for the Fabian Society in 1890 as a campaigning socialist and cultural critic in a series called "Socialism in Contemporary Literature"; the following year this led to the writing of his first major essay in philosophic criticism, *The Quintessence of Ibsenism*.[5] Shaw, the author of the novel *Love Among the Artists*, never lost an opportunity of deconstructing the notion of "art for art's sake" and protested at the end of the preface that his book "is not a critical essay on the poetic beauties of Ibsen, but simply an exposition of Ibsenism" (*Non-Dramatic*, 208). This study of Ibsen probably prompted the resumption and completion of *Widowers' Houses* in 1892, although a more immediate incentive was that J. T. Grein's Independent Theatre, which had put on Ibsen's

Ghosts to scandalous effect in 1891, was looking to produce an English play to appeal to the same audience. In this, *Widowers' Houses* with its social theme of rack-renting proved as successfully scandalous as Ibsen's play on social hypocrisy and syphilis.

The Pleasures (and Pains) of the Critic

The critic G.B.S., a subjectivity with text as its object, was susceptible to what Barthes has called "pleasure" in *The Pleasure of the Text*. Barthes's book, consisting of forty-six short sections, is aphoristic, rather than a fully argued theory, and can be useful for considering Shaw's critical writing. Just as Shaw maintains in "The Religion of the Pianoforte" that feeling sets a man thinking (not the reverse) so Barthes writes: "Pleasure's force of *suspension* can never be overstated . . . what pleasure suspends is the *signified* value. . . . That is the pleasure of the text: value shifted to the sumptuous rank of the signifier. . . . The pleasure of the text is that moment when my body pursues its own ideas—for my body does not have the same ideas I do" (Barthes, *Pleasure*, 16–17). Whereas Shaw refers to both pleasure and passion in the essays he wrote during his time as critic, Barthes bifurcates the concept into *plaisir* (pleasure) and *jouissance* (bliss): the former tends to reinforce the self, enabling analytical or critical judgments within the context of a tradition, but the latter dissolves the self (as happens in sexual enjoyment), which prevents reasonable (objective, analytic, or critical) judgments being reached on the text. This distinction leads to Barthes positing both a split subject and two types of text, one of pleasure, linked to a comfortable practice of reading, and the other of bliss, which brings to a crisis the reader's relation with language: "the subject who keeps the two texts in his field and in his hands the reins of pleasure is an anachronic subject . . . : he enjoys the consistency of his selfhood (that is his pleasure) and seeks its loss (that is his bliss/jouissance). He is a subject split twice over, doubly perverse" (Barthes, *Pleasure*, 14).

Barthes's plaisir/jouissance distinction is similar to Nietzsche's distinction between the Apollonian (associated with the rational) and the Dionysian (associated with the irrational). In abstract terms, plaisir and jouissance are mutually exclusive concepts, although in practical terms there can always be a mixture, more or less, of the two types. Barthes approached the question of pleasure as a reaction to his earlier more theoretical writings on semiological and narrative codes: "I felt that today's intellectual language was submitting too easily to moralizing imperatives that eliminated all notion of enjoyment, of bliss. In reaction, I wanted therefore to reintroduce this word [pleasure] within my personal range, to lift its censorship, to unblock it, to *un-repress* it" (Barthes, *Grain of the Voice*, 205).

Jouissance, bliss, is particularly associated with the new, the modern. It cannot apply to something experienced before. While bringing bliss to some, and pain to others, jouissance cannot be appreciated in reference to previous pleasures or previous texts as can plaisir. This reaction to the experience of jouissance can only be, to use Barthes's term, hysterical ("in the psychoanalytic sense"), and all a critic can write in response becomes a form of hysterical affirmation: "the writer of bliss (and his reader) begins the untenable text [which] is outside pleasure, outside criticism, unless it is reached through another text of bliss: you cannot speak 'on' such a text, you can only speak 'in' it, *in its fashion*, enter into a desperate plagiarism, hysterically affirm the void of bliss (and no longer obsessively repeat the letter of pleasure)" (Barthes, *Pleasure*, 19–22).

Shaw's equivalent in his criticism is "passion," where objective analysis, a supposed goal of criticism, goes by the board: "really fine artists inspire me with the warmest possible regard, which I gratify in writing my notices without the smallest reference to such monstrous conceits as justice, impartiality, and the rest of the ideals. When my critical mood is at its height, personal feeling is not the word: it is *passion*: the passion for artistic perfection, for the noblest beauty of sound, sight, and action that rages in me" (*Music 2*, 169; my italics).

Barthes says very little about the pain, as opposed to the pleasure of the text, except insofar as pain pertains to bliss/jouissance. Shaw, however, raises it in respect of his own criticism, which cannot help but be cruel on occasion to the primary reader of the criticism, the original artist/writer: "No man sensitive enough to be worth his salt as a critic could for years wield a pen that, from the nature of his occupation, is scratching somebody's nerves at every stroke, without becoming conscious of how monstrously indefensible the superhuman attitude of impartiality is for him. If the countless injustices which I have done in these columns had been perpetrated in that attitude I should deserve hanging" (*Music 3*, 237–38).

The critic might even argue that two types of pain supplement Barthes's two types of pleasure associated with critical writing. The first, as above, is an unintended consequence for the artist/writer, often the object of the criticism who reads the critique, which, if necessarily partial, at least seeks to maintain a level of coherent discourse. Shaw describes a second type of pain, that inflicted on the passionate critic by bad art: "The artist who accounts for my disparagement by alleging personal animosity on my part is quite right: when people do less than their best, and do that less at once badly and self complacently, I hate them, loath them, detest them, long to tear them limb from limb and strew them in gobbets about the stage or platform" (*Music 3*, 168–69).

This Dionysian critical rage may be the negative counterpart to Barthes's "hysterical affirmation," where the critic's text can be read as an expression of hysterical negation resulting from the experience of pain, rather than pleasure in reading the artwork/text. We might add here that, according to Derrida's translator, the etymology of the word *critic* comes from the Greek *Krinein*, which means to decide, to judge, to separate, to cut into.[6] Shaw might well have been aware of this etymology when he called for Rembrandt's *Anatomy Lesson* to be a prop in the final act of *The Philanderer*. This double aspect of pleasure—and pain—has implications for criticism and indicates two sides of Shaw as critic: incisive critical analysis and abandoned enthusiasm or deprecation.

A major implication of Barthes's notion of "the pleasure of the text" is what he calls an erotics of the text, where the text becomes a fetish object of desire, an object, therefore, that seduces the reader with a perverse (in the Freudian sense) pleasure: "How can we read criticism? Only one way . . . I can make myself its voyeur: I observe clandestinely the pleasure of others, I enter perversion. . . . The writer's perversity (his pleasure in writing is *without function*), the doubled, the trebled, the infinite perversity of the critic and his reader" (Barthes, *Pleasure*, 17). Elsewhere, Barthes speaks of "the Don Juanism of the text" (Barthes, *Grain of the Voice*, 159), a potent metaphor in relation to the author of the Don Juan play *Man and Superman*. The phrase "body of the text" thereby acquires erotic undertones where the text as fetish object induces a perverse pleasure, which in turn provokes a further insatiable desire: a desire for the author, whom Barthes has already exposed as a fiction: "lost in the midst of the text (not *behind* it, like a deus ex machina) there is always the other, the author. As institution the author is dead . . . but in the text, in a way, I *desire* the author" (Barthes, *Pleasure*, 27). The reader of criticism, Barthes goes on, is doubly perverse, fetishizing not only the primary artwork/text, but also the secondary text of criticism.

The reader of criticism thus takes pleasure in another's pleasure—or pain. We might suppose that Shaw, the taboo-breaking but still pre-Freudian critic, would not concur with such language. But the Epistle

Dedicatory to *Man and Superman*, which juxtaposes the generation of texts with human sexual generation, explicitly presents the artist as genius, as artist-philosopher, precisely in the context of sexual perversity.

> Hence it is that the world's books get written, its pictures painted, its statues modeled, its symphonies composed, by people who are free from the otherwise universal dominion of the tyranny of sex. Which leads us to the conclusion, astonishing to the vulgar, that art, instead of being before all things the expression of the normal sexual situation, is really the only department in which sex is a superseded and secondary power, with its consciousness so confused and its purpose so perverted, that its ideas are mere fantasy to the common man. (*Prefaces*, 157)

Whether Shaw considered the reader of the text as perverse as the writer is not clear, although he did ironically use the word *degenerate* in referring to himself as critic in the title of his open letter review of Nordau's *Degeneration*, "A Degenerate's View of Nordau." The writer's perversity lies in being driven by a need to write more powerful than that of "normal" sexuality. To the extent that a similar need may be expressed by a desire to read, the reader-critic can be called perverse.

Barthes's *Pleasure of the Text* details implications for the reader's subjectivity, a subjectivity as theater, which we might extrapolate to the spectator-reader-critic of Shavian drama whose subjectivity is social—belonging to the theater of society—not personal, in spite of the fictive individual who feels the pleasures of his body: "A certain pleasure is derived from a way of imagining oneself as *individual*, of inventing a final, rarest fiction: the fictive identity. This fiction is no longer the illusion of a unity; on the contrary, it is the theater of society in which we stage our plural: our pleasure is *individual*—but not personal" (Barthes, *Pleasure*, 62).

The Perversity of the Skilled Voluptuary

Two of Shaw's major critical essays written in the 1890s, "The Religion of the Pianoforte" and "A Degenerate's View of Nordau," express his approach to reading, pleasure, art, passion, and sensuality. In the first, he writes explicitly of the rewards of the ability to read music, which he sees as a unique type of textuality, a language of feelings. Yet it is clear that he wrote his plays, as he claims Shakespeare wrote his, as a type of music, as verbal music, where the "word-music" in his dramatic writing becomes a theater of feelings, of emotion. But this word-music is bifurcated: phonetic as well as phonological, to use Barthes's distinction derived from his appreciation of classical singing. Phonetic writing displays what Barthes calls "the grain of the voice," regardless of semantics. He uses the phrase "writing aloud" to indicate that aspect of writing concerned only with the signifier, the articulation of language, not with either meaning (signifiance) or the signified. "Writing aloud" is phonetic rather than phonological.[7] This points to a distinction not often made in Shaw's theater of sounds. The element of music in his dramatic writing is sometimes acknowledged, but usually in the context of what is proposed here as a theater of emotions at the service of the clarity of messages. Such generation of meaning belongs to the geno-text, as Barthes terms it, to the process of signifying (signifiance) in relation to the signified. But, as we saw in chapter 1, Shaw himself pointed out in the Epistle Dedicatory that style may have nothing to do with the signified, with ideas or opinions, but rather with "amorphous qualities of temper and energy." Style results from what he calls "effectiveness of assertion," an "articulation of the body," in Barthes's phrase, present only in the form of absence, as Derridean traces after the "signifieds" of the artwork/text become otherwise untraceable. "All the assertions get disproved sooner or later; and so we find the world full of a magnificent débris of artistic fossils, with the matter-of-fact credibility gone clean out of them, but the form still splendid" (*Prefaces*, 166), writes Shaw.

In his 1898 review of Tolstoy's *What is Art?* Shaw had noted approvingly Tolstoy's definition of art as "an activity by means of which one man, having experienced a feeling, intentionally transmits it to others," but he felt that it should be supplemented with "William Morris's definition of art as the expression of pleasure in work" (*Non-Dramatic*, 429–30). "The Religion of Pianoforte" argues that reading/appreciating texts/artwork only happens through the senses, through sensual pleasure, and through feelings. The essay especially emphasizes the cultural implications of the particular pleasures of reading musical texts that allow for the elaboration of a language of feelings, in which the sound is not a description or sign of a feeling, but *is* the feeling: "[without 'music wisdom'] you are an ignoramus, however eagerly you may pore in your darkened library over the mere printed labels of those wonders that can only be communicated by the transubstantiation of pure feeling for musical tone. . . . Thus to the whole range of imaginative letters . . . you have a parallel range of music

... conveying to your very senses what the other could only suggest to your imagination" (*Music 3*, 105–14).

Whereas Barthes can write: "The pleasure of the text is that moment when my body pursues its own ideas—for my body does not have the same ideas I do" (Barthes, *Pleasure*, 16–17), Shaw puts it like this:

> Asceticism [life without music] will not save us, for the conclusive reason we are not ascetics. Man, as he develops, seeks constantly a keener pleasure, in the pursuit of which he either destroys himself or develops new faculties of enjoyment. He either strives to intensify the satisfaction of resting, eating, and drinking, the excitement and exercise of hunting, and the ardor of courtship, by "refining" them into idleness, gluttony, dipsomania, hideous cruelty, and ridiculous vice, or else he develops his feeling until it becomes poetic feeling, and sets him thinking with pleasure of nobler things. Observe, if you please, the order of development here: it is all-important. . . . It is feeling that sets a man thinking, and not thought that sets him feeling . . . . Taking it then as established that life is a curse to us unless it operates as pleasurable activity, and that as it becomes more intense with the upward evolution of the race it requires a degree of pleasure which cannot be extracted from the alimentary, predatory, and amatory instincts without ruinous perversions of them . . . are we to deliberately reverse our Puritan traditions and aim at becoming a nation of skilled voluptuaries? Certainly. (*Music 3*, 116–19)

Two years later, "A Degenerate's View of Nordau" (or "The Sanity of Art," as Shaw later retitled it) sought to defend modern artists from Nordau's accusation of pathological "degeneration." Shaw does not deny the charge so much as turn it on its head by showing that Nordau's own writing reveals all the symptoms of degeneration he ascribes to the modern artists and critics he criticizes. Shaw argues that Nordau's charge does not account for the specific cultural, social, and moral implications of the work of these artists. But while admitting that art involves perversion, he is less certain than Barthes about the text as fetish, or Nordau who sees art as a symptom of disease, or Freud (influenced by Nordau), who would see it as a symptom of sexual repression. Shaw quotes favorably the Danish critic Georg Brandes, who is quoted unfavorably by Nordau, as representing his own long-held opinion: "To obey one's senses is to have character. He who allows himself to be guided by his passions has individuality"

(*Non-Dramatic*, 354). Although this might lead art to be perverse, that is not the same as being psychologically unhealthy, and Shaw saw as unsettled "the main question as to how far genius is a morbid symptom" (*Prefaces*, 802). Nordau's *Entartung* was published in 1893, the year Shaw wrote *The Philanderer*, but *Entartung* was not translated into English as *Degeneration* until 1895; it is therefore difficult to know if Shaw had Nordau in mind in that play, which has a running joke where the establishment drama critic à la Nordau, Cuthbertson, accuses the Ibsenists of suffering "like all advanced people" from "neurasthenia" (Act II).[8] This psychological disease, *qua* disease of the artist-intellectual, is as nonexistent as Dr. Paramore's physiological disease of the liver (note the pun) proves to be in the same play. But the apposition makes clear that Shaw sees the metaphor of disease (imaginary or not) to art as applicable.

Nordau in *Degeneration* is one example of a critic reacting hysterically to the perversions of late nineteenth-century modern art. Such criticism foregoes all analytic or logical coherence because the subjectivity of the critic clashes socially, culturally, or psychologically, in short, ideologically, with the subjectivity that the reader is invited to assume in enjoying the artwork/text. The critic, in hysterically refusing the invitation, often confuses (by projection) his own subjectivity with what he assumes is the artist/writer's. The critic's reaction as hysteria exposes a type of overdetermined subjectivity where the individual is obscured by the ideological, as Althusser might argue. Or in Shaw's terms, the critic's ideals (Lacan's Imaginary) by which he lives and which he has hitherto taken as reality are stripped away. Shaw's fellow London drama critic Clement Scott, whom Shaw dramatizes as the theater critic in *The Philanderer*, in his reaction to productions of Ibsen's *Ghosts* and Shaw's *Widowers' Houses* epitomized such hysterical criticism.

The Quintessence of Ibsenism—The Reader-Critic as Philosopher-Writer

Shaw's major essay on Ibsen, *The Quintessence of Ibsenism*, taken in tandem with his second play, *The Philanderer*, can tell us about the wider context of his critical writing. To read his criticism means reading more than his criticism; a critique always assumes at least one other text, just as any text always assumes a critique. The essay gives a persuasive reading of the implications in terms of social relations that can be drawn from Ibsen's plays, the later realistic ones in particular, but they are not our concern here.

The initial three chapters ("The Two Pioneers," "Ideals and Idealists," and "The Womanly Woman") elaborate the general critique. The first chapter describes what he calls the "crablike progress of social evolution" (*Non-Dramatic*, 212), which consists of succeeding waves of orthodoxies and heresies, of what we might now call metanarratives and their deconstructions, where each new heresy becomes the next orthodoxy. For example, just as the heresies of rationalism and materialism overturned the orthodoxy of the churches, rationalism in its turn became an orthodoxy, a dominant ideology (Barthes points out that any ideology is necessarily "dominant"). Shaw cites Voltaire as an heretical First Pioneer in regard to the old orthodoxy of the churches, while being an upholder of the new orthodoxy or ideology of eighteenth-century rationalism. When Voltaire wrote, "I don't see the necessity," in response to the assertion that "one must live," he was guilty, according to Shaw, of what the Church he was fighting would have called *"mala fides"*—Sartre's *mauvais fois* (bad faith). Voltaire, wrote Shaw, was "face to face with the very necessity he was denying . . . [and] since all human institutions are constructed to fulfill man's will, and that his will is to live even when his reason teaches him to die, logical necessity . . . is not necessity at all" (*Non-Dramatic*, 214). After this assault on Logos, Shaw continues, but he refuses to elaborate an ideology of the Schopenhauerean will: "Thus we are landed afresh in mystery; for positive science gives no account whatever of this will to live . . . [and scientific] Materialism . . . only isolated the great mystery of consciousness by clearing away several petty mysteries with which we had confused it; just as rationalism isolated the great mystery of the will to live." Barthes echoed this criticism, when he accused the human sciences of adopting general scientific language operating within the "image-repertoire" (similar to Lacan's Imaginary) and are thus ignorant of ideology and the unconscious "which by definition elude the subject who writes, who does not know exactly in which ideology he is entrapped and who does not know his own unconscious" (Barthes, *Grain of the Voice*, 212).

Shaw calls the heretics "Pioneers" and the upholders of orthodoxy "Idealists." He argues that Ibsen is a First Pioneer, the type "who declares it is right to do something hitherto regarded as infamous," with the result that he is "stoned and shrieked at" and considered "an unnatural corrupter of public morals and family life" (*Non-Dramatic*, 209). A Second Pioneer, by contrast, declares it wrong to do something considered heretofore as right—for example, bear-baiting, slavery, colonialism; unlike a First Pioneer, a Second Pioneer is often labeled a "Good Man" while being hated "like the devil" (*Non-Dramatic*, 209). That Ibsen was hysterically shrieked at in print by Clement Scott, the dramatic critic of the *Daily Telegraph*, according to Shaw "the English newspaper which best represents the guilty conscience of the middle-class, or dominant factor in society today" (*Non-Dramatic*, 210), almost certainly meant the Norwegian playwright was a First Pioneer. Shaw claimed that Scott's review of the 1891 production of Ibsen's *Ghosts*, which accused Ibsen of "dramatic impotence, ludicrous amateurishness, nastiness, vulgarity, egotism, coarseness, absurdity, uninteresting verbosity and suburbanity," was written "in an almost hysterical condition." Shaw asks the question: "How then is it that Ibsen, a Norwegian poet of European celebrity, attracts one section of the English people so strongly that they hail him as the greatest living dramatic poet and moral teacher, whilst another section is so revolted by his works that they describe him in terms which they themselves admit are, by the necessities of the case, all but obscene?" (*Non-Dramatic*, 211).

But Shaw does not accuse Scott or the other establishment critics who reacted similarly of being dishonest, hypocritical, or bad critics (the subjective cannot be abstracted from the objective): "Mr Clement Scott's judgment has not misled him in the least as to Ibsen's meaning. Ibsen means all that most revolts his critic." And so the critic is "impelled to denounce Ibsen as he does, Ibsen being equally impelled to propagate the convictions which provoke the attack" (*Non-Dramatic*, 211).

In his second chapter, Shaw breaks down his picture of the composition of society into three notional categories: Philistines, which was presumably borrowed from Matthew Arnold's *Culture and Anarchy* (1869), Idealists, and Realists. The Pioneers are always Realists, whereas the upholders of the status quo are always Idealists. The third chapter deals with one of the greatest of the ideals (or ideological constructions) of a patriarchal, capitalist society that depends on the sale of women between men in marriage as its basis: the Womanly Woman. Feminist critics, influenced by Lacan, describe what Shaw called the Womanly Woman in terms of gender construction, of "Woman as masquerade," where femininity becomes a socially assumed masking.[9] At the beginning of his second chapter, Shaw speaks of an "Ideal" being "a mask for the reality, which in its nakedness is intolerable to [the Idealists]" (*Non-Dramatic*, 219). Lacan receives greater attention in chapter 4, but relevant here is an equivalence between Shaw's three social types of subject—Philistine, Idealist, and Realist—and Lacan's three types of object (reality)—the Real, the Imaginary, and the Symbolic, respectively.[10] The Philistine, unlike the Realist and the Idealist, does not relate to his world either critically or uncritically, either realistically or idealistically, either working out his symbolic subjective position in terms of childhood family history and society or as being lost in his Imaginary. That is why the world in which the Shavian Philistine lives is the Lacanian Real—a realm in which we all live when not otherwise engaged with linguistic (Symbolic) relations or (Imaginary) relations of desire. To write of Shaw's social types in relation to Lacanian psychoanalysis should not necessarily surprise us; Richard Dietrich's article "Shavian Psychology" has already considered them as psychological types. And Matthew Arnold had already gone some way to psychologizing the classes with his trinity of categories (Barbarians, Philistines, and Populace), which retained the link to the old social classes: upper, middle, and lower. Shaw, the prospective dramatist, took from Arnold the character-type model, but he broke the alignment with the old class model because he was not a class warrior in Marx's mold. Thus Shaw's types, both psychological and social, allow of both internal and external application, a distinction implicit in the modern discourses of psychoanalysis and ideology (Freud/Marx or Lacan/Althusser) and taken up by such writers as Lévi-Strauss, Barthes, and Derrida. Barthes had Marx and Freud in mind when he said in relation to subjectivity and discourse that "utterance is affected by two factors previously unknown to us: ideology and the awareness of ideology, and the unconscious and an awareness of the unconscious" (Barthes, *Grain of the Voice*, 212).

The Shavian Realist is the Barthesian reader who does not draw on the image-repertoire of scientific writing for any explanation of the pleasures of the text, or, indeed, of textuality itself; this is in direct contrast to Idealist critics like Clement Scott or Max Nordau, who remain hysterically trapped in the Imaginary, logocentrism, ideology, and the image-repertoire. The Shavian Realist provides the model for the reader-critic who writes, the critic-writer. The year after writing *The Quintessence*, Shaw portrayed a Shavian realist as an Ibsenite philosopher-critic and the Idealist critic as a theater reviewer in his second play, *The Philanderer*. This discussion resumes in chapter 6, the shadow of chapter 2.

The Quintessence of Ibsenism was the first of an important series of critical essays as exercises of reading that Shaw wrote as critic in the 1890s that presents his worldview, a philosophy constantly reworked during the rest of his writing career. In these essays Shaw insists on the vivification and corporeality, the dramatization of the pleasures and the pains, of the critic as reader. The critic or critic-philosopher is the Shavian realist who deconstructs the culture's texts and reads the ideological in terms of economic and social relations, the fractured subject who, by navigating his way within the Lacanian Symbolic, creates his subjectivity. Reading and writing are shown as processes in which objectivity is inseparable from subjectivity. These essays are exercises in reading critically in which Shaw as writing subject figures himself as the feeling critic, as *Corno di Bassetto*, as G.B.S., as "the degenerate," as the skilled voluptuary. The critic, the reader who writes and the writer who reads functions as the paradigm of Shaw's reader.

3   Authorial Identity

Promethean Strategies of a Pantomime Ostrich

> *The celebrated G.B.S. is about as real as a pantomime ostrich. . . .*
> *I have never pretended that G.B.S. was real: I have over and*
> *over again taken him to pieces before the audience to shew the*
> *trick of him.*
>
> Bernard Shaw, "The Chesterbelloc" (1908) in *Pen Portraits and Reviews*

The Authorial Subject

The fictional dramatic character figured as the subject in Shaw's writing, the so-called author, is an identity comprising many shadows. One might say that the largest shadow cast by Shaw's writing is Shaw himself, and, indeed, different combinations of Shaw shadows produce different Shaws. As intimated in chapter 2, an element in Shaw's writing as critic was the construction of an authorial identity, the inscription of a corporeal subjectivity in his writing, which this chapter examines further in various autobiographical writings. Following Barthes's declaration of the death of the author, which puts the concept of authorship into question, chapter 7 (as a shadow of this chapter) discusses how Shaw's self-reflexive concerns about authorship, text, and writing are manifest in the textual design or structure of several plays. Chapter 3 concentrates on the authorial identity of that fluctuating subject-object within the Shaw text, the writer Bernard Shaw.[1]

Authorial identity can generally be described as unenunciated subjectivity, Barthes's "paper-*I*." Unlike the novelist, the playwright cannot use the self-referential first-person singular pronoun. Thus the appearance of the author in the text, which happens often enough in Shaw's plays, is something of a textual scandal. One well-known example of such authorial transgression is the artist's declaration to both his audience of doctors and the audience in the theater in *The Doctor's Dilemma*: "I am a disciple of Bernard Shaw." However, the general absence of authorial presence, in both writing in general and dramatic writing in particular, creates a literary vacuum, which the Shavian pen did not hesitate to fill with a bewildering array of supplementary personae. Needless to write, a superfluous authorial identity was thus created, "a fantastic personality" that Shaw boasted had no existence at all. Thus a special problem arises in the Shaw text, which becomes complicated by a cast of fabricated fictional Shaws; as with Barthes and Derrida, authorial identity is not unitary. Some, though not all, of these fictions were deliberately created out of this abundance of authorial production. Rather than being a totally empty "paper-*I*," Shaw as author, as the text's shadow, becomes a site of playful linguistic and fictional dramatic discourse, a play of competing and inconsistent fictions with, by way of a Derridean supplement to this authorial abundance, a disavowal and a calling into question, a deconstruction of the authorial subject.

Chapter 1 tentatively proposed translating Shaw's Creative Evolution into poststructuralist terms as a process of subject-object relations to be read within the sentence structure of language, where neither subject nor object is an abstract unitary coherent given. The two Creative Evolution or Life Force plays *both* foreground writers and texts in the context of species generation (and Derrida describes the play of deferring differences, of traces, of inscription, of writing in terms of generation and force).[2] *Man and Superman* pronounces that there is an impulse to greater knowledge and self-consciousness; *Back to Methuselah* suggests that the only thing a person can finally create is "self." Shaw's strategies in his own writing in regard to the creation of self therefore must be examined. The context the strategies provide is invariably that of writing and of textuality; moreover, they warn that there is no ultimate or "real" self. The Shaw text is an always ongoing work, and this chapter continues that textual process in relation to the writer named Shaw. Shaw's autobiographical strategies of self-creation, not dissimilar from Yeats's poetic conception of masks, constitute a distinctive aspect of the Shaw text. The sheer playfulness around this pole of the subject-predicate structure of writing might trick the reader into ignoring another aspect of this problem: any sense of the other of this fiction-subject. By that is not meant the material world, reality, or facts, or a final, real, or factual Shaw. "Facts mean nothing by themselves," wrote Shaw to H. G. Wells (*Shaw-Wells*, 152–53). Rather, both Shaw's and Derrida's concept of force in writing (similar to Lacan's notion of desire at work in language) might be pertinent here to refer to that impulse toward meaning (signifiance) within language, toward the creation of self, which might be translated as force of feeling or sensibility in the interaction of the subject with those objective structures called the world, however imaginary.

How do you articulate feeling in language? Shaw's answer seems to have been by the music in his writing, or, to put it in terms of structuralist linguistics, by a shifting metonymy of signifiers, referred to in chapter 1, inscribed into the grain of the text. A dynamic of fluctuating authorial identity is traceable as a shadow-play of the dramas of feelings that are the play-texts. Indeed, a type of mirroring oscillation between the play with identity and the text produces, in its turn, a sense of an other of the other, the sensibility of an aesthete/artist writer/dramatist. This sensibility, similar perhaps to Keats's notion of "negative capability," is an absence of authorial identity, as Shaw paradoxically suggests in the previously quoted comment to Frank Harris: "I am of the true Shakespearean type: I understand everything and everyone, and I am nobody and nothing" (Shaw, *Letters 4*, 189). Chapter 3 therefore traces different aspects of this autobiographical play of authorial subjectivity within the Shaw text that exemplifies the problematic of subjectivity in writing.

Biography as Myth

Drawing on the standard biographies, a quick thumbnail sketch traces Shaw's early life, which may be entitled: "The Myth of the Birth of the Author."[3]

"Sonny" Shaw was exposed to a domestic background of what was certainly an unhappy marriage. The immediate household was large: Shaw and his two older sisters, Lucy and Agnes; his unconventional society-defying opera-singing mother, Bessie Shaw née Gurley; her brother and ship's doctor, Uncle Walter, when home on leave and whose conversation was "Rabelaisian"; her music teacher and partner, George John Vandeleur Lee; as well as her rather despised alcoholic husband, George Carr Shaw, who displayed his own brand of anticlimactic humor that left its mark on his son. In different ways all were dramatic personages, to which might be added a supplementary cast of numerous uncles, aunts, and cousins. Despite being brought up in a musical background, Sonny's great artistic interest as an adolescent was painting. He prowled the recently opened National Gallery of Ireland, located about a half-mile away from his

Hatch Street home in Dublin. He and his school friend, Edward McNulty, enrolled in art classes run from London's Kensington Art School. His declared ambition was to be an artist along the lines of Michelangelo, but McNulty refused to pose nude for him! A musician friend of his mother's gave him access to art books, and he bought issues of Vasari's essays on Florentine artists when he could afford them, which was not often. As he later freely admitted, he was not particularly talented in drawing and painting, and his artistic ambitions lapsed. His surviving drawings, not surprisingly, have a certain anecdotal humor about them, but they totally lack ease of execution and fluidity of line. Nevertheless, in later life he provided sketches for the set designers of his plays and for the artist John Farleigh to work from for wood-cuts illustrating *The Adventures of the Black Girl in her Search for God*. If anything, his drawing illustrates an energetic jerkiness that eyewitnesses remarked on in his public-speaking persona, as well as that power of comic observation he admired so much in Hogarth.[4]

From an early age, he was an avid reader of *The Arabian Nights*, Bunyan, Shakespeare, Byron, Scott, Lever, and Dickens, and, as an adolescent, he came under the spell of the poet revolutionary, Percy Bysshe Shelley. His favorite subject at school was English composition. At the age of fifteen he left school to become a clerk and pursued his writing career with McNulty, his associate in most of these activities. McNulty had joined the staff of a bank in Newry, a town fifty miles from Dublin, and in their almost daily correspondence the boys sent each other their latest literary productions. Because his mother was one of Dublin's leading amateur opera singers, music was the art to which he had most exposure in his childhood. Rehearsals for opera productions were often held in the Shaw home, which gave Sonny an experience of theater at an early age. Through his musical connections, for instance, the young Shaw was able to go backstage during a Dublin performance by two of the leading international opera singers of the day, Trebelli and Tietjens.[5] When Lee went to London (to be quickly followed by Mrs. Shaw and her two daughters), the teenage Shaw had no other recourse for filling the resultant musical void than teaching himself how to play the piano. He learned well enough to become an accompanist at social events in his early years in London. At the same time he frequented the Dublin theaters, especially the largest and most respectable, the Theater Royal, where there were regular visits from touring companies. The most memorable experience of the literary theater for the young Shaw was the appearance of the great Shakespearean actor of Irish extraction, Barry Sullivan. His theatrical instincts were also furthered by his model theater, which he supplied with his own dramas. This varied exposure to the arts established the cultural background of Shaw's early life that was artistic father to the literary man.

One reason for his mother's going to London with her two daughters, apart from her partnership with Lee, was to see if Lucy could make a career for herself as a singer on the stage; George, as he had become, was set up as a clerk in a Dublin land agency and lived with his father in lodgings, a type of boarding house (now a hotel) in Harcourt Street. Late in life Shaw wrote a piece of nonsense prose as a test piece for a phonetic alphabet based on the famous provision for it in his Will. Glimpsed through its Joycean stream-of-consciousness prose and Beckettian characters, a rather sad piece of autobiographical writing might be read on the period when Shaw and his father lived together in Dublin after Mrs. Shaw and her daughters had moved to London:

> Hear the queer story how father and son one time sat in the house man to man eating bread and telling the tale of the fir on the road to the city by the sea following the coast to its fall full two fathoms deep. There they lived together served by the carrier, whose narrower mind through beer was sore and whose poor boy shivered over the fire all day lingering in a tangle of tactless empty instinct, ineptly swallowing quarts of stingo. (Richard Wilson, *Language*, 27)

Shortly before his twentieth birthday, and just after his sister Agnes had died from tuberculosis on the Isle of Wight, Shaw himself emigrated to London.

In the second half of the nineteenth century London was a smoggy, foggy, filthy city; most of its population lived in dire poverty. Yet the young provincial Irish aesthete reveled in it, while, paradoxically, he never ceased to revile the Dublin of his childhood artistic education. "A devil of a childhood," he lamented to actress Ellen Terry. At some stage between leaving school at the age of fifteen and writing both the prose work *My Dear Dorothea* (1878) and the unfinished satirical verse *Passion Play* (1878) two years after arriving in London, Shaw had decided that he was going to be a writer.[6] The childhood ambition to become a painter in the mode of Michelangelo and the clerk's adolescent ambition to be an opera singer had been transposed. Instead, he sought to become a novelist by combining the reforming poetic zeal of a Shelley with a capacity for the dissection of society worthy of George Eliot, whose novels he had also devoured. He was also bolstered by an imaginative facility for creating fictional characters to match that of another literary hero, Charles Dickens. The Dublin background, which had included the beginning of a lifelong intimate knowledge of the King James authorized version of the Bible, the plays of Shakespeare, and Bunyan's *Pilgrim's Progress* (hence his later claim to have been born in the seventeenth century) was reinforced in London by his economic studies and encyclopedic reading in the British Museum. This formative experience in both cities enabled him to become one of the most self-conscious (that is, allusive) of modern literary writers.

He soon started writing his first novel, *Immaturity* (not published until 1930 as the first volume of the Collected Works of a seventy-four-year-old world-famous author). Four others quickly followed, but none was accepted for immediate publication, and he soon abandoned the beginning of a sixth novel. How, then, did this ambitious, but unsuccessful novelist discover that his real vocation as writer was that of playwright? Part of the myth of the great dramatist called Shaw is that the radical campaigning journalist and critic G.B.S. created the conditions for a serious drama, which Bernard Shaw the playwright then exploited.

But how tenable is this self-fulfilling myth? This myth purports to reveal his early yearning to be an artist of some sort and his exposure to somewhat unconventional paradigms of several distinct branches of the arts, all of which he used in his later career as a critic. In fact, his ambition to be a creative writer lay dormant for eight years until he removed from a drawer his abandoned, half-written, jointly authored play with William Archer. By completing that play, he jump-started a career as playwright that ended as one of the most successful in the history of theater. Thus there remains a disjunction, a lacuna, in all the biographical accounts between the childhood of artistic ambitions and the achievement of the fin-de-siècle playwright that several critical studies, like those of Dietrich, Carpenter, Sally Peters, and Bertolini, seek to account for with their different emphases.[7]

Posterity Shaw

One unusual feature of this biographical account is its source: most information originated with Shaw, who published disparate autobiographical writings aimed to manufacture the fiction labeled here "Posterity Shaw." After his death, his information was supplemented by the publications of his *Collected Letters* and the *Diaries*, which, as Shaw well knew, would eventually be published. To a great extent, the *Letters* and *Diaries* corroborate the veracity of Shaw's published autobiographical pieces, and surprises have been few in biographical research since Shaw's death in 1950. Ten years after his death, an affair of Shaw's from the late 1920s and early 1930s with a young American actress/sculptor, Molly Tompkins, was revealed when her son published both Shaw's letters and a separate account of the affair.[8] It seems to have echoed Shaw's most famous extramarital affair, the one with Mrs. Patrick Campbell around 1912–1913, and so it did not greatly shock students of Shaw. In a more recent type of exposé Sally Peters in *The Ascent of the Superman* speculated on a homosexual aspect of Shaw's creative personality. Although the evidence is circumstantial, Shaw, the advocate of the Womanly Man and the Manly Woman, would have been the last person to deny a feminine aspect of his self.[9]

As an old man, Shaw did confess to suppressing one biographical fact in his autobiographical *Sixteen Self Sketches* (1949). That title is significant because it suggests that, until his death, Shaw's opinion of self, in terms of both multiplicity ("Sixteen") and incompleteness ("Sketches"), was neither unitary nor necessarily coherent; it also neatly encapsulates two types of inscription or line drawing: sketching and writing, the image and the word. John O'Donovan has argued that Shaw's confession of shame or "wounded snobbery" at being sent to the Central Model School in Dublin obscures, rather than reveals, the real cause of shame.[10] Shaw's explanation was one of caste: the son of a respectable middle-class, if relatively impecunious, grain wholesaler should not have been sent to a school, where he would mix socially with the sons of tradesmen and retailers. O'Donovan's explanation is that, by attending a school which, although nominally nondenominational, consisted mostly of Roman Catholics, the young Protestant boy lost caste with his coreligionists, for not so much social as religious reasons. O'Donovan further explains that the shame was compounded by his being sent there on Lee's suggestion, his mother's possible lover who was Catholic. In his copious writing on Lee, O'Donovan explains, Shaw never mentions Lee's Catholicism.[11] Moreover, this association with a Catholic, rather than his father's drinking (Shaw's explanation), may well explain why the Shaws of Synge Street were ostracized by the rest of the resolutely Protestant Shaw clan. Along with Rosset's research that Shaw's mother left Dublin much sooner after Lee's departure for London than Posterity Shaw would have us believe, this would be a significant, if rare, exception to the general reliability of Shaw's accounts.[12] In Shaw's defense, it could be countered on the first point that he had never made a secret of his inculcated childhood anti-Catholicism; so it would not have been a great revelation to make after eighty years. But the social snobbery did have relevance for one of the great socialists of the day and demanded explanation. In relation to the second point, he freely admitted a rather cavalier approach to dates, although here he specifically denied that his mother could have gone as quickly after Lee as ship's records indicate she did.[13] That there have not been more discrepancies is, perhaps, more surprising, and something rather anticlimactic remains about Shavian biography where there is little new to discover, as Holroyd's massive biographical work testifies. The lines of all Shavian biography have been laid down, seemingly, into perpetuity by the autobiographical writing of Posterity Shaw, and they are thus programmed as an extension of the Shaw text.

Quite early on, Posterity Shaw began establishing the broad outlines of the biographical myth. The article "How to Become a Man of Genius" written for a New York magazine, *Town Topics*, December 6, 1894, begins pithily: "The secret at the bottom of the whole business is simply this: there is no such thing as a man of genius. I am a man of genius myself, and ought to know" (*Non-Dramatic*, 341). Shaw's statement provides a succinct example of Shaw's tendency to make the language of his writing completely bypass Aristotelian logic. This flexibility in language allows him to make simultaneously several different and contradictory statements, as when the denial of the existence of "the man of genius" is expressed by affirmation of same. More relevant here, this article along with the construction and deconstruction of the writer as genius contains a consideration of identity and subjectivity:

> Pray, amiable sir or madam, what is the thing you call yourself? Is it yourself as you are with people you like or as you are with people who rub you the wrong way? Is it yourself before dinner or after it? . . . If your enemy might select some one moment of your life to judge you, would you not come out mean, ugly, cowardly, vulgar, sensual, even though you be another Goethe; or if you might choose the moment yourself, would you not come out generous and handsome, though you may be, on an average of all your moments, a most miserly and repulsive person? . . . Our experience does, then, provide us with material for a concept of a superhuman person. You have only to imagine someone always as good as you in the very loftiest ten seconds of your life . . . . Wise indeed and wisest among men

would be he who could now say to me: Why should I deceive myself thus foolishly? Why not fix my affections, my hopes, my enthusiasms on men and women as they are . . . instead of on these ideal monsters who never existed and never will, and for whose sake men and women now despise one another and make the earth ridiculous with Pessimism which is the inevitable end of all Idealism? (*Non-Dramatic*, 341–42)

He continues by playing another variation on Shakespeare's "all the world's a stage" metaphor:

[On] Shakespeare's great stage of "all the world," . . . there are many parts to be cast, since the audience will have its ideal king, its President, its statesman, its saint, its hero, its poet, its Helen of Troy, and its man of genius. No one can *be* these figments; but somebody must act them. . . . Napoleon, called on, as a man who had won battles, to cast himself as Emperor, grasped the realities of the situation, and, instead of imitating the ideal Caesar or Charlemagne, took lessons from Talma. (*Non-Dramatic*, 343)

Shaw used this idea of role playing in his Napoleon play, *The Man of Destiny*, written the following year (see chapter 5), but he applied it negatively to himself and his most recent play at the time:

Very recently the production of a play of mine [*Arms and the Man* (1894)] in New York led to the appearance in the New York papers of a host of brilliant critical and biographical studies of a remarkable person called Bernard Shaw. I am supposed to be that person; but I am not. You may take my word for this, because I invented him, floated him, advertised him, impersonated him, and am now sitting here in my dingy second floor lodging in a decaying London Square, breakfasting off two penn'orth of porridge and giving this additional touch to his make-up with my typewriter. (*Non-Dramatic*, 344)

This passage is worthy of Swift at his best and positively vertiginous in its logical and linguistic implications. At the outset of the essay, Shaw outlines his equivalent to the Lacanian Imaginary using, not for the first time, the metaphor of man as a child: "When a child wants something it has not got, what does it do? It pretends to have it. It gets astride of a walking stick and insists on a general conspiracy to pass that stick off as a horse" (*Non-Dramatic*, 341). This is precisely what man as (metaphysical) Idealist does, which leads Shaw, among the passages of high satire, to exclaim with feeling (and pointing to the distinction Lacan would make between the Imaginary and the Real):

> But pray where do these idealists and cynics get their fundamental assumption that human nature needs any apology? What is the objection to man as he really is and can become any more than to the solar system as it really is? All that can be said is that men, even when they have done their best possible, cannot be ideally kind, ideally honest, ideally chaste, ideally brave and so on. Well, what does that matter, any more than the equally important fact that they have no eyes in the back of their heads (a most inconvenient arrangement), or that they live a few score years instead of a few thousand. (*Non-Dramatic*, 345)

This, note well, from the future author of *Back to Methuselah*!

So what parts did Shaw cast for himself? What were the authorial strategies of Posterity Shaw? Although Shaw knew all autobiography to be false, it did not prevent him from producing a deluge of autobiographical material, which he justifies as follows: "Only when I can make a case of myself, economic, artistic, sociological, or what not, can I make literary use of myself" (*Autobiography 1*, viii). And Shaw does appear to have conceived an autobiographical project in the early 1920s, when thinking of publishing a Collected Edition of his works. Around this time he started writing the significant autobiographical prefaces to his first (hitherto unpublished) novel, *Immaturity*, to his correspondence with Ellen Terry, and to the music criticism that had originally appeared under the pseudonym *Corno di Bassetto*. This was the beginning of the autobiographical project that lasted for the best part of thirty years until the very publication of *Sixteen Self Sketches* in 1950.

A parallel autobiographical strategy for Posterity Shaw was to assist with the writing of his biographer's books on him. Indeed, this activity had begun even earlier, when on January 3, 1905, some six years before Archibald Henderson's first official biography was published in 1911, Shaw wrote him a fifty-three-page letter filled with autobiographical information, from which thereafter Shaw himself would cull for his own autobiographical pieces. Shaw even suggested calling the work "G.B.S.: Biography and Autobiography" (*Letters 2*, 480). Pearson's much later biography (1942) has large chunks of direct quotation from Shaw, which Pearson insisted be put into quotation marks to make clear what his subject had written. Even biographies published posthumously, like Henderson's last and St John Ervine's, can be said to have been written, in part, with Shaw's assistance.

Shaw's authorial shadow is practically inescapable in the biographies, even in Holroyd's more recently researched multivolume work, but its pervasiveness has compensations. For instance, the Frank Harris biography can be read as an autobiography written in the third person, as, to all intents and purposes, Shaw rewrote the book after Harris's death (his excuse was to make sure that the facts were correct, while providing some much needed income for Harris's widow).[14] It is significant that this volume "by" Harris was published in 1931 at the height of Posterity Shaw's putative autobiographical project. As "An Unauthorized Biography Based on First Hand Information"—according to the title page—it complemented Henderson's second "official" biography, published in 1932.

A more questionable autobiographical strategy was a refusal to allow some material to be published at all. In relation to the Harris biography, it has been suggested that his bantering with Harris, over what should and what should not be included in the biography, put unnecessary stress and strain on Harris toward the end of his life, if it did not actually hasten the inevitable. Mrs. Patrick Campbell, when short of money in later life, was very keen to publish Shaw's letters from the period of their affair because she knew that Shaw's correspondence with Ellen Terry (from their purely epistolary relationship) had already been published. After some seemingly callous equivocation, Shaw, to her rueful incomprehension, refused permission to publish. Shaw most questionably frustrated the publication of a proposed biography by an Irish-American, Demetrius O'Bolger, to whom he had provided a great deal of autobiographical information and encouragement in correspondence. This refusal greatly distressed O'Bolger, who, as Shaw rather callously put it, died "a man with a grievance." Shaw had felt that O'Bolger's forensic instinct (being the son of a policeman) got the better of him when speculating on the relationship between Bessie Shaw and Lee.

Such negative activity and interference by the subject, seen in the retrospective light of biographical propriety, may seem reprehensible. But it may also represent some problems of being one of the more famous men in the world with a reputation, a name worth money, and legal responsibilities to nurture and protect. Indeed, regardless of any judgment by posterity, Shaw, when he lived, was obliged often to protect his name in legal, financial, and literary terms while endeavoring to control the development of his reputation and identity as an author. As a long-time journalist he knew how publicity worked, and so he could manipulate this publicity more effectively than most, while, as a businessman, he also knew how the law worked. He undeniably enjoyed exercising the power and freedom of writing his own part to play in the world, but there were likewise other considerations. His wife, Charlotte, had been much hurt at the time by the affair with Stella Campbell, and Shaw had no wish to revive those painful memories by publishing their correspondence.

Shaw sought out different writers to write about him. When he referred to Shakespeare in his autobiographical comments to Frank Harris, he did so because not only was Shakespeare to him a literary touchstone and forefather against whom he waged a perpetual Oedipal battle but also Harris considered himself an expert on the Bard. Thus he directed to Harris his revealing comments on authorial subjectivity and objectivity in relation to Shakespeare: "I am of the true Shakespearean type: I understand everything and everyone, and am nobody and nothing" (Shaw, *Letters 4*, 189); "Have you not found out that people like me and Shakespear *et hoc genus omne* have no souls? We understand all the souls and all the faiths and can dramatize them because they are to us wholly objective. We hold none of them" (Harris, *Shaw*, xiii). In spite of those Shaw shadows, the cast of fictional Shaws, authorial subjectivity is reduced to nothing as the writing becomes "wholly objective." But what does Shaw mean by that? A clue comes in another statement of his: "Things have not happened to me: on the contrary, it is I who have happened to them, and all my happenings have taken the form of books or plays. Read them, or spectate them; and you have my whole story: the rest is only breakfast, lunch, dinner, sleeping, wakening, and washing" (*Autobiography 2*, viii).

In other words, to produce a wholly objective relation the writer as subject disappears, yet, paradoxically, that "wholly objective" production of writing enables the "author" to be read. There is a peculiar subject-object relation in writing where the author may return, as Barthes puts it in "From Work to Text," as a guest in his text: "It is not that the author may not 'come back' in the Text, in his text, but he then does so as a 'guest.' If he is a novelist, he is inscribed in the novel like one of his characters, figured in the carpet; no longer privileged, paternal, aletheological, his inscription is ludic. He becomes no longer the origin of his fictions but a fiction contributing to his work" (Barthes, *Image-Music-Text*, 161).

Barthes made this comment in relation to his distinction between the work and the text. The Work as a product of the Author is subject to what he calls "filiation" (a term borrowed from Kristeva who, in turn, borrowed it from psychoanalysis), meaning "a line of paternity." The text is not subject to any such condition of linear paternity, which seems to have been how Shaw understood the way his literary products might be used by his readers and audiences. As the production of the author, "Bernard Shaw," they, of course, can be consumed, and he (and, after his death, the Shaw estate) can make money; but as texts they are at the disposition of their audience and readers to treat as flexibly as he treats the subject-object relation in language.

Among famous writers, perhaps only Goethe was as assiduous in the writing of his own biography. This ludic aspect of the writing, as a type of patchwork of subjectivity with the author as one of the text's fictions mentioned by Barthes, helps readers to understand why (apart from psychological reasons, which are not a concern here). The authorial shadow called Shaw is merely a site of discursive operations involving different subject-writers (biographers) in the extended Shaw text, where Shaw becomes an object, a fictional creation or character, of his and others' writing. Of course, Shaw as a dramatist possessed more than most a specific talent for writing from another's point of view, which, in a spirit of compulsive playfulness, made it impossible for him to avoid retouching his biographers' various portraits of him. However, Shaw as authorial-subject felt it important, even essential, that he be written about from someone else's point of view. If as writer he was "nothing and nobody," "Shaw," like Lacan's subject, can only come into existence from the point of view of others: "the audience will have . . . its man of genius."

Autobiography for Shaw, therefore, meant provoking others to write extensive, if necessarily partial, biographical accounts or portraits. None could be the true or final account, so he encouraged as many biographers as possible. Biographers depended for whatever truth they might have on their own viewpoint and abilities, not on their subject. Different biographies cast separate shadows, separate works of fiction, in which the character Shaw was created, exactly as Socrates was created by Plato and Dr. Johnson by Boswell. For Shaw, the more biographers the merrier. He can thus be presented from a multiple, rather than a singular, perspective, where each biographer provides *a* true view, rather than *the* true view, which simply does not exist. As he explained in relation to one biographical portrait:

> I have been asked whether the portrait resembles me. The question interests me no more than whether Velasquez's Philip was like Philip or Titian's Charles like Charles. No doubt some mean person will presently write a disparaging volume called The Real Shaw, which will be . . . true in its way. . . . Perhaps some total stranger to the Irish-British environment may produce a study as unexpected, and as unflattering, as the very interesting picture of Nelson by a Turkish miniaturist which hangs in the National Portrait Gallery.

He goes on:

> Like all men I play many parts; and none of them is more or less real than another. . . . I am, in short, not only what I can make out of myself which varies greatly from hour to hour and emergency to no-emergency, but what you can see in me. And the whole difference between an observer of genius and a common man is not a difference in the number of objects they perceive, but in their estimate of the importance of the objects. Put one man into Fleet Street and ask him what he sees there; and he may give you an accurate description of the color of the buses, the sex of the horses, the numbers of the motorcars, the signs of the public houses, and the complexions and probable ages of the people. Another man, who could not answer a single question on these points, may tell you that what he sees is a Jacob's ladder with angels moving up and down between heaven and earth. (*Autobiography* 2, 1–2)

This last, incidentally, is most likely a reference to his favorite painter-poet-engraver-bookmaker, the Londoner William Blake. And there is no doubt that he considered the angel-seeing Blake, called mad by some, an "observer of genius." Wanting to promote biographical diversity, Shaw sought as biographers those who might not have been the most obvious candidates for the job from a literary point of view. Henderson, his official biographer, was a professional mathematician at Princeton. Harris, the scabrous autobiographer and unofficial biographer, was already mentioned. And not content with mere biographies, he diversified his insatiable penchant for (auto)biography toward other forms of inscription. As a keen amateur photographer, he encouraged leading photographers to photograph him at every opportunity in all states of dress and undress (Evans, Coburn, Steichen, Karsch, Freund, and so on), as well as painters (most notably Augustus John's three portraits) and, especially, sculptors

(Rodin and Epstein). His association with the BBC and the movies ensured plenty of sound recordings of his mellifluous Irish voice from his later years, as well as film records of the bearded visage. There are, perhaps, more disparate indexical representations of Shaw than of any other well-known writer before the age of television. The sheer quantity of this material defies us to make a coherent individual that we can call the author. Equally, such variety allows for multiple fictional individual portraits. As he said in the postscript to the Harris biography: "Nothing can be more unnatural and biographically worthless than a rigid single estimate with everything else forced into harmony with it: it is like an instantaneous photograph of a horse transfixed by the camera in the act of galloping" (Harris, *Shaw*, 426).

For the Shaw text, posterity, and not Posterity Shaw, is the final arbiter on Shaw in an arbitration that is never final. The reputation conscientiously assembled as a result of a variety of authorial strategies by Posterity Shaw is after all a work of multiple fictions; not all of them are of Shaw's invention. An earlier, and more famous, fabrication entirely of his own making was known worldwide simply as G.B.S.; he called it a "pantomime ostrich."

Pantomime Ostrich

Shaw frequently commented on how he deliberately created the literary persona that became famous as the set of initials, G.B.S. Those were the initials over which his music and theater criticism and much of his other journalism was printed, after his stint of music criticism on *The Star* as *Corno di Bassetto* ended. The fictional and dramatic corporeality of the writing subject of chapter 2, the critic as Punch, that he inserted into his critical writing was a fictional persona he later described as being as "real as a pantomime ostrich." Such a self-portrait was a caricature, a monstrous and insufferable parody of his own aspirations. Yet this theatrical shadow, the pantomime ostrich, reflects a complex project that involves acting, fantasy, and imagination on the parts of both actor and audience. It raises the question: Who is the "real" Shaw?

> I have never pretended that G.B.S. was real: I have over and over again taken him to pieces before the audience to shew the trick of him. And even those who in spite of that cannot escape from the illusion, regard G.B.S. as a freak. The whole point of the creature is

that he is unique, fantastic, unrepresentative, inimitable, impossible, undesirable on any large scale, utterly unlike anybody that ever existed before, hopelessly unnatural, and void of real passion. Clearly such a monster could do no harm. (*Autobiography* 2, 1)

In a parody (before the fact) of poststructuralist literary theory, which holds the author to be a fiction, Shaw decided to enjoy himself and fabricate the author as textual product himself. Our knowledge of him/it may only come through representations of what he/it is not, as that bogus Superman, the "pantomime ostrich," among other biographical fabrications.

G.B.S.'s notice in *The World* of February 4, 1891, of Sullivan's *Ivanhoe* provides an example of Shaw's deliberate deconstruction of G.B.S. in the very act of constructing his construction. The opera was adapted from one of Shaw's favorite novelists, Walter Scott, which might account for the review's withering tone. "On second thoughts I have resolved to suppress my notice of *Ivanhoe*" (*Music* 2, 253) is the opening gambit in a devastatingly satirical critique of Sullivan's attempt to compose a serious opera away from the influence of the librettist of his comic operas, W. S. Gilbert. Shaw's wicked sense of tact leads him to make all the necessary gestures of obeisance to the late Victorian British Imperial institution, Sir Arthur Sullivan, and to declare that he will not reveal the review he originally wrote of the opera. He then quotes long paragraphs from the suppressed review. Having finished with that gambit, he performs a variation on it by declaring he will not compare the two different casts for the opera (he had conscientiously attended the rehearsals and so had heard both casts) and proceeds to make exactly such a comparison. The review is a typically brilliant Shavian performance of writing as a play of language, texts, and discourse, and, as a shadow of that brilliance in the writing, the fictional persona G.B.S. was created. The character of the pantomime ostrich seems to leap across (or out from) the pages of the reviews as well as the prefaces to his first three volumes of plays.

D'Oyly Carte, the impresario behind Sullivan's operas, had managed the press so successfully that hyperbole reigned supreme in the London press. As Shaw put it: "The innocent people who believe whatever they see in print—and among those are a considerable section of the playgoing public—are convinced that something magnificent and momentous beyond all parallel in the annals of music has just happened" (*Music* 2, 263). According to Shaw, this "puffery" had merely made Sullivan ridiculous.

To deflate the hype, he added a second critique of *Ivanhoe* the week after his original notice. The conscientious critic had returned to hear a couple of acts from the opera again. As an "instructive" lesson to D'Oyly Carte, Shaw discusses G.B.S.'s intellectual strategy in public relations and outlines how he created the G.B.S. persona:

> I yield to no man in the ingenuity and persistence with which I seize every opportunity of puffing myself and my affairs; but I never nauseate the public by getting myself praised. My favorite plan is to seek some gentleman who has a weakness for writing to the papers, and who writes rather well when his blood is up. Him I provoke by standing on his tenderest corn, to write to the papers saying that I have no sense of humor, of morals, of decency, of art, of manners, or what not. This creates an impression that the national feeling on these points runs so strongly the other way as to require urgent correction; and straightaway many people who never heard of me in their lives become ashamed of their ignorance. Then all the enemies of my assailant constitute themselves my partisans; and so I become famous to a degree that goads those who see through the whole puff to write fresh letters and paragraphs denying that I am famous at all, thereby making me more famous, or infamous, or what you will; for any sort of notoriety will serve my turn equally. All this would be the easiest thing in the world did not so much depend on the adroitness and opportuneness of the original provocation; and here, no doubt, my well-known critical insight, developed by profound economic, historic, artistic, and social studies, give me an advantage. (*Music 2*, 264–65)

This willfully misleading self-portrait as writing subject was created in the crucial period before he burst into prominence as a published playwright. Moreover, G.B.S. carried this pose and strategy beyond the weekly columns of music and later dramatic criticism; for example, he begins such brazen articles as "Mr Bernard Shaw's Works of Fiction: Reviewed by Himself" in *The Novel Review*, February 1892: "The need for getting me to review my own works of fiction has arisen through the extreme difficulty of finding anyone else who has read them." To a great extent the two autobiographical prefaces to the first publication in 1898 of his first seven plays in the two volumes known as *Plays Pleasant and Unpleasant* (the title reversing the order of volumes, as well as the chronology of their composition) continued the construction of, as well as deconstruction of the journalistic "figment," G.B.S. They finally announced the arrival of "Bernard Shaw" as a published author at the relatively advanced age of forty-two. The preface to *Plays: Pleasant and Unpleasant. By Bernard Shaw. The First Volume, containing the three Unpleasant Plays* (to give it its full and orthographically correct title) is entitled "Mainly about Myself," and the preface to *The Second Volume, containing the four Pleasant Plays* continues that theme. These prefaces announce how Shaw became a playwright. As a slice of cultural history, they sketch in the theatrical background, but their brilliance, a shadow of the alleged brilliance of G.B.S., obscures the fact that the text "Mainly about Myself" nowhere reveals how Shaw decided to become a dramatic writer. Events happen to the failed novelist, a mere cork floating along on this late Victorian sea of events—this from a Schopenhauerean philosopher of the Will ("Shawpenhauerism," William Archer called it!).[15] His career of novel writing is dismissed with the phrase "once I gave up writing novels," and the bridge from novels to plays—G.B.S. as critic—he labels Punch. This deconstructing construction, another version of the pantomime ostrich, contributed to what became a living legend. Meanwhile, Shaw insisted on its unreality as "the most successful of my fictions" (*Non-Dramatic*, 454) because he had created it. Still, that is not to say there is no truth in the myth; in fact, it resembles the original, as a caricature might resemble its subject, an actor his character, or a shadow the man.

Promethean Shaw

One paradoxical effect of both the pantomime ostrich and Posterity Shaw (part of whose project in the 1920s and 1930s was to blunt the textual effect of the earlier fabrication) has been obscuring the impact of another myth, another biographical shadow once powerfully cast by Shaw's writing: the Promethean writer, who, as playwright, reached the apex of his achievement with the publication in 1903 of *Man and Superman* (writing had begun in May 1900), the Court Theatre productions of *John Bull's Other Island* in November 1904, of *Man and Superman* in May 1905, and of *Major Barbara* in November 1905, and the publication of *John Bull's Other Island* and *Major Barbara* in 1907.[16] These three masterpieces (literally what a journeyman creates to show that he has become a master after a long period of apprenticeship) cemented the myth of a Promethean, who, as a well-known socialist, was working to bring a new world into existence. If these extraordinary plays were all we knew of Shaw as dramatist, then the Shaw text might be easier to appreciate today and, in some ways, better appreciated.

Eric Bentley noted Shaw's Promethean, rather than the more usually recognized Puritan, tendencies: "might one not add that he is the first unsentimental *naturalist*? For him life is a Promethean adventure which may entail Promethean tortures to be borne with Promethean fortitude" (Bentley, 29). But the pantomime ostrich prevents viewing Shaw in this Promethean light. He explained the relation between the two dispositions, if we accept the equivalence of the metaphor of creeping under the bed to that of a pantomime ostrich burying its head in the sand: "Intellectual courage is the courage of my profession; and I possess it in the highest degree; but when the shooting begins I claim the right to creep under the bed and leave the fighting to people whose lives, being of no value, are not providentially protected by a good sensible dastardly poltroonery" (Harris, *Shaw*, 229).

Shaw never made any secret that he did not feel bound to bring general theory or writing into line with his individual practice; that would constitute an idealism he had spent his whole intellectual life fighting against. Critics stuck in the groove of binary thinking were unable to comprehend this distinction, so Shaw became the object of attack for being a Rolls Royce-owning socialist, for having conservative capitalists like Nancy Astor as his friends, and for consenting to liver injections to fight pernicious anemia as an old man although he was a vegetarian.[17] But he did have a conscience and was not a hypocrite. As a socialist, he always supported Trade Unions and insisted that his publishing contracts, for instance, require using "union houses" whenever possible. That, however, did not mean he felt in any way constrained from criticizing unions for being right-wing inclined, rather than socialist, the tendency with larger trade unions in any capitalist society.

The Mercurial (as in messenger of the gods) aspect of Shaw as authorial subject makes it easy to ignore its Promethean tendencies (as antagonist of the gods). Prometheus was a legendary character of great symbolic importance to both the young Shaw and two of his great culture heroes, Shelley and Beethoven. To Shaw, both Shelley and his best-known character were Promethean, and Shelley's influence extended from his adolescence through the period that is mainly under discussion in this chapter. That reading of Shelley, especially *Prometheus Unbound*, was as powerful and lasting an influence as Shaw's later reading of Marx. *The Perfect Wagnerite*'s Marxist reading of Wagner's tetralogy, *Der Ring des Nibelungen*, explicitly equates Wagner's hero, Siegfried, with Shelley's Prometheus, and the other great critical essay of the 1890s, *The Quintessence of Ibsenism*, opens by discussing Shelley's type of revolutionary.

Prometheus has three relevant characteristics: (1) as a Titan, he was neither man nor god; (2) with the gift of fire/life, he was a creator of and a benefactor to men; and (3) he defied the gods for the sake of man and suffered accordingly. In terms of Nietzsche's Dionysian/Apollonian opposition in *The Birth of Tragedy*, Prometheus—defier of the law—was the equivalent to Dionysus, who represented the irrational beneath the rational. For Nietzsche, who held Goethe to be the epitome of the creative artist, the artist must comprise *both* the Dionysian *and* the Apollonian. Ancient classical drama, the subject of Nietzsche's *The Birth of Tragedy*, originated at more or less the same time as Socratic philosophy in a celebratory rite performed in honor of Dionysus, as Shaw well knew. Occasionally a powerful production in the theater reminds us with a shock of the full Beethovenian or Dionysian force of Shaw's major plays. Part of the twentieth-century reappreciation of Mozart (usually considered Apollonian compared to the definitely Dionysian Beethoven) was recognizing a strong aspect of the Dionysian in his music. As with Mozart, the Victorians had turned the Promethean Shelley into an effete Apollonian, so that Matthew Arnold could say of Shelley that he was "a beautiful and ineffectual angel, beating in the void his luminous wings in vain." Shaw in *The Quintessence of Ibsenism* took severe exception to that remark and sought to restore an appreciation of the Promethean force in Shelley's writing. Perhaps the same needs to be done in a reappreciation of Shaw's writing. Prometheus was a defiant moral force, unlike Mozart's Don Giovanni, who, although possessed of similar defiance and energy, is totally amoral. Appropriately, the Promethean puritan, Beethoven, famously criticized Mozart for devoting his highest powers to the creation of such an amoral hero. Indeed Mozart's and Shaw's Don Juans might be nearer to Nietzsche's Dionysus than to Beethoven's Prometheus in the ballet *The Creatures of Prometheus*, which supplied the theme for the last movement of his most Promethean later work, the *Eroica* symphony.

Immediately after writing *The Perfect Wagnerite* about Wagner's *Ring* and its Promethean hero, Shaw "pillaged" Nietzsche's own Promethean character, the Superman, albeit with some ambivalence (see chapter 1). *Superman* is a word Dietrich and Peters both incorporate into the titles of their critical studies that concentrate on this early part of Shaw's writing life. Their books are particularly useful in examining Promethean Shaw in, respectively, his novel-writing phase and the whole period from his arrival in London to his overnight success nearly thirty years later. Dietrich's book, on Shaw as apprentice novelist, has shown how progressively in each of the five novels he figured his own developing sense of self as a young superman. Peters argues that Shaw's sense of his own difference during this period enabled him to fashion the persona of writer as superman. Bertolini's *The Playwrighting Self of Bernard Shaw* took up the procedure in respect of the mature master playwright who figured different aspects of his *writing* self in the major plays. These studies suggest a strong conscious or intentional element in Shaw's endeavor to become an artist-philosopher, brushed over by Shaw's contentions that he became a playwright more or less by accident, that his texts more or less wrote themselves, and that he was only their barely conscious agent or amanuensis. At a certain level Shaw might be right, but, given the alternative readings in the above studies, it may also be both the exact opposite of what happened and possibly intentionally misleading.

That Shaw did not pursue a career for which he had the talent, and which would have been easier to understand retrospectively, say as librettist of comic burlesques and operas in the style of W. S. Gilbert, might be because at the root of all his ambitions was a long-held desire to be a Promethean mold-breaker in the vein of his artistic heroes: Michelangelo in painting and sculpture, Shelley in poetry, and Beethoven in music. The two major critical studies, *The Quintessence of Ibsenism* and *The Perfect Wagnerite*, were about the two great Promethean artists of the last half of the nineteenth century, Ibsen and Wagner. When he created his first artist as hero, the composer Owen Jack in his third novel, *Love Among the Artists*, he used both Shelley and Beethoven as his Promethean models: Jack, like Beethoven, is a crusty bachelor of a composer and his major composition in the novel is an oratorio based on Shelley's *Prometheus Unbound*.

If Shaw's career as dramatist is considered in historical terms up to the time of *Major Barbara*, then there is no doubt that the Promethean was exactly the type of artist Shaw had succeeded in becoming and what he represented for his adopted culture in the early years of the twentieth century. However, Shaw—the Shaw who would rather creep under the bed than risk his life for his principles while simultaneously insisting that to be someone in social-cultural terms meant playing or acting a part—was simply not typecast to play the role of Prometheus. Without positing a real or essential Shaw, there was a disjunction in his assumption of the role not apparent in such Promethean exemplars as Beethoven and Ibsen, who made the sheer force of their powerful personalities so much a part of their art. Shaw was his own living deconstruction of the concept of superman. Nevertheless, considering this largely ignored Promethean factor in Shaw's art may help account for the transformations of his artistic ambitions both during his childhood and youthful writing and during his mature career in the forty-five years as a creative writer after *Major Barbara*. Mozart, who had done so much so early and who died so young, never had to face that problem. But, as a dramatic writer, Shaw had to keep reinventing himself throughout his very long creative life. The fictional Shaws are traceable throughout the Shaw text; they are as much a part of Shaw's writing as the creation of the plays as texts.

The ellipsis in the chronology, between abandoning novel writing and starting to write plays, was the time of the creation of the reputation and persona of G.B.S., the pantomime ostrich, the critic as Punch, not of a Promethean dramatist Bernard Shaw. Yet this gap extended eight years *after* he assumed, apparently, that his destiny was to be a writer of Promethean proportions from age twenty-eight through thirty-six, the years often thought of as the most productive in an artist's career. Nevertheless, behind the facade of this literary persona as clown, he expended Promethean energies in several different areas during this period, even if no finished pieces resulted. One area was socialism, for which he acted as writer, orator, and organizing committeeman. In another area of culture, he was the voice of the deconstructing iconoclastic anti-idealist journalist-critic of the arts. Yet another area of expertise was philandering; in its way, this activity required considerable writing, which allowed his later boast that all the great romances have been paper affairs.[18] Thus his Promethean energies and his published and unpublished political and polemical writing were working at full steam during this period of intense creative journalism, which might account for his later puzzling statement that the highest form of writing is journalistic—a tendency more in keeping with recent literary theory, perhaps, than with any traditional concept of high art, to which Shaw always gave short shrift.

This Promethean Shaw shadow was reflected in or mirrored by a string of Shavo-Promethean characters in the texts written during the period of novel writing and early playwrighting: Owen Jack in *Love Among the Artists*; Trefusis in his last novel, *An Unsocial Socialist*; Charteris in his second play, *The Philanderer*; Napoleon in *The Man of Destiny*; Valentine in *You Never Can Tell*; Dick Dudgeon in the aptly titled *The Devil's Disciple*; Caesar in *Caesar and Cleopatra*; Captain Brassbound in *Captain Brassbound's Conversion*; Jack Tanner in *Man and Superman*; and Andrew Undershaft in

Major Barbara. No two of these characters are the same, though they all exude the Promethean force—reflecting that force that both Shaw and Derrida see as a mark of writing—of cultural transgression. These fictional characters, personifying the life force that John Tanner makes so much of, came not only knocking at, but positively knocking down, the doors of Victorian convention that made the Promethean authorial persona of their creator such an overpowering presence at the turn of the twentieth century. Indeed, these characters helped produce the terms of the new age. Such Promethean authority, though, is only one aspect of the writing, and Shaw was quite happy, even insistent, that it not be taken too literally. Writing still in the nineteenth century, he prognosticates at the end of the preface to *Three Plays for Puritans*:

> But the whirligig of time will soon bring my audiences to my own point of view . . . by that time my twentieth century characteristics will pass unnoticed as a matter of course, whilst the eighteenth century artificiality that marks the work of every literary Irishman of my generation will seem antiquated and silly. It is a dangerous thing to be hailed all at once, as a few rash admirers have hailed me, as above all things original: what the world calls originality is only an unaccustomed manner of tickling it. . . . Reputations are cheap nowadays. Even were they dear, it would still be impossible for any public-spirited citizen of the world to hope that his reputation might endure; for this would be to hope that the flood of general enlightenment may never rise above his miserable high-watermark. . . . We must hurry on: we must get rid of reputations: they are weeds in the soil of ignorance. Cultivate that soil, and they will flower more beautifully, but only as annuals. If this preface will at all help get rid of mine, the writing of it will have been well worth the pains. (*Prefaces*, 753)

To this rhetorical challenge the response should be careful. As with all writing, Shaw's texts deserve critical reading. That is a burden that Shaw puts on the reader, in much the same way that the poststructuralists dispense with authors and instruct readers to create the text. Shaw's Promethean reputation need not be swallowed whole, yet neither should the Promethean force present in the writing, so evident to his contemporaries and in good productions of the plays, be ignored. Bertrand Russell's comment, which I quoted in chapter 1, remains pertinent: "We all talk in a different way from that in which people talked before Shaw."

Irish Exile/Alien

Yet another authorial shadow bears some discussion. Shaw's concrete artistic ambitions as a playwright crystallized some time after writing *Candida* in 1894, a very unPromethean play with its Parsifalian associations and a very unShelley-like poet. By 1899, despite a lack of production opportunities, he had written a total of ten major plays in seven years, an astonishing rate of production in English literary theater. Unlike his aborted novel writing, Shaw did not give up playwrighting for the rest of his very long life, although there was a hiatus in the 1920s after *Saint Joan*. At the beginning of the new century, playwrighting became his principal literary activity, and it eclipsed even the political and critical journalism that had catapulted him to fame—or notoriety—in the previous decade.

If Promethean Shaw has been lost among the shadows of time and obscured by the sheer plenitude of authorial Shaws, then a more personal or private Shaw shadow might have become equally obscured. In terms of his unconscious ambition, as he called it, he spent fifteen years wandering in the wilderness before reaching the promised land of publication as the author Bernard Shaw. One major piece of autobiography written by Posterity Shaw, the preface to *Immaturity*, refers to two aspects of this other Shaw: the raw Irish provincial in an empire's capital and an even more alienated young man suffering from what would later be called existential *Angst*.

> [*Immaturity*] is the book of a raw youth, still quite out of touch with the country to which he had transported himself; and if I am to be entirely communicative on this subject, I must add that the mere rawness which so soon rubs off was complicated by a deeper strangeness which has made me all my life a sojourner on this planet rather than a native of it. Whether it be that I was born mad or a little too sane, my kingdom was not of this world: I was at home only in the realm of my imagination, and at my ease only with the mighty dead. Therefore I had to become an actor, and create for myself a fantastic personality fit and apt for dealing with men, and adaptable to the various parts I had to play as author, journalist, orator, politician, committee man, man of the world, and so forth. . . . At the time of which I am writing, however, I had not yet learnt to act, nor come to understand that my natural character was impossible on the great stage of London. When I had to come out of the realm of imagination into that of actuality I was still uncomfortable. I was outside

society, outside politics, outside sport, outside the Church. If the term had been invented then I should have been called The Complete Outsider. (*Prefaces*, 680)

Shaw rarely refers to himself as "me," as he does in the above paragraph, although he uses the first person singular pronoun, Barthes's "paper-*I*," more than most. And two interpretations might be offered for the phrase: "a deeper strangeness that has made me all my life a sojourner on this planet." One is a recognition that everything is written under the auspices of death. The "I" of any of us is merely a temporary usage, whether as a habitation and refuge in history on this earth or as the subject in a sentence. Shaw was always aware of this absence that is always present with presence in the utterance and especially the writing of "I." By writing that only with "the mighty dead" could he feel at home, in the realm of his imagination, Shaw implies that he exists as a textual fiction among fictions, a subject of many subjectivities, as a presence with no absence, as already an absence. Perhaps his Irishness made palpable to him this feeling of presence in absence and absence in presence, which gives a lurking sense of alienation, or otherness, to everything he wrote.

If the Shaw text could be represented as a landscape, it would not be Dublin, the small provincial city by the sea surrounded by hills with a few prominent and beautiful buildings in which he had been born, but rather London, the sprawling, filthy city that was the hub of empire, to which he arrived in 1876, one of thousands of Irish exiles trying to make their way in the social and cultural spheres of that great metropolis. His feelings as a complete outsider upon his arrival in the "landscape" through which only a William Blake can see angels is understandable. The young "devil's disciple" tried to turn that world upside down following the mid-1880s in his efforts to build the New Jerusalem. Later, when the playful feelings of the masterful critic and the budding playwright gave way to the triumphant feeling of the Promethean's success at the beginning of the new century, he used the city as the stage for the several parts he played, including that novel feeling of coupling when one identity merges with, or attaches itself to, another in marriage—in his case, to fellow Irish Fabian Charlotte Payne-Townshend. The final phase of the ascent of this superman was framed at the outset by this marriage in 1898 and at the conclusion with his first return to Ireland in 1905 since leaving Dublin nearly thirty years before. Within this time frame, he wrote three plays about places where heaven can become hell, and hell heaven, *Man and Superman*, *John Bull's Other Island*, and *Major Barbara*. All end with an accepted marriage proposal between two opposites; all involve both a loss of identity and a mediation of identities.

During all this time, an accompanying feeling of exile, both as Irishman and as artist, had persisted.[19] One of these plays is set in Ireland, another has a seemingly extraneous, yet major Irish character in its last act, and the third, without any Irish connection, was largely written in Ireland during the 1905 visit. As an indication of the emotional effect on him of this visit, although he blamed it on the climate ("the moisture that passes for air in Ireland"), he had to rewrite most of the last scene of *Major Barbara* after returning to London. That was a rare, but not unique, undertaking, as it had happened before with *The Philanderer* and happened later with *Back to Methuselah: Part II*.

John Bull's Other Island provides the best text for reading this double aspect of exile in Shavian identity. This play about Ireland, one of only three set in the country (and none at all in his native city), raises the question as to what extent his dramatic writing is autobiographical. Two of its three major characters, Larry Doyle and Peter Keegan, are Irish and have particular relevance here.[20] The third, the quintessential liberal Englishman Tom Broadbent, is shown to be the most genial and possibly most destructive of devils and certainly a close relation of that archfiend and proud possessor of Shavo-Promethean energies, Andrew Undershaft. But Protestant Shaw figures his Irish sense of artistic identity in the two quarreling Catholic Irishmen. Whereas *Major Barbara* ends with an extended trio between two men, the practical man and the intellectual, engaged in a battle of wits for the salvation of the third, Barbara, who represents the spiritual principle, *John Bull's Other Island* ends with a dialogue between that insider of insiders, God's Englishman, Tom Broadbent, and the "mad" Irish neo-Platonic religious mystic and outsider, Peter Keegan, with acerbic interjections from the third, Laurence (Larry) Doyle, an intense Irish melancholic and exile.

A digression on melancholy may be useful here. *John Bull's Other Island* specifically associates it with not one character but two, both Irish and sometime exiles, Larry Doyle and Peter Keegan, who figure this aspect of the writing subject. Their separate vocations of scholarly priest and engineer share the visionary aspirations personified in Albrecht Dürer's saturnine figure of Melencolia. Later, in *Heartbreak House*, Shaw combined the mystic and engineer-inventor in a single character, Captain Shotover, who—appropriate to the tradition of melancholy—needs darkness in order to create: "Give me deeper darkness" (*Plays*, 775), he cries at the end of Act I. Shaw may have known of that seventeenth-century cornucopia of intertextuality, Robert Burton's *Anatomy of Melancholy* (1621), and it might be worth speculating on his understanding of melancholy in the light of, say, Frances Yates's studies of the subject in relation to neo-Platonism in Renaissance art.[21] In *Occult Philosophy in the Elizabethan Age* (1979) Yates analyzes Dürer's engraving *Melencolia I* and suggests that it be viewed as part of a series, in which another of Dürer's best-known engravings, *Saint Jerome*, could be called "Melencolia II" (Yates, 49–59).[22] Shaw's *Androcles and the Lion*, of course, retells the story of Saint Jerome and his lion, pictured lying peacefully in the scholar's study in Dürer's engraving.

Shaw was a great admirer of Dürer and certainly knew *Melencolia I*. The engraving of Saint Jerome in his study at work translating the Bible into the Vulgate might even have given Shaw a visual reference for the setting of *The Gospel of the Brothers Barnabas*; the play opens with Franklyn Barnabas writing his "Gospel" in a sun-filled book-lined study featuring a prominent window equipped with window seats, just as in Dürer's picture. The setting of Act I of *John Bull's Other Island* in combination with the personality of Larry Doyle might similarly be read in terms of *Melencolia I*. In that engraving, Melencolia's face is occulted in shadow, while her wings and surrounding paraphernalia, which include tools, geometrical forms, plans, and a ladder, are symbols of her aspirations and of the means to realize them. The stage directions for the offices of Messrs. Doyle and Broadbent, civil engineers, in Act I of *John Bull's Other Island* describe something similar: *"a table consisting of large drawing boards on trestles, with plans, rolls of tracing paper, mathematical instruments, and other draughtsman's accessories on it. . . . On the walls hang a large map of South America, a pictorial advertisement of a steamship company"* (*Plays*, 405). The character whom the text associates with this paraphernalia is Larry Doyle, although he does not appear until well into the middle of the act: *"He goes up to the table where the plans are, and makes a note on one of them, referring to his pocket book as he does so"* (*Plays*, 409).

Doyle's melancholic, saturnine temperament is soon revealed to us: "Why are you so bitter?" "Never mind my temper . . . You know the way I nag, and worry, and carp, and cavil, and disparage, and am never satisfied and never quiet . . ." "Of course you have the melancholy of the Keltic race" (*Plays*, 410). After which, he launches into one of the great Shavian long speeches, here full of self-castigation precisely because of his melancholic qualities of imagination, dreaming, and derisive humor. The closest modern literary parallel to Larry Doyle is Joyce's Stephen Dedalus in

Ulysses, another intense, brainy, melancholic returning Irish exile. In 1904, the year of Shaw's play, Joyce returned home and met Nora Barnacle; Shaw's own return came the year after, at the instigation of his Irish wife. Both leading characters, Doyle and Stephen, are overshadowed, occulted as befits their melancholic natures, in their different narratives by others, by Broadbent and Bloom, respectively. Both stories are ostensibly about homecomings that develop in quite different directions as their inner dramas are displaced onto the external experiences of other characters. The literary model for both Larry and Stephen is the most famous returning melancholic exile of all, Shakespeare's Hamlet, who, dressed in his "inky cloak," even refers to himself as "melancholy." Like Hamlet, Larry refuses the responsibilities of his birthright—the parliamentary seat that his father has contrived for him—and lets his Falstaffian Laertes, Broadbent, take both the seat and his Ophelia, Nora, who has been waiting patiently for him during his exile; this provides a more realistic, if no less harsh, ending for Nora than Ophelia.

Act II begins with Shaw's description of the other melancholic Irishman, Peter Keegan, the defrocked priest, in which the word *melancholy* again features: "*A man with the face of a young saint, yet with white hair and perhaps 50 years on his back, is standing near the stone in a trance of intense melancholy, looking over the hills as if by mere intensity of gaze he could pierce the glories of the sunset and see into the streets of heaven*" (*Plays*, 416).[23] This is, of course, a cliché of nineteenth-century romantic Ireland as the land of saints and scholars, but as always in a Shaw play several things happen simultaneously. Indeed, in this play of all plays, a double process seems constantly to be taking place: exploding generalizations contrast with the specifics of generalization. This Irish play opens with a deconstruction of the myth of the stage Irishman in the character of Tim Haffigan, who happens not to be Irish at all. But Shaw also gives enough information to show that Tim *is* a decidedly Irish phenomenon, although this slant, occulted like Larry Doyle's personality, may at first escape the reader and audience. He was born in Scotland, the product of his Irish parents' forced emigration from Ireland following the great famine a generation earlier, like Malone, the Irish-American millionaire in *Man and Superman*. And later, when the setting moves to Ireland, we encounter Tim's very Irish Uncle, Matt Haffigan, who, although a caricature, represents the harsh realities of nineteenth-century Irish rural life.

Likewise with Keegan, the text suggests there is something more to him than an Irish cliché. He is represented as being mad in the way William Blake was mad, and Broadbent more than once refers to him as an "Irish Ruskin" (Ruskin suffered bouts of insanity). Shaw's irony is at work here in these English associations because, although Keegan is an extraordinarily well-traveled, well-educated, and urbane man, he is also intensely, though not virulently, anti-English. Keegan possesses something of the "severe indignation" of Swift at his most anti-English. In this, he is unlike Larry, or Shaw for that matter, and it causes great friction between them. In other respects, however, they are similar, and the most obvious is their shared characteristic of melancholy. They both possess imaginative, critical, saturnine intelligences, which are not simply characteristic "of the Keltic Race," as Broadbent would have it.

One trait of the writing in *John Bull's Other Island* (indeed of Shaw's dramatic writing in general), taken to an extreme with Broadbent, is to make his characters unaware of their own motivations while simultaneously making them crystal clear to the other characters and the audience. Often, as with Broadbent, the language that the character uses to explain himself or herself betrays his or her meaning. Socratic self-knowledge distinguishes Keegan in this respect, especially from Broadbent: he knows that he does not know. Keegan's Socratic enlightenment occurred at the hands of a "black man. . . . an elderly Hindoo" (*Plays*, 440), whose revelation was that this world is hell. Thus fortified, Keegan, the mad priest, is not subject to the meliorist delusions of others.

Both Doyle and Keegan left Ireland as soon as they could. Both became highly educated and extremely well traveled. Doyle first went to Dublin, which gave him the education to go farther afield. As a youth in Rosscullen he dreamed of going to London and America and Rome and the East, an itinerary similar to Keegan's. Doyle spent some time in America, he now lives in London, and the map of South America indicates that some engineering projects may have brought him there. In the preface, Shaw, in unusual fashion, reveals something about his character: "Doyle's special contribution was the freedom from illusion, the power of facing facts, the nervous industry, the sharpened wits, the sensitive pride of the imaginative man who has fought his way up through social persecution and poverty" (*Plays*, 442).

Keegan is a representative of pre-nineteenth-century Irish Catholicism. He pointedly says he is not a Maynooth man; Maynooth is the Roman Catholic theological college set up by the British government in the middle of the nineteenth century to educate Irish priests in Ireland after centuries of religious repression against Catholics. The parish priest of

Rosscullen, Father Dempsey, represents the new type of Maynooth priest in the play, which placed the Irish Catholic ever more firmly under the joint yoke of Rome and England. By contrast, Keegan represents the older tradition of an Irish priest's education: exile and traveling; *peregrinatio* is a narrative form for recounting lives of the early Irish saints and scholars, who as missionaries re-Christianized Western Europe and with whom Keegan is associated. Keegan's peregrinations took him to the great universities of Rome, Paris, Jerusalem, Salamanca, and Oxford. The difference between the two melancholic visionaries, Larry and Keegan, is best represented in their chosen professions of priest and engineer: one belongs to the spiritual world, the other to the material world. But in talking of his Catholicism in Act I, Larry associates himself with Keegan rather than with the modern nationalist Roman Catholicism represented by Father Dempsey: "My Catholicism is the Catholicism of Charlemagne or Dante, qualified by a good deal of modern science and folklore which Father Dempsey would call the ravings of an Atheist" (*Plays*, 413). Toward the end of the act, Larry speaks of his troubled relation to his native land in terms of dreaming, which Keegan echoes at the end of the play: "[The Irish charm is] the charm of a dream. Live in contact with dreams and you will get something of their charm: live in contact with facts and you get something of their brutality. I wish I could find a country to live in where the facts were not brutal and the dreams not unreal" (*Plays*, 415). More elaborately and memorably, Keegan offers his own dream in Act IV in terms of the doctrine of the Trinity, famously associated with Saint Patrick:

> [Heaven] is a country where the State is the Church and the Church the people: three in one and one in three. It is a commonwealth in which work is play and play is life: three in one and one in three. It is a temple in which the priest is the worshipper and the worshipper the worshipped: three in one and one in three. It is a godhead in which all life is human and all humanity divine: three in one and one in three. It is, in short, the dream of a madman. (*Plays*, 452)

The three in one and one in three reveals something about the logic of Shavian dialectic. This notion also comments on the three characters taking part in the climactic trio, and thus it elucidates something about the nature of Shavian drama—in particular, its tendency to take nothing in itself as final. As one of the most eloquent illustrations of the flexibility of the subject-object relation within Shavian discourse, the theme of trinity suggests why drama is such a good linguistic tool or "apparatus" (his word) for Shaw as linguistic/grammatological bricoleur. As characters there can be no reconciliation between their expressed views, except symbolically in terms of marriage or friendship, or negatively as personal antagonism. The apparatus, however, allows for the almost simultaneous expression of logically contradictory propositions, which *must* all be expressed but which Western discourse positively discourages.

Thus, both Keegan and Doyle, in their similarities and differences, represent a matrix of different aspects of Shaw's identity, the national and the international, the spiritual (the artist/mystic) and the material (the socialist social engineer) that he points to in the *Immaturity* preface: the Irish writer working in England; and the alienated exile or outsider, not really belonging to the world, but working out his destiny as best he can as visionary. These two facets do not make for easy bedfellows, as the intensity of Larry Doyle's and Peter Keegan's argument with each other makes clear.

> KEEGAN. When I went to England, Sir, I hated England. Now I pity it [*Broadbent can hardly conceive an Irishman pitying England; but as Larry intervenes angrily, he gives it up and takes to the hill and his cigar again*].
>
> LARRY. Much good your pity will do it!
>
> KEEGAN. In the accounts kept in heaven, Mr Doyle, a heart purified of hatred may be worth more than even a Land Development Syndicate of Anglicized Irishmen and Gladstonnized Englishmen.
>
> LARRY. Oh, in heaven, no doubt. I have never been there. Can you tell me where it is?
>
> KEEGAN. Could you have told me this morning where hell is? Yet you know now that it is here. Do not despair of finding heaven: it may be no farther off.
>
> LARRY [*ironically*] On this holy ground, as you call it, eh?
>
> KEEGAN [*with fierce intensity*] Yes, perhaps even on this holy ground which such Irishmen as you have turned into a Land of Derision.
>
> BROADBENT [*coming between them*] Take care! You will be quarreling presently. Oh, you Irishmen, you Irishmen! Toujours Ballyhooly, eh? (*Plays*, 451)

But earlier, in the contrast between the English Broadbent and the Irish Keegan, Shaw makes the point, to which he would return twenty-five years later in the preface to *Immaturity* when he wrote of the "deeper strangeness which has made me all my life a sojourner on this planet rather than a native of it":

> BROADBENT. I find the world quite good enough for me: rather a jolly place, in fact.
>
> KEEGAN [*looking at him with quiet wonder*] You are satisfied?
>
> BROADBENT. As a reasonable man, yes. I see no evils in the world —except, of course, natural evils—that cannot be remedied by freedom, self-government, and English institutions. I think so, not because I am an Englishman, but as a matter of common sense.
>
> KEEGAN. You feel at home in the world, then?
>
> BROADBENT. Of course. Don't you?
>
> KEEGAN [*from the very depths of his nature*] No. (*Plays,* 441)

In dramatizing these aspects of his own identity, the writer's subjectivity, the shadows of Shaw's Irish play inscribe his autobiography. These less obvious authorial personae inscribed therein can be added to those others delineated in this chapter. The resulting variety of autobiographical writing, though, adds to that unfolding drama of a Shavian subjectivity (the fictional author as subject), which readers bring to the texts: the drama of an authorial shadow-play cast by the drama of the writing, the drama of the characters, and the drama of the readers' lives. Shaw's playwrighting provides a stage for not only the multiple subjectivities in the writing and of his characters but also his audience-readers, whereby they may lend or introduce their own subjectivity into the text. Shaw's writing, as he wrote of Ibsen's plays, makes "the spectators themselves the persons of the drama, and the incidents of their own lives its incidents" (*Drama 4,* 1300).

4 The Spoken/Written Subject

The Machine in the Ghost

> *I have an instinct which tells me that death plays its part in life.*
> Cain in Act II of *In the Beginning, Back to Methuselah: Part I* (1921)

The Mechanical Shadow

The Infidel Half Century, published as preface to *Back to Methuselah*, traces the ideological consequences following the publication of Darwin's *On the Origin of Species* on the social and political history of the last half of the nineteenth century. Shaw's essay provides a rare cogent critique of neo-Darwinian evolutionary theory in the context of writing and its relation to on-going discourse in culture.[1] The piece treats the discourse of modern science, and biology in particular, as a metanarrative, a mythic discourse the text offers for deconstruction; meanwhile, Shaw proposes his own myth, that of creative evolution, which stems from the philosophy of Schopenhauer and Bergson as inflected by Nietzsche, crossed with what he called "the 1790–1830 theory of Evolution" (*Agitations*, 119) epitomized by the biology of Lamarck as well as the theory of natural selection of Darwin, as developed by Weismann and as critiqued by Samuel Butler.[2] Creative evolution as a science of life is a myth of metaphysical vitalism, what Shaw calls metabiology, which he offers alongside his critique or deconstruction of biological discourse. In social terms, this means religion. In philosophical terms, it means acknowledging the necessity for a *new* metaphysics of consciousness as a supplement to the discourse(s) of modern science necessary for coming to an adequate understanding of the process of subject-object relations. This chapter proposes that Lacan and Derrida in their different ways have answered this call for a new metaphysics, although Derrida would not use that word.

Chapters 2 and 3 discussed the deconstructive or critical aspect of Shaw's writing and the multiple authorial subject, and now this chapter considers the object or, rather, the subject-object relation in language by enlarging on the suggestion of previous chapters that would read creative evolution as a philosophy of the relation between subject and object in language, in writing. In science, the object is usually understood as the material world—where the material is real—in relation to an abstract human subject. In the face of the abstract metaphysics of such materialism, Shaw declared: "I am contemptuously and implacably anti-rationalist and anti-materialist" (*Agitations*, 117). Chapter 2 views subjectivity in criticism, as the insertion of the corporeal subject into the writing, as a staging of the subject as dramatic character. It should not be surprising that Shaw wanted to examine the other side of the relation and critique the modern science of biology in a discourse that marks the intersection of the living subject and the material world, sometimes described as the ghost in the machine. Shaw's claim to be a biologist thus offers an opportunity to read another type of his writing, one whose shadow is traceable across different types of discourse in unexpected ways.[3]

A "metonymy perpetually at work on the same metaphor" is what Derrida calls Freud's search for a model of the psyche in a series of texts beginning with the unpublished *Project for a Scientific Psychology* (1895), taking in "Two Principles of Mental Functioning" (1911) and *Beyond the Pleasure Principle* (1920) among others, and ending with *The "Mystic Writing Pad"* (1925). This chapter is also a "metonymy perpetually at work" in a series of texts: Shaw's *The Infidel Half Century*, Freud's *Beyond the Pleasure Principle*, Lacan's *The Seminar of Jacques Lacan: Book II*, including his "Seminar on [Poe's] 'The Purloined Letter,'" Derrida's "The Postman of Truth" and "Freud and the Stage of Writing," and back to *In the Beginning*, Part I of *Back to Methuselah: A Metabiological Pentateuch*. Each text is concerned with the same thematic of language, meaning, and writing based on a necessity (*pace* Derrida) for a new metaphysics in the context of the death/life distinction, a metabiology or metapsychology to follow the demise or deconstruction by, among others, Nietzsche, Shaw, and Derrida of the old abstract metaphysics of Cartesian dualism.

Lacan based his "return to Freud" in *Seminar II* on a clinically observed phenomenon from which Freud had derived his "death instinct" in *Beyond the Pleasure Principle*, that of the "compulsion to repeat." This led Lacan to reinterpret psychoanalysis in terms of structural linguistics in opposition to the Freudian ego-based psychology that had become so popular in the

United States. Derrida, for his part, was also powerfully exercised by Freud's *Beyond the Pleasure Principle* and other metapsychological writings, which he reinterpreted as the basis for the new science of writing he called grammatology in the essays "Freud and the Stage of Writing" and "Différence."[4] Later, as Cain to Lacan's Abel and perhaps suffering from sibling rivalry with his elder Freudian reinterpreter, Derrida attacked Lacan's interpretation of the Poe story "The Purloined Letter" in an essay entitled with some sarcasm "The Postman of Truth." To appreciate the relevance of these texts of Lacan and Derrida with respect to Shaw, a consideration of Freud's *Beyond the Pleasure Principle*, from which they acknowledge their several texts derive, will be useful. As "metapsychology," this work first proposed the concept of a "death instinct," and Shaw's exactly contemporaneous *The Infidel Half Century* with its similar thematic provides a link to Freud's text. The "beyond" of a pleasure principle, a death instinct derived from a compulsion to repeat, provided a basis for both Lacan's idea that the unconscious as the Symbolic is structured like a language, and Derrida's notion of différance as writing. Thus the move from Shaw's and Freud's interest in the death/life (or *thanatos/eros*) opposition in relation to repetition and the living machine leads to Lacan's and Derrida's transmutation of these concepts as metaphors into language and writing. Both Lacan and Derrida confront that old Cartesian dualism of mind and matter exemplified in the simple metaphysical basis of modern science and biology, of which Shaw was so critical, but to which Freud nevertheless adhered. Their texts imply that it might be more a question of the machine in the ghost rather than the ghost in the machine. For Lacan, the machine becomes the Freudian Unconscious, what he calls the Symbolic or language that constitutes the subject, and for Derrida, différance as (*archê*) writing.

This chapter, therefore, takes a circuitous route from biology and metabiology to grammatology by way of psychology and metapsychology, psychoanalysis, literary analysis, and drama, to unravel a few textual threads from this densely knotted weave of intertextuality and to suggest how Shaw's texts and theater practice may perform on this particular "stage of writing."

The Infidel Half Century

Although Shaw's interventions in politics and economics might have been worthy of some intellectual and academic respect, his interventions in other areas of scientific discourse were seen, and continue to be seen, as more problematic.[5] Thus, his crusade against the medical profession, its ideology, its ritual practices, and its economics contributed to the establishment of a National Health Service in Britain in the 1940s, but his intervention in the debates on animal experimentation and biological theories of evolution, particularly his antagonism to the hegemony of Darwinian theory, earned him a reputation as an idiosyncratic heretic. His most powerful critique came in *The Infidel Half Century*, which began as a paper on Darwin read to the Fabian Society on March 23, 1906.[6] This text could have been titled a "General Inquiry into the Causes and Effects of the Publication of Darwin's Book on Western Culture and Civilization." As a textual inquiry into the cultural background from which Darwin's writing arose, and the economic, political, and social implications of its theory, the resulting essay offers a critique of natural selection as an ideology, though he does not use the word. *The Infidel Half Century* carries on where Marx left off with his denunciations of the workings of unfettered capital, reinforced by Darwin's theory with its seeming justification of competition and survival, where the empires engaged aggressively in competition for international markets. Indeed Shaw is alert to the possibility that such a theory not only produces ideological effects but is also itself an ideological product: "Darwinism was so closely related to Capitalism that Marx regarded it as an economic product rather than as a biological theory" (*Prefaces*, 531).[7] He then cites Malthus, Lyell, the French physiocrats, and Ricardo, who supplied the theoretical basis for late nineteenth-century capitalist economics, as all contributing to the theoretical foundations for Darwin's book.

Insisting on natural selection as the sole explanation for evolution was to Shaw as much an expression of nineteenth-century fundamentalism as that manifested earlier by the Bible thumpers who had done away with the "compromise made [in the Middle Ages] by which two different orders of truth, religious and scientific, had been recognised" (*Prefaces*, 518). This nonlogocentric demand for "two different orders of truth," for a discourse of metaphysics to accompany the discourse of science, has proved an insurmountable difficulty for *both* modern scientists *and* Bible fundamentalists in their respective debates with poststructuralists and neo-Darwinians. Shaw's metabiological writing, therefore, rather than providing *the* truth of one biological theory over another, offered a critique of scientific discourse as ideology along with a deconstruction of its metaphysical assumptions and at the same time argued for the necessity for a new metaphysics as a critique of materialism.

Yet Shaw, appreciative of Darwin's work in natural history and intent on a cornerstone for his own social philosophy, adopted Darwin's arguments on sexual selection that called for maximizing the pool of intermarriageability in the preservation of the species. Such egalitarianism prevented Shaw from going down either the racist or elitist paths that tainted the new so-called science of eugenics (a development of Social Darwinism) first proposed by Francis Galton, another grandson of Erasmus Darwin and Charles Darwin's cousin, of which he was otherwise a notable supporter.

The Infidel Half Century comprises forty-nine newspaper-type sections with separate subheadings that fall into five distinct divisions: first, a general anecdotal introduction to the impact of Darwin on Victorian culture; second, a history of evolutionary theory *before* the contributions of Charles Darwin and Alfred Wallace, the codiscoverer of natural selection; third, the immediate, generally positive impact on cultural life and intellectual debate following publication of Darwin's book; fourth, the consequential, generally negative effects on European civilization of neo-Darwinism during the ensuing fifty years, which culminated in the Great War; and, finally, a reaction to Darwinism in religion and art at the beginning of the new century leading to the writing of the accompanying text, the play-cycle *Back to Methuselah*.

The early part of Shaw's preface, after the introductory sections, is devoted to showing how the 1780–1830 theoreticians of evolution had sprung up around the eighteenth fin de siècle and that Charles Darwin's grandfather, Erasmus Darwin, had been prominent among them. The grandson hijacked, as it were, the concept of evolution as a misnomer for his own theory of natural selection, which Shaw perceptively describes as "pseudo-evolution at best":

> [Darwin] was conscious of having discovered a process of transformation and modification which accounted for a great deal of natural history. But he did not put it forward as accounting for the whole of natural history. He included it under the heading of Evolution, though it was only pseudo-evolution at best; but he revealed it as *a* method of evolution, not as *the* method of evolution. He did not pretend that it excluded other methods, or that it was the chief method. . . . In short, he was not a Darwinian, but an honest naturalist working away at his job. (*Prefaces*, 522)[8]

In fact, the rhetoric of later Darwinians continues to suggest that Darwin's book, which barely mentions evolution, developed and decided the theory all at once. Herbert Spencer's catchphrase "survival of the fittest" became, and remains, the rhetorical war cry of Darwin's followers, although Darwin himself did not care for it. As a truism (the fittest survive; who survive? the fittest), it does not lend weight to the argument one way or another. And Shaw, ever ready to deconstruct Darwinian language and rhetorical procedures, refers through much of *The Infidel Half Century* to natural selection as "Circumstantial Selection," an unnatural selection that acts in response to global catastrophes and other accidental external conditions.

More important, Shaw argued that, on its own terms, the Darwinian theory requires the incorporation of a metaphysical or vital concept, a concept of self-control similar to Freud's Reality Principle, although Darwinian rhetoric had seemed to eliminate such metaphysics:

> Yet self-control is just the one quality of survival value which Circumstantial [i.e., Natural] Selection must invariably and inevitably develop in the long run.... The self-controlled man survives all such changes of circumstance, because he adapts himself to them, and eats neither as much as he can hold nor as little as he can scrape along on, but as much as is good for him. What is self-control? It is nothing but a highly developed vital sense. (*Prefaces*, 526–27)

For a theory of evolution, Shaw, influenced by Samuel Butler, turned to the leading pre-Darwin evolutionist, Jean Baptiste Lamarck (1744–1829), who had coined the term "biology" (science of life). That introduced a metaphysical difficulty into the whole subject, as Lacan pointed out:

> Vitalist thought is alien to biology . . . life was going to be defined in relation to death . . . the character of the reference to the machine [is decisive] so far as the founding of biology is concerned. Biologists think they devote themselves to the study of life. It's not clear why. Until further notice, their fundamental concepts' point of origin has nothing to do with the phenomenon of life, which in its essence remains completely impenetrable. (Lacan, *Seminar II*, 75)

The metaphysical concept of life has continued to shadow biology, and both Shaw and Freud, in their efforts to take it into account as metabiology or metapsychology, turned back to Lamarck and his idea of functional adaptation.[9] As Shaw explained it, Lamarck's functional adaptation was a theory of use and disuse in terms of willing, albeit unconscious. Speaking of species development, he explained: "If you have no eyes, and want to see, and keep trying to see, you will finally get eyes. If, like a mole or a subterranean fish, you have eyes and don't want to see, you will lose your eyes" (*Prefaces*, 509).

It remains doubtful whether experiments can be devised to prove either Darwinian natural selection or Lamarckian functional adaptation. Shaw, the antivivisectionist, castigated the cruel experiments on mice by the German biologist and leading neo-Darwinian, August Weismann (1834–1914), whom he described as "a very clever and suggestive biologist who was unhappily reduced to idiocy by neo-Darwinism" (*Prefaces*, 506).[10]

Weismann was the scientist who brought Darwin's theory into line with what later developed into the science of genetics. He was largely responsible for the neo-Darwinian denial of the inheritance of acquired characteristics, to which Shaw quipped that all inherited characteristics are acquired. More forcefully, Shaw was scathing of both the cruelty of Weismann's experiments designed to see if acquired characteristics could be inherited, which involved cutting off several successive generations of mice's tails, and the logic behind the experiments, which argued that cutting off a mouse's tail might lead to a descendant of that mouse being born with a shorter tail. "This experiment," claimed Shaw, "is impossible because the human experimenter cannot get at the mouse's mind. And that is what is wrong with all the barren cruelties of the laboratories" (*Prefaces*, 525–26). Shaw's alternative proposal to hypnotize a mouse in an experiment to discover "musque" evolutionary methods, while hilarious, has not made him any less of a pariah as far as humorless neo-Darwinians are concerned.[11]

The inheritance of acquired characteristics (Shaw called them habits) became the major bone of contention between neo-Darwinian and neo-Lamarckian theories. Neo-Darwinians attribute individual characteristics to genetic mutation occurring at the time of conception of the individual or before. To put it at its simplest, in genetic terms the reproductive cells are not, and cannot be, influenced by other body cells. Neo-Lamarckians claim—and neo-Darwinians deny—that characteristics, or characteristics of those characteristics, acquired after the conception of the individual can be genetically passed on in some way. An individual's life experience, according to neo-Darwinians, cannot affect the process of generation (that is, of evolution); species change, therefore, can only happen as a result of accidental individual genetic mutations favored by chance external circumstances. Neo-Lamarckians argue that somehow experience matters and that the process of species evolution may be affected by individual experience between the conception of a child and the conception of its child.

Several twentieth-century attempts to find evidence one way or another failed, whether on the neo-Lamarckian side with Lysenko in the Soviet Union and the unfortunate Paul Kammerer as related in Arthur Koestler's *The Case of the Midwife Toad*, or on the neo-Darwinian side with the equally unfortunate H.B.D. Kettlewell and E. B. Ford and their peppered moths as told in Judith Hooper's *Of Moths and Men*. Although the neo-Darwinian position has generally been fortified by advances in genetics since the 1950s (the discovery of chromosomes, DNA, and so on), Shaw, with some consistency and pertinence, could still write as late as 1945 that biology's "new knowledge of chromosomes and hormones only substitutes millions of miracles for the single mystery formerly called the soul or the breath of life" (*Methuselah* [1945], 299).

The general critique of science in *The Infidel Half Century* seeks to be persuasive rather than conclusive, and Shaw's general argument is best summed up in the statement: "Our minds have reacted so violently towards provable logical theorems and demonstrable mechanical or chemical facts that we have become incapable of metaphysical truth" (*Prefaces*, 538). The paradox, according to Shaw, is that modern education has made the necessary metaphysical thinking impossible.

One aspect of the argument in *The Infidel Half Century* is to expose neo-Darwinian biology as riddled with metaphysical assumptions and incapable of resisting drawing metaphysical conclusions at the same time as it uses reductive arguments to rule out other forms of discourse that would seek to (re)introduce metaphysics. Thus Shaw argues for a new metaphysics to accompany scientific discourse, a metaphysics beyond the simplistic metaphysics of an abstract human subject observing the material world. *The Infidel Half Century*, therefore, alongside its critique or deconstruction seems to make a logocentric demand: to acknowledge the necessity for a discourse of the metaphysical, of life, or, in less strictly philosophical terms, of religion.

Shaw's metaphysics derived from Schopenhauer's distinction between the world as will and as representation. Schopenhauer, in a way, went back to Plato's dichotomy between reality (the world of ideas, reason, or Logos) and appearance, except that for Schopenhauer, reality is the will, not reason. According to Schopenhauer, as individuals we can apprehend the world in two different ways: either by submitting to the general will, of which we can have no direct knowledge, or by reasoning derived from the world of appearances or re-presentation (similar to Freud's distinction between the unconscious and the conscious and Lacan's between the Symbolic and the Imaginary). Shaw adopted Schopenhauer's metaphysics but not his generally pessimistic philosophy involving Buddhist-like resignation.[12] His version of Schopenhauer's will, the Life Force, despite all the disadvantages and suffering caused by it working itself out in a process of trial and error, is on balance, it is to be hoped, beneficent.

Shaw's metaphysics—as distinct from the simplistic metaphysical basis of material science, or the abstract metaphysics of logical reason, or an essentialist metaphysics of liberal humanism—might find its contemporary philosophical counterpart, not so much in Bergson, but in Edmund Husserl (1859–1938), who proposed a phenomenological analysis of the relations between the human subject and the world as object in such works as *Ideas* (1913) and *Cartesian Meditations* (1931). In the words of Derrida's translator of *On Grammatology*, Gayatri Spivak: "The question asked by Husserl is precisely a question of the relationship between subjective and objective structures" (Derrida, *Grammatology*, li). That is the question the Shaw text proposes with the term "creative evolution," as outlined in chapter 1. Husserl's phenomenology, however, requires a transcendental subject and a world of essential ideas, which became a prime target of Derrida's deconstruction. Although similar to Husserl's phenomenology as a problematic, Shaw's general refusal of the abstract, the essential, and the transcendental, may bring his new metaphysics closer to Derrida's différance as (archê) writing than to the logocentric metaphysics of presence (the privileging of the identity of the spoken word with the thing, signifier with signified) epitomized by Husserl.

Shaw, an artist with a mystical bent, refers admiringly in *The Infidel Half Century* to the biologist Lorenz Oken, who wrote in 1807 of "the science of the everlasting transmutations of the Holy Ghost in the world." This, for Shaw, was biology as metaphysics from a writer "scientific enough to see that the Holy Ghost is a scientific fact" (*Prefaces*, 513–14). Such metabiology would become an hermeneutics of metaphor and analogy with both the Bible and cellular biology as its object, as is the case in the play-cycle *Back to Methuselah* (see chapter 8). This metabiology would be open to the science of the religious imagination that Shaw himself proposed in *On the Prospects of Christianity* (the preface to *Androcles and the Lion*), *The Infidel Half Century*, the preface to *The Black Girl in Search of God*, the preface to Wilson's *Birth of Language*, as well as in many plays, lectures, and other occasional writings.

Shaw was not alone in holding that modern science has either a simplistic or inadequate metaphysical basis for explaining its own procedures. Without an adequate metaphysical discourse, science, especially biology, risks becoming what Marx and Althusser call an ideology with ruinous social and political consequences, which Shaw describes in *The Infidel Half Century*. That problem preoccupied not only Husserl in his phenomenology, but also other early twentieth-century thinkers like Bergson (to whom Shaw acknowledged intellectual kinship) in his *L'Evolution créatrice* and Alfred North Whitehead (1861–1947) in his process philosophy. They all understood that the inevitable metaphysical assumptions and conclusions to be traced within a scientific discourse that disdains metaphysics require something like a critique "in the Kantian sense," as Shaw puts it in *On the Prospects of Christianity*. And Husserl's disciple, Martin Heidegger, went beyond phenomenology in his existential inquiry into what he called Dasein, how the human existent or being could come to know itself, rather like the artist-philosopher of *Man and Superman*.

The attempts of these philosophers to provide a new metaphysical basis for science, while admirable and ingenious, have not been easy for the layman to understand; Shaw, a professional thinker if not an academic philosopher, indicated the difficulty facing the untrained yet interested thinker:

> Evolution as a philosophy and physiology of the will is a mystical process, which can be apprehended only by a trained, apt and comprehensive thinker. Though the phenomena of use and disuse, of wanting and trying, of the manufacture of weightlifters and wrestlers from men of ordinary strength, are familiar enough as facts, they are extremely puzzling as subjects of thought, and lead you into metaphysics the moment you try to account for them. (*Prefaces*, 521)

Here the biologist and logician might accuse Shaw of making a "category mistake" in equating a theory of use and disuse in the evolution of species with the phenomenon of individual weight lifters putting on muscle. But that, whether we like it or not, is precisely Shaw's argument. His equation of our understanding of the process of cellular biology with the workings of the religious imagination in sacred literature is similar. His rhetoric forces us either to refuse to consider these analogies or to take them into account somehow.

As for Shaw's logic in its confrontation with Cartesian dualism, the most difficult and at the same time the most crucial part of *The Infidel Half*

Century comes in its presentation of the age-old conflict between mechanists and vitalists. What is admissible in scientific method he discusses in the context of mechanists, vitalists, antimechanists, materialists, and old and new vitalists in a key paragraph "The Homeopathic Reaction against Darwinism" that develops in somewhat Hegelian fashion.[13] Stemming from the distinction among physiologists between mechanists and vitalists, Shaw contends that those antimechanists who do not want to be called vitalists believe in two contradictory postulates, both incorrect: first, a vital force is unscientific; and second, the concept of a force is a mechanical conception. According to Shaw, "The New Vitalists . . . regarded the Old Vitalists as Mechanists who had tried to fill up the gulf between life and death with an empty phrase denoting a physical force" (*Prefaces*, 537). Shaw's language here can easily make us overlook exactly what he is saying: life is not solely a physical force. Shaw continues, "the Old Vitalist, who was essentially a materialist has evolved into the New Vitalist, who is, as every genuine scientist must be, finally a metaphysician . . . he will cease to boggle at the name Vitalist, or at the inevitable, ancient, popular, and quite correct use of the term Force to denote metaphysical as well as physical overcomers of inertia."[14] With this metaphysical concept of life (*vis inertiae* or *vis naturae*), Shaw's new metaphysics (surprisingly, given the logocentric terminology) opens itself to the Derridean notion of the force of différance and his new science of writing, grammatology.

Although Shaw acknowledged that Deism served as part of the intellectual background to the 1780–1830 evolution theory, he criticized the eighteenth-century Deists for believing in a mechanical universe set in physical motion by an uncritiqued metaphysical entity called God (a clockwork God!), but who thereafter does not interfere in its workings. He is similarly critical of neo-Darwinians who combined natural selection "with a force as inhuman as we conceive magnetism to be." As the "red-haired Irishman" says in *The Black Girl in Search of God* (1932): "theres somethin in us thats dhrivin at him, and somethin out of us thats dhrivin at him." Shaw's metaphysical Life Force, therefore, can be read within the Western philosophical tradition as analogous to Plato's demiurge, Aristotle's unmoved mover, Thomas Aquinas's sustaining cause, Kant's categorical imperative, Hegel's spirit, Schopenhauer's will, and Nietzsche's will to power. Similarities with the writing of his contemporaries Bergson, Husserl, Whitehead, and Heidegger have already been mentioned, and kinship to later writings is suggested here. Most pertinent is its relation to force in Derrida's sense as emerging from différance as writing, the force of the breaching or pathbreaking that makes inscription possible (a notion borrowed from Freud, as we shall see), which leaves behind those traces of differentiating differences he calls archê-writing.

The Great War gave a sense of urgency to Shaw's requirement for a mediation between those discourses of truth, religion and science, with metaphysics as a "mental apparatus" or "frame of reference" for the science of biology. The postscript to *Back To Methuselah*, written in 1944, might be useful to bear in mind in the light of the more recent science wars, not to mention C. P. Snow's concerns in the 1960s about the two cultures:[15]

> Professional science must cease to mean the nonsense of Weismann and the atrocities of Pavlov, in which life is a series of accidents and reflexes, and logic only a thoughtless association of ideas. Still less must it mean mere erudition in the scriptures of the saints, prophets, and metaphysicians from Augustine and Aquinas to Butler and Bergson and Shaw. It must renounce magic and yet accept miracle; for as biology is still in the metaphysical stage . . . and as physics, in spite of its miraculous electrons and its abolition of matter, is nearer to the positive stage, the metaphysicians and artist-philosophers must co-operate with the astronomers and physiologists in separate but friendly and at the edges overlapping departments of social service. (*Methuselah* [1945], 298–99)

The final part of *The Infidel Half Century* argues that if a credible religion were to emerge from the proposed new metaphysics, it would be expressed in the art of the times. He therefore reads art history and dramatic literature to detail the aesthetic genesis of the writing of his preface and play. In intertextual terms, his "metabiological pentateuch" rewrites *both* the Bible *and* Darwin's most famous book. The discourse of the new metaphysics is presented, for the moment, in writing both as dramatic poetry and as a reflexive critique of imagination (see chapter 8).

Beyond the Pleasure Principle

Sigmund Freud's *Beyond the Pleasure Principle*, of fundamental importance to the writings of both Lacan and Derrida, can be read as a counterpart in many ways to *Back to Methuselah*. How, then, do the Shaw text and the Freud text intersect? Is there meaning to be extracted from this textual intersection? Thematic coincidences between Freud's metapsychology and Shaw's metabiology give us a context by which to relate Shaw's demand in *The Infidel Half Century* for a new metaphysics to crucial texts of the two major poststructuralist thinkers, Lacan and Derrida, while a consideration of their texts may retrospectively help with a reading of Shaw's.

At the same time as Shaw was writing *Methuselah* in the wake of World War I, Freud, who had founded the new science of psychoanalysis in Vienna in the last years of the nineteenth century, was also reflecting on the war and writing on one clinically observed phenomenon in particular, that of former soldiers reliving the horrors of their wartime experiences. Freud called this phenomenon a "compulsion to repeat" and wrote a short book, *Beyond the Pleasure Principle* (roughly sixty pages, almost the same length as *The Infidel Half Century*), on its metapsychological implications. The book proposed a biological death instinct to explain this unpleasurable behavior, which meant revising the dynamic of how the pleasure principle (sexual libido) worked with the reality principle in Freud's theory; the death instinct, in large part, replaced the working of the reality principle.[16]

As the luck of cultural and intellectual history will have it, Freud associated the reality principle with none other than Bernard Shaw, as evidenced in his footnote on what is translated as "the reality-ego" in his paper on "Two Principles of Mental Functioning": "The superiority of the reality-ego over the pleasure-ego has been aptly expressed by Bernard Shaw in these words: 'To be able to choose the line of greatest advantage instead of yielding in the direction of least resistance.' (*Man and Superman: A Comedy and a Philosophy*) [A remark made by Don Juan towards the end of the Mozartian interlude in Act III]" (Freud, *Metapsychology*, 41).

The necessity for a Shavian counterpart to the pleasure principle, the vital sense of self-control mentioned above, had already led Freud to hypothesize the *reality principle*, which "does not abandon the intention of ultimately obtaining pleasure, but it nevertheless demands and carries into effect the postponement of satisfaction ... on the long indirect road to pleasure" (Freud, *Metapsychology*, 278). However, Freud claimed that the reality principle could not explain all the occasions of unpleasure, especially instinctive ones, so he posited what he called a death instinct beyond that of libido.

Methuselah, published in 1921, was mostly written by 1919, and the preface, *The Infidel Half Century*, was composed in 1920. Freud wrote the first draft of his work in 1919 and revised it in 1920, the year it was published in German as *Jenseits des Lustprinzips*, before going on to be translated into English and published as *Beyond the Pleasure Principle* in 1922. Both authors were outsiders (an Irishman and a Moravian Jew) living in imperial capitals (London and Vienna, respectively), and both works were major reconsiderations of their earlier thinking in the immediate aftermath of the Great War. Definite themes are shared between the texts, especially the theme of death central to both works—the word *beyond* in Freud's title is the very last word in the text of *Methuselah*, a synonym in both cases for death. *Beyond the Pleasure Principle* is so called to announce Freud's famous "discovery" of the "death instinct." *Back to Methuselah* is so called to announce an evolutionary fantasy, in which mankind conquers that oldest of old bogeymen: death. Ironically, the progressive optimist's title is backward looking, while the regressive pessimist's is outward looking.

Shaw and Freud were both rather cagey about each other's work and not because they were unacquainted with it. By 1920 Shaw was well known in Freud's Vienna, where his plays had been frequently performed in the main theaters. His German translator, Siegfried Trebitsch, was Viennese, from a Jewish background like Freud, and a novelist and playwright in his own right in the circle of Schnitzler and Hofmannsthal.[17] Indeed the shadow of Freud seems to loom large over Trebitsch's play *Frau Gittas Sühne*, which Shaw began to translate as *Jitta's Atonement* when revising *Methuselah* in 1920.[18]

Freud's most famous English disciple, his biographer Ernest Jones, was a keen Fabian supporter who knew Shaw well enough to be asked to the Shaws' house for lunch. To Jones, Freud and Shaw were—with all due deference to the acknowledged founder of his chosen profession of psychoanalysis—the leading intellectual lights of the age, and, with some persistence, he urged Freud to an appreciation of Shaw.[19] Freud tried hard but failed to rally much enthusiasm for Shaw's work. It had been for Jones's sake, apparently, that Freud had referred to Shaw in "Two Principles of Mental Functioning."

Shaw was acquainted with that other great contemporary writer on sex, Havelock Ellis, and had read the first volumes of Ellis's *The Psychology of Sex* as early as 1898. Although Freud's *Interpretation of Dreams* (1900), which first posited the Oedipus complex, was not translated into English until 1913, Shaw had certainly come across Freud before this. This can be seen in an astonishing letter of March 14, 1911, to his friend, classics scholar, and translator of Euripides, Gilbert Murray, that displays a more than superficial acquaintance at a very early stage with the Oedipus complex:

> I very seldom dream of my mother; but when I do, she is my wife as well as my mother. When this first occurred to me (well on in life), what surprised me when I awoke was that the notion of incest had not entered into the dream: I had taken it as a matter of course that the maternal function included the wifely one; and so did she. What is more, the sexual relation acquired all the innocence of the filial one, and the filial one all the completeness of the sexual one . . .
>
> I am not very appreciative of the psychiatrists; but there may be something in their theory that repressed instincts, though subconscious, play a considerable part in our lives, and that the first child's jealousy of the second, and even of its father, is the jealousy of Othello in a primitive stage of passion, before the specialization of a part of it takes place for reproductive purposes. The completeness with which that specialization is suppressed does not eradicate the passion; and in my case the suppression apparently vanishes in sleep, though it is perfectly effective when I wake. Dr. Ernest Jones contends that Hamlet's inability to kill the king is produced by his subconsciousness that he was jealous of his father and would have done the same thing himself to get possession of his mother. (*Letters 3*, 13–19)

Jones's essay "The Oedipus Complex as an Explanation of Hamlet's Mystery" had been published in 1910.

The great Irish scoffer was not shocked by Freud's theories. As early as 1901, Shaw had declared his desire to "found a genuine psychology of fiction by writing down the history of my imagined life, duels, battles, love affairs with queens and all" (*Non-Dramatic*, 451). When he reprinted this article, long after his exposure to Freudian theory, very late in his life in the autobiographical *Sixteen Self Sketches*, he added the sentence: "The difficulty is that so much of it is too crudely erotic to be printable by an author of any delicacy." That Shaw was thinking of Freud, and even identifying with him in this added phrase, is shown by another quotation from the same text, in which Shaw marvels "that an author so utterly devoid of delicacy as Sigmund Freud could not only come into human existence, but become as famous and even instructive by his defect as a blind man might by writing essays on painting." Freud's writing amounts to displaced sexual exhibitionism in Shaw's reading, and so he remains apart from, rather than the type of, most men. Yet this is no more than what Shaw wrote about the artist in relation to sexual behavior in the Epistle Dedicatory to *Man and Superman*: "the artist never catches the point of view of the common man on the question of sex, because he is not in the same predicament. I first prove that anything I write on the relation of the sexes is sure to be misleading; and then I proceed to write a Don Juan play" (*Prefaces*, 161). So, in spite of Shaw's ambivalence toward Freud and his theories, Freud provided one of the best examples of the type of scientist that Shaw would champion: one who uses his imagination rather than, for example, torturing animals as a basis of scientific inquiry.

Both *The Infidel Half Century* and *Beyond the Pleasure Principle* share an interest in biology and Darwinian theory. "The attributes of life were at some time evoked in inanimate matter by the action of a force of whose nature we can form no conception" could easily be from Shaw's text, yet it comes from Freud's (Freud, *Metapsychology*, 311). Moreover, both writers derived their ideas on death, crucial to both works, from the preeminent neo-Darwinian, August Weismann. Freud writes: "The greatest interest attaches from our point of view to the treatment given to the subject of the duration of life and the death of organisms in the writings of Weismann" (Freud, *Metapsychology*, 318). Shaw, for his part, writes in the postscript to *Methuselah*: "Readers of my preface will remember that it was a remark by Weismann that set me on the track of Methuselah. He suggested that death is the result of Natural Selection, not 'natural' in the ordinary sense, lifetimes varying in duration from the immortality of the eternally splitting amoeba to the brief span of the drosophila fly" (*Methuselah* [1945], 294). In *The Infidel Half Century* Shaw had written: "Among other matters apparently changeable at will is the duration of individual life. Weismann ... pointed out that death is not an eternal condition of life, but an expedient introduced to provide for continual renewal without overcrowding" (*Prefaces*, 506). There are other common points. Freud's notions of pleasure, eros and libido, Shaw had already made his themes in his first great evolutionary parable and part dream play, *Man and Superman* (composition began May 1900, the year *The Interpretation of Dreams* was published in German). Shaw's life force contained Freud's libido in it—not surprising because both were heavily influenced by Schopenhauer's *World as Will and Representation* (1819). Freud, for his part, rather disingenuously dismisses the connection in *Beyond the Pleasure Principle*: "We have unwittingly steered our course into the harbour of Schopenhauer's philosophy" (Freud, *Metapsychology*, 322), while Shaw in *The Infidel Half Century* frankly acknowledges Schopenhauer's book as "the metaphysical complement to Lamarck's natural history" (*Prefaces*, 514).

Both writers had been reading Lamarck, Weismann, Schopenhauer, Plato, and Samuel Butler, Shaw's great anti-Darwinian evolution theory teacher.[20] And both refer to recent scientific studies in embryology. Butler's notion of the unconscious influenced Freud as well as Shaw's life force as the unconscious will on the macrocosmic level and evidenced on the microcosmic level in the aphorism from *The Revolutionist's Handbook*: "The unconscious self is the real genius."[21] Freud's notion of "the compulsion to repeat," which led him to theorize the death instinct, is echoed in Shaw's treatment of habits in evolution theory, which becomes a more classically philosophical consideration derived from the dialectic of master and slave in Hegel's *Phänomenologie des Geistes* (1807) in *Part V* of *Methuselah*. There, the body, starting out as slave of the mind, through habit (Freud's "compulsion to repeat") becomes its master.

Freud had realized from his patients in analysis, and particularly those with war experiences, that unpleasurable experiences from the war were replayed constantly in their minds. The "compulsion to repeat," he connected with behavior shown by both young children at play and his adult patients during psychoanalytic sessions. In trying to explain this phenomenon, Freud assumed that nothing in nature seeks to go beyond itself, that nature's ideal is stasis; thus, he defines an instinct as "an urge inherent in organic life to restore an earlier state of things" (Freud, *Metapsychology*, 308). He points out that this might strike readers as strange because they usually think of instincts as "a factor impelling towards change and development." Pursuing his usual metaphor of force, Newton's *vis inertiae* to which Shaw also seems to refer in *The Infidel Half Century*, he explains this urge as "the expression of inertia inherent in organic life" (Freud, *Metapsychology*, 309). Shaw, proponent of the life force and anti-Newtonian vitalist in the tradition of English poet William Blake, might have pointed out that Freud's use of the metaphysical term "life" undercuts his scientific language and therefore his definition.[22] Lacan in his turn was perfectly aware of this, and he devotes much of *Seminar II* to transferring the metaphorical basis of *Beyond the Pleasure Principle* from biology, Newtonian physics, and the steam engine onto yet another new technology, information theory.

Part of the conceptual structure of the drama *Back to Methuselah* is that man's confrontation with the concept of death launches him on an evolutionary trajectory out of the static biblical paradise of Eden (*the* state of inertia) presented as an allegory of early cell evolution, as described by Freud and also by the Brothers Barnabas in *Back to Methuselah: Part II*. Indeed, the five parts of the play present an analogy/allegory of the evolution of the species, as well as of the life span of an individual, in which death, for Shaw as for Freud, figures largely as a psychological mechanism and, following Weismann, a voluntary action. Though not quite the death instinct of Freud, Shaw's use of the implications of death for the metaphysics of consciousness or metabiology is an exact equivalent of Lacan's association of the realm of the Symbolic with death, where the concept of death arises at the moment when a child emerges into the realm of the Symbolic by acquiring language. This is shown at the beginning of *In The Beginning*, when Eve, confronting the dead fawn, speaks the first metaphysical word or concept, "dead," learned from the Serpent (Hegel's "negative reason"), although the Serpent taught herself to speak by listening to the nominal (that is, Imaginary for Lacan or metaphysical for Derrida in identifying signifier/name with signified) language of Adam and Eve. The Serpent advises Adam and Eve: "Choose a day for your death; and resolve to die on that day. Then death is no longer uncertain but certain." That makes Adam, who prefers the stasis characteristic of Freud's death instinct, very happy: "Yes, that is splendid: that will bind the future." Thus, corresponding to Freud's "organism wishing to die only in its own fashion," they invent death.

Later Eve asks the Serpent to explain another metaphysical concept, analogous to Heidegger's Dasein and unknown in her purely nominative speech, but a word that she has heard the Serpent use:

EVE. What is the life?

THE SERPENT. That which makes the difference between the dead fawn and the live one.

EVE. What a beautiful word! And what a beautiful thing! Life is the loveliest of all the new words. (*Plays*, 857)

Life as metaphysical existence, therefore, is defined for Shaw in terms of death, in terms of Saussurean difference. And if "signifier" is exchanged for "word" and "signified" for "thing" in the above dialogue, Shaw's meaning becomes clearer in terms of Saussurean linguistics. "Life" and "death" arise as signifiers in this new world of language, the Symbolic.

Drawing on Nietzsche, perhaps, *Methuselah* is structured as an eternal cycle of repetition(s), and Freud's "compulsion to repeat" in its psychological sense is best echoed in a curious little scene in *Part II* involving a bird in the silly young rector's garden. The brothers Barnabas have just revealed to the visiting clergyman their new gospel: women and men do not have to die at "three score year and ten," but they could live as long as the biblical Methuselah if they wanted. Conrad Barnabas, Shaw's evangelical "new vitalist" biologist, sarcastically suggests to the rector:

> CONRAD. Are you sure you might not become a good clergyman if you had a few centuries to do it in?
>
> HASLAM. Oh, there's nothing much the matter with me. It's quite easy to be a decent parson. It's the Church that chokes me off. I couldn't stick it for nine hundred years. I should chuck it. You know, sometimes, when the bishop, who is the most priceless of old fossils, lets off something more than usually out-of-date, the bird starts in my garden.
>
> FRANKLYN. The bird?
>
> HASLAM. Oh yes. There's a bird there that keeps on singing "Stick it or chuck it: stick it or chuck it"—just like that for an hour on end in the spring. I wish my father had found some other shop for me. (*Plays*, 870)

Shaw here is criticizing the church, personified by the bishop, and its language as being out of date and fossilized; the geological metaphors, prompted by the influence the geologist Lyell had on Darwinian theory, recur throughout the play. The rector then refers to the bird in his garden, Shaw's version of the bird of prophecy, in an allusion both to the Garden of Eden (the setting of *Part I* of *Methuselah*) and Act II of Wagner's opera, *Siegfried,* when Siegfried comes to understand the language of birds.[23] Linguistically, Shaw emphasizes the assonance of the bird's song ("Stick it or chuck it: stick it or chuck it," repeated endlessly) to intelligible English. The clergyman understands the bird's language, as Adam and Eve understood the animals and "the Voice" in Eden—and probably as much as we understand anyone's language. The equivalence is between not only bird song and human language but also the bird's predicament and the parson's. For, just as the bird in the garden is condemned to repeat compulsively his song, so the rector is stuck in his role in the church (that is, habitual or compulsively repeating behavior) from which he cannot for the moment escape. This, surely, recognizes "a compulsion to repeat," and with classic Shavian logical ingenuity, the expression of the bird's predicament contains its own release-cure. A "talking-cure," Lacan might note approvingly, where the refrain "stick it or chuck it" is the paradoxical call to action that lies at the heart of the play—and at the heart of the phenomenon of the "compulsion to repeat," where seeking to go beyond compulsively repeating behavior can be seen as the goal or end of Freudian and Lacanian psychoanalysis.

Freud's argument in *Beyond the Pleasure Principle* is desperately tentative as it comes to an abrupt pause: "It may be asked whether and how far I am myself convinced of the truth of the hypotheses that I have set out in these pages. My answer would be that I am not convinced myself and that I do not seek to persuade other people to believe in them. Or, more precisely, that I do not know how far I believe in them. There is no reason, as it seems to me, why the emotional factor of conviction should enter into this question at all" (Freud, *Metapsychology*, 332). That extraordinarily unconvincing statement obviously gave Lacan, who refused to follow Freud in his biological speculations, pause. The word *conviction* in the last sentence is the great "Freudian" giveaway. Why is he positing a thesis that cannot be proven if conviction is *not* part of his motivation? Perhaps any aspiration of conviction contradicts what he is positing. That notion is in stark contrast to the rhetorical procedure of Shaw, who sought in *The Infidel Half Century* to be persuasive rather than conclusive: "You can only tell him from the depths of your inner conviction." And indeed, Freud's own prescription at the beginning of chapter 3 in *Beyond The Pleasure Principle* insists that therapeutic success can only happen if "the patient's sense of conviction is won" (Freud, *Metapsychology*, 289).

When Freud writes: "the attributes of life were at some time evoked in inanimate matter by the action of a force of whose nature we can form no conception" (Freud, *Metapsychology*, 311), he sounds like what Shaw called an Old Vitalist, essentially a mechanist. Moreover, Freud maintained in *Beyond the Pleasure Principle* that he was always a dualist.[24] Shaw, in contrast, sometimes adopted a dualist position, as in *Part V* of *Methuselah*, but he felt free to adopt other positions depending on the context. Sometimes life is matter. Sometimes matter is in opposition to life. Sometimes matter does not exist, as in Shaw's general critique of Enlightenment rationalism and materialism in his critical essays of the 1890s. Where science understands force as physical within a dualism, Shaw's discourse of metaphysics proposes a metaphysical force. This adoption of various stances in different types of discourse in relation to dualism, differing textual positions with their own textual histories, is a consequence of the flexible signifier/

signified relation that leaves the Shaw text surprisingly open to the Lacanian and Derridean readings attempted in the rest of this chapter. Refusing any notion of logocentric truth, Shaw declared in the Epistle Dedicatory to *Man and Superman*: "I plank down my view ... for what it is worth. It is a view like any other view and no more, neither true nor false, but, I hope, a way of looking at the subject which throws into the familiar order of cause and effect a sufficient body of fact and experience to be interesting to you" (*Prefaces*, 161).

As Shaw saw the need for a metaphysical New Vitalism (beyond the body/soul, life/matter binaries) to replace the clockwork mechanics of the Deists and of the Old Vitalists, so Freud, the rationalist-materialist, sought in evolutionary biology an explanation for the psychological "compulsion to repeat." Both rooted their speculations on a seemingly discredited Lamarckian concept of biology. The reinterpretation of Freud's compulsion to repeat and the death instinct in terms of language by Lacan (transposing the problematic to a theory of the unconscious, language, and the Symbolic) and of writing by Derrida (finding writing as the root metaphor in Freud's search for a suitable model for the psychic apparatus—the machine in the ghost), may provide suitable analogies for Shaw's new metaphysics and a basis for a new reading of the Shaw text.

Seminar II: The Ego in Freud's Theory

The key work in Lacan's "back to Freud" movement is his *Seminar II*, in large part a commentary on Freud's *Beyond the Pleasure Principle*. In the post–World War II era, after irreconcilable differences arose between the psychoanalyst Jacques Lacan and the official keepers of Freud's legacy in France, the *Société Psychanalyse de Paris*, Lacan and others seceded from that group in 1953. Eventually, he was expelled from the International Psycho-analytic Association in 1963. Like any true heretic, he maintained that he, rather than the IPA, was remaining faithful to Freud, the founder of psychoanalysis. The official organization, according to Lacan's group, had continued after Freud's death to work on theories of the ego and depth psychology in uncovering hidden childhood neuroses while attempting to reintegrate the individual's ego into his immediate environment. Lacan contended that such a view of Freud's writings was erroneous because it was based on a fundamental mistake: the ego as such does not exist. The ego, an imaginary split unity, as misrecognition of self as subjective identity cannot be reintegrated into anything. That such a concept of fragmentary subjectivity has become so familiar makes it difficult to appreciate this radical gesture on the part of Lacan, for he, with Althusser, spelled out to us that the "I" is not a singular, unified, essential entity.[25]

Taking from Freud that there is a difference between the conscious ego and the subject of the unconscious, Lacan's revolutionary postulate is that the unconscious works like a language, its rules are those of language, the rules of symbolic representation, association, and repetition. Whereas a system of signifying elements that involves the Other creates the subject, the ego is caught in a mesh of Imaginary relations with shadowy others. Lacan stressed what had heretofore been considered merely an aspect of Freud's writing, its emphasis on language, of psychoanalysis as the "talking cure." Psychoanalysis functions within the realm of language, the Symbolic where the subject is to be found or, rather, from which the subject emerges and into which the subject will eventually disappear; the symbolic makes possible notions of birth and death. Language is where the subject's mistaken identity, or confusion, with the ego, with its Imaginary shadow, takes place. Lacan also posits two other realms: the Real, about which there is not much to say except that, in some sense, it is there, rather like Kant's *Ding an sich*; and the Imaginary, the realm of the ego and the libido where the story of our lives takes place as in a play of shadows, to borrow Plato's metaphor of the cave in the *Republic*.[26] Shaw in *On the Prospects of Christianity* says "the world is full of these Adams and Smiths and men in the street and average sensual men and economic men and womanly women and what not, all of them imaginary Atlases carrying imaginary worlds on their insubstantial shoulders" (*Prefaces*, 589), which is as good a description of the Imaginary as is available before Lacan. The job of psychoanalysis is to effect harmony between the Symbolic and the Imaginary by exposing the gaps and fissures in language, the Symbolic, caused by the Imaginary. It seeks to bring language more in line with the Real, in what Lacan calls a "true speech," and to write a new text within the Symbolic by "going behind the scenes" of the Imaginary to take account of what is happening in *both* the Symbolic and Imaginary. In terms of the Shaw text's demand for a new metaphysics, Lacan's reinterpretation of Freud's Unconscious as the Symbolic proposes just such a radically new language-based discourse of truth, as opposed to that of science based on the Imaginary mind-body distinction.

A fundamental thesis of *Seminar II* is that the "I" is a construct, that it only becomes possible with language, that the subject is in effect constituted by language—the symbolic machine in the ghost. Indeed language, the realm of the Symbolic, is only possible with both language and the subject occurring as a result of the Oedipus complex. As structures based on differences provide the basis of language, according to Saussure, Lacan's stroke of genius was to associate this with Freud's Oedipus complex. The recognition of the possibility of difference, and therefore the possibility of signification, arises with what Lacan calls the Phallus. The ego operates in the realm of the Imaginary, which is anterior (logically) to the Symbolic and associated for Lacan with the mirror stage, the (mis)recognition of the ego in its desire for the (m)other. He developed this dynamic of desire in *Seminar I* in terms of an optical schema, similar to the development of the theme of vision and the image in Shaw's *Back to Methuselah* (see chapter 8). As Forrester puts it: "Lacan goes so far as to say that the most important thing about the mirror stage is its sudden disappearance in the moment when the symbolic takes over the functions that up until then had been served by the recognition of desire in the other" (Forrester, *Seductions*, 122).

There is a Shavian analogy to Lacan's construction and misrecognition of the "I" in *Back to Methuselah: Part V*, to which the rest of the play-cycle has been leading. Shaw narrows his focus from the biological drama of the evolution of the species to the creation of the self, or rather the ego, a Fichtean "I am I": "the only thing that I can create is myself." What Shaw seems to be proposing here is an Husserlian phenomenological reduction that ends with a transcendental ego in which the transcendental subject's ideal object is itself. Just as Husserl held that perception is intentional (derived from Franz Brentano's psychological concept, which in its turn was derived from Aristotle), so Shaw, in the postscript to *Methuselah*, writes: "attention is the first symptom of thought."[27] Starting with conscious experience, Shaw reveals an Husserlian process of "intentionality" through various stages. The subject ascribes meaning to the external world—gives "life to the doll," to use Shaw's metaphor—which is then worked through several stages before reaching the end of the process (an end, "the creation of self," that is not an end but an ongoing process). Unlike Husserl, Shaw, who was not a transcendentalist, shared Lacan's view that the "I" exists only within language, as part of the metaphysics of consciousness or mode of subjectivity associated with the experience of life and death of the body. Shaw's Ancients, however, look forward to a release from the body in death to become, as they put it, "a vortex," a concept that alludes to both Descartes and a modernist art movement. Shaw's unattainable vortex probably best represents Husserl's transcendental ego, where what was once pure object has become pure subject. As Lilith describes it: "the vortex freed from matter, to the whirlpool in pure intelligence that, when the world began, was a whirlpool in pure force."

According to Lacan, relations between the individual or ego and the other can only be Imaginary. She can only create herself through outside agencies, which the Ancients call "dolls," a metaphor drawn from the experience of very young children with their dolls. What the child does with a doll is what Lacan's younger child does with his mirror image. He misrecognizes it by ascribing an imaginary unity or life to it. In the case of a doll, the child ascribes to it a life of its own, as the child might to her own shadow. In other words, the child creates for the doll what the doll lacks. Pursuing the metaphor, as the child grows, she wants to repeat the experience with the doll. In science, as a Cartesian dualist, the child actually tries to create life out of inanimate matter. The child continues to ascribe imaginary life (signifiance) to new texts and cultural Symbolic creations in art, which functions as a Lacanian mirror of the soul. The child also treats her own body as a doll and ultimately realizes that the only thing that can be created is self as ego. "It was to myself I turned as to the final reality," says Shaw's She-Ancient echoing the He-Ancient's earlier "truth that you can create nothing but yourself." In the end they discard their dolls, their metaphors (see *Part IV*), their language, and their bodies for "a direct sense of life." That, though, is not possible in the Imaginary or, rather, without the Imaginary. For without body, speech, and matter, life—as imaginary as the self or ego—does not exist.

That is the tragedy, according to Shaw. Having created life and having misrecognized subjective identity as an imaginary ego, beings cannot make themselves self-sustaining. They are always, inevitably, subject to death and disintegration. Life is always born under the sign of death, "in the beginning." This tragic inevitability is Shaw's recognition of Lacan's theory of misrecognition of identity. The only way out lies in the realm of the Symbolic, represented in *Part V* of *Methuselah* by the "children" growing up and giving up all the delights of their Imaginary relations for those of the Symbolic, mathematics in particular. The Imaginary is caught in the trap of the Symbolic by death, Shaw's and Freud's "beyond." Shaw would lead us back therefore, beyond both the metaphysical and the Symbolic, at the very end of the play-cycle, to before the beginning, to the time of Lilith, the first undivided mother.[28] After all, Freud *begins* analysis with a repetition and *ends*, after a series of repetitions, with the original trauma or event.[29]

In the first play of the cycle, the serpent sings her great hymn to imagination: "Imagination is the beginning of creation. You imagine what you desire; you will what you imagine; and at last you create what you will." Thus, at the outset, Shaw links the world of imagination with desire as the "desire of the other," which is the motor of Lacan's Imaginary, and can be traced in the Symbolic in terms of lack. One of Lacan's most important points is that the Imaginary and the Symbolic are not homologous. There is no simple translation between the one and the other. The Symbolic is expressed in structural relations, in the structures of language, the unconscious as a movement of signifiers, whereas the Imaginary is expressed in nominal or metaphysical one-to-one relations (whether in Platonic metaphysics or modern scientific discourse) between signifier and signified. The relations of the Imaginary are just that, as imaginary as the shadows in Plato's cave, as matter was for Berkeley, as causality was for Hume, and as what we usually think of as the world was for Schopenhauer and Shaw.

Lacan jettisoned Freud's biological speculations as the foundation for the death instinct, his Cartesian dualism, and focused instead on the death instinct as the clinical phenomenon of a "compulsion to repeat." Lacan does point out that death only arises in the realm of the Symbolic, or language, and that is precisely Shaw's point. For Lacan, the Symbolic is made possible by the recognition of difference, by the signifying possibilities of the Phallus, by the difference between presence and absence. For Shaw, this emergence into language is due also to a lack that would be a presence, one of life itself (or, rather, its absence), death, a difference inscribed in memory as a Derridean archê-writing, when Adam and Eve encounter the dead fawn at the beginning of the act. *In the Beginning* begins with, of all Lacanian things, a gaze, as Adam, in an existential moment of fear and trembling, stares "in consternation at the dead body." It anticipates Lacan's contention in "Function and Field of Speech and Language": "The first symbol in which we recognize humanity in its vestigial traces is the sepulture, and the intermediary of death can be recognized in every relation in which man comes to the life of his history" (Lacan, *Écrits*, 104). At the end of Act I of *In the Beginning*, as in the Bible itself, this initiation into language is associated with sexual knowledge, as Eve learns from the serpent, the feminized phallus, how she and Adam can conceive, the primary creative act.

"The Purloined Letter"

Lacan rewrote a section of Seminar II and published it separately as "Seminar on 'The Purloined Letter.'" He used Edgar Allan Poe's detective story to illustrate his understanding of the compulsion to repeat in the context of psychoanalytic practice. Here the story helps to explicate two distinct aspects of the Shaw text: its practice as both theater and writing.

For his part, Shaw, a great admirer of Poe, had written that Poe's incomparable artistry was such that even his detective stories could not help but be edifying. He also remarked that "in Poe's stories the sun never shines" (*Pen Portraits*, 225). Perhaps for this reason, hidden away among the shadows, far from the metaphor of light and the realm of the Imaginary, Lacan found edification in the third of Poe's Detective Dupin stories. Interestingly, given Lacan's later use of Aristotle's concept *automaton*, Shaw compared Detective Dupin favorably to Sherlock Holmes and called Dupin "that ingenious automaton" (*Drama 2*, 682). Need it be pointed out that a synonym for detective is shadow? "The Shadow's Shadow," an essay written by Liahna Klenman Babaner, suggests that Dupin the Detective and the Minister D. are brothers, doubles, each the shadow of the other. That would not surprise the author of *The Devil's Disciple* and *The Doctor's Dilemma*. In the latter, the shadow as death is personified on stage as Old Father Time in Act IV, and the doctor's shadow, the artist as double, dies. The symmetry (on one axis) of the letter "D" in both Poe's story and Shaw's titles indicates the reflexive shadowing process of "'D' for doubling" at work in these texts.[30] Poe's story becomes the exemplary text for Lacan, and many texts surrounding the use Lacan made of Poe's text in his "Seminar on 'The Purloined Letter,'" including Derrida's riposte "The Postman of Truth," have been assembled in Muller's and Richardson's *The Purloined Poe* and can be studied in detail there.

It should be clear by now how Lacan's distinction between the Imaginary and the Symbolic bears on the Shaw text that, in its own way, makes the same distinction. For both Freud in writing *Beyond the Pleasure Principle* and Lacan in delivering *Seminar II*, a major motivation was explicating their own practice of psychoanalysis, in which they attempted to account for their own behavior. In "The Function and Field of Speech and Language in Psychoanalysis," Lacan opens the possibility for the new metaphysics that Shaw called for: "it is impossible not to make a general theory of the symbol the axis of a new classification of the sciences where the sciences of man will once more take up their central position as sciences of subjectivity" (Lacan, *Écrits*, 73). In the symbolic situation of the psychoanalytic session, Freud discovered the phenomenon of the compulsion to repeat, and in Poe's story of "The Purloined Letter," Lacan found a symbolic representation of that symbolic repetition.

Just as Shaw often draws on the polyvalence of the word *letter* in his plays (see chapter 5 in relation to *The Man of Destiny* and *Village Wooing*), so Lacan gives three different meanings in the "Seminar on 'The Purloined Letter'": "typographical letter, epistle, or what makes one a man of letters" (Muller and Richardson, *Purloined*, 39). Lacan uses this polyvalence in his exemplary reading of Poe's text. There the letter (epistle) is to stand as a symbol for the symbolic letters of the alphabet that constitute written language. For Lacan as for Shaw, the subject functions as a letter in a symbolic alphabet, a signifier rather than a message, as in a letter sent through the postal system. For Lacan the subject is, in fact, constituted by language. Language is a symbolic system of repetitions, and what Lacan finds in Poe's story is the repetition of a symbolic situation where meaning is attached to the letter whose contents (the message, the signified) are never revealed. Meaning is constituted by whichever position the subject occupies in relation to the letter among other subjects (Lacan's intersubjectivity). Shaw's *The Man of Destiny* makes similar play with a sheaf of *letters* whose contents are never revealed but whose meaning depends on where any particular character is placed in relation to whoever is in possession. As in the Poe story, the letters change hands from time to time and implicate personages too high up in the social scale to mention.

In the first scene of Poe's story, the Minister D steals a compromising letter addressed to the queen from right in front of her. She watches, unable to protest, because her protest would alert the King, who notices nothing. In the second scene, Detective Dupin purloins the letter from under the minister's nose when visiting the minister's apartment (because the queen is not present, this time she is the one who sees nothing). Lacan's description of these first two scenes in Poe's story, each involving three (different) characters, two men and one woman, shows that the structure, decided by whoever is in possession of the letter, of the second scene is similar to that of the first; furthermore, this sequence might also apply to a third scene and so on in a continuum. Lacan applies this tripartite intersubjective structure to the psychoanalytic session, and it might also suggest a model for the practice of Shavian theater. The triangular structure of the symbolic situation Lacan presents is based on three glances, or "gazes," to use the term that took on increasing importance for him: "Three moments, structuring three glances, borne by three subjects, incarnated each time by different characters" (Muller and Richardson, *Purloined*, 32).

The three glances/positions can be generalized as follows: (1) a glance (the Law) that does not see (the letter); (2) a (feminine) glance that sees (the letter being stolen) but is powerless—the reading subject lost in her Imaginary; (3) a glance (the detective/analyst) that sees both the glance that sees and the glance that does not see, thereby empowering the subject to purloin the letter—the reader-critic of the Symbolic. Lacan's point is that the position/possession of the letter determines which position the subject occupies in this triangular relationship; the subject is constituted by the itinerary of the signifier. These positions can be seen to correspond to Lacan's three realms: in the first, the Real has no relations; in the second, the ego is caught in an Imaginary relation with the shadow, the double, the dupe ("Dupin"), "Should they pass beneath (the letter's or the signifier's) shadow they become its reflection" (Muller and Richardson, *Purloined*, 44); in the third, the detective-analyst lurks in the shadows and contemplates in the dark or shuns the (metaphor of) light by wearing green glasses. He is thereby enabled to deduce a system of relations, an articulate(d) system, the Symbolic. This third position can be called symbolic because, like a language, it expresses an articulated relation involving other subjects.

One of Lacan's points is that the letter, as signifier like all signifiers signifying difference, remains indivisible, an integer, and thus can suffer any amount of deformation and even substitution as *the* letter. The minister, for example, turns the letter inside out and supplies it with a new address. Dupin replaces it altogether with a new one for the minister with a new message. Unlike the original contents, which are never revealed, this replacement message is a quotation from *Atrée et Thyeste*, a play by Crébillon (1674–1762) on a classical theme in which a man who commits adultery with another man's wife is forced to eat his own son from that illicit union. This unsavory analogy leads Lacan to make the point that the sender always gets back his own message (the conception of his son) in reverse form (his dead son); thus, "a letter always arrives at its destination," which is wherever it happens to be when someone, not necessarily the addressee, reads it. The reader reads, "sees" in a letter ("projection" was Freud's term), just what the reader's situation prescribes, but the prescription is reflected in reverse, as a mirror image.

Freud's great breakthrough was in seeing that there was something to be explained beyond the energetics of the machine, although a highly symbolic model, as Lacan insists. To be explained was the insistence of the "compulsion to repeat," repetition. A repetition always connotes absence, which at one extreme is death. To keep his science within the mode of Newtonian mechanics/physics, Freud posited a biological compulsion to death, the death instinct. But Lacan proposes "the compulsion to repeat" as a function of language, which is always a repetition, a presence of an absence, "the letter killeth." As with Shaw, language, the Symbolic, separates man from the animal world.

Lacan suggests that subjects function as letters within a larger textual discourse called culture or society. People arrive in that text by the accident of birth and given an(other's) name, "in the Name of the Father," and so—as subjective identity—integrated into the Law, into the text of our culture. In a way, analysis consists in reading that textual discourse into which man or woman has been so arbitrarily inserted at a certain place and named. The difficulty in making such a reading is that the ego is usually caught in Imaginary relations. In the psychoanalytic session, these are epitomized by that Imaginary relation with the shadow or double, the "other" of Lacanian terminology, who, the analysand believes for the moment, is the analyst. Freud called this phenomenon of repetition with the analyst "transference." The analyst/detective therefore sets out to discover the patient's "truth," as Lacan calls it: "The register of truth, located where the subject can grasp nothing but the subjectivity which constitutes the Other as absolute" (Muller and Richardson, *Purloined*, 35). By means of this intersubjectivity, a concept he took from Hegel mediated by way of Lévi-Strauss, the subject is constituted by this absolute Other, the Symbolic, the machine in the ghost.[31] "The task of the analysand, with the help of the analyst holding the place of the Other, is . . . to discover itself as subject, . . . to distinguish itself from its own ego caught up in imaginary intercourse with other egos" (Muller and Richardson, *Purloined*, 71–72).

The third scene, occupying only a page at the end of Poe's tale, becomes the focus of Lacan's attention in the "Seminar on 'The Purloined Letter.'" Dupin, without Minister D's knowledge, purloins the letter from the minister's apartment and, for a fee, returns the original letter to the Prefect of Police, who presumably will return it to the police. Minister D., the original purloiner of the first scene, who was so vigilant with the police in the second (that is, caught in the Imaginary) that he failed to notice being seen by Dupin, comes to occupy in the third scene the position of the one who does not see. But then that exemplary Detective M. Dupin is himself caught unawares in the Imaginary in two ways: by demanding payment for the return of the letter and by substituting another letter with the vengeful quotation from Crébillon's play in order to repay the minister (now his shadow) for an old hurt. The question remains: who is in the third position? The answer most commentators give is that Lacan as analyst-critic of Poe's story, as master of the Symbolic, occupies that position. But by following the structure of Poe's text, the reader comes into possession of and purloins the text of "The Purloined Letter." In this reading, the reader occupies the third position, which for a moment (enough time to deliver his allegory of psychoanalysis in the seminar) had been occupied by Lacan. As before, possession of the letter soon places the possessor in the second position, in a mesh of Imaginary relations. Lacan, the master analyst, is soon demanding money from his patient as Dupin did; he abandons the position of the Symbolic, of the absolute Other, in his relation with the patient. Insofar as Lacan is author of the seminar expounding how the structuring of the Symbolic constitutes the subject, he now stands in an Imaginary relation with his own theory and proceeds to attach a number of propaedeutic texts to his primary text (not that there was a primary text, it was extracted from *Seminar II*). Obsessed by this Imaginary situation, Lacan—the postman of truth—is powerless to stop the reader of his seminar Jacques Derrida—the grammatological detective—stealing along to expose him as being caught in an Imaginary relation with the truth and the spoken word, complicit, after all, with Western metaphysics, with phonocentrism in its suppression of writing and différance. Hardly was the ink dry on Derrida's text of "The Postman of Truth"—the Derrida who had ruefully pointed out that "speaking frightens me because, by never saying enough, I also say too much" (Derrida, *Writing and Difference*, 9)—then, powerless in his turn, there came a whole series of texts and writers with each (not excluding this one) finding the previous commentator/analyst locked in an Imaginary relation with his shadow, all reading their own messages backwards, if we subscribe to Lacan's analysis.

Poe, of course, built this structure into his story, almost demanding that the reader would be foolish enough to analyze the text. One writer, interestingly, who refused to do so was Bernard Shaw, famous for never being at a loss for words. Shaw, however, preferred to remain mute: "There is really nothing to be said about it: we others simply take off our hats and let Mr Poe go first" (*Pen Portraits*, 225). Shaw, uttering his own paradox, claimed that "Poe's supremacy . . . has cost him his reputation.

This is a phenomenon which occurs when an artist achieves such perfection as to place himself *hors concours*" (*Pen Portraits*, 224). Perhaps Shaw knew what he was writing about. Lacan, in a footnote to "The Seminar on 'The Purloined Letter,'" refers to, perhaps, Poe's only successor in this type of storytelling, the twentieth-century blind Argentinean poet and writer, Jorge Luis Borges; Lacan maintains that Borges's "works . . . harmonize so well with the *phylum* of our subject." Given this account of circularity and repetition, it is noteworthy that for Borges the preeminent modern writer was Bernard Shaw.[32]

In conclusion two points suggest a relation between two otherwise disparate texts in this mesh of intertextuality. First, Lacan's understanding of the analyst's role in the subject finding "true" speech in the Symbolic (Lacan's new metaphysics of language) might parallel Shaw's New Vitalist's search of "metaphysical truth" while negotiating between different levels of discourse, between the abstract metaphysics of science (the Imaginary) and a discourse (the Symbolic) that allows for the articulation of metaphysical subjects such as subjectivity, the soul, the mind, consciousness, life, reason, will, desire, imagination. Second, the reader may appropriate Lacan's use of the concept of intersubjectivity, as delineated in Poe's story, as a tool in appreciating Shaw's practice of theater. In the theater the letter as text is the play, and in most theater (West End, Broadway, or Hollywood) the spectator stands in an Imaginary relation watching the actors (Shakespeare's "shadows") act out a story. Adopting Lacan's triangular model of glances, the writer as author, standing in a position of authority (the Law) over the text, is the personification of the Real who does not see. The spectator does see, but sees only the spectator's shadow(s), the Imaginary, the self's message reversed, and remains powerless. And the third position is occupied, perhaps, by that indispensable adjunct to the text, the reader-critic as analyst-detective, who has come to understand what the spectator sees. As discussed in chapter 2, the critic can either read the Symbolic as a Shavian Realist or remain, as spectator, caught in the Imaginary of the theater. I will pass over where this text as literary criticism, which you, the reader, are reading, enters into this symbolic repetitious insistent circularity and attempt to adjust the model in respect of Shavian theater. Shaw's theater demands—as Poe's tale does, and as Brecht's theater later demands—a spectator as reader-critic who, in the act of watching the play, purloins it in full view of the writer and actors. They, while locked in Imaginary relations with the box office and with putting on the play, cannot prevent the theft. The blind position, the

Law, is occupied in this case by mainstream theater, the culture or society who does not see the text, and would not know whether it was purloined. In this situation, the Shavian spectator as subject has, for the moment, come into human time with a chance of occupying the position of the analyst/detective, where the play as text becomes the Symbolic, the Other.

Shaw's theater represents that insistent repetition of the symbolic Symbolic scene where night after night the audience steals the text, the purloined letter, from under the author's nose, as it were. In her turn, and Lacan is adamant that the second (passive) position dons "the attributes of femininity and shadow, so propitious to the act of concealing" (Muller and Richardson, *Purloined*, 44), the spectator as subject succumbs to immobile imaginings unable to prevent the text/letter's theft by—and at this point we break off to adopt the Shavian pose: we take our hats off and let M. Jacques Lacan go first.

"The Postman of Truth"

Derrida's difficulty with Lacan was that Lacan was proposing a regime of truth: that Lacan posed, as the title of Derrida's essay puts it, as a "postman of truth."[33] But readings of both Derrida and Lacan deserve caution. Barbara Johnson has suggested that Derrida's attack on Lacan might have been a pseudodeconstruction, although the personal accounts of Derrida's occasional rage against, and irritation with, the mischievous analyst have a humorous, anecdotal type of truth to them.[34] His method of purloining the letter may have been to feign being caught up in an Imaginary relation himself with Lacan, rather than the other way around. Perhaps, even for Lacan himself, the reading presented in the "Seminar on 'The Purloined Letter'" is a deliberately misleading pseudoreading.[35] So although the master analyst proclaims identification of the analyst with the master detective, Lacan is really identifying the analyst with the rather uninvolved general narrator of Poe's story without explicitly stating his intention. In other words, Lacan was wary of expressing himself in terms of the truth, although he might imply the reverse, while Derrida is deliberately misleading the reader into thinking he is not wise to Lacan's duplicitous strategy. Truth, it seems, is a tricky concept for anyone who strays from the logocentric fold, whether it be Poe, Shaw, Lacan, or Derrida.

Of most concern here in Derrida's critique of Lacan is the critique of its phonocentrism, difficult to avoid when both Lacan and Shaw practice disciplines involving so much speaking. Most difficult to stomach for Derrida were Lacan's statements about truth in relation to the practice of psychoanalysis. And the purpose of Lacan's "Seminar on 'The Purloined Letter'" was precisely to discover how the analysand could come into a relation of truth in terms of his place within the Symbolic, although Lacan places the truth purely in terms of a movement of a signifier among signifiers, which is no more than Derrida could reasonably desire. But therein lies the rub. Reason pertains to logocentric metaphysics, and Derrida is not reasonable. Derrida, the reader-critic, is assuredly adopting a more subtle deconstructive strategy in adopting such a blatantly antagonistic strategy against a writer saying much the same thing except for the utterance (the *enunciation*) of the word *Truth*—uttered, doubtless, with a whiff of irony, if not sulfur, by Lacan.

Shaw could be guilty of similar phonocentric utterances on truth. It certainly might become problematic for Lacan or Shaw if they posited their techniques as the true techniques of analysis or the only possible practice of drama. But Lacan's notorious use of indirect language was precisely to avoid such an identification of his highly idiosyncratic analytic practice with *the* practice, although, of course, he defined his practice in contrast to those other practices he declared false. The same is true of Shavian theater. Shaw rejoiced in many theater practices different from his own (Euripides, Shakespeare, Molière, Goldsmith, Ibsen, Wilde, Barker, Chekhov, Strindberg, Tolstoy, Pirandello, Eliot, O'Casey), yet, as his criticism makes more than clear, he founded his practice, his method, specifically in contrast to both contemporary (Pinero and Jones as well as the late nineteenth-century theater of romance) and past forms (Shakespeare, Sheridan), which become "idealistic" and therefore locked into the Imaginary. False for both Lacan and Shaw are those practices based on an identity between signifier and signified, which, insofar as they posit truth, are false. That is the basis of Shaw's iconoclastic, anti-idealist campaigns as a critic in the 1890s, as well as Lacan's attacks on ego-based misinterpretations of Freud.

Rather than *the* truth, both Shaw and Lacan end up with a cacophony of true voices, nowhere better illustrated than in the climaxes of two of Shaw's short plays, *O'Flaherty V. C.* (1915) and *The Six of Calais* (1934), themselves exemplary of the longer plays. In the first, all four characters *"are soon all speaking at once at the tops of their voices,"* where, despite the written text, the signifieds of the phonological text disappear in the noise. In the latter, the signifieds disappear even in the written text as the two adversaries Edward III and Piers de Rosty, the king and his captive, square off with each other at the climax of the play and engage in a shouting match as barking dogs: *"They repeat this performance . . . until it develops into a startling imitation of a dog fight."* In other words, what is left is a play of signifiers without signifieds.

Derrida's attack on Lacan as "the postman of truth" has something of the snarling dog about it. The attack would be strengthened if either Lacanian or Shavian discourse tended toward a truth, a single signified, or set of signifieds. Certainly the Shaw text is vulnerable to this criticism if concepts such as life force are understood simplistically or abstractly, rather than along the lines of, say, Heidegger's Dasein, which the complexity of *Back to Methuselah* would encourage. Shaw invariably put such terms under erasure, as in his "claim to know as much about the origins of life as the professionals, this being exactly nothing" (Richard Wilson, *Language*, 13).

"Freud and the Stage of Writing"

Both Lacan and Derrida concentrated, in their different if overlapping ways, on the same set of Freud's texts associated with *Beyond the Pleasure Principle*, where Freud raises the questions of death, repetition, and a model for the mind incorporating a principle beyond or supplementary to the libido or eros of the pleasure principle. As with Lacan in *Seminar II*, Derrida in "Freud and the Stage of Writing" traced this development from Freud's unpublished *Project*, through chapter 7 of *The Interpretation of Dreams, Beyond the Pleasure Principle*, to "The Mystic Writing Pad." Derrida found this last text to be Freud's radical breakthrough in his repeated efforts to elaborate a psychic model, "the metonymy perpetually at work on the same metaphor" (Derrida, *Writing and Difference*, 228). Significantly all Freud's models for the *psyche* are different types of writing machines, of inscription supplements. Derrida seizes on Freud's need for a metaphor of a writing apparatus to suggest what he calls a necessary supplement to the movement of metaphor in language, "a supplementary machine, added to the psychical organization in order to supplement its finitude," the machine in the ghost (that shady subject), writing, just as Lacan's Symbolic is the "supplementary machine" in relation to the subject. And Derrida's writing, like Lacan's Symbolic, as repetition, as representation (re-presentation), as machine, is death.

This notion of a metaphorical supplementary psychical apparatus would not be news to Shaw. In "The Illusions of Socialism, he writes of "a necessary illusion . . . the guise in which reality must be presented before it can rouse a man's interest, or hold his attention, or even be consciously apprehended by him at all" (*Non-Dramatic*, 408). He continues: "The human mind is like the human hand in being able to grasp things only when they are shaped in a certain way . . . if you ask him to exercise his brain on subjects of thought, you will find him under . . . [a] necessity to have a handle to his subject, so to speak, before he can apprehend it. And a logical theory, with its assumptions of cause and effect, time and space, and so on, is just such a mental handle and nothing else" (*Non-Dramatic*, 411). In "How to Become a Man of Genius" Shaw even uses Derrida's word, *apparatus*: "the ordinary man very seldom thinks, and finds it so difficult when he tries that he cannot get on without apparatus. Just as he cannot calculate without symbols and measure without a footrule, so, when he comes to reason deductively, he cannot get on without hypotheses, postulates, definitions, and axioms that do not hold good of anything really existent" (*Non-Dramatic*, 345).

Freud's thinking on dreams and the unconscious formed the basis for Derrida's view of writing as a deconstruction of the metaphysics of presence: "The Freudian break [conceives] of the dream as a displacement similar to an original form of writing which puts words on stage . . . a model of writing irreducible to speech. . . . The unconscious text is already a weave of pure traces . . . consisting of archives which are *always already* transcriptions . . . the present . . . is not primal but, rather, reconstituted . . . there is no purity of the living present—such is the theme, formidable for metaphysics" (Derrida, *Writing and Difference*, 209–12).

A reading of "Freud and the Stage of Writing" is essential to understand how Derrida's idea of writing as différance is derived from Freud's attempts to describe the psychical apparatus, which invariably involved a system of traces, a metaphor for writing. One crucial aspect is that of breaching or pathbreaking force. For perception to be possible, a sensation must leave behind a trace on the perceptual apparatus, which for Freud is physiological, a trace as a presence of an absence that is an absence of a presence. As Freud describes it, physiological perception requires at least two *strata*, one offering resistance to the experience, but not so permeable that it will not leave any traces, and the other capable of retaining the traces so inscribed.[36] Thus from the very first, as with Bergson, perception is memory as a representation (that is, a re-presentation) or repetition of the experience that left its trace. This provides Derrida with a foundation for his attack on presence in logocentric philosophy, particularly in that of Husserl. For Derrida, there is no pure present; just as there is no pure life without death (the trace of life), presence is always re-presented. There can be no origin, but there is the experience of time. The present is always the difference between now and then, between two non-presents, between two differences. Because it is impossible to speak of a pure present, it is likewise impossible to speak of a pure origin "in the beginning" or of an end; there is only difference and delaying or deferring. Neither is pure force possible, as Derrida explains: "The distinction between force and meaning... belongs to the metaphysics of consciousness and presence... Force produces meaning... through the power of 'repetition' alone, which inhabits it originarily as its death. This power, that is, this lack of power... institutes translatability, makes possible what we call 'language'" (Derrida, *Writing and Difference*, 213).

Force can be *read* only from traces of differences that mark both a heterogeneous space and a heterogeneous temporality, from which logical, linear, homogeneous, logocentric Kantian time and space or a Shavian life force emerges or, rather, can be inferred and is constructed. This force of difference and deferral can be read, however, precisely because of the breaching, the pathbreaking, of différance as tracing or writing. Freud finally found his best metaphor of writing as a model of the mind in a child's toy, known as the Mystic Writing Pad (or block), a slab of wax first covered by a layer of greased paper and then by a layer of cellophane. A stylus is used to write on the layer of cellophane, and the written trace becomes visible as the greased paper sticks to the wax slab along the path the stylus has traced. Thus for Freud, the cellophane is analogous to our organs of perception, forming both a barrier and a receptacle of the experience, yet not itself retaining the tracing, whereas the greased paper is analogous to the physiology of the nervous system in retaining traces of the perceptual experience. One chief feature of this toy writing tool is that tracings can be erased, which is necessary if new tracings are to be read, by a simple mechanism that lifts the layer of greased paper from the wax slab. New writings must be preceded by the erasure of the old tracings, just as past experiences are replaced by present experiences, or as death makes way for new life. Again Derrida contends that "the 'subject' of writing does not exist if we mean by that some sovereign solitude of the author. The subject of writing is a *system* of relations between strata: the Mystic Pad, the psyche, society, the world. Within that scene, on that stage, the punctual simplicity of the classical subject is not to be found" (Derrida, *Writing and Difference*, 226–27).

Here is Derrida's version of Barthes's "death of the author," a shadowy ghost or a ghostly shadow of a "system of relations." For Derrida, as for Lacan," that the machine does not run by itself means something else: a mechanism without its own energy. The machine is dead. It is death. Not because we risk death in playing with machines, but because the origin of machines is the relation to death" (Derrida, *Writing and Difference*, 227).

> The Mystic Pad ... still participates in Cartesian space and mechanics.... The machine—and, consequently, representation—is death ... *within* the psyche.... Metaphor ... is possible here only through ... a *supplementary* machine, *added to* the psychical organization.... Writing, here, is *technê* as the relation between life and death, between present and representation, between the two apparatuses (psychical and nonpsychical) ... writing is the stage of history and the play of the world. (Derrida, *Writing and Difference*, 227–28)

Of special interest in relation to Shaw as a dramatic writer is Derrida's metaphor for writing as a type of staging. A major part of Freud's model of the mind as he had developed it from about 1900 was the unconscious, for which the slab provided a peculiarly apt metaphor as traces remain in the wax block after being erased from the greased paper. The wax becomes a palimpsest retaining heterogeneous traces of many inscriptions. This led to Derrida's idea of a heterogeneous spacing, what he calls the "scene (i.e. stage) of writing": a space with vertical depth for the inscriptions that are spatially separated on a horizontal level—but not only spatially. Derrida points out that Freud links "a discontinuist conception of time, as the periodicity and spacing of writing" (Derrida, *Writing and Difference*, 225). Derrida's time does not conform to the logocentric time of Western metaphysics or to the homogeneous Enlightenment clockwork universe of "Cartesian space and mechanics" and Newtonian physics.[37] Rather Derrida describes "the fundamental property of writing ... [as] *spacing*: diastem and time becoming space" (Derrida, *Writing and Difference*, 217–18). Again, as for Bergson, there is no abstract time outside the writing's own time. Thus, where Shaw could write that "writable language made Time historical and Thought philosophical" (Richard Wilson, *Language*, 15), Derrida wrote that "time is the economy of a system of writing." The metaphor of the mystic writing pad suggests that writing is "the interruption and restoration of contact between the various depths of psychical levels: the remarkably heterogeneous temporal fabric of psychical work itself. We find neither the continuity of a line nor the homogeneity of a volume; only the differentiated duration and depth of a stage, and its spacing" (Derrida, *Writing and Difference*, 229).

Writing for Derrida, then, is the machine in the ghost, the Imaginary subject, and his following comment, presented with seemingly light irony, comes as a new variation on the openings of Genesis and Saint John's gospel that makes the link to Freud's *Beyond the Pleasure Principle* (and, unwittingly, to Shaw's *In the Beginning*): "Life must be thought of as a trace. . . . This is the only condition on which we can say that life *is* death, that repetition and the beyond of the pleasure principle are native and congenital to that which they transgress. . . . It is thus delay which is in the beginning" (Derrida, *Writing and Difference*, 203).

Derrida's essay provides a (con)text for reading Shaw's great dramatic essay on "origins," *In the Beginning*. As with Derrida, there is neither punctual simplicity, nor a "big bang." Shaw explains: "Instead of dwelling morbidly on the quite unedifying and not too interesting inference that in the beginning the earth was a wisp of blazing gas torn off from the sun, the votary of Creative Evolution goes back to the old and very pregnant lesson that in the beginning was the Thought; and the Thought was with God; and the Thought *was* God, the Thought being what the Greeks meant by "the word" (*Methuselah* [1945], 296). He goes back to a text, writing, *the* book, to Logos, not as an eternal idea but as language and writing. He presages a new metaphysics of language or writing, of différance, rather than the old metaphysics of presence. Derrida acknowledges we cannot escape the language of metaphysics (tying a signifier to a signified), as even différance "remains a metaphysical name; and all the names that it receives from our language are still, so far as they are names, metaphysical . . . What is unnamable is the play that brings about the nominal effect . . ." (Derrida, *Speech and Phenomena*, 158–59). (This "play" of naming constitutes a large part of Shaw's dramaturgy. This idea connects in chapter 7 with *Getting Married*, but the action of *Major Barbara*, for instance, culminates in the renaming of Adolphus Cusins as Andrew Undershaft as yet another name-mask of "Dionysos.")

In the Beginning

In the Beginning: B.C. 4004 (In the Garden of Eden), the first "book" of Shaw's metabiological pentateuch, re-presents metabiology as a metaphysics defined in terms of death, representation, and writing, as a science of life with several beginnings (in Derrida's phrase "always already" beginning). These are the Bible, Genesis, Adam and Eve, the Babylonian Lilith, splitting and pain, differences, a poem, a look, death, language, negation, imagination, sex, and even the play's preface, *The Infidel Half Century*. Especially is there a coming into heterogeneous time. *In the Beginning* is marked by both a simplicity and a complexity. Take the gaze with which the play *begins*: Adam staring at a dead fawn—an existential moment that is of its very "essence" of the present, of life, but which only exists in terms of absence and non-presence, of death, of memory and difference, of the dead body as a trace, of re-presentation as a primordial writing. Or take Lilith, who is the principle of imagination in the play, the very force of imagination, that force of meaning in writing, of différance, that Derrida speaks of. She is the creative principle who conceives life as a writing, as a poem. She is, thus, both Shaw's play and the story of life as writing—of Adam and Eve and their descendants. She is the "pathbreaking" differentiating force that creates meaning, that leaves behind disseminating traces. Lilith (in the biological allegory, the original cell) forged the path of difference by splitting herself, with great pain (as Freud and Derrida would insist), into two. Two differents, yet similar, Adam and Eve are themselves writing, as traces of that breaching, of that force that Derrida (invoking "the hidden epigraph which has silently governed our reading") refers to Freud, who, alluding to sexuality, "tells us *worin die Bahnung sonst besteht . . .* in what pathbreaking consists" (Derrida, *Writing and Difference*, 229). These heterogeneous times ("Johnswort" in Genesis!) are played out for us in the simplicity of Shaw's stage trio: Adam and Eve (as disseminating and fecund différance) and the Serpent (as negation and abstraction in language, naming as metaphysics). Lilith is present only in her absence, as memory, as traces. Lilith, the beginning ("it is thus delay which is in the beginning"), will be deferred to return as dream to Shaw's stage—a Derridean space of dream writing ("a model of writing irreducible to speech")—in the epilogue to the last play of the cycle: Lilith, a mythical last as she was a legendary first, as supplement, as a beyond, as a fiction of force and meaning, as dramatic poem, as writing, as death.

Simply to question the privilege given to the spoken word within Western metaphysics, to point out what Derrida calls "symptoms" of the repression of writing, was deconstruction's great rhetorical beginning to its work. Writing, according to Derrida's view in *Of Grammatology* has always been understood in the tradition of Western metaphysics from Plato to Heidegger as a mere "supplement" in two contradictory senses: (1) as an unnecessary incidental addition to the spoken word; and (2) as necessary to make up for a deficiency in the spoken word. Yet Derrida always recognized a certain complicity between deconstruction and the metaphysics it deconstructs, which was "always already" present in the etymology of the word he used to describe his science of writing: grammatology (*gramme* + *logos*).[38]

Back to Methuselah not only positively boasts of its Platonism, derived especially from Plato's *Republic*, but Shaw's work also describes a Platonic ascent derived from the *Symposium* and *Phaedrus* to a world of pure thought, as indicated in the title of the final play, *As Far as Thought Can Reach*. If the Shaw text subscribed to a Platonic world of Ideas *tout court*, then its deconstruction as an epitome of logocentrism might be more than justified. Yet, apart from the polytextuality and intertextuality in the play, this title, like the *aporia* that is the title *Too True to be Good*, points to limits to Platonism—with its suggestion of a "beyond" beyond thought or *logos*. Furthermore, a strand of anti-Platonism can be found or traced in the text's emphasis on the very "supplement" that Derrida finds has been suppressed in Western metaphysics, "writing." What can be read in the Shaw text is that *both* the force of the meaning in the writing *and* the discourse of spoken language are favored. Shaw's poetic structuring of his dialectical drama emphasizes both speech and writing—Logos inextricably implicated with différance. The play begins, as it ends, with a vision of death, and the end of Act I of *In the Beginning* shows Eve discovering, with some puritanical disgust, that the first supplement is the physical mechanism of sexual regeneration. At the end of Act II, for Adam the digger and Eve the spinner, the supplement, the "something else," becomes *manna*:

ADAM. What is manna?

EVE. Food drawn down from heaven, made out of the air. . . . Man need not always live by bread alone. There is something else. We do not yet know what it is; but some day we shall find out; and then we will live on that alone. (*Plays*, 868–69)

Part II: The Gospel of the Brothers Barnabas opens with the following sentence in the stage directions: "*In the first years after the war an impressive-looking gentleman of 50 is seated writing in a well-furnished spacious study. . . . The walls are covered with bookshelves*" (*Plays*, 869). This apposition of Franklyn's *writing* with Eve's *manna* can be read as her "something else," as a movement of delay and difference, of différance, where the possibility of a supplement, of *mana*, of signification, has become a writing that allows for disseminating imagination and meaning. This idea of writing, as the possibility of "something else," provides a Derridean anti-Platonic thread running through *Methuselah*. Franklyn's writing, a metaphysics of science, is itself supplemented by his brother's writing, a science of metaphysics. Conrad's book, a biological treatise, a metabiological rewriting of *On the Origin of Species*, sets the rest of the play in motion when the parlormaid, one of the first of the longlivers in *Part III*, *reads* it. As she succinctly puts it: "Me and cook, had a look, at your book" (*Plays*, 872).

This thread of the supplement extends to the very end of the playcycle, to the dream Epilogue of *Part V*, when Lilith's last word "beyond," like Freud's "beyond" of the pleasure principle, takes the reader beyond "as far as thought can reach," beyond heliocentrism and metaphors of the image: "for what may be beyond, the eyesight of Lilith is too short. It is enough that there is a beyond" (*Plays*, 962). And that "beyond," that death as re-presentation, is an echo, a gram-ic disseminating shadow, of the end of the preface, where Shaw calls for other texts, writing by other hands, to supplement his own: "It is my hope that a hundred apter and more elegant parables by younger hands will soon leave mine as far behind as the religious pictures of the fifteenth century left behind the first attempts of the early Christians at iconography" (*Prefaces*, 546).

Shaw's *Infidel Half Century* began this textual journey as a series of detours that casts many shadows and leaves many traces (more closely examined in chapter 8). The Shaw play-texts become the focus of Part 2, as a symbolic discourse where Lilith's "silent language (for there were no words then)" is read (*Plays*, 858). The play-texts offer a supplementary apparatus of machines and ghosts (shades, shadows) played out on a stage of heterogeneous spacing with its own heterogeneous time (out of logical time) and capable of appreciation on a combination of several levels. There were many stages in Shaw's life: the model theater he played with as a child, the chess board he used to work out his characters' moves in productions of his own plays, the stages on which he directed productions of his own plays, the stage of his mind's eye, as the machine in this playwrighting ghost. He wrote to his German translator on two occasions describing, contrary to his usual organic metaphor for writing, this stage using the words *mechanical* and *staging*: "You see I have the whole thing in my head: you have only read it and made a version of it; and though you remember the poetic connexion and course of the feelings and the more touching ideas of the characters, you cannot remember the mechanical connexions nor the comic incongruities" (*Shaw-Trebitsch*, 26–27). Shaw elaborates: "barbarous as my drawings of scenery are, a great deal depends on them. Even an ordinary modern play . . . depends a good deal on the author writing his dialogue with a clear plan of stage action in his head . . . the staging is just as much a part of the play as the dialogue" (*Shaw-Trebitsch*, 59).

The theater in the Shaw text is the machine in the ghost, a Derridean writing apparatus as spacing and temporality with the stage as palimpsest. This writing as a staging of traces, of shadows (a)mended by imagination, presents a cacophony of texts and spoken words, of force and meaning, from which emerge those other fluctuating shadows: the writer Shaw and his reader.

PART II

Reading the Plays

The reading must always aim at a certain relationship, unperceived by the writer, between what he commands and what he does not command of the patterns of the language that he uses. This relationship is not a certain quantitative distribution of shadow and light, of weakness or of force, but a signifying structure that critical reading should produce.

Jacques Derrida, *Of Grammatology* (1967)

5 A Writing Machine

> *I am only a writing machine.*
> A in Bernard Shaw's *Village Wooing*

As a prelude to this second part of the book, it might be useful to retrace the steps in approaching Shaw as writing machine, as a shadowy ghost of the machine, a *phasma* or *umbra ex machina* in his world as theater. Chapter 1 serves as an introduction to both part 1 and the book as a whole: it opens the topic of what it means to (re)read the writing of Bernard Shaw by considering the relation of the author Shaw to the writing called here the Shaw text; it discusses aspects of poststructuralism associated with particular writers useful for this reading; and it designates the epistemological and ontological implications of poststructuralism in respect of subjectivity, language, writing, and meaning, analogous to Shaw's own understanding of the world, that can be used as a basis for reinterpreting his philosophy of Creative Evolution in terms of language, and of reading and writing.

Chapter 2 looks at Shaw's (writing as) critical writing in terms of bodily pleasures and pains, perversion and anatomical dissection, suggesting that its strand of critical deconstruction is woven inseparably into the threads of the fabric of all Shaw's writing.[1] His iconoclastic philosophy of critical realism makes Shaw one of the most suitable candidates for poststructuralist consideration among his contemporaries.

Chapter 3 considers how subjectivity was treated, especially in his autobiographical writing, and noted its openness and similarity to poststructuralism's view of a fractured, mutable, inconsistent, partial, multiple, authorial subjectivity.

Finally, chapter 4 embarks on a journey of intertextuality starting out from Shaw's critique of Darwinian science in *The Infidel Half Century* to see how themes shared in a chain of texts can lead in their consideration of the material world and metaphysics to an understanding of Lacan's Symbolic (as opposed to the Imaginary) and of writing as Derrida's différance (as opposed to logocentrism). Moreover, Lacan's analysis of Poe's paradigmatic story *The Purloined Letter* can be transposed to an understanding of how Shaw's theater works and that Derrida's "stage of writing" offers a potent metaphor for Shaw's dramatic writing.

Now part 2 considers the dramatic writing, the play-texts, and this reading begins in chapter 5 with three of Shaw's short plays. Shaw himself cautioned in a letter to *The Saturday Review* on June 30, 1910, that understanding must take place over time: "It is not in the nature of things possible for a person to take in a play fully until he is in complete possession of its themes; or to put it another way, nobody can understand the beginning of a play until he knows the end of it: a condition that cannot be fulfilled on first hearing" (*Drama 3*, 1224).

The following chapters retrace the themes of their respective shadow chapters in Part 1: criticism in chapter 6, subjectivity and authorial identity in chapter 7, and, finally in chapter 8, how a theory of dramatic poetry can emerge from the opposition of the Image and the Word in a new metaphysics of human aspiration.

Losing the Plot

As a dramatist Shaw was always against plot. The result was that his contemporaries at the end of the nineteenth century, friends and foes alike, who believed that drama consisted above all in the construction of plot, would never admit him to be a dramatic artist. Even these earliest of Shaw's critics: Archer, Walkley, and so on, happily conceded his nonplays to be greatly entertaining and, in their idiosyncratic way, successful, while criticizing the deficiency of artistically constructed plots.[2] Such criticism might puzzle practitioners of modern theater and their readers—except perhaps Hollywood screenwriting gurus who hark back to the well-made three-act play of the mid-nineteenth century as their model.

To the late nineteenth-century dramatic critics, plot, although derived from Aristotle's *Poetics*, meant plot as developed for the mid-nineteenth-century novel. In this sense plot had to be unitary to produce a coherent narrative. Many nineteenth-century novels were serialized, as were Shaw's own, so their trajectory was not always as smooth as the proponents of the good plot might have wished. Dickens, Shaw's great precursor as creator of extraordinary fictional characters, was never a model for that type of contrived narrative.[3] In late nineteenth-century theater the exemplars of plot production in the theater were the French adapters, Scribe and Sardou, whose artistry could restore a truly logocentric sense of coherence and unity to the somewhat rambling narratives of the novels they adapted. Shaw ridiculed this authorial combination as "Sardoodledom," and he launched a critical onslaught on formulaic plot production, from which, with the exception of their late twentieth-century descendants—those Hollywood screenwriters and their script-gurus—it has never recovered.[4]

Plot was to nineteenth-century narrative art what perspective and shadows were to fifteenth-century representational art, what Aristotelian logic was to thought, what Cartesian dualism and Kantian space-time was to science, or what Derrida maintains the spoken word and presence has been to language. Perspective in the fifteenth century resulted, as did opera and the development of diatonic music at the end of the sixteenth century, from a typical Italian Renaissance project in the application of the new knowledge derived from the study of the Ancients. The highly theorized mathematical technique of perspective based on monocular vision—human vision being, usually, binocular and difficult to represent on a flat surface—propagated a conventionalized ideology of realism where an identity (truth) was assumed between an abstract mode of representation and reality, the image as signifier and the real as signified. As discussed at the beginning of chapter 1, the use of shading and shadow was a necessary supplement to convey the realism of this new type of conventionalized visual representation. The nineteenth-century novel and other narrative literary forms like theater as well as early twentieth-century film scripts adopted this realist representational ideology uncritically. Indeed, the ideology of perceptual realism replaced religion as superstructure to such an extent that it became a truism to assert that the represented is the real, that the signified *is*. Science became the dominant discourse, where to be perceived or represented was to be. The keepers of the discourse, the scientists, those abstractly objective perceivers and measurers of Newton's Royal Society so wickedly satirized by Swift in Book Three of *Gulliver's Travels*, replaced Berkeley's all-*seeing* god. Although highly artificial and conventionalized, plot reinforced this representational illusion of realism in works whose only relation to reality, to Shaw's way of thinking, was the commercial exigency to fill theaters with paying customers. Walter Scott, whose fiction Shaw grew up on and which provided the basis for many nineteenth-century operas he saw in his childhood, might now be an acquired taste, but the modern equivalent is the Hollywood spectacular, which, significantly, has not forgotten Walter Scott. Hollywood's improbable fancies (fantasies) are remote from either any reality within the experience of the spectator or any other possible historical reality. Nevertheless, they *seem* real enough given their conventional mode of representation. This is, primarily, because as dramatic narrative they are stuffed full of old-fashioned plot and reinforced by those other Aristotelian *desiderata*, the classical unities (the unity of time, place, and action as well as the unity of character), which had been rigidly codified in seventeenth-century French tragedy.

In dispensing with plot, Shaw became the first dramatic modernist. At the beginning of the new century, Picasso and his friends in Paris were deconstructing representational art by resorting to newspaper cuttings as the primary representational elements of their collages and montages, what Lévi-Strauss in the tradition of Saussurean linguistics calls double articulation. Shaw claimed to be doing the same thing, as is clear from the title, in his short play *Press Cuttings: A Topical Sketch Compiled from the Editorial and Correspondence Columns of the Daily Papers during the Woman's War in 1909*. More sober-minded modernists like Eliot, Yeats, and Pound failed to recognize such modernist tactics in Shaw's work, and indeed it could never be said that Shaw was simply a modernist. Ironically, they suspected Shaw of being a rather frivolous exponent of the old realist school, whose socialist politics gave a deceptive modern air to his masquerading, while providing his texts with message, anathema to modernists like Eliot and Joyce who adopted the late Victorian "arts for art's sake" aesthetics of Walter Pater.[5] Message as truth is also anathema to the procedures of deconstruction. Yet the latter is concerned with nothing but messages; if Shaw's insistence on message is taken, as this book argues, as the dissemination of meaning rather than of truth, then it becomes quite possible to align Shaw with poststructuralism. Shaw ironically propagated his didacticism with not only varying degrees of rhetorical relish but also an insistence that an author's view of his text is only one possible reading and in no way author-itative. As for realism, Shaw considered himself a dramatic realist in contrast to the plot-ridden confectioners of "Sardoodledom." In the *Quintessence of Ibsenism* he described himself, if pressed, as a Platonic realist. In producing his plays, he cautioned a doctrine of realism on the actors in his plays. Yet he did not confuse these realisms with the ideology of realism that arose between the fifteenth and eighteenth centuries. He was never a Zolaesque naturalist, and to apply the label realist without qualification to Shaw's play-texts would be a serious misrepresentation, although at the time of composition their realism *did* give them values of novelty and originality.

Modernists certainly foregrounded as their subject the material aspects of their art that gave their works a strong element of reflexivity, while those who are called postmodern under the influence of poststructuralism consider their work as culturally produced and culled from disparate and heterogeneous sources, from different significatory modes and types of discourse, confined to neither a single culture nor a single society. They are concerned with language and the production of meaning in their writing or art, where the material components have mutable status as signifiers. They construct and deconstruct anyoldhow with manifold inquiries into meaning, différance, signification, language, and discourse where the artist is also cultural critic. The filmmaker Jean-Luc Godard and the playwright Bertolt Brecht are striking examples of this tendency of artist as bricoleur.[6] Before them, Shaw was perhaps the most notable bricoleur of European culture. Shaw, like Godard a critic and a political activist with a highly developed aesthetic sense, was primed by his cultural inquiries and political activities to go beyond modernism almost before any of the modernists were modernist. Reading the Shaw play-texts as being open to a certain poststructuralism can, therefore, be more useful than considering them as either modernist or premodernist.

This chapter now reviews from different stages of his career three of Shaw's short plays, which tend to be critically overlooked: *The Man of Destiny* (1895), *How He Lied to Her Husband* (1904), and *Village Wooing* (1933). These texts embrace a reflexive technique of signification in insisting on the problematic of identity and the subject in terms of language and writing. These readings clarify how even the shorter Shaw play-texts are not without the poststructuralist textual implications of the larger works.

The Man of Destiny

Shaw began writing his first short or one-act play, *The Man of Destiny*, on May 10, 1895. Remarkable in many respects, the play is deliberately conceived as both a textual parody and a riposte to Sardoodledom. On July 8, 1895 (right in the middle of writing his play), he saw Sardou's Napoleon play, *Madame Sans-Gêne*, at which he expostulated, "I have never seen a French play of which I understood less" (*Drama* 2, 389–90). With rarely used sarcasm, Shaw inserts into the text of *The Man of Destiny*, after some Sardoodly play involving a scented handkerchief (and incidentally illustrating the heterogeneous time of Shaw's text), the following intertextual reference: "[*The scented handkerchief reappears, eighty years later, in M.*

Victorien Sardou's drama entitled 'Dora']" (*Pleasant*, 172).⁷ Also notable is his caustic comment that refers to Sardou's other dramas *Diplomacy, Dora, Théodora,* and *La Tosca,* in reviewing a production of *Fedora*: "Of course I was not altogether new to it, since I had seen Diplomacy Dora, and Theodora, and La Toscadora, and other machine dolls from the same firm" (*Drama* 2, 353). In the same vein, and sounding very like a Lévi-Straussian structuralist, Shaw characterized the narrative technique in *Fedora* in terms of: "The postal arrangements, the telegraphic arrangements, the police arrangements, the names and addresses, the hours and the seasons, the tables of consanguinity, the railway and shipping time-tables, the arrivals and departures, the whole welter of Bradshaw and Baedeker, Court Guide and Post Office Directory" (*Drama* 2, 354).

The Man of Destiny turns on a packet of despatches containing *papers* and *letters,* the elements of writing. Indeed, as the play opens the stage directions comically describe the young Napoleon involved in his own idiosyncratic form (bricolage) of writing: "*Napoleon . . . is working hard, partly at his meal . . . and partly at a map which he is correcting from memory, occasionally marking the position of the forces by taking a grapeskin from his mouth and planting it on the map with his thumb like a wafer*" (*Plays*, 154). Like Poe's purloined letter, Napoleon's packet of despatches is stolen—by a Strange Lady—and its trajectory can be taken as an analogue for both the play itself and writing as language in general. The text, directly self-reflexive in its play with the packet of papers and letters, foregrounds itself. And this playing suggests, as with Lacan, that as subjects with identities and gender-determined sexuality the characters are constructed by their position in relation to the packet, to letters, to the itinerary of the signifier, to writing.

In the text of Shaw's play, the Strange Lady threateningly enumerates a list of Sardoodly situations, which Napoleon might expect to find revealed if he reads the purloined letter. Such a revelation might then force him to play out his own life in the Imaginary as if it were a Sardou play:

NAPOLEON. I am to read the letter then? [*He stretches out his hand as if to take up the packet again, with his eye on her*].

LADY. I do not see how you can very well avoid doing so now. [*He instantly withdraws his hand*]. Oh, don't be afraid. You will find many interesting things in it.

NAPOLEON. For instance?

LADY. For instance, a duel, . . . a domestic scene, a broken household, a public scandal, a checked career, all sorts of things.

NAPOLEON. Hm! [*He looks at her; takes up the packet and looks at it, pursing his lips and balancing it in his hand; looks at her again; passes the packet into his left hand and puts it behind his back, raising his right to scratch the back of his head as he turns and goes up to the edge of the vineyard, where he stands for a moment looking out into the vines, deep in thought. The Lady watches him in silence, somewhat slightingly. Suddenly he turns and comes back again, full of force and decision*]. I grant your request, madam. Your courage and resolution deserve to succeed. Take the letters for which you have fought so well. (*Plays*, 165)

Napoleon's stage-business with this letter displays this battle of wits as a visual analogue of doubtful experience in reacting to Shaw's play. Napoleon later leaves the room to read the letters, from which he returns *"pale and full of gnawing thoughts"* (*Plays*, 168).

Into this parody of nineteenth-century mechanically plotted drama Shaw built a subtext of an earlier genre, the Italian *commedia dell'arte*. On finishing the first draft of the play (a long gestation for a short play) he wrote to Janet Achurch (August 24, 1895): "It is not exactly a burlesque; it is more a harlequinade, in which Napoleon and a strange lady play harlequin and columbine, and a chuckle headed, asinine young sublieutenant . . . and an innkeeper . . . play clown and pantaloon" (*Letters 1*, 546). With the *commedia dell'arte* in mind and against the backdrop of Sardoodledom, Shaw wrote in the preface to *Plays Pleasant*, in which *The Man of Destiny* was first published: "I was more than willing to shew that the drama can humanize these things as easily as they, in undramatic hands, can dehumanize the drama" (*Prefaces*, 730). Shaw has in mind here the heterogeneity of human time as opposed to the logocentric homogeneity of clockwork time. He wants to introduce the complexities of subjectivity into his writing to be distinguished from the whole array of abstract, machine texts that constituted Sardou's writing. Shaw's writing or drama is not a clockwork machine producing Imaginary shadows, but a Symbolic one—sometimes labeled as the play of ideas, "a factory of thought" (*Prefaces*, 779).

One previous battle along these lines in the history of European theater had been fought between the *Comédie Française* and the Italian Players in early eighteenth-century Paris. The painter Watteau, much of whose painting is theatrically inspired, depicted both groups in performance, but, like Shaw, his sympathies were with the naturalness of the Italian players as opposed to the mechanical artificial rigidities of the French. Watteau, of course, is *the* painter of the commedia dell'arte, and Shaw's description of the dress of the Strange Lady (his "Columbine") notes Watteau's signature style: "*She is not, judging by her dress, an admirer of the latest fashions of the directory. . . . Her dress of flowered silk is long waisted, with a Watteau pleat behind*" (*Plays*, 158). The suggestion is that Shaw wanted her, when dressed as a woman, to look as if she had stepped from a Watteau painting from the beginning of the eighteenth century into a drama of revolutionary France at the century's end. That this reference to Watteau is not fortuitous we can infer because *Fanny's First Play* makes the same association between Watteau and the Italian comedy, when Count O'Dowda anticipates that his daughter's play will be "like a Louis Quatorze ballet painted by Watteau. The heroine will be an exquisite Columbine, her lover a dainty Harlequin, her father a picturesque Pantaloon, and the valet who hoodwinks the father and brings about the happiness of the lovers a grotesque but perfectly tasteful Punchinello or Mascarille or Sganarelle" (*Plays*, 653).

Charles Berst has examined how *The Man of Destiny* can be seen as a play about performance, and in this context that means its own performance.[8] For instance, early on, when the lieutenant reports on his earlier encounter with the Strange Lady disguised as a man, he explains that she exploited his good-nature by making him give a proof "to shew his confidence in me" (*Plays*, 157). When she repeats the same phrase later to Napoleon, it becomes a cue. In fact, it actually becomes Napoleon's cue to react in anger as he realizes that he has almost let himself be duped by the Lady into a *repetition* of the lieutenant's encounter. But by recognizing his cue, Napoleon can extricate himself from the Imaginary trap, the compulsion to repeat, she had been setting for him in this cat-and-mouse game of a play. A further authorial intervention in the stage directions refers us to another theatrical tradition as represented by the great French tragic actor of the Napoleonic age, Talma, and again, by mentioning Corneille, he refers further back in time to the Golden Age of seventeenth-century French theater. Napoleon is preparing himself to deliver (that is, give a performance of) his great final long speech (or *aria*) on the English for the benefit of the Strange Lady—and the audience: "*His style is at first modelled on Talma's in Corneille's 'Cinna'*" (*Plays*, 171).

In relation to the despatches, the Strange Lady refers to one particular "stolen letter: a letter written by a woman to a man—a man not her husband—a letter that means disgrace, infamy." That might remind us of the allegory that Lacan would make of Poe's *Purloined Letter* based on the pun to be made on the word letter, as indicated in chapter 4. This metaphor was so important to Lacan that Derrida was able to make fun of him as "the postman of truth." And, given Shaw's critique of Sardou in the terms of "postal arrangements" and the "Post Office Directory" mentioned above, it has similar significance for Shaw. In fact, two of the three scenes in *Village Wooing* are set in a post office. In *The Man of Destiny*, as in Poe's *Purloined Letter*, the letter has been intercepted in its intended circuit, its relay from specific sender to specified receiver, and put into more general circulation where an individual's relation to the letter (in respect of possession/dispossession, and whether to read it or not) determines (the power of) his/her position in the chain. And, as in Poe's story, the contents of the letter, while strongly hinted at, are never explicitly revealed. Lacan's repeating triadic situation is understandably more fluid in Shaw's text as the French state in 1798, the Law, following the executions of the king and queen followed by the fall of the Directoire was in a precarious state of revolutionary balance. Engaged in a European war, the future emperor, the embodiment of the future Law of France and much of Europe, is portrayed as a young ambitious soldier who has not yet arrived, although his destiny, which gives the play its title, is suggested in the dramatic narrative. The drama of this mastery of self consists of Napoleon and the lady oscillating between the second and third positions of the Lacanian triangle in their struggle, first for possession of the stolen letter and then whether he should read it. If he reads it, then he will be plunged into a further struggle of the Imaginary (the compulsion to repeat), into a struggle with his wife not only parallel to that depicted in the play with the Strange Lady but also ripe with consequences for both the state and his destiny. The mission of both the lady and the play is to rescue Napoleon from such a repetition, from that Imaginary trap, thereby allowing him to fulfill his destiny, his Symbolic position in history. In this way the play as an encounter exemplifies the use Lacan made of Aristotle's concepts of *tuche* and *automaton* in *Four Fundamental Concepts of Psychoanalysis*.[9] Yet unlike Lacan's application of his schema to analysis where analyst and analysand occupy in their encounter a fixed relation (albeit involving transference and countertransference), in Shaw's play those positions are continually shifting. Napoleon's destiny, his mastery of self, is continually in the balance.

Lacan was at pains to point out, in regard to his triadic scheme, that the second position, caught in the Imaginary and unable to prevent the letter being stolen, is characteristically feminine. For Lacan femininity was an Imaginary construction, as in his famous formula: "~~The~~ woman does not exist." One of Shaw's versions of this, as we have seen, was "a woman is only a man in petticoats," and this play makes much of the old theatrical convention of cross-dressing, in which the woman plays a man's role, a travesty role. A man is a woman in breeches, perhaps. The Strange Lady is both feminized and defeminized, but, significantly, so is the young soldier Napoleon demasculinized.

> LADY [*disappointed*] Oh, then you are only a womanish hero, after all.
>
> NAPOLEON [*greatly astonished*] Womanish!
>
> LADY [*listlessly*] Yes, like me. (*Plays*, 161)

And Napoleon changes the implications of this degendering by realizing that it can be empowering rather than enfeebling as the Strange Lady "listlessly" hints, although her listlessness is but a performance. Only by feminizing himself as woman can Napoleon escape the Imaginary relation with the Lady, in which she seeks to trap him.

> NAPOLEON Suppose I were to allow myself to be abashed by the respect due to your sex, your beauty, your heroism and all the rest of it! Suppose I, with nothing but such sentimental stuff to stand between these muscles of mine and those papers which you have about you, and which I want and mean to have: suppose I, with the prize within my grasp, were to falter, and sneak away with my hands empty; or, what would be worse, cover up my weakness by playing the magnanimous hero, and sparing you the violence I dared not use! would you not despise me from the depths of your woman's soul? Would any woman be such a fool? Well, Bonaparte can rise to the situation and act like a woman when it is necessary. Do you understand?
>
> *The lady, without speaking, stands upright, and takes a packet of papers from her bosom.* (*Plays*, 163)

The farcical lieutenant had originally mistaken the woman for a man and, after later making the same mistake when she is dressed as a woman (accusing her of being her supposed brother), explains the fluidity of gender: "I thought you were the same person, only of the opposite sex; and that naturally misled me." Part of the comedy of the lieutenant, the Philistine as clown, is that he is lost in both the Imaginary and the Symbolic: he lets himself be seduced by the woman pretending to be a man, which is only possible because the lieutenant, in contrast to Napoleon, is neither an adept in the Lacanian Symbolic nor a Shavian realist. He cannot play out the Symbolic game of destiny like Napoleon, and the comedy is exacerbated when, despite his foolishness, the lieutenant—the philistine as representative of the Real like Colonel Craven in *The Philanderer*—expresses the truth in his interpretation of history (as opposed to the accounts of the historians): he recounts that his bolting horse, which led the charge, won the Battle of Lodi, not the young General Bonaparte.

Napoleon, although an adept of the Symbolic, who knows how to play his role in the Shavian theater of the world, remains nevertheless susceptible to the Imaginary of femininity. He becomes comically alert and attentive the instant he hears the Lady's offstage musical voice, and when Giuseppe identifies the handkerchief as a woman's, Napoleon immediately takes the handkerchief and *"smells it."* Like Aeneas, who has to leave Dido in Carthage to found Rome and fulfill his and the world's destiny as the founder of a new empire Rome in Virgil's *Aeneid* (the story of Dido and Aeneas is another likely model for Shaw's play), Napoleon escapes from the Imaginary shadows of his sexual struggle with the lady at the end to emerge into the realm of the Lacanian Real.[10] In that escape lies his destiny, the Law of France, the Napoleonic Code, and the future of Europe. In the last part of the play, the lady demasculinizes her (re)adopted masculinity when, dressed as a man, she surrenders her saber to the lieutenant, somewhat to the disgust of Napoleon (forgetting how he feminized his own masculinity) after the duped lieutenant leaves

[*The lady*] *seats herself . . . enjoying the sensation of freedom from petticoats.*

LADY. Well, General: I've beaten you.

NAPOLEON [*walking about*] You have been guilty of indelicacy—of unwomanliness. Do you consider that costume a proper one to wear?

LADY. It seems to me much the same as yours. (*Plays*, 170)

The Man of Destiny is one of the more blatantly sensual of Shaw's plays, always allowing for the blind if ever-present eye of the stage censorship. When the lieutenant accuses the Strange Lady of being a man in disguise early in the play, she runs to Napoleon. To protect her, he holds his arm in front of her brushing against her breast as she clutches it. Napoleon thus can assure the lieutenant immediately that the lady is indeed a lady: "This is certainly a lady [*she suddenly drops his arm and blushes*]" (*Plays*, 158). This strand of sexual by-play leads directly through a series of similar bits of stage business right to the play's end. At one point the text identifies the despatches (the letters and papers, the text) with the lady's breast when Napoleon tells her that: "No: I have already told you where they are [*pointing to her breast*]." This action is repeated in reverse in a later scene, again filled with blatant sexual innuendo, when the lady pretends to be a witch for the benefit of the others. This time Napoleon has the despatches hidden inside his breast pocket:

> LADY. General: open your coat: you will find the despatches in the breast of it. [*She puts her hand quickly on his breast*]. Yes: there they are: I can feel them. Eh? [*She looks up into his face half coaxingly, half mockingly*]. Will you allow me, General? [*She takes a button as if to unbutton his coat, and pauses for permission*].
>
> NAPOLEON [*inscrutably*] If you dare.
>
> LADY. Thank you. [*She opens his coat and takes out the despatches*]. (*Plays*, 169)

Finally, given the romance of the setting, Napoleon's sense of destiny, which we have seen is so precarious in Shaw's Symbolic rendering, is associated with an image of explicit sexuality.

> [*(Napoleon) goes meditatively into the moonlit vineyard and looks up. She steals out after him. She ventures to rest her hand on his shoulder, overcome by the beauty of the night and emboldened by its obscurity*].
>
> LADY [*softly*] What are you looking at?
>
> NAPOLEON [*pointing up*] My star.
>
> LADY. You believe in that?
>
> NAPOLEON. I do. [*They look at it for a moment, she leaning a little on his shoulder*].
>
> LADY. Do you know that the English say that a man's star is not complete without a woman's garter?

NAPOLEON [*scandalized: abruptly shaking her off and coming back into the room*] Pah! The hypocrites! If the French said that, how they would hold up their hands in pious horror! (*Plays*, 172)

Despite his being morally scandalized, the play ends with Napoleon and the lady intending, presumably, to spend the night together. They sit at the table, against the background of a moonlit starry night, looking into each other's eyes in the light of the flames of the burning purloined letter, which has finally reached its destination. In Lacan's words from "The Seminar on 'The Purloined Letter'": "a transition is made . . . to the register of truth . . . situated at the very foundation of intersubjectivity . . . located . . . where the subject can grasp nothing but the very subjectivity which constitutes the Other as absolute" (Muller and Richardson, *Purloined Poe*, 35). This ending, one of the most beautiful in the Shaw canon, depicts sexuality with a directness rare in Shaw. Possibly because of the complications in his own personal life at that time, Shaw needed to express it. Yet it also suggests how sexuality can entrap viewers/readers in a play of shadows that is the Imaginary, and from which Napoleon and the lady, as in Lacan's paradigmatic analytic situation, escape for the moment at the end by deconstructing/degendering themselves. Such possibilities, of course, were not open to the prurient drama of Sardoodledom, the inspiration of this short play's parody.

How He Lied to Her Husband

In 1904, Shaw wrote a short play, *How He Lied to Her Husband*, as a curtain-raiser for a production of *The Man of Destiny*, in which he shares authorship with his fictional character, a young poet. The drama revolves around Mr. Bompas's discovery of the poet's manuscript of poems dedicated to his lady, Mrs. Aurora Bompas; the drama is resolved when the husband decides to have the poems published under the title Shaw gives his own play. There are thus two texts with the title *How He Lied to Her Husband*, which, in addition to describing the action, serve as the last line in the play.[11] Of the two texts the reader has access to only one: the play itself, and not the manuscript of poems, although the reverse is true for the theater audience, which sees the manuscript of poems, but *not* the text of the play it is spectating. The only example of the poet's poetry that Shaw gives us is when the poet repeatedly apostrophizes his lady with her name, Aurora, which ironically alludes (as the poet makes clear when he says "Aurora, you know: rosy fingered Aurora") to the first poet, Homer, as well as Shaw's own Candida. The bathetic irony is amplified when set against Aurora's married name: Mrs. Bompas.

How He Lied to Her Husband was a deliberate parody, a rewriting, of Shaw's earlier play *Candida* (1894), which also has a poet as a principal character who figures, in part, as the author.[12] Both plays share the thematic of writing and authorship, as well as that of marriage, with *Man and Superman*, written immediately before *How He Lied*, which also features a poet in the character of Octavius.

Candida was on Shaw's mind in 1904: that was the year the play eventually received its first public production in London by becoming the first great success of the Royal Court Theatre repertory experiment with Harley Granville Barker that secured Shaw's reputation as dramatist. In *Candida*, the central triangle consisted of a young poet falling in love with an older woman married to a Christian Socialist minister. The ambivalent portrait of the eponymous Candida shows her as both a goddess of the Imaginary and a bourgeois philistine housewife. Because some of the audience seemed to miss the point and saw only the goddess, Shaw wrote *How He Lied to Her Husband* as a satiric parody on his earlier play. Shaw refused to be locked into the Imaginary of his own art, and in *How He Lied* there is no mistaking the philistine nature of the married woman, Mrs. Bompas, with whom the young poet becomes infatuated.

In his short preface, Shaw gives a rare glimpse of what exactly he set out to accomplish. He explains how he took two stage genres, the romantic triangle and knockabout farce, and made an original play out of them precisely by not following the romantic assumptions and stage genre conventions of a play like *Othello* (he does not mention *Candida* in this context). Although, in its light way, this short farce parodies both *Othello* and *Candida*, Shaw does not proclaim any thematic connection to *The Man of Destiny*, which it was designed to supplement. However one similarity is significant: the use of writing to propel the action. Where the action of the earlier play turned on a sheaf of letters, *How He Lied to Her Husband* turns on a manuscript of poems, and like the despatches in the Napoleon play, the manuscript operates much as the letter operates in *The Purloined Letter*. Thus *writing* as the itinerary of a signifier again acts as a narrative device or catalyst. Whereas in *Candida*, Shaw figured himself in both the young poet and in the second male of the triangle, the husband, Morell, there is no such identification with the husband in *How He Lied*. Nevertheless, the epistemological relation between the poet's perceptions and mundane reality is central in the short play and parallels what Shaw highlights about his method in the preface (as he had in his preface to *Plays Pleasant* in relation to *The Man of Destiny*): to treat stage conventions in the light of "an observed touch of actual humanity," which resulted in an original play.

How He Lied To Her Husband presents the spectator/reader with a play, a manuscript, a poet, a source for his inspiration, a human situation, and stage conventions. Shaw underlines this list with the play insisting on its own theatricality. The characters are mirror images of the audience dressed-up to take their part in the theatrical rite in evening dress. The very first stage directions specify that the action begins at *"eight o'clock in the evening,"* the usual hour for a performance to begin in the theater. Later the poet and the lady reveal that they were, indeed, scheduled to go to the theater that evening. According to the holograph manuscript, their choice was to have been between *Candida* or *Parsifal*, a link explored in more detail in chapter 7. By not going, they act out their drama as characters in front of a theater audience who have gone to the theater. To hammer home this reflexivity, when the husband appears on the scene he exclaims: "Hallo! I thought you two were at the theatre." Of course, that is where they both are and are not. This reflexivity, in which the text becomes its own object, is clearly signaled when the poet picks up a mirror to look at himself right at the beginning of the play before the woman enters. This piece of mime functions in the stage directions as a one-sentence play in itself.

> *He is, be it repeated, a very beautiful youth, moving as in a dream, walking as on air. He puts his flowers down carefully on the table beside the fan; takes off his cape, and, as there is no room on the table for it, takes it to the piano; puts his hat on the cape; crosses to the hearth; looks at his watch; puts it up again; notices the things on the table* [previously described as *"a hand mirror, a fan, a pair of long white gloves, and a little white woolen cloud to wrap a woman's head in"*]; *lights up as if he saw heaven opening before him; goes to the table and takes the cloud in both hands, nestling his nose into its softness and kissing it; kisses the gloves one after another; kisses the fan; gasps a long shuddering sigh of ecstasy; sits down on the stool and presses his hand to his eyes to shut out reality and dream a little; takes his hands down and shakes his head with a little smile of rebuke for his folly; catches sight of a speck of dust on his shoes and hastily and carefully brushes it off with his handkerchief; rises and takes the hand mirror from the table to make sure of his tie with the gravest anxiety; and is looking at his watch again when*

She comes in, much flustered . . . [He] hastily puts down the mirror as she enters. (Plays, 452–53)

This mime of the Imaginary signals that the narcissistic motivation of his art, of the play, of the poems, of language, is desire. The desire is acted out as he glimpses her belongings, those signifiers that metonymically denote her, the "other" of Lacanian terminology (the misrecognition of self and the mother at the mirror stage), even before the audience has seen her. Indeed this mimed prologue mirrors the progress of the play to follow, as the poet's infatuation with his lady is first shown before he becomes concerned with himself, his image, in the mirror, a mirroring analogy for the playwright's writing of his text.

A material counterpart to the poet's manuscript as an objective correlative of desire for the woman in the play appears as her jewels in the form of a diamond necklace. They denote her sexuality, of course, but they also denote her belonging to her husband, of major significance in her social currency as woman, as Lévi-Strauss might put it. By displaying his/her diamonds in dressing up for that social ritual of going to the theater, she presents herself as a signifier denoting ownership by both her husband and his status. In a similar situation her counterpart in *Candida* had declared to both her husband and his poet rival that she was not for sale to the highest bidder. That play has been read in the light of Chaucer's parody of courtly love, "The Franklin's Tale."[13] Here, using farce rather than the domestic drama, the text again alludes to the tradition of courtly poetry, in which the poet is conflicted between his honor and the necessity to lie to preserve his lady's virtue, a literary tradition reflected in the title itself (remember the stress Lacan put on lying in relation to the Symbolic—without the lie we would be locked into the Imaginary). The serious intent behind the farce is to show that people's perceptions of the same thing (in this case the woman), as well as of social relations, can be as radically different as the two material signifiers of their desire for her: shiny lumps of stone and pieces of paper with ink tracings (paper shadows) on them. Significantly, as Philistine she shows as little respect for her husband's diamonds as she shows for the poet's poems.

Shaw in the preface uses the word *trifling* in relation to this play. He often used such a put-down, like a magician's sleight of hand, to deflect attention away from the *écrivance* in his texts. Such a seemingly throwaway line in the preface, "Trifling as it is, I print it as a sample of what can be done" (*Prefaces*, 282) refers, in fact, to the end of the play when the husband wants to publish the poems the poet has written to and about his wife. The husband understands how the poems may be read, as his diamonds as signifiers are read. Presumably, both the poet and the object of those poems, the wife, read the poems in differing ways. The play ends when the husband asks the poet what the volume should be called; the poet responds: "I should call it How He Lied to Her Husband" (*Plays*, 460). The manuscript is the shadow of the drama of its own text or the play is the shadow of the drama of the manuscript. Even in his trifles, Shaw was an artist to his pen-wielding fingertips.

By putting a question mark against the unitary text by providing two texts with the same title, and again raising that relation between a text and material reality, a relation woven both thematically and in technique into this little play, Shaw anticipates Barthes, who championed the text produced by the reader against the primacy of the author. This applies to all his plays in the relations between the play-texts and the actors in the rehearsals for the play, and between the enacted play and its audience. Later chapters expand on this exposition to trace or unravel complexities in Shaw's play-texts, which call for a complexity of critical response, an act of imaginative reading as a playful response to the artistic skill of the writing.

Village Wooing

Shaw's *Village Wooing*, written in 1935, has particular pertinence here because it exemplifies in concise and obvious form concerns of much later poststructuralist writing. Primarily these derive from a concern with language, with reading and writing that dominated much of twentieth-century philosophical and cultural writing from Shaw's contemporary Saussure through Whitehead, Russell, and Wittgenstein, to Jakobson, Lévi-Strauss, and the structuralists, and on to Derrida and the deconstructionists, poststructuralists, and postmodernists. *Village Wooing*, intricately concerned with language and modes of discourse, offers a shift from actual speech to language and from the story to its telling. As such, it becomes an exemplary text.

The formal concerns are made very clear in its full title *Village Wooing: A Comedietina for two Voices in three Conversations*; this title parallels those familiar structuralist distinctions of *histoire/discours* (story/discourse) and *parole/langue* (speech/language). The word *comedietina* seems to be a neologism with its source in two different Italian words with historical connotations to both drama and music: *commedia* and *sonatina*. *Commedia* suggests the commedia dell'arte with its Columbine and Harlequin. *Commedia* can mean any type of play, not necessarily comedy, so it is not beyond the bounds of possibility that he was nodding here in the direction of Dante's *Divina Commedia* with the three scenes as a little parody on Dante's Hell, Purgatory, and Heaven, similar to the evocation of Homer in *How He Lied*. *Sonatina* within the Western classical music tradition means a little sonata, which, at its simplest, can be any piece of instrumental music based on a combination of voices or lines. This combination is carried over into the other two terms in the subtitle, the voices and conversations, which are the components of the play. The two unnamed characters, the man and the woman, the alpha and omega, are designated in the text by the letters A and Z to suggest the alphabetic series: a, b, c, and so on, while the progression in the subtitle of "a," "two," "three," suggests the numerical series: 1, 2, 3, and so on.[14] The language of mathematics and numbers is thus immediately posed as an alternative or supplement to phonetic language provided by letters and speech. In late plays like *Saint Joan*, *The Simpleton of the Unexpected Isles* (1934), and *Geneva* (1938/1939) the metaphor of a trial, the balancing of opposing sides in a court of law to yield an anthropometric judgment, came to the fore. These Shavian courts ask how the worth of the subject can be judged in a society or in a society of nations where the law socially places or stitches the subject into the Symbolic weave. *Village Wooing* introduces number (as calculation and measurement) as the possibility of a Symbolic anthropometry. The conception of mathematics as a function of language or language as a function of mathematics is a moot point theoretically, and Shaw seems happy enough to acknowledge the coexistence of this other language with the one of which he was master; the combination allows subjects different means to symbolically relate to the world (as object). The initial letters of the title even combine the two systems, insofar as W is as written, double-V (2xV), or as spoken, double-U(2xU), and where the double-U (you) might indicate the coupling of subjective identities in marriage. The Village of the title is, of course, ironic, as the wooing begins on a round-the-world cruise ship before ending up in the village, modeled on Ayot Saint Lawrence, where Shaw lived in England.

Village Wooing follows the courtship in three scenes of the man A, who begins the play as a globe-trotting travel writer and ends as the owner of a village post office in rural England, and the woman Z, a post office shop assistant and telephone operator, who has won a round-the-world cruise in a newspaper contest. In the first scene, they meet for the first time on board ship while waiting for lunch. He is *writing*, and she is (bored with) *reading*. The play, thus, becomes an encounter between writer and reader (as well as between the written and spoken word, that is, writer and phone operator), which ends in their marriage. It will be a marriage of language and calculation, reinforced at the beginning of the second scene with her offstage voice (*phonê*) on the phone saying the words "three, nine," while the third scene starts with his writing (*grammê*) what he calls "a balance sheet." This last scene ends with her once again on the phone spelling words out loud. She is just about to utter their hitherto unmentioned names when the play-text abruptly ends.

In a key joke in the text, the man suggests to the woman that her father must have been "a man of letters" (*Plays*, 1170), to which she replies that indeed he was: he was a postman. Now to consider this joke simply as a pun is easy, but it can also be remembered that the two unnamed characters in the play are only known by the single letters A and Z (whereas names are usually composed of at least two letters). Shaw in this simple playlet elaborates a complex linguistic or Symbolic ontology that parallels and supplements an Imaginary materialist metaphysics, in which letters, not atoms, function as basic elements. Shaw, as we have seen, did not subscribe to logocentric metaphysics of either science or of personal identity, and this play makes clear that the latter is a product of the *play* of arbitrary signifiers. The text articulates a Lévi-Straussian argument that language, like any other system of cultural signification, is always in circulation within and between sociocultural groups as in the writer and reader going round the world, the letters passing through the post office, the despatches being stolen in *The Man of Destiny*, and the poems being discovered in *How He Lied to Her Husband*. This is so whether it be the plays of Shakespeare, or letters sent and circulated through the postal machine, or human beings interacting with each other in relations of desire and organizing themselves in societies with writing, language, currency, and calculation. Letters in circulation in both this joke and the play become the ruling metaphor for how all language is constituted; how we are and what we do are constituted in and by writing and language. Thus the man of letters (a writer) known in the text only as a letter becomes a man of letters (a postman) in a post office, a hub for the exchange and circulation of letters: identity in difference, difference in identity. By the end, the play has, at last, given us enough information so that the characters can be named, but leaves the audience in suspense and refuses the spectator the pleasure of the metaphysical act of naming, of spelling their names out.

Shaw's counterstrategy here is more blatant when compared with his other plays, especially the late ones, where he positively heaps different names on his major characters; this results in confusion and conflation of subjective identities and thus forestalls the logocentric metaphysics associated with naming, as Derrida describes it. Lacan emphasizes "The Name of the Father" as a mechanism for assuming identity, the point of insertion into the Symbolic order of language and the relation to the Law in the social world. Shaw, like Lacan, specifically relates naming, and therefore identity, to the father and the Law. The following dialogue in *Village Wooing* makes the general point about the arbitrary Saussurean nature of language and how language regenerates itself:

A. We are on the Red Sea.

Z. But it's blue.

A. What did you expect it to be?

Z. Well, I didn't know what color the sea might be in these parts. I always thought the Red Sea would be red.

A. Well, it isn't.

Z. And isn't the Black Sea black?

A. It is precisely the color of the sea at Margate.

Z. [*eagerly*] Oh, I am so glad you know Margate. There's no place like it in season, is there?

A. I don't know: I have never been there.

Z. [*disappointed*] Oh, you ought to go. You could write a book about it.

A. [*shudders, sighs, and pretends to write very hard*]!

A pause.

Z. I wonder why they call it the Red Sea.

A. Because their fathers did. (*Plays*, 1168)

Significantly the reason their names are about to be uttered at the end is because the two characters have, finally, agreed to marry. The forthcoming marriage of A and Z, of writer and reader, of grammê and phonê, will presumably generate more letters as in Derrida's perpetually signifying metonymy of différance or *dissemination*. Readers and spectators continue that literary circulation after the play. And as a marriage of employee and employer in a business that sells food to generate money, and where food is the basis of all economics according to Shaw's own seminal essay, "The Economic Basis of Socialism" in *Fabian Essays*, the play reminds its readers that money as currency is also a signifying system whose signifiers are always circulating among subjects.

Generically every comedy ends with a marriage, as does this "comedietina," and Shaw's comedy in general is self-reflexive. Shaw seems to be saying that marriage is the end (that is, the goal) of all language as well; compare this to the joke at the end of *Man and Superman* where the last line of the play, just after Jack and Anne have announced that they are going to marry, is "Go on talking." "Talking!" he expostulates, which brings both the rest of the characters and the audience in the theater down in what the stage direction calls "universal laughter" (*Plays*, 405). Marriage, with its implications of generation, is a metaphor for the process of language itself, though Derrida would caution that dissemination often falls on fallow ground.

John Bertolini has pointed out that this is "a play of reading and writing" (Bertolini, *Playwrighting Self*, 165), and he has shown how Shaw consistently found analogues in his plays for his own artistic activities. These reflexive concerns are modernist, whereas the concerns with language itself are poststructuralist. Both reading and writing are essential to what Barthes calls the text. Ironically—Shavian irony is always present because the text's language is always multiple or layered in meaning—the writer A, the author of a series of chatty travel books, hates idle conversation, but Z, the reader bored with her book, insists on engaging him in conversation. If she is stereotyped as a chatty female, then the other action of the text might go missing, particularly if the critical eye has been directed elsewhere. By the end of the play, the woman also assumes the role of the (procreative) woman in search of a mate, an important Shavian archetype, of which Ann Whitefield is the most prominent example. But Shaw deliberately undercuts such unambiguous and romantic symbolism not once, but twice. At the end of the first conversation, once the soup has come round, the woman loses all interest in the conversation. Perhaps she was simply filling in the time until the soup came round. But, in fact, she deliberately undertook to engage the notoriously uncommunicative—at least to the other passengers on board—writer of "the Marco Polo Series of Chatty Guidebooks" (*Plays*, 1169) in conversation as a result of a bet.

If such undercutting of both the text and its philosophy is ignored, then a disservice is done to the understanding of both reader and writer. Shaw's play-texts are deeply implicated with concerns of writing, language, subjectivity, and meaning; without reading their ambiguity, complexity, and subtlety the play-texts will indeed appear—in the snooty characterization of the usually astute T. S. Eliot—as no more than "the potent voodoo of Mr. Shaw's life force." From such simplification this book wishes to rescue the reader by offering alternative strategies of reading that can unravel the Shaw text's larger complexities.

Like Jason in his encounter with the Medusa, the reader must look at Shaw indirectly, by foregoing the Imaginary relation with the author. The following chapters offer critical readings of some longer play-texts, those reflected shadows in that Symbolic textual mirror-shield that is the Shaw text, the stage of Shaw's writing.

6   The Playwright and the Critics

I'm Fanny.

Bernard Shaw in a letter to Viola Tree, December 17, 1911

Written in the wake of his critical writing on Ibsen, the second and most autobiographical of Shaw's early plays, *The Philanderer*, makes criticism one of its themes and is the first to feature a critic; the other is *Fanny's First Play*, discussed later in this chapter.[1] *The Philanderer* offers an opportunity to examine the imbrication of his critical and dramatic writing (referred to in chapter 2) and to understand how the dramatic writing can complicate the thematic of criticism in his writing. The play portrays two types of critic, personified by Shaw and Clement Scott in the London of the early 1890s; the play also provides a vivid picture of London intellectual life at the time. *The Philanderer* combines a theatrical snapshot of Shaw's personal life as philanderer in its scandalous dramatization of his confrontation on February 4, 1893, with his two mistresses, five weeks before starting to write the play on March 14. *Fanny's First Play* recalls the Ibsen controversies of the early 1890s, as well as the aesthetic controversies that Shaw engaged in as a mature critic later in the decade; the shade of the great English art critic John Ruskin casts his shadow over the whole design.

The Philanderer

Shaw's full title of his second play, *The Philanderer: A Topical Comedy in Four Acts of the Early Eighteen-Nineties*, refers to the cultural impact of the first productions of Ibsen's plays in London, during which he had played a prominent role as writer of *The Quintessence of Ibsenism* and crusading journalist for the Ibsenist cause.[2] As early as 1886, he had taken part in a public reading of *A Doll's House* with Eleanor Marx, daughter of Karl, and her common law husband and the translator into English of *Das Kapital*, Edward Aveling. On his first trip to the continent, he attended a production of *A Doll's House* in Amsterdam on April 21, 1889. His friend William Archer (with his brother Charles Archer) had been working on Ibsen translations since the late 1870s, and the first complete production of *A Doll's House* using Archer's translation (a couple of earlier productions had used other, less than adequate translations) came on June 7, 1889. Shaw did some prepublicity journalism for this production and wrote a review for the *Manchester Guardian*, covering for Archer, who would not review his own work. The production featured Janet Achurch as Nora, to whom Shaw became romantically attached in the mid-1890s and who inspired Shaw's *Candida* of 1894, written as a variation on *A Doll's House*. On July 18, 1890, Shaw delivered his lecture on Ibsen to the Fabians, presumably with input from Archer to whom he read a large portion before he delivered it.[3] Another production of *A Doll's House* in January 1891 was followed a month later by a production of *Rosmersholm*, prompted by Shaw himself, with his mistress Florence Farr as both producer and actor.[4] *Rosmersholm* provoked contentious debates in the Playgoers Club with Shaw and Eleanor Marx as leading protagonists. Shaw, in particular, denounced Clement Scott who had, in fact, praised Miss Farr, if not the play, in his notice. The most controversial production during this Ibsen "boom" came in March 1891 with the production of *Ghosts* by J. T. Grein's newly formed Independent Theatre. As Shaw wrote to Janet Achurch's actor-husband, Charles Charrington: "Scott . . . went stark raving mad, and produced not only a column of criticism but a leading article . . . in which he compared an Ibsen play to 'a dirty act done publicly,' 'an open drain,' and so on, demanding that the Independent Theatre should be prosecuted, suppressed, fined and deuce knows what" (*Letters 1,*289).[5] Elizabeth Robbins, an American actress resident in London, who—in spite of his entreaties—never warmed personally to Shaw, produced *Hedda Gabler* in April 1891. Shaw was occupied for much of this Ibsen year with developing his 1890 Fabian lecture into a book, *The Quintessence of Ibsenism*, which was published in October. His own first play, *Widowers' Houses*, featuring Florence Farr as Blanche, was finally completed and produced at the Independent Theatre in December 1892. The reaction of the critics, in particular that of Clement Scott, was as hysterically negative as it had been toward *Ghosts*.

Such was the topical background to *The Philanderer*, which had caused it to seriously date by the time of its first public production fifteen years later in 1907. In the text of Shaw's play, the Schopenhauerean philosopher of the will, the Shavian Realist and philanderer, is called "the Ibsenist philosopher" (*Plays*, 35). He is not referred to as a critic, but, knowing anything of the myth of this particular author as philosopher-critic, the reader is invited to presume "the Ibsenist philosopher" could well have written a book called *The Quintessence of Ibsenism*, who might even have gone on to write a play called *The Philanderer*. However, the text displaces the question of writing toward the body and its pleasures, toward sensuality. Moreover, the text mentions among the writings of the philandering philosopher only his love letters. The Ibsenist critic-philosopher of the will, the Shavian Realist, pursues his pleasures and passions as a first pioneer in defiance of the dominant ideology, especially the ideals of Victorian marriage and the gender construction of Woman on which it is premised. Thus, as a dramatic character, the philosopher-critic becomes the very incarnation of the author of the third chapter of *The Quintessence*, a promiscuous philanderer, a Don Juan, an early incarnation of John Tanner in *Man and Superman*, where Shaw made even more explicit the relation between sensuality and textuality.

The Ibsenist philosopher critiques/dissects/deconstructs the theater, not of Ibsenist realism, but of that Imaginary, the nineteenth-century theater of romance and its greatest fabrications, the Womanly Woman with its corollary, the Manly Man. Cuthbertson, the play's theater critic, modeled on Clement Scott, believes in these two fictions above all others. His job, as he puts it, involves him witnessing "scenes of suffering nobly endured and sacrifice willingly rendered by womanly women and manly men" (*Plays*, 36). Such deconstructions of gender as Shaw proposed have become commonplace in feminist and psychoanalytic discussions in literary theory in recent times, but the pre-Freudian Shaw, the Ibsenist philosopher, although inspired by Ibsen, Mary Wollstonecraft, and Harriet Taylor-J. S. Mill, was striking out here more or less on his own. The play's drama critic is neither a bad critic nor intellectually dishonest; just as Shaw described Clement Scott in *The Quintessence* as "a good-natured gentleman, not a pioneer, but emotional, impressionable, zealous, and sincere," so the philosopher-critic Realist makes clear to the Philistine Colonel Craven that the Idealist Cuthbertson is a good critic, in spite of his opinions:[6]

> CRAVEN. Isn't it ridiculous for a man to talk like that? I'm hanged if he don't take what he sees on the stage quite seriously.
>
> CHARTERIS. Of course: that's why he is a good critic. Besides, if you take people seriously off the stage, why shouldn't you take them seriously on it? (*Plays*, 38)

While the Shavian Realist deconstructs the theater of romance, the Shavian Philistine is quite indifferent to the Imaginary of the theater of romance in which the Shavian Idealist lives both on- and offstage. *The Philanderer* presents us with a clash of two theatrical metaphors of personal relations: Ibsenite-Shavian realism and the theater of romantic ideals. The philanderer's two mistresses, modeled on Shaw's own, personify these two types of theater as well as two types of woman, the Womanly Woman (Julia) and the New Woman (Grace) of the 1890s. The representative Womanly Woman was based on his first lover, the needy and jealous widow Jenny Paterson, whose fate in the play can be regarded as a real tragedy. The representative New Woman was based on Florence Farr, the Ibsenist actress, who had played Rebecca West in her own production of *Rosmersholm*. Shaw's dramatic point in the play is that the clash of theatrical metaphors and ideological fictions has, nevertheless, human, even tragic consequences. Even while laughing at the Womanly Woman, the unintended cruelty caused by the impervious philosopher's relentless pursuit of his own pleasures becomes apparent and contributes to this play's unpleasant quality. The New Woman, not the philandering philosopher-critic, is able to read and understand the tragedy of the Womanly Woman.[7]

The first scene in the play portrays some rather risqué lovemaking between the philosopher-critic and the New Woman, followed by the intrusion of the Womanly Woman and the ensuing confrontation. Julius Novik contends that:

> we are to understand that Charteris has been sexually intimate with Julia, and probably with Grace as well... the somewhat jejune opening dialogue... though at the immediate level a passage of mainly verbal "love-making," can also, I believe, be understood, however inexplicitly, as a conventional substitute for "love-making" in an unshowably different sense. That Shaw meant sex to be understood *somewhere* in *The Philanderer* is clear from a letter he wrote in 1896: "In 'The Philanderer' you had the fashionable cult of Ibsenism and 'New Womanism' on a real basis of clandestine sensuality." (*The Philanderer: Holograph*, xviii)

The scene, while real in being based on a very unpleasant incident in Shaw's own life, seems to come straight out of melodrama. The stage directions can illustrate the subtlety of Shaw's dramaturgy here. The theatricality verging on melodrama that Shaw satirizes, Sardoodledom, derived from the French theater of Sardou and Scribe. Yet French literature was also famous for its sexual frankness, which often caused problems with the

English censor. The literary naturalism of Zola, a French parallel to the realism of Ibsenism, provided one example, while another was a more popular literature that went untranslated, an example of which, *"a yellow backed French novel lying open"* (*Plays*, 28), is highlighted in the opening stage directions of Shaw's play. Its importance is revealed later in the act in a scene between the philandering philosopher and the Womanly Woman. She reacts to the *open display* of the French novel with disgust— and some hypocrisy—that implicates all three in the "clandestine sensuality" of the play.

> JULIA [*She sees the yellow backed French novel*] Ah, look at that [*holding it out to him*]! Look at what the creature reads! filthy, vile French stuff that no woman would touch. And you—you have been reading it with her.
>
> CHARTERIS. You recommended that book to me yourself. (*Plays*, 34)

The presence of "the yellow backed French novel" makes quite clear the sexual underpinnings of the play and establishes a relation between the two, by having textuality represent sexuality. Reading, thus, becomes a sign for the sexual act, which leaves little doubt as to what had been happening immediately before the beginning of Act I.

The play's three settings are signposts to the ideological confrontation between a theater of romantic Idealism that dominated the London scene in the early 1890s (becoming the object of Shaw's critical derision as a dramatic critic later in the decade) and a theater of Ibsenite-Shavian Realism. The settings thus become symbolic ("Symbolic! That is an accusation of Ibsenism" (*Plays*, 60), declares the Idealist dramatic critic) sites for the cultural wars of the early 1890s. The drama critics, Clement Scott and A. B. Walkley (the dedicatee of the Epistle Dedicatory who was later lampooned as the critic Trotter in *Fanny's First Play*), were champions of the French well-made play, and both translated them for the London stage. One irony, from Shaw's point of view, was that his friend and ally in the cause of Ibsenism William Archer was another champion of the well-made play. Archer never ceased to criticize Shaw's plays for their failings in terms of (plot) construction, and he particularly disliked *The Philanderer*.[8]

Shaw insists on the thematic of theatricality in the setting. The first act takes place in the living room of the drama critic modeled on Scott, the establishment representative of the Old Drama. The stage directions detail the room's theatrical accoutrements:

> *The walls are hung with theatrical engravings and photographs: Kemble as Hamlet, Mrs Siddons as Queen Katherine pleading in court, Macready as Werner (after Maclise), Sir Henry Irving as Richard III (after Long), Ellen Terry, Mrs Kendal, Ada Rehan, Sarah Bernhardt, Henry Arthur Jones, Sir Arthur Pinero, Sydney Grundy, and so on, but not Eleonora Duse nor any one connected with Ibsen . . . [there is] a turret window filled up with a stand of flowers surrounding a statuet of Shakespear.* (Plays, 28)

This graphic representation of the history of British theater before the advent of Ibsen, complete with its altar to Shakespeare, brings viewers both directly to signifiers of that theater, visual reproductions of Shakespeare's shadows (the actors), and reflexively to this particular drama's process of signifying (how it creates meaning). But for the critic of the Old Drama, the representation functions as the Imaginary in which he lives, as his ideological signifieds (Ideals in Shaw's word), as real to him as the equally ideological signifieds in the world beyond the theater. Lest the audience overlooks this insistence on signifying, on theatricality, the Ibsenist realist sums up the action (the signified) to the establishment critic at the end of the act in terms of pure theatrical convention (the signifiers):

> CHARTERIS. I tell you seriously, I'm the matter. Julia wants to marry me: I want to marry Grace. I came here tonight to sweetheart Grace. Enter Julia. Alarums and excursions. Exit Grace. Enter you and Craven. Subterfuges and excuses. Exeunt Craven and Julia. And here we are. That's the whole story. (Plays, 38)

The second act, set in the library of a fictional Ibsen club, inspired possibly by the debates in the Playgoers Club after the production of *Ghosts*, presents us with a site for an alternative theater: a Theater of Ibsenite-Shavian Realism. The room, a perfect den of textuality, is dominated by a "*fireplace, surmounted by a handsome mantlepiece, with a bust of Ibsen, and decorative inscriptions of the titles of his plays,*" and with one of the characters "*reading a volume of Ibsen*" (Plays, 39). Thus, the settings of the first two acts visually present the clash of two theatrical metaphors as modes of "being-in-the-world" (if I may adapt Heidegger's term), analogous to the two types of criticism that constitute the major thematic in the play. Shaw's writing as dramatic text seeks to contrast the Lacanian Imaginary, where a theatrical audience is usually trapped in the theater of romance by the visual, from the Symbolic, where the reader may begin to read how each is interwoven into the text of contemporary culture, both individually and socially (psychoanalytically and ideologically, as Barthes suggested).

Echoing Shaw's use of anatomy as a metaphor for economics as a methodology and, perhaps, drawing on the etymology of the word *critic*, the metaphor of anatomist dissector/vivisector is one the play proposes for the moral philosopher-critic.[9] Another character is a doctor, who works at the literal cutting edge of medical science for he experiments on live animals. This vivisecting doctor, specializing in diseases of the liver, functions within the structure of the play more as the philosopher-critic's shadow or Doppelgänger than does the theater critic. Shaw was, of course, a well-known antivivisectionist, but the text makes clear that the Ibsenist philosopher of life, whose sense of personal relations is based on a willful sensuality, on pursuing his own pleasure rather than romantic ideals, is also a vivisectionist, an emotional vivisectionist whose interest is in the anatomy of human relations.

> JULIA [*earnestly*] It is you who are the vivisector: a far crueller, more wanton vivisector than he [the doctor].
>
> CHARTERIS. Yes; but then I learn so much more from my experiments than he does! And the victims learn as much as I do. (*Plays*, 57)

The doctor, like the Idealist drama critic but unlike the Ibsenist philosopher-critic, is caught in his own Imaginary, the image-repertoire of scientific language with its own codes of textuality. As with the metaphor of theatricality, that of medicine runs thematically through the play; indeed they are linked. Early on, the representative Philistine, the retired army colonel, on hearing the Idealist drama critic's description of his work in the theater as being witness to "scenes of suffering nobly endured and sacrifice willingly rendered by womanly women and manly men," automatically and surreally assumes that the critic must work in a hospital! The action of the second half of the play turns on the doctor *reading* the latest issue of the *British Medical Journal* (at the beginning of the second half of the second act in later editions, of the third act in earlier ones). Specifically he reads an article rebutting his own published *writing* that claimed to discover a new disease of the liver—a disease as chimerical as the drama critic's ideals of marriage, the Womanly Woman, and the modern artist's malady of neurasthenia.

The third setting in the play replaces (or, rather, conflates) the theatrical metaphor of the previous two with a medical one. This transition from the theater (the Ibsen library) to medicine (the doctor's waiting room) moves the focus from the social body (a theater where social and sexual relations—whether romantic or not—are depicted) to the individual body and mortality: from the theater of pleasure to the anatomy school (or theater) of pain and death, from the pleasant to the unpleasant. The stage directions describe *"a cabinet of anatomical preparations, with a framed photograph of Rembrandt's School of Anatomy"* (*Plays*, 54–55) prominently displayed in the doctor's reception room. Rembrandt's famous painting, also known as "The Anatomy Lesson of Dr. Nicolaes Tulp" (1632), shows a seventeenth-century lesson in anatomy as a form of theater with the dissection of a cadaver as its chief, ghastly feature watched by an audience of Dutch burghers. The character the text associates with this representation of an anatomical dissection is the Ibsenist philosopher-critic, the critic-vivisector of human feelings, who enters later in the act and strolls *"across to the cabinet, and pretends to study the Rembrandt photograph"* (*Plays*, 56).[10] Although his philanderer is unconscious of the connection, Shaw —the playwright as theatrical dissector, who declared "if the playgoer could see the dramatist's mind, all the dramatists would be hanged" (*Non-Dramatic*, 455)—is not. Moreover, Shaw, the art critic, is conscious of both the theatricality and the self-reflexivity in Rembrandt's painting where the relation between the artist and his subject is as much his theme as that between Dr. Tulp and the corpse. Shaw, the vivisector/analyst of social relations as well as artist as theatrical dissector, recognizes the anatomy lesson as an illustration of his dual role as social critic and dramatist. Whatever the beneficial result of the clash of theatrical metaphors or of the two types of criticism might be, as with the scientist's vivisection experiments or the philosopher's philanderings or the critic's criticism, Rembrandt's painting shows that the theater of Shavian Realism (before Brecht or Artaud) can always have cruelty as either an incidental or intentional result (*The Philanderer* is intentionally one of the *Plays Unpleasant*). This recognition of human feeling in relation to the body from which thinking can never be entirely abstracted—the beyond of the writing, the pleasure or pain of the text that insists on corporeality while, at the same time, constituting the metaphysics of the text—is key to Shaw's drama of criticism and criticism (critique) of drama. There can be no such human feelings between those Ideals as masks, those social constructions as masquerades: the Womanly Woman and the Manly Man. A complete denial of feeling separates the doctor-scientist and the animals he tortures, although he is a naturally affectionate man.[11] And in the critical repudiation of sentimental theatrical romance by the Ibsenist Realist as philanderer lies the danger that all feelings involving human relations will be repudiated.

The novel topical basis of the play made it date very quickly in its own time, but its dated aspect makes the play all the more interesting now.[12] Primarily it provided Shaw with a means of representing the subjectivity of the writer as philosopher-critic, as Realist, in contrast to the theater critic as Idealist. In its later chapters, *The Quintessence* elaborated the disastrous social consequences as worked out in Ibsen's plays of the Idealist trying to live up to his or her ideals and expecting everyone else to do the same, in spite of practical experience. One irony in *The Philanderer* is that the Idealist theater critic, who upholds the romantic ideal of marriage above all else, is revealed, in prosaic fact, as having more or less happily separated from his own wife. However, another irony is that the emotional consequences of the Ibsenist Realist's critiques and personal behavior, which are shown as cruel and painful, whether beneficial or pleasurable, question Shaw's own critical writing and drama. The play is a warning: just as Shaw's 1890 lecture on Ibsen warned his Fabian audience against turning socialism into an ideal and as *The Quintessence* warned against turning Ibsenism into an ideal, so also *The Philanderer* warns that in attempting to deconstruct ideals, deconstruction itself may become an ideal.

The end of the play shows us the realization of sympathy for the Womanly Woman by the New Woman (the female Shavian Realist), in contrast to the unconscious cruelty of the philanderer (the male Realist) and the anatomical devastation he wreaks on the emotional life of others.

> SYLVIA [*whispering quickly behind Charteris as he is about to advance*] Take care. She's going to hit you. I know her.
>
> *Charteris stops and looks cautiously at Julia, measuring the situation. They regard one another steadfastly for a moment. Grace softly rises and gets close to Julia.*
>
> CHARTERIS [*whispering over his shoulder to Sylvia*] I'll chance it. [*He walks confidently up to Julia*]. Julia? [*He proffers his hand*].
>
> JULIA [*exhausted, allowing herself to take it*] You are right. I am a worthless woman.

CHARTERIS [*triumphant, and gaily remonstrating*] Oh, why?

JULIA. Because I am not brave enough to kill you.

GRACE [*taking her in her arms as she sinks, almost fainting away from him*] Oh no. Never make a hero of a philanderer.

Charteris, amused and untouched, shakes his head laughingly. The rest look at Julia with concern, and even a little awe, feeling for the first time the presence of a keen sorrow. (Plays, 61)

Shaw's play, typically, complicates the categories he set out in *The Quintessence*. His Womanly Woman is strongly Philistine, but her attempt to embrace Ibsenist Realism ends as an Idealist's tragedy. This Shaw text exemplifies a textual dialectic of drama and criticism, which becomes a complicating process, akin to Hegelian dialectic, that allows much of the comedy and the tragedy to emerge, thus immediately making Shavian drama something different from Ibsen's. Bearing in mind Shaw's essay "The Religion of the Pianoforte," music might offer another way to understand this complicating process in Shaw's writing, and he certainly had it in mind when he was writing *The Philanderer*. Two years later, after finishing *Candida*, he wrote to Charles Charrington (March 1, 1895): "When you see a man like me, trying to do in counterpoint in even as few as three real parts, as in Candida, or in seven, as in the finale to The Philanderer, never tell him he ought to go and write choruses instead" (*Letters 1*, 491).

Art, texts, and criticism form a nexus, an interweaving, of social, cultural, and personal relations from which *both* Shaw's critical *and* dramatic writing can be said to emerge. Such works from the early 1890s as the critical essays and *The Philanderer* provided a tissue of writings densely interwoven with others of their time that allows the reader to read and discern the threads in these disparate texts as both history and critical writing. It remains, Barthes might say, the reader's doubly perverse pleasure to continue reading them. Shaw's later play on critics, *Fanny's First Play* resurrected this thematic of criticism from the 1890s.

Fanny's First Play

Fanny's First Play is a dramatic inquiry into art and criticism, a point Shaw makes by deliberately evoking the first literary and drama critic, Aristotle (known as the Stagirite), at the end of the Induction. The Induction with the epilogue form a frame play that is a satire on critics. And Shaw's model critic, John Ruskin—author of both *Modern Painters* (5 volumes, 1843–1860) and *The Stones of Venice* (1851–1853), perhaps the best known of Victorian books of art or architectural criticism, permeates the whole play. *Fanny's First Play* opened in London on April 19, 1911; that performance began the longest first run of any of Shaw's plays in London, with more than six hundred performances.[13] Shaw, however, was embarrassed by this success and referred to the play disparagingly as a potboiler. In the middle of a newspaper controversy with the art critic Roger Fry, he wrote a letter to *The Nation* on March 1, 1913, in which he referred to Ruskin as "a quite abysmal juggins" (*London Art*, 425). Juggins is, in fact, the name of the footman in the play, who presides over its events; whether Shaw's calling Ruskin by that name was coincidental or intentional, the conflation nevertheless gives the reader a clue as to the writing process of his play-texts. As critic, the shadow of Ruskin—a prime influence in shaping Shaw's views on art—looms large over the text of his satire on critics, *Fanny's First Play*, then fresh in the minds of London theatergoers.

Seldom revived and critically ignored nearly a century after it was written, *Fanny's First Play: An Easy Play for a Little Theatre* is one of Shaw's funniest comedies, which, along with *Village Wooing*, can be read as one of his most self-reflexive plays about drama and authorship in line with poststructuralist themes. The play functions in Shaw's oeuvre much as Mozart's piano *sonata facile* or *Eine kleine Nachtmusik* functions in his. However easy these little works might be, neither Shaw nor Mozart left artistry behind in creating these minor masterpieces. Because of its critical frame and context, *Fanny's First Play* can be read as a mine of information on the technique of the Shaw play-texts and his methodology of creating poetic structures in his dramatic writing.[14]

Inspired, perhaps, by Buckingham's *The Rehearsal* (1671) and Sheridan's *The Critic* (1779), *Fanny* is about drama and criticism, comprising both inner and outer plays where one fits inside (a part of) the other. The inner play is self-contained and can be played without the outer play (Shaw wrote a prologue in rhymed doggerel to substitute for it if only the inner play was being performed). Shaw used the title *Fanny's First Play* to describe the combination of inner and outer plays, so that the play's title becomes somewhat uncertain, as does the name of its author. The inner play is significantly not given a title, but it does have an author, whom we eventually discover to be Fanny (a fictional character belonging to the outer play); thus, the title is Fanny's first play. Fanny's name suggests that Shaw almost certainly drew on the life of Fanny Burney (1752–1840), writer and friend of Dr. Johnson, as a real life model, for not only the name of his heroine and the incidents in the outer play in which she figures but also something of her personality. Burney had famously written her first novel, *Evelina: or, a Young Lady's Entrance into the World*, unbeknownst to her father, the well-known music-historian Charles Burney. When published anonymously in London in 1778, *Evelina* became a literary sensation and raised the big question to which everyone wanted an answer: who was *Evelina*'s author? It was commonly assumed that the writer was a man. When Fanny's sister told their father that his daughter Fanny was the author, Charles Burney was as surprised as anyone. Subsequently Fanny wrote a play, *The Whitlings*, for production at Richard Brinsley Sheridan's Theater in Covent Garden, but she withdrew it herself, under pressure from her father, when it became evident that its satire contained recognizable portraits of society figures who were his patrons.[15] Fanny in Shaw's play revolts against her pampered upbringing and, by writing a modern socialist-inspired realistic play, scandalizes her father, an aesthete living in an imaginary eighteenth-century world of art, beautiful things, and beautiful actions. Shaw's irony is that Fanny's so-called realist play, as *both* father *and* daughter suppose, can be read in a way *neither* understand: informed by the textual history of Western drama.

The whole raison d'être of the outer play as a frame, its drama, as with the publication of Burney's *Evelina*, is to ask the question: Who is the author of the inner play? Thus the critics, all but one of whom are modeled on London critics of the time, in the outer play speculate about the inner play's possible writers, including Shaw himself! This questioning mirrored the predicament of the actual critics at the play's first London performance when confronted by advertisements naming its author as, Xxxxxxx Xxxx. In their speculations on the identity of the writer, in their desire to know and name the author, the critics reveal their own particular prejudices, as well as more general ones on authorship, writing, and criticism, consistent with what Barthes writes in "The Death of the Author": "To give a text an Author is to impose a limit in that text, to furnish it with a final signified, to close the writing. Such a conception suits criticism very well, the latter then allotting itself the important task of discovering the Author beneath the work: when the Author has been found, the text is 'explained'—victory to the critic" (Barthes, *Image-Music-Text*, 147).

Subjectivity is a crucial aspect of any writing, and throughout his literary career Shaw sought to bring it into question, nowhere more so than in *Fanny's First Play* with its strategy of suppressing its authorship.[16] The point of such suppression is to dissociate author and text and, as Barthes puts it, focus attention on the text: "The Author, when believed in, is always conceived of as the past of his own book: book and author stand automatically on a single line divided into a *before* and an *after*. . . . In complete contrast, the modern scriptor is born simultaneously with the text, is in no way equipped with a being preceding or exceeding the writing, is not the subject with the book as predicate" (Barthes, *Image-Music-Text*, 145).

Shaw plays with and beyond the frame of his work (*parergon*) and extracts his comedy by withholding the name of the author from both the fictional critics in his play and the real critics who attended the first performance of *Fanny's First Play*. As he wrote in the preface—incidentally identifying himself as writer with a puppet character related to Punch and derived from the Italian Comedy: "The concealment of the authorship, if a *secret de Polichinelle* can be said to involve concealment, was a necessary part of the play" (*Plays 4*, 346). He had to insist that the author of the authorless, nameless inner play was Fanny O'Dowda—not Bernard Shaw. Perhaps Fanny is Shaw's shadow, but now, even more than at the time it was written, it can be said that Shaw is Fanny's shadow. He withdrew his own name as author and substituted her name in the title of both inner and outer plays for the benefit of his audience, not Fanny's, as the onstage critics have to speculate on the author of Fanny's titleless play. It could be further argued that Shaw wrote the inner play in the character of Fanny by splitting his own authorial persona in two, thereby making the play both a fictional and real production (but, notice how slippery is this border between fiction and reality). Shaw signals authorial identity with his fictional author, his authorial shadow, in a bold dramatic stroke. But such identity is necessarily a misrecognition with Lacanian overtones, where Shaw's stage is the mirror, in which this (mis)identification is made.

The deliberate structural strategies at work in *Fanny's First Play* indicate the manifold levels on which this Shaw text operates. Shaw in the preface to *The Black Girl in Search of God* made the Saussurean observation that an ability "to distinguish similars and dissimilars" was "the most elementary test of intelligence" (*Prefaces*, 651). So, as an easy play, key elements (whether of themes, names, or relations) at a purely formal level in *Fanny's First Play* are reduced to simple conceptual (often textual) pairs of either similarity or difference. From these, complex structures of meaning are built up in which the larger thematic of an Oedipal struggle between children and their parents in both inner and outer plays is paralleled by aesthetic and ethical conflicts as represented by the figure of Ruskin in his life and role as critic. This, in a way, shadows Shaw's own Oedipal relationship as art and cultural critic with Ruskin. Both sets of problems in the play, aesthetic and ethical, can be acted out and resolved by practical action in real life. Shaw explained in the preface: "I hate to see dead people walking about: it is unnatural. And our respectable middle-class people are all as dead as mutton." Thus he "is driven to offer to young people in our suburbs the desperate advice: Do something that will get you into trouble" (*Prefaces*, 138). All this is presented at the self-reflexive level of reading and writing in the context of the theatrical textual tradition: a drama about drama within the critical context of a satire on contemporary London theater critics; a playwright figures himself as a playwright who figures herself as a major character; and her fictional play figures as an integral, if separate, part of his or her larger play. The entire Western dramatic literary tradition is invoked to build an astonishingly complex textual edifice. That is Shaw's joke. If the irony in the subtitle "Easy Play" is a clue to such elaborate structures of meaning, then the implication for his other plays is obvious: their even more complex structures are also designed to elicit both critical and creative readings from their audiences. To read critically is a lesson Shaw, the critic as artist, wanted to teach his critics in his parody of them in *Fanny's First Play*.

By displacing its comic surface, and Shaw had insisted in a letter to Siegfried Trebitsch on October 23, 1911, that Acts I and III should be "wildly comic" (*Shaw-Trebitsch*, 158), *Fanny's First Play* can be read as having serious concerns. In the formal terms already discussed, Shaw anticipates the linkage between structure and signification of similarities and differences in structuralist writing inspired by Saussure. In exposing the drama as a product of a particular intellectual cultural tradition, it touches on the hermeneutic concerns of Paul Ricoeur, who argued that new meaning can only be produced through a symbolic detour and interpreted within the context of a particular tradition, within the conceptual framework provided by that tradition. In terms of reflexive writing and authorial subjectivity, Shaw puts at center stage a major concern of poststructuralists. The rest of this chapter traces connections between Shaw's frame play and the traditions from which it sprang, as well as with later twentieth-century poststructuralism, to suggest how it may be (re)read and, by extension, used as a framework to read and critically reinterpret the entire Shavian dramatic corpus.

The Shadow of Ruskin

Fanny's First Play, as a title in lieu of a title, already points to Shaw's play with language and meaning: Fanny's first play as the untitled (inner) play within a larger play entitled *Fanny's First Play*. The inner play concerns two families living in the London suburb of Denmark Hill, the Gilbeys and the Knoxes, who are in partnership as shopkeepers selling underwear. Other characters include a cockney prostitute, a French sailor (who gives a splendid parody of the Shavian long speech, exemplified by Napoleon's speech on the English at the end of *Man of Destiny*), and—an old theatrical staple—the footman, Juggins, who is brother to a duke. An Induction and Epilogue comprise the outer play, providing the frame for the inner one. The Induction introduces: Fanny O'Dowda, the author—at this point unknown—of the inner play, Cambridge student, Fabian socialist, and suffragette; Count O'Dowda, her father, a papal knight of Irish descent who resides in Venice; Savoyard, her impresario for this first performance of her first play; and, finally, four dramatic critics, three of whom are caricatures of contemporary London critics. Because the central action in both the inner and outer plays consists of a rebellion by children against their parents and their upbringing, the play asks a moral question, a constant in the Shaw text: what is the basis for what Kant called practical action by the autonomous subject? Shaw's answer lies within a nexus of social, cultural, and textual concerns that may be called passionately informed moral action. This moral question provides the context for the large shadow cast over the play by the formidable artistic and moral-social conscience of late Victorian England, the critic John Ruskin. And Shaw frames the moral question with the aesthetic question of authorship in *both* his own *and* Fanny's play.[17]

Although his name is mentioned only once in the entire play, several clues point to the significance of Ruskin in the play's poetic construct. The singular instance happens in the Induction of the outer play, when the aesthete Count O'Dowda claims that he left nineteenth-century post-industrial revolution England to live in Venice so as to escape from: "soot and fog and mud and east wind; out of vulgarity and ugliness, hypocrisy and greed, superstition and stupidity. Out of all this and [live in Venice] in the sunshine, in the enchanted region of which great artists alone have had the secret, in the sacred footsteps of Byron, of Shelley, of the Brownings, of Turner and Ruskin" (*Plays*, 652).

The major result of Ruskin's experience in Venice was the three-volume *The Stones of Venice*. In a 1893 review of Wagner's prose works, Shaw wrote humorously on how Ruskin's book could inspire a journey to Venice, which might reveal something about the count's Idealist aestheticism (with the proviso that the count is Irish, not English, and so *is* susceptible to art):

> the Britisher reads his "Stones of Venice" until he trembles and thrills with enthusiasm for Carpaccio and Tintoretto, counting himself not happy before the day when he books with Cook or Gaze to Venice, where he hastens, suffocating with emotion, to San Giorgio Schiavone, only to stand chapfallen in a dirty little church, seeing nothing that he likes half so well as the chromo-lithograph he bought with the last Christmas number of the *Illustrated London News*. (*Books 2*, 168–69)

When Shaw, the music critic, wrote to Golding Bright on December 2, 1894, with a list of critics for the aspiring critic to read, Ruskin was the first he named (Wagner, Lessing, Lamb, and Hazlitt were the others).[18] Ruskin was a powerful influence on not only Shaw but the whole cultural life of late Victorian Britain. In 1878 the famous libel trial between Ruskin and the American impressionist painter James McNeil Whistler, who lived in London, focused the debate in art criticism on the conflict between the ethical concerns of Ruskin and the aesthetic concerns of Whistler. Ruskin lost the suit, and his reputation as a critic of modern art was over. Whistler won a farthing in damages with no costs and went bankrupt. Ironically, the painter then went off to Venice to recuperate financially by executing a commissioned series of etchings of the city of art most associated with Ruskin. More than thirty years later, Shaw resurrected this Ruskin-Whistler ethics-aesthetics debate in *Fanny's First Play*.

Another germ for the play came, when as music critic, Shaw reviewed on May 2, 1894, a collection of Ruskin's essays, *On Music*, which he found "infinitely suggestive and provocative." Shaw explained: "It is at once the strength and weakness of Mr Ruskin in dealing with music that he is in love with it . . . and so am I; but I am married to her, so to speak, as a professional critic, whereas he is still a wooer, and has the illusions of imperfect knowledge as well as the illuminations of perfect love" (*Music 3*, 193–200).

To Ruskin's contention that "true music is the natural expression of a lofty passion for a right cause," Shaw retorts, "I entirely agree with Mr Ruskin in this; but it will not hold water, for all that;" and Shaw added, "Music will express any emotion, base or lofty. She is absolutely unmoral."

Shaw points to an example Ruskin himself gives, in contradiction of his own premise when he refers to Mozart, "who used the greatest power . . . to follow and fit with perfect sound the words of the Zauberflöte and of Don Giovanni—foolishest and most monstrous of conceivable human words and subjects of thought." Shaw, the Mozart lover, not content with pointing out Ruskin's own contradiction, continues: "This is a capital instance of Mr Ruskin's besetting sin—virtuous indignation." He later describes another example as "an explosion of pious horror of the best Denmark Hill brand." Ruskin, Denmark Hill (the London suburb in which Ruskin lived and wrote *Stones of Venice*), and the relation between aesthetics and morality all reappear in *Fanny's First Play*, within the framework or context of criticism.

Worse than Ruskin's virtuous indignation at Mozart, from Shaw's point of view, was his advice to the girls of England: "From the beginning," counsels Ruskin, "consider all your accomplishments as means of assistance to others." "This," insists Shaw, "is Denmark Hill with a vengeance. But the artist in Mr Ruskin is always getting the better of Denmark Hill; and on the very next page he says, 'Think only of accuracy; never of effect or expression.'" Shaw advises "the young ladies of England, whether enrolled in [Ruskin's] Guild of St George or not, to cultivate music solely for the love and need of it." Shaw's writing of *Fanny's First Play* in the persona of a young woman suffragette works as a riposte (more than fifteen years later) to Ruskin's ambivalent moralizing toward "the young ladies of England." Fanny in the play seems to have taken to heart Ruskin's advice on the education of women in *Sesame and Lilies* (1865): "Let a girl's education be as serious as a boy's . . . Turn her loose into the old library . . . and let her alone. She will find what is good for her; you cannot."

Denmark Hill, perhaps not coincidentally, is also the setting for Act I of Granville Barker's *The Madras House*, in which one character actually points out Ruskin's house in the distance. Barker's play, specifically referred to in the epilogue of *Fanny's First Play*, is a play about the rag trade (the clothes and fashion business), and the lower middle-class shopkeepers of *Fanny's First Play* sell underwear. Written a year before *Fanny*, Shaw's play *Misalliance*, about a wealthy middle-class family of an underwear manufacturer, had borrowed its sartorial thematic from Barker's play. The metaphorical or semiotic significance of clothes in all these plays, including *Getting Married* (see chapter 7), possibly derived from Carlyle's *Sartor Resartus* (1831) and works as a formal device with social, psychological, and metaphysical connotations, which Roland Barthes, who wrote on the semiotics of fashion might have appreciated.[19] One principal function of clothes, apart from comfort, adornment, and warmth, is to hide the naked body. Underwear, however, has a peculiar semiotic status as a type of clothing that has itself to be hidden, being metonymically linked to the genital areas and therefore with generation. These plays seem to delight in *writing* with those sartorial signifiers that have been hidden primarily for social reasons, so that society, its people, and how it reproduces itself might be better *read* by its members, the theater audience, and play readers. The light relief of *Fanny's First Play* and its featured underwear functions in relation to the three large-scale plays in much the same way, perhaps, as a satyr play did to a trilogy of tragedies in Greek theater.[20]

Other clues indicate the importance of Ruskin to the play, in both his character and his thinking. Immediately obvious is the count's effete aestheticism. The aesthete was a late nineteenth-century English phenomenon inspired by the writings of Ruskin and Pater and personified in such London dandies as Whistler, Aubrey Beardsley, and Oscar Wilde; Shaw himself was an aesthetically minded anti-aesthete in this tradition with his Jaeger clothing and vegetarianism.[21] As he wrote to Charles Charrington (March 1, 1895): "I have my feeling for the exquisitely cultivated sense of beauty—an almost devotional sense—and the great pains and skill of execution which produces work of [this] kind" (*Letters 1*, 490–91). But there was a great gulf between Ruskin and his one time pupil, Pater, in their understanding of the aesthetic. Ruskin inextricably linked aesthetics with moral virtues and a fidelity to nature, while Pater, displaying an indifference to ethical concerns, preferred to embrace the decadence associated with "the art for art's sake" school. These contrasting attitudes led each to champion different periods in the history of art. For Ruskin Venetian Medieval Gothic was superior to the Florentine Renaissance, whereas Pater found the reverse to be true. The comedy of the count in Shaw's play comes from his unwittingly being *both* a Ruskinite *and* Pateresque aesthete, but at different times. Ironically, Shaw, perhaps because of his own innate aestheticism, always gleefully and somewhat perversely set himself against the "art for art's sake" school. As he had put it in the Epistle Dedicatory from *Man and Superman*: "But 'for art's sake' alone I would not face the toil of writing a single sentence" (*Prefaces*, 165).

Ruskin's importance elsewhere in the Shaw text seems to lie less in his role as art critic than in his role as a prophet of economics. *Fanny's First Play*, however, draws on the shadowy presence of Ruskin as both aesthete and exemplary critic. Shaw described *The Stones of Venice*, in a lecture on Ruskin as economist, as being "about art, but [also] very largely about the happiness of workingmen who made the art: for the beauty of Venice is a reflection of the happiness of the men who made Venice."[22] Ruskin's aesthetic theories, with their economic and moral implications, appealed to Shaw in his role as the proverbial mischievous cat among the aesthetic pigeons.[23] Possibly because of his own obsessions with the world of art, moving beyond the Imaginary of art into a Symbolic social and textual nexus of aesthetics, ethics, politics, and economics became a constant theme in his writing, which ended with passionately informed practical action.

Ruskin, notoriously, had been raised in a rarefied atmosphere by wealthy idealistic parents who allowed him no contact with the outside world and exposed him only to what they thought good for him. Count O'Dowda brought up his daughter Fanny in similar seclusion. He claims that she "has never seen an ugly sight or heard an ugly sound that I could spare her; and she has certainly never worn an ugly dress or tasted coarse food or bad wine in her life. She has lived in a palace and her perambulator was a gondola" (*Plays*, 652).

The outer play of *Fanny's First Play* dramatizes two distinct but interrelated aspects of Ruskin's work, the aesthetic and the ethical in the related characters of father and daughter. Shaw had written about a similar conflict of generations in *The Perfect Wagnerite* in relation to Wagner's treatment in *Die Walküre* of the allegorical relationship of Wotan with his daughter, Brünnhilde: "Brynhild is the inner thought and will of the Godhead [Wotan], the aspiration from the high life to the higher that is its divine element, and only becomes separated from it when its resort to kingship and priestcraft for the sake of temporal power has made it false to itself" (*Music 3*, 453). The revolt of a daughter against her father provides the drama in both Shaw's play and Wagner's opera, but a variation on this theme of generational conflict is mirrored in this staging of reflections and shadows in the inner play, where the principal dramatic conflict is between a mother and daughter: the religious, if puritanical Mrs. Knox and her rebellious strong-willed daughter, Margaret. Again, both names conceal and suggest connections to Ruskin. Ruskin's mother, born Margaret Cox, was a strongly evangelical Protestant like Mrs. Knox, whose religion Ruskin eventually rejected after fervently espousing in his youth.

Margaret's discussion in Act II with her mother, after she has been released from prison, is the centerpiece of the inner play, which parallels

Shaw's deconstruction of Ruskin's views of Mozart's music—as both moral and unmoral—in the review quoted above. Here Shaw deconstructs the binary opposition of good and evil in relation to freedom:

> MRS KNOX. I know that prayer can set us free; though you could never understand me when I told you so; but it sets us free for good, not for evil.

> MARGARET. Then what I did was not evil; or else I was set free for evil as well as good. When I was at home and at school I was what you call good; but I wasnt free. And when I got free I was what most people would call not good. (*Plays*, 667)

The splitting of personal traits into different characters is a paradigmatic technique in the Shaw text. The generational conflict of the Ruskins, mother and son, is transposed to the mother-daughter relationship in the inner play and to the father-daughter relationship in the outer one. Meanwhile Ruskin's religious conflicts with his parents are displayed in the ethical conflicts of the inner play, and his moral-aesthetic-critical synthesis in the moral-aesthetic-critical arguments of the outer play (shadows of the Whistler trial). These variations of simple patterns figured in particular individual characters or traits develop into a systematic elaboration of paired oppositions of similarities and differences, from which meaning emerges.[24]

The contrast between the wealthy count's artistic dilettantism and his socialist daughter's artistic practical action shadows the revolt of the children in the inner play against their Philistine petit-bourgeois shopkeeping parents. The crucial dialectical distinction between art and life, between, in Kantian terms, aesthetic judgment and moral action (practical reason) is laid bare, paralleling that between his own text and its practical effect on the lives of his audience in their critical reading of this Shaw play-text. This conflict culminates in the Epilogue with the count's tragic realization of the full horror of his daughter's play. In his reference to the collapse of the great Venetian tower in 1902, the count announces that the Oedipal drama is over in distinctly phallic terms: "She will never return to Venice. I feel now as I felt when the Campanile fell" (*Plays*, 684). This can also be read as an implicit deconstruction of the aesthetics of Ruskin's *Stones of Venice*, liable to collapse at any time. The stones, the aesthetic expression of the labor of Venetian workmen, need to be rebuilt by each new generation. As such, the fall of the Campanile represents the climax of the Oedipal struggle Shaw, the literary artist-critic, was having with the father-figure shadow of Ruskin, the literary art critic, in the course of this play.

That Shaw was circumspect about the formal concerns in his plays has been discussed in other chapters, so the unheralded significance of Ruskin in *Fanny's First Play* should not come as a surprise. Why did Shaw camouflage the significance of Ruskin to the thematic of the play? This is, perhaps, best answered in the contention of this study that the play-texts can be read on many different levels. Margery Morgan, for instance, has written of "the careful planning that went into Shaw's often apparently careless playwriting. It brings out the fact that he was writing, as Shakespeare was supposed to have written, on different levels to suit the tastes and capacities of different sections of his audience" (Morgan, *Shavian Playground*, 94).

Shaw, it seems, had begun by writing the inner play set in Denmark Hill.[25] Perhaps when Lillah McCarthy asked him for a play in a hurry for her Little Theatre, he elaborated the framing play from the Ruskin associations of the setting and Barker's use of the same location for Act I of *The Madras House* in order to build up a poetic structure around the personality and writings of Ruskin, which bear on the artistic and moral concerns of all these plays, as well as their critical reception.

Satire on Critics

By 1911, Shaw's own career as "critic of all the fine arts in succession"—and as radical avant-garde comic playwright trumpeting in the new century at the head of a new generation of playwrights at the expense of the old—was behind him. As an established literary artist, he now suffered the stings and arrows of outrageous, or, at least, what he considered inadequate criticism. For those critics *Fanny's First Play* was written as both a retort as well as a lesson.

To understand the significance of the satire of the critics in the epilogue, remember that Shaw at the time, although highly influential in intellectual, political, and cultural circles, especially among young people, was not yet a popular playwright. By 1911, he was well known as a dramatist in Britain and Ireland, North America, and Germany. He had indeed made money from his plays, but had not had a fashionable and popular West End success—that came with *Pygmalion* in 1914. In a letter to Charles Ricketts, who designed the costumes for the play, Shaw lamented that *Fanny's First Play* had become "the Charley's Aunt of the new drama

... [changing] a desperate artistic enterprise into a sordid commercial speculation" (Dukore, *Shaw's Theater*, 133–34). As dramatic critic and later as member of the executive committee of the Stage Society, he had been an early champion of such European playwrights as Ibsen, Chekhov, Strindberg, Tolstoy, Hauptmann, Sudermann, and Brieux. However, his experience with Granville Barker in setting up the Court Theatre as an experiment to show the feasibility of and necessity for a national repertory theater made him the leading exponent of the New Drama in England. The novelty of the plays caused each new production to become a victim of critical attacks that, while acknowledging their success, denied their right to be called plays, their characters to be real characters, or Shaw to be a true dramatic writer. The epilogue to *Fanny's First Play* directly confronts these criticisms, which had been leveled at his plays since the 1890s. Shaw had become increasingly exasperated at these attacks; more than the direct criticism of him as playwright, these critics diverted attention from the Court Theatre experiment itself and the other playwrights associated with it, like Murray, Galsworthy, Barker, and St. John Hankin. In response Shaw wrote a popular drama, *Fanny's First Play*, as a drama about drama. In much the same way, *You Never Can Tell* was written as a comedy about comedy when he had great difficulty in getting any of his plays produced in the 1890s. Both plays allude to the commedia dell'arte. Moreover, Shaw picked up the thematic thread of criticism from *The Philanderer*, and in *Fanny's First Play* his more obtuse critics became the butt of an unmalicious satire as a dramatic exercise on how to read—and how not to read—a play-text.

All but one of the critics in the play are modeled on actual London critics. Indeed, two of them are also partial self-portraits of Shaw, the critic from the 1890s. Vaughan was primarily modeled on music and drama critic Edward A. Baughan (1865–1938), with whom Shaw engaged in artistic controversies from the early 1890s. Like Shaw, Vaughan is both a music and drama critic; yet unlike Shaw, Vaughan is without a shred of humor. In this respect Vaughan may also be a partial portrait of critic and close friend William Archer, who was congenitally incapable of showing his feelings and remained to the end of his life critical of Shaw's dramaturgy. Gunn's original model was Gilbert Cannan (1884–1955). When Shaw opposed a Stage Society production of his first play, Cannan had exclaimed: "Christ betraying Judas!" A post-Ibsenist playwright-critic like Shaw, Cannan is portrayed as an avant-garde intellectual who utterly despises, unlike Shaw, his elders and antecedents in the theatrical tradition.[26]

That Shaw, like Gunn, was brilliantly original and intent on overturning all previous types of drama was a commonplace of the 1890s, which prompted Shaw to insist in the preface to *Plays for Puritans* that his plays were, on the contrary, so steeped in the theatrical tradition as to seem hackneyed as soon as they were written. Shaw's joke in the context of *Fanny's First Play* is that these two critics, partial parodies of the critic G.B.S., fail to guess the identity of the author of Fanny's/Shaw's play. The other two critics, antitheses of Shaw as critic, guess differently, and paradoxically, both are correct: one guesses Fanny, the other Shaw. As is well known, one of these critics was based on *The Times* A. B. Walkley, the dedicatee of the Epistle Dedicatory to *Man and Superman*, who is called Trotter in the play; Walkley, in on the joke, helped with the make-up for the actor who played his character. The other, Flawner Bannal, is a generic representative of the ever-present popular, opinionated, and misinformed type of journalism.[27]

On June 13, 1894, a month after the review on Ruskin quoted earlier, Shaw had cited both Walkley and Clement Scott, the critic so scandalized by the productions of *Ghosts* and *Widowers' Houses* in the early 1890s and whom Shaw had lampooned as the drama critic in *The Philanderer*. This review, which provided another germ for the play he wrote sixteen years later, asserted that both wrote their critiques as "impressionists." This characteristic is attributed to Trotter in the play, who should therefore probably be read as an amalgam of both Walkley and Scott. The hysterical reaction of moral outrage, so characteristic of Scott, is split in the play between the critic Trotter and the aesthete Count O'Dowda. In line with Shaw's systematic pairing-off in the play, Trotter is in several respects identified with the count: both, for example, wear old-fashioned formal dress and both dote on their daughters. One of the play's many ironies— and one difference between the two—is how the urbane critic Trotter, who holds that Aristotle laid down the ground rules for drama for all time, is *morally* shocked by Fanny in person, whereas the count is *aesthetically* shocked by her play.

In the Epilogue, at the height of an argument about the identity of the author, three critics simultaneously shout the name Shaw (all for different reasons) at the very moment Fanny appears between the curtains. A clash of cymbals and drums could not have been more emphatic at this climactic moment in the thematic of authorial identity: the text uses both visual and verbal signifiers to express not a case of simple identity, but rather of identity in difference. Shaw identifies himself with his own fictional character, but the authorial confusion is even more complicated. The resolution of the inner play occurs when Margaret decides to marry Juggins—the name Shaw used to refer to Ruskin. If Fanny is Shaw's alter ego in the outer play, then Margaret is Fanny's in the inner play and must therefore also be an (alter-) alter ego for Shaw.[28] So is Juggins: the master of ceremonies, a sort of theatrical producer/director for the occasion, who presides over and seemingly controls the drama's events. The proposal of marriage between Margaret and Juggins is, in effect, the marriage of two aspects of the authorial self that takes place at the end of a theatrical rite, whose analogue is the afternoon tea served to the Knoxes and the Gilbeys by Juggins in Act III of the inner play. It serves the same function as, and possibly alludes to, the meal in *You Never Can Tell* presided over by the waiter, William, who is named after Shakespeare.[29] Following this string of identifications Shaw also identifies himself with his famous predecessor.

Simple Structures of Differences

Beyond the structural use Shaw made with the associations of the critic Ruskin, other formal elements in *Fanny's First Play* have received scant critical attention. However they may be easier to read as a paradigm of his dramatic method than those in the better-known plays because they so patently build complex structures out of simple elements.[30] Shaw was never a mere formalist, as the discussion of ethics and aesthetics implies, but he was much more interested in the formal elements of a text and their relation to its thematic than has generally been realized. If the matter of the play, despite appearances, is not simple, then neither is its form where Shaw is, if anything, even more daring. A foundation for Shaw's formal scheme has already been suggested: pairing off everything into a system of binary oppositions, "similars and dissimilars," which Saussurean structuralists saw as the basis for language or any other semiological system. As Saussure put it, "each linguistic term derives its value from its opposition to all the other terms. . . . The linguistic mechanism is geared to differences and identities, the former being only the counterpart of the latter. . . . in language there are only differences. . . . The entire mechanism of language is based on oppositions and on the phonic and conceptual differences that they imply" (Saussure, *General Linguistics*, 88, 108, 120, 121). The result for Shaw in this play, in spite of its simplicity, is dazzling in its brilliance and bewildering in its intricacy. It becomes a play of shadows and reflections played out on a Shavian stage—Plato's cave as a linguistic-textual hall of mirrors. For instance, two Byrons are mentioned in the Induction, seemingly in passing: Lord Byron, the early nineteenth-century Romantic poet and, incidentally, a dramatist who lived for a while in Venice, which provided the setting for his own first play, and H. Byron, a mid-nineteenth-century dramatist and author of the popular *Our Boys*. Shaw extracts comedy from this identity in difference. Apart from their names, the obvious similarity is that both Byrons were dramatists, but from entirely different literary/theatrical traditions. Shaw uses that difference to stress the distinction between the two characters onstage at the time: Count O'Dowda (ennobled like Byron) and the theatrical impresario, Savoyard, who claims he had a job in the original production of *Our Boys*; Savoyard's name alludes to yet another theatrical tradition, Gilbert and Sullivan operetta. The implied irony is that the ethically rigid aesthete, Count O'Dowda, who objects in the Epilogue to the scandal of his daughter's much less fervid revolutionary tendencies, should have been inspired by such a morally scandalous political revolutionary as Lord Byron.

As opposed to the difference in identity of the two Byrons, there is the example of the paired opposition of Oxford/Cambridge, which Shaw uses not once but, predictably, twice. In the outer play, the count associates Cambridge with eighteenth-century values, but his daughter, a student at Cambridge, considers the school the most up-to-date institution for its stance on socialism and suffragettism of the early twentieth century. Oxford is associated for the traditionalist critic Trotter with Aristotle, the Stagirite, who laid down the rules for drama.

It is both coincidental and ironic in terms of the history of English literary criticism that in 1911 Shaw's Fanny, the eponymous neophyte playwright and suffragette at the height of the Woman's War, was at Cambridge, not Oxford. In fact, that very year Cambridge broke with tradition by setting up its first course in English Literature, some time after a more language-based course in English had been set up at Oxford. Cambridge became dominant in the study of English literature in the English-speaking world of the twentieth century. F. R. Leavis was better known later in the century, but I. A. Richards, whose book *Practical Criticism* was published in 1929, set the course for later study. Richards's approach to criticism followed directly on, whether intentionally or not, from the conundrum posed by Shaw's play: is it possible to judge/criticize a literary work without knowing its provenance?[31] As Peter Barry puts it in *Beginning Theory*:

I. A. Richards, finally, is the pioneer of the decontextualised approach to literature which became the norm in Britain from the 1930s to the 1970s as "practical criticism" and in America during roughly the same period as the "New Criticism." Richards's experiments in the 1920s of presenting students and tutors with unannotated, anonymous poems for commentary and analysis gave rise to the ideal of removing the props of received opinion and knowledge and fostering a "true judgement" based on first hand opinion. (Barry, *Beginning Theory*, 30)

This was precisely how Cambridge student Fanny presented her play to the four critics in Shaw's play and how Shaw presented his play to both the London critics in 1911 and, more important, to the audience whom he invited to read the play as something more than their own preoccupations and prejudices based on knowing the identity of the author. Although Shaw uses the decontextualized situation as a starting point for contextualizing the text in criticism, rather than coming to a "true judgement" based on "opinion." And, of course, Theory, including poststructuralism, set itself against the hegemony of New Criticism from the 1970s onward.

Fanny's clashes with her father and Trotter in the academic sphere occur on aesthetic and political points, as befits an encounter between academic institutions. These are contrasted with the quite unacademic behavior in the inner play, when the events following the Oxford-Cambridge annual boat race precipitate the going to jail of Margaret and Duvallet. With such simple structuring of oppositions and doublings the textual thematic extends to that of practical education, as Margaret learns from her experience.

Here is a list of some of the paired opposites in *Fanny's First Play*:

2 plays	Shaw's *Fanny's First Play* & Fanny's first play
2 authors	Shaw & Fanny
2 audiences	for Fanny's play & for Shaw's play
2 sets of critics	at Fanny's play & at Shaw's play
2 Byrons	Lord Byron & H. J. Byron
2 footmen	footman in Induction & Juggins
2 noblemen	Count & Juggins
2 prostitutes	Mrs. William Tinkler (?) & "Darling Dora"
2 families	Knoxes and Gilbeys
2 single fathers	The Count & Duvallet
2 criminal incidents	Margaret's & Bobby's

2 French names	Delaney & Duvallet
2 absurd jokes on cats	Trotter's (Induction) & Bobby's (Act III)
2 cultural outsiders	Duvallet & Darling Dora
2 generational conflicts	Fanny's & Bobby and Margaret's
2 children	Bobby & Margaret; Duvallet's two daughters
2 shopkeepers	Mr. Gilbey & Mr. Knox
2 big houses	Florence Towers & Venetian palace
2 middle class houses	Knox's & Gilbey's
2 pairs of sets	Country house & stage; Knox's & Gilbey's houses
2 theaters	For Fanny's play and Shaw's play respectively
2 exact halves	Induction, Acts I, II/Act III and Epilogue[32]

Duvallet's name even suggests two (*deux*) valets.[33] The following is certainly an incomplete list of the play's several binary oppositions:

> inner/outer play
> female author/male author
> fiction/reality
> aesthetics/ethics
> historical tradition/contemporary life
> past/present
> actors/real people
> upper-class/middle-class settings
> industrialism/culture
> social respectability/individual freedom
> conventional hypocrisy/considerate manners
> prison/home
> freedom/habitual behavior
> parents/children
> husbands/wives
> Harlequin/sailor/boy/girl/prostitute/Columbine
> Cambridge/Oxford
> English/French
> Puritanism/Catholicism
> author/critics
> master/servant
> play/audience
> religious experience/theatrical experience

Any of these pairs or combinations of pairs, of signifiers and their shadows, can be taken and their ramifications traced through both inner and outer plays. In the pairings, the difference in identity is emphasized, while in the binary oppositions the identity is in difference. Thus, whole webs of meaning woven throughout the text are set up on the simplest basis. Meaning is fluid, not fixed, in this theatrical machine and to trace those structures based on signifying differences, those conceptual and contextual conflicts, requires critical and preferably creative responses to the Symbolic of the text by the reader/spectator. Once realized, this design becomes patently clear and can be read. The implication is that Shaw understood the construction or generation of meaning by conflicting concepts and contexts and therefore constructed the play in this manner, although Shaw, abjuring authorial intent, might have said the play generated itself in this way.[34] Few playwrights, apart from Shakespeare, have reflected on and analyzed drama and their own technique of dramatic writing in their plays as intensely as Shaw. To recognize this is enough to encourage the type of readings attempted in this study.

Textual Tradition

As a dramatic exercise, like one of those pedagogical musical forms such as *essercizi*, *études*, or *leçons*, *Fanny's First Play* shows that Shaw both knew the rules (or dramatic codes) and could be a popular playwright if he chose. If he did not choose, the implication must be that his texts have other concerns of both form and content. Having undertaken a popular work, he was incapable, given this technique of dramatic-poetic construction/generation that characterizes his dramatic writing, of making this "easy" play facile. The play can be understood only in a wider context. Again Barthes's essay "The Death of the Author" supplies some useful critical hindsight: "a text is not a line of words releasing a single 'theological' meaning (the message of the Author-God) but a multi-dimensional space in which a variety of writings, none of them original, blend and clash" (Barthes, *Image-Music-Text*, 146).

Insofar as the play touches on questions of authorship and subjective identity, Shaw comes close to what Ricoeur calls "an opaque subjectivity." Like Lacan with his misrecognition of identity and Barthes with his concept of the split subject, Ricoeur's view on subjectivity deviates from that of a coherent unitary ego: "To dispense with the classical notion of the subject as a transparent cogito does not mean that we have to dispense with all forms of subjectivity. My hermeneutical philosophy has attempted to demonstrate the existence of an opaque subjectivity which expresses itself through the detour of countless mediations—signs, symbols, texts and human praxis itself" (Kearney, *Dialogues*, 32).

By suppressing the name of the play's author, the text lets the writing be read simply as text, but a text comprised, or generated by other texts. Any drama is created from within its own tradition, and *Fanny's First Play* is no exception. Its deliberate construction in the full knowledge of that tradition provides an additional layer of signification (another text), which the reader may choose to acknowledge and read, or not.

On the question of subjectivity within a sociocultural tradition, Richard Kearney in a commentary on Ricoeur's hermeneutics observes:

> Ricoeur point[s] out that human consciousness can never know itself in terms of an intuitive immediacy, as Descartes or the early Husserl believed: consciousness must undergo a hermeneutic detour in which it comes to know itself through the mediation of signs, symbols and texts. In other words, consciousness cannot intuit (*anschauen*) its meaning in and from itself, but must *interpret* (*hermeneuein*) itself by entering into dialogue with the texts of a historical community or common tradition to which it belongs (*zuhören*). (Kearney, *Dialogues*, 128)

More, perhaps, than any other major dramatist, Shaw, the formidable theater critic, was steeped in dramatic tradition. Although all new art is a reaction to and revolt against what came before, it cannot be separated from its history. Appropriate clues are provided in the play-text for the critics and critical readers to read if they are alert to them. The question becomes: Can the critics of Fanny's and Shaw's play(s) read in this multithreaded text, which they claim is not a play, a self-reflexive critical inquiry pertaining both to the history and forms of drama? The audience/reader, in her turn, is encouraged to supplement the critical supplements, both those supplied in the play itself and those coming from outside the text. The question is not whether the critics' opinions are right or wrong, but how they are expressed in a nexus of relations: critic to society, artwork/text to culture, audience to artwork/text, and so on. The play suggests that criticism is more complicated than a simple question of close readings and decontextualization. Both, however, may become part of a critical reading that comprehends historical tradition and social reality, and the subject-reader's relation to these as well as to the text. Even in a piece as apparently slight as *Fanny's First Play*, the dramatic tradition, of

186 · Part II: Reading the Plays

which it is inextricably a part, can be read as part of its text. Here the method is one of textual allusion, rather than the pairing off of binary oppositions:

classical drama	the "Stagirite" (Aristotle)
Shakespearean drama	inversion of *Romeo and Juliet*
restoration drama	Buckingham's *The Rehearsal*, Sheridan's *The Critic*
commedia dell'arte	reference to Harlequin and Columbine
opera buffa	Pergolesi and Cimerosa
operetta	naval lieutenant and Savoyard
pantomime	nineteenth-century English pantomime
religious meeting	Salvation Festival at Albert Hall
nineteenth-century comedy	Act I
nineteenth-century melodrama	Act II
nineteenth-century farce	Act III
tragedy	for the count in the Epilogue
Ibsenist drama	three-act domestic drama and problem play
Shavian drama	Fabian socialist play of ideas
variety theater	where Margaret is inspired
repertory theater	which Fanny advocates
The New Drama	Pinero and Granville Barker

Not only does the text allude to these forms or genres, but *Fanny's First Play* literally parodies most of them.

For example, the inner play as a parody of Shakespeare's *ROmeo and JuliET* could, perhaps, have been called *RObert and MargarET*, with their echoing names. The young couples in Shaw's comedy choose mates contrary to their parents' wishes as in Shakespeare's play, but, contrary to the form of Shakespeare's play, they do not choose each other.

The outer play, the critical prism through which the action and textual context of the inner play is reflected, raises direct questions about plays, their authors, and their critics. In the Induction, not even Savoyard and the count know the identity of the author, which is deliberately withheld from the critics. All they know is that Fanny wants this play—without title or known author—to be produced for a select audience of the leading London critics. In the Epilogue the critics are shown as incapable of bringing more than their idiosyncratic prejudices to bear on their judgment of the play and its ambitious scope. They are not reading the Symbolic of Shaw's play; instead, they relate only to what they think they see on the Imaginary of the stage in terms of the imaginary author. The outer play provides the frame whereby the question can be asked of how a modern work fits, if at all, into the dramatic tradition that begins with the tragedies of ancient Greece and whose first theoretician was Aristotle (the Stagirite) in his *Poetics*. The Induction ends with the count having to explain to Fanny who Trotter meant when he referred to the Stagirite. That the neophyte playwright and Cambridge student Fanny was ignorant of the textual tradition of which her play is merely the latest product, does not tell against Shaw's or the poststructuralists' argument or against the qualities of her play.

These alternating textual shadows and reflections of the writing become a text of *play* with no final signifieds, where all signifieds become signifiers. The text becomes a matrix of nonunified meanings, strategies, and discourses eliciting a plurality of meanings without stable signification or truth to be sought in an homogenizing power of a single author. Meaning, rather, emerges in a text, a space or network of a constantly deferring or disseminating metonymy of signifiers (signifiance, or dissemination, never yielding one concrete signification), in a text within a much larger discourse.

Fanny's First Play is open to such manifold textual interpretation, a variety of readings with implications for the corporeal subject's subsequent interaction in the real world as informed and passionate practical action. Fanny, because of her principled militancy as a suffragette, has spent time in prison. She writes from experience, a writing, Derrida would say, as a necessary supplement of that experience. Such an experience, although denied to Shaw, the firebrand socialist orator who faced the risk of it more than once, was open to his dramatic imagination to stage, and to that of his audience. In *Fanny's First Play* the exposure of authorial strategies at work within its own text and in the critical discussions of what a play is, what this particular play is, and of authorship in general can all be read as the text's own deconstruction. Because the author is stripped of authority, the drama rises phoenixlike from the ashes of such acrobatics of autodeconstruction in the theater as the generation of new meaning. The last word in the Epilogue is addressed to the shadows of the theatrical Imaginary, the actors, and, by inviting a response from the audience, underlines both as indispensable participants or hierophants in theatrical ritual (see chapter 7). The final tableau, then, presents an analogue of communication between writer, audience, actors, characters, producers, and—even—those reading-writers called critics:

> *The curtains are drawn, revealing the last scene of the play and the actors on the stage. The count, Savoyard, the critics, and Fanny join them, shaking hands and congratulating.*
>
> THE COUNT. Whatever we may think of the play, gentlemen, I'm sure you will agree with me that there can be only one opinion about the acting.
>
> THE CRITICS. Hear, hear! [*They start the applause*]. (*Plays*, 684)

While *Fanny's First Play* is Shaw's *apologia* for his profession both as writer-critic and playwright, no critical or literary analysis can convey the pleasures of the rhythm, pitches, tempi, tones, dynamics, and cadences of the music of his "writing aloud," to use Barthes's term. Yet these are among the more powerful signifying elements in Shavian drama, by means of which the reader is invited to engage in the critical discourse both of the play and the culture from which it emerges, and to write the text that is the reader's own. To paraphrase Barthes's famous remark: the birth of the reader/spectator must be at the cost of the death of the author.[35]

7 Mystery and Ritual

Theater and Textuality

> *A theatre to me is a place "where two or three are gathered together." The apostolic succession from Eschylus to myself is as serious and as continuously inspired as that younger institution, the apostolic succession of the Christian Church. . . . The artists of the theatre. . . . [have a] deeper claim to be considered . . . [as] hierophants of a cult as eternal and sacred as any professed religion in the world.*
>
> Bernard Shaw, preface to *Our Theatres in the Nineties* (1906)

Mystery of the Text

Part 1, as well as chapter 6, suggests that Shaw's theater is deliberately antithetical to a theater of the Imaginary. Chapter 3 focuses on how Shaw played with his authorial identity by creating several distinct personae to supplement the "paper-*I*" in his autobiographical writing, including the play *John Bull's Other Island*. This chapter considers two more plays, *Candida* and *Getting Married*, to see how they may be read rather as belonging to a theater of a Symbolic beyond the Imaginary and how Shaw again inscribed his own subjectivity as dramatic writer into their design. At one level, both plays take as their subject their own drama as Symbolic rite. *Candida*, one of Shaw's more popular plays, presents a particular challenge because its very popularity stems from the attractions of this pleasant play for Imaginary consumption by the reader-spectator, who becomes as enamored of Candida Morell as is the young poet in the play, Eugene Marchbanks. Yet the play's very theme of poetic vocation as antithetical to marriage demonstrates how to escape from thralldom to the Imaginary; that is, to write poetry the poet must leave the doll house in spite of its enchantments (a leaving as misunderstood as Eliza Doolittle's leaving Henry Higgins at the end of *Pygmalion*). Shaw knew this, and, as shown in chapter 5, wrote *How He Lied to Her Husband* as an antidote to the Imaginary attractions of the earlier play. Building on the work and hints of others, but constructed in a different way, chapter 7 presents a reading of *Candida* as a work of Symbolic (inter)textuality, albeit one functioning in the context of the social ritual that is theater.

In the context of such a demystifying discipline as poststructuralism the question is raised about what happens in terms of human experience when viewers spectate a Shaw play or readers read its text. How does speaking of Shaw's drama as ritual affect its reading as text? Undoubtedly the experience of a play in a theater is not an entirely abstract act of reading, but watching a performance involves pleasure and its desires, as Barthes and Shaw would insist; it becomes a subjectivity of feelings that mirrors, without clear delineation, those of the characters, the readers/spectators, and the author (returning as guest in his fiction). The Shaw theater experience, therefore, although liable to become a ritual event, does not reinforce the social status quo or an ideologically produced ego; rather it becomes an experience where subjectivity is symbolically remade. The two Shaw plays discussed here self-reflexively build mythology, ritual, and initiation thematically into their textual, dramatic, poetic structures and touch on the implications of ritual and initiation in terms of textuality and identity. By making myth flexible within the writing of his poetic-dramatic discourse, Shaw makes the audience and the reader interpret and critique the Symbolic of the play, a Symbolic comprising a textual history reaching back to the beginnings of Western poetry, drama, religion, and mythology. By means of this complex of textuality, the plays display unsuspected levels of meaning waiting to be unearthed, a significant metaphor in regard to a play like *Candida* that invokes the myth of Demeter (Earth-Mother) and Persephone (or Proserpine).

Both these marriage plays, *Candida* and *Getting Married*, question the extent to which the reenactment of a Shaw text in the theater becomes an initiatory rite. Care must be taken in reading—Shaw was not a hermetic writer like his Irish contemporary W. B. Yeats, who criticized Shaw for his "cold logic," although both trod similar thematic ground.[1] The "Mystery" of *Candida*'s subtitle, apparently signaling a hermetic aspect of Shaw's play shared with *Getting Married*, has rather nonesoteric textual connotations that emerge in the course of this chapter. As others have pointed out, understanding is a keyword in *Candida*, which is simultaneously both understanding and misunderstanding of textuality and intertextuality, of knowing and not knowing; communication becomes divination of mysteries and secrets (all keywords in the text) of death and sex.[2] But rather than reading these Shaw play-texts as having hidden or secret meanings awaiting divination, a critical or hermeneutical inquiry might be a more useful way to read the authorial messages of the text, whether consciously or unconsciously embedded. And the initiation mystery most relevant here concerns not mystical knowledge, but a mode of knowledge nonetheless. The writer as poet passes through the Imaginary into the Symbolic and thereby acquires a mastery of his vocation as artist, of language as writer. The writing of *Candida* seems to have provided a threshold in Shaw's writing life: his own initiation as playwright. Immediately after finishing it, he expressed a completely new certainty about his own capacity as dramatist in a letter to fellow playwright Henry Arthur Jones: "you will at once detect an enormous assumption on my part that I am a man of genius. But what can I do—on what other assumption am I to proceed if I am to write plays at all?" (*Letters 1*, 462).

Shaw's simple drama of *Candida*, which consists of one set and six characters with the action taking place in three acts in a single day, aims to be a textual Gesamtkunstwerk with references and allusions to many texts and different arts, including music, the visual arts, mythology, poetry, as well as drama. Whereas Wagner's sense of the total artwork is an Imaginary manifestation of many different arts, Shaw's play-texts draw on the *textual* elements of different arts as signifiers within the textuality of his own work. Thus, there is always a movement from the image to the word, from the Imaginary to the Symbolic in the Shaw text, as well as a going beyond. The Shaw text as drama, in this sense, has much in common with the "glass-bead game" played in Hermann Hesse's novel of that name, in which reading, even for the spectator in the theater, becomes a game, a social ritual, a playing with counters of heterogeneous signifiers of signifiers (rather than of signifieds) drawn from many different cultural source-texts played out on Shaw's stage, a textual heterogeneous space-time beyond the homogeneous logocentric diegesis of the Imaginary narrative. The spectator-readers can decide at what level of participation they will play, and the simpler levels of the play-text allow for the spectator-readers' Imaginary satisfactions. Thus Candidamaniacs, as Shaw called them, can flourish and such entertainments as *My Fair Lady* or *The Chocolate Soldier* can be extracted from the Shaw text. Even a theater for puritans can allow the spectators to be seduced by the pleasures of the text in the theater before they adopt a more participatory and critical attitude to the reading-game in the library.

Candida and Its Mystery

Three disparate texts published in serial form in London in the early 1890s seem to have had an influence on the textual Gesamtkunstwerk that is *Candida*: the famous Kelmscott Press publication of Chaucer's *Canterbury Tales*, printed by Shaw's friend and pre-Raphaelite poet-designer, William Morris; the English translation of Wagner's major prose work, *Opera as Drama* (1852); and James Frazer's *The Golden Bough*, which supplied Shaw with an anthropological/mythological background, for not only *Candida* but probably also *Getting Married* and other plays. The influences of Wagnerian opera and classical mythology are discussed later, but first the Morris reference can prize apart a few strands of the text. The most obvious are Morris's pre-Raphaelitism and the importance to the pre-Raphaelites of the art of the late Middle Ages and early Renaissance. Pre-Raphaelitism as an art movement allowed Shaw to claim, in relation to *Candida* (his "pre-Raphaelite play"), that "religion was alive again, coming back upon men, even upon clergymen, with such power that not the Church of England itself could keep it out" (*Prefaces*, 728). Links have been made between *Candida* and Chaucer's "Franklin's Tale": both are parodies of the literary tradition of honor and courtly love in the triangle between the knight, his liege, and his lady (the wife of his lord). As suggested in chapter 5, the title of Shaw's parody of *Candida*, *How He Lied to Her Husband*, refers ironically to this literary tradition of courtly love and poetry. Shaw probably had Chaucer in mind as a form of textual counterpoint to his more modern allusions to Ibsen's *The Doll's House*, about which many commentators have written, including Shaw himself. Shaw typically complicates the reference; that is, while the Lancelot figure of Marchbanks assumes for the most part the role of the perfect Christian knight, so also in some aspects does the Reverend James Mavor Morell, Eugene's antagonist and Candida's husband, the crusading Christian Socialist pastor who fights against the evils of capitalism and poverty in a poor district of the East End of the thriving imperial metropolis that was late nineteenth-century London. As Shaw put it in the preface: "To distil the quintessential drama from pre-Raphaelitism, medieval or modern, it must be shewn at its best in conflict with the first broken, nervous, stumbling attempts to formulate its own revolt against itself as it develops into something higher" (*Prefaces*, 729). Hope for restoring the wasteland (Chaucer's "droghte of March") of sick Christian civilization lies with not only Morell's Christian Socialism but also the "mad" poet, Eugene Marchbanks. Eugene, in choosing chastity (according to genre convention), incarnates the pure fool persona in Wagner's *Parsifal*—another work rooted in medieval literature, Wolfram von Eschenbach's *Parzifal*. Not at all coincidentally, Chaucer and *Parsifal* also contributed to T. S. Eliot's famous twentieth-century depiction of the modern wasteland.

Both *Candida: A Mystery* and *Getting Married: A Disquisitory Play* deal with their own writing as drama; both draw on their textual history and social function in terms of quasireligious ritual. Like the medieval play-cycles presented by the trade guilds, they are dramatic-religious "Mysterys" that matter-of-factly fuse the human and the divine. Shaw invokes this connection to the guilds by describing the Reverend Morell as *"an active member of the Guild of Saint Matthew."* Thus, Shaw draws on at least two medieval literary traditions: courtly poetry and the Mystery plays. In a letter to his translator Trebitsch (August 18, 1906), Shaw explained that, "I often have to go behind the popular use of a word into its etymology to get it quite right" (*Shaw-Trebitsch*, 110), and in etymological terms *mystery* here is associated with the word *master, mister,* or in German *Meister*. Another source meaning for "mystery" is *mystes*, the word for the initiate in the classical Mysteries, both Eleusinian and Dionysian (see later). But for now, insofar as Eugene is the initiate in the play, Shaw seems to be speaking of self-mastery. And, shortly after Shaw has again mentioned the Guild of St Matthew in the stage directions, the word *master* is given special emphasis in the dialogue leading into the famous final discussion in the last part of Act III.

CANDIDA. Eugene: I asked you to go. Are you going?

MORELL [*putting his foot down*] He shall not go. I wish him to remain.

MARCHBANKS. I'll go. I'll do whatever you want. [*He turns to the door*].

CANDIDA. Stop! [*He obeys*] Didn't you hear James say he wished you to stay? James is master here. Don't you know that?

MARCHBANKS [*flushing with a young poet's rage against tyranny*] By what right is he master?

CANDIDA [*quietly*] Tell him, James.

MORELL [*taken aback*] My dear: I don't know of any right that makes me master. I assert no such right. (*Plays*, 149)

The apposition of the title and subtitle, *Candida: A Mystery*, serves as a typical Shavian deconstruction. As Margery Morgan has noted, Candida has connotations of white, as well as shining and bright, which applies also to other Shaw heroines such as Blanche Sartorius and Ann Whitefield.[3] Candida in incarnating the nexus of metaphors of vision, light, sight, and image might appear as an epitome of heliocentric logocentrism, of that eighteenth-century rationalism that Voltaire satirized in his blank (*blanc*) slate, *Candide*. Yet, as connotations associated with the word *mystery* include obscuring and shutting one's eyes, Shaw's full title may be read as an aporia with something of the contradictory meaning evident in the title of a much later work on marriage as mystery, Stanley Kubrick's last film, *Eyes Wide Shut* (1999).[4]

On the subject of names, Shaw deliberately exploited the fin-de-siècle concept of aesthetic degeneracy in *The Philanderer* and "A Degenerate's View of Nordau." Moreover, the name of the poet in *Candida*, Eugene ("well-born"), refers with some irony to Francis Galton's new science of eugenics. Certainly, Eugene, who might have been partly modeled on the pre-Raphaelite—and masochist (that is, degenerate)—poet Swinburne, is seemingly the reverse of the mentally and physically superior man, like Morell perhaps, that the so-called science of eugenics was supposed to develop for the maintenance and development of Galton's British Empire. Eugene, although well born in having upper-class connections (a grand-nephew to an earl), displays all the symptoms of the late nineteenth-century degenerate neurasthenic type of artist criticized by Nordau in *Degeneration*.

Another tradition beyond poetic literature that contributes strongly to the textual Gesamtkunstwerk of *Candida*, as to so many Shaw plays, is visual iconography. Shaw's appreciation of the figurative arts and their history is as fundamental to *both* the Imaginary *and* the Symbolic of his theater as is his better-known understanding of music, which he always maintained was a more powerful influence on his writing than literature. His ideas on art were heavily influenced by Ruskin and the pre-Raphaelites, including Morris, and a major visual reference for the title character is the well-known painting of Proserpine by the leading pre-Raphaelite painter, Dante Gabriel Rossetti. In like fashion, Burne-Jones's series of Pygmalion paintings probably provided a more immediate source than Ovid for Shaw's later play, *Pygmalion* (Mrs Higgins, an older Candida possibly, is specifically associated in that text with Burne-Jones and Rossetti). In the summer, *before* beginning to write *Candida*, Shaw had scoured Europe looking at visual representations of the Virgin Mother. He made a detour to Darmstadt to see a Madonna by Holbein on a visit to Bayreuth, and he had seen a Botticelli Madonna among others on a trip to Florence earlier in 1894. In the preface to *Plays Pleasant* Shaw writes about the context for the composition of *Candida*: when he returned to England after his 1891 trip to Italy he visited the Birmingham art gallery, where he had been more impressed by the contemporary British (that is, pre-Raphaelite) art than by that of the old masters in Italy. In the published play, the stage directions specify "*a large autotype of the chief figure in Titian's Assumption of the Virgin*" (*Plays*, 124) above the fireplace although the holograph manuscript had specified a "Large photograph of the Madonna di San Sisto [Raphael's painting located in Dresden] above the mantelshelf" (*Candida: Holograph*, 7). The irony, in a play that proclaims its pre-Raphaelitism, is that *neither* of these chosen depictions of the Virgin is pre-Raphaelite (in either the fifteenth- or nineteenth-century sense)—and one is actually painted by Raphael. Yet again Shaw's inclusiveness refuses to make an either/or distinction. His characteristic both/and provides us with a *textual* contrast and an invitation to read beyond the binary opposition.

Rossetti's painting of Proserpine with her dark brown hair and pomegranate in hand, as well as Titian's and Raphael's paintings, seem to have provided the visual models for his title character, which could be why Shaw was outraged when Janet Achurch, for whom the part was written, dyed her hair "a refulgent yellow" (*Letters 1*, 506) before going on tour with *Candida* in the United States (a production that did not come off).[5] Rossetti's actual model for this painting and many others was William Morris's wife, Jane Burden, who might have lent the first three letters of both her married and maiden names to Candida MORell, née BURgess. Mrs. Morris, the pre-Raphaelites' most notable model and whose affections lay more with Rossetti than with her husband, certainly represented a living example of the fantasy/reality dichotomy in art for Shaw, as she was relatively commonplace in person, at least in Shaw's experience at meals in the Morris home.[6] Part of the secret in the poet's heart at the end of *Candida* is that the scales have dropped from his eyes in respect of this dichotomy; the mystery regarding the object of his affection is no longer mysterious. He has learned from Candida to distinguish the divine from the merely human (or the human from the merely divine) and so fades into the night—in this reading, out into the Symbolic dark, into that world beyond the light of the sun and the Imaginary of Platonic reason (beyond the metaphor of light and light of metaphor)—to pursue his vocation as poet, as writer. Notwithstanding his scolding of Janet Achurch, Shaw must have mischievously enjoyed the disjunction between the most famous pre-Raphaelite pictorial representation of Proserpine and *his* Proserpine, whose name is given not to Candida, but to her husband's secretary "Prossy"—whom he describes as *"a brisk little woman of about 30 . . . cheaply dressed"* (*Plays*, 124).

Another visual source on the classical side worth considering, given its thematic relevance to the reading proposed here, might have been a little-known engraving by William Blake of the famous Portland Vase, on which Keats later wrote his possibly even more famous "Ode to a Grecian Urn"; this attribution raises the possibility that, when considering Keats's poem and Shaw's *Candida*, the Portland Vase gave rise to at least two major works of nineteenth-century English literature.[7] The provenance of Blake's engraving was Erasmus Darwin's book, *Botanic Garden* (1791), an early evolutionary text, which makes it more likely that Shaw, with interests in both Blake and evolutionary theory, might have known it. The actual representations on the urn are difficult to ascertain now, but for both Blake and Darwin the designs no doubt represented a mystery of a neo-Platonic variety, which depicted the visit of a soul to the Underworld ruled by Hades and his wife, Persephone or Proserpine. Darwin and Blake derived their knowledge of neo-Platonism (as did most writers in English until the end of the nineteenth century) from the work of their friend Thomas Taylor, translator of Plato and Plotinus, and in particular from Taylor's *On The Eleusinian and Bacchic Mysteries* (Amsterdam, 1790), a text that makes explicit the connection between the Eleusinian and Bacchic mysteries imputed to Shaw in this chapter. Taylor indeed might well have been another source, along with Frazer, for the mythological background to Shaw's play with its allusions to the myths of Demeter and Proserpine and of Dionysus. Blake's engraving of the second compartment of the vase provides a striking visual analogy for the tableau at the end of *Candida*, where the spirit or soul, depicted as a young man preparing to leave the underworld, refuses the blandishments to remain there with its Lord, Hades, and his wife, Proserpine.

By suggesting analogies between Blake's engraving and Shaw's last act, questions of textuality are raised in relation to both classical mythology and neo-Platonism. Shaw's visual analogies invariably lead toward the textual by showing how the Imaginary of the Shaw theater functions as part of its Symbolic. Indeed, Blake's engraving depicts the neo-Platonic journey of the soul into and out of Hell that became part of Shaw's general thematic iconography in not only *Candida* but also the three later Heaven and Hell plays, especially the *Don Juan in Hell* scene, where hell is the home of ideals, of death, a world of the Imaginary from where the artist-philosopher Don Juan seeks the way to heaven at the end. In *Candida*, the poet also leaves the Imaginary underworld at the end to pursue his vocation as poet in the Symbolic night, as suggested by Blake's engraving.

For this reason, an alternative title for *Candida* might be "Eugene in Hell." In mythic terms, the play is a drama of a young poet's journey to the underworld ruled over by Hades and his wife Persephone in the persons respectively of the poet Eugene Marchbanks, a latter-day Orpheus who does not look back, and the Reverend James Mavor Morell and his wife, Candida ("Morell" could be seen as a conflation of "moral" and "hell"!). Yet this encounter with death in life, a descent into the underworld, has its own deconstruction, a visual/textual context, where, as always in the Shaw text, the visual elements specified for the staging in the text have textual thematic significance: the reproduction of *"the central figure"* of Titian's *Assumption of the Virgin*. Thus, not only is the underworld differed and deferred from heaven (that is, descent from ascent, the poet from the muse, the man from the woman), but so also is the classical world differed and deferred from the Christian world; the post-Raphaelite world in the person of Titian is contrasted to the pre-Raphaelite, and the Protestant clergyman's home to the Catholic representation of the Virgin Mary. "There is only one religion, though there are a hundred versions of it," Shaw wrote in the preface before insisting that unity "is fatal to drama; for every drama must present a conflict" (*Prefaces*, 728–29). The allusiveness in the textuality of the play, therefore, is presented in terms of contrasts, often where one supplants the other, as Christianity supplanted the religion of the classical gods.

In Catholic doctrine, where the Assumption of the Virgin is the fourth of the Glorious Mysteries, the Christian sacraments are understood in terms of the mystery of the second person of the Trinity taking human form, so that human experience becomes part of divine experience · (*Et incarnatus est de Spiritu Sancto, ex Maria Virgine: et homo factus est*). The specific sacrament expressing this mystery is marriage in which identities are dissolved and reformed. In classical terms, this becomes a reenactment of the sacred marriage between the Hierophant and the priestess in the Eleusinian Mysteries, which supplies the main subject of both this play and, especially, *Getting Married*. Christ, however, like Marchbanks in the play, forwent marriage, and his unlikely equivalent in the classical world was Dionysus, a god who was also killed and resurrected and whose festival marks the beginning of classical drama.

Dionysus, as Nietzsche famously argued in *The Birth of Tragedy* (1872), epitomized the irrational beneath the rational Apollonian surface of the classical world. Shaw had probably read Nietzsche by the time he wrote *Candida*, as the Dionysian or Bacchic allusions are made quite clear with almost everyone in the play being called "mad" at one stage or another, with Marchbanks's wild dance in Act II, and with the drunken scene in Act III. The name Marchbanks may well refer to the month (March) when the dramatic religious festival of classical tragedy and the satyr plays was held in honor of Dionysus. If so, it would function as a counterpoint to October, specified as the time when both the play's action occurs and the Eleusinian Mysteries were celebrated in honor of Demeter. As a phonetic spelling of the original Marjoribanks with its suggestion of March flowers, Marchbanks may also indicate spring (although it could likewise refer to Chaucer's "drought of March"), which makes sense in a play drawing on the Proserpine legend.[8] Dionysus, a god of vegetation (of corn like Demeter) was famously associated with grapes, with wine and harvest time, when the play is set. Thus each myth refers to the time associated with the other. According to Frazer, "pomegranates were supposed to have sprung from the blood of Dionysus" (Frazer, *Golden Bough*, 389), and pomegranates, of course, are associated with Proserpine. Dionysus was variously presented as being the son of Zeus and Demeter or Persephone or Semele. In one form of the myth, he descended into Hades to bring up his mother (Semele) from the dead. Again, as with Persephone, this represents the experience of winter before the promise of spring. Moreover, like that of Orpheus mentioned earlier, Dionysus's fate lies in being torn apart—by his own followers. Thus, by partaking in the drama of *Candida*—as in the ritual of classical drama, as in attendance at the Christian liturgy—the spectators are visited by the god with Marchbanks adopting the mask of Dionysus. In a letter to James Huneker of April 1904, Shaw wrote of Eugene's leaving the Morell house and going out into the night at the end as "really a god going back to his heaven, proud, unspeakably contemptuous of the "happiness" he envied in the days of his blindness" (*Letters*, 415). He probably had Dionysus in mind. Given the iconography of the play, visitors to the theater play out a somewhat unwitting role as celebrating Bacchantes, an experience of visitation from the young god, Bacchus (Dionysus), perhaps. But Shaw, being Shaw, was not content with a male divinity and insisted also on the feminine, whose visual analogue in the set is the depiction of the Christian Mother of God ascending to heaven.

Nietzsche's *Birth of Tragedy*, which promoted the view of the importance of the Dionysian element—most evident in the festival of Greek tragedy held in honor of Dionysus—to balance that of the Apollonian in Greek life, can be used as a textual background for Shaw's play. The Apollonian is associated with dreams, the visual, and the rational (the principle of individuation—*principium individuationis*), and the Dionysian with intoxication, music, and madness. Nietzsche also makes the link between the mysteries of Dionysus and those of Demeter by referring to tragic heroes like Aeschylus's Prometheus and Sophocles's Oedipus:

> mere masks of this original hero, Dionysus . . . the one truly real Dionysus appears in a variety of forms, in the mask of a fighting hero, and entangled, as it were, in the net of the individual will. . . . the suffering Dionysus of the Mysteries, the god experiencing in himself the agonies of individuation . . . as the origin and primal cause of all suffering. . . . In this existence as a dismembered god, Dionysus possesses the dual nature of a cruel, barbarized demon and a mild, gentle ruler. But the hope of the epopts [those already initiated into the mysteries] looked towards a rebirth of Dionysus, which we must now dimly conceive as the end of individuation . . . this hope alone . . . casts a gleam of joy upon the features of a world torn asunder and shattered into individuals; this is symbolized in the myth of Demeter, sunk in eternal sorrow, who rejoices again for the first time when told that she may *once more* give birth to Dionysus. (Nietzsche, *Tragedy*, 72–74)

Wagner and Drama

At the time of writing *The Birth of Tragedy*, Nietzsche was inspired by Wagner as the exemplar of a new modern Dionysian art of music-drama corresponding to classical tragedy. Wagner's music-dramas are strongly present in the textuality of Shaw's play. But Shaw was thinking of more than Wagner's music; he had recently read the English translation of Wagner's most important prose work mentioned above, *Opera and Drama*, which attempted to lay a theoretical basis for his later operas (or music-dramas, as he preferred them to be called)—parts of *Der Ring*, *Tristan und Isolde*, and *Parsifal*. These last two operas contain elements of courtly love in the Arthurian context, present also in Shaw's play, characteristic of the pre-Raphaelites and as parodied in Chaucer. *Opera and Drama* sought to deconstruct "Opera," particularly the Parisian variety of Grand Opera, to make room for his notion of music-drama, which he proposed as a modern incarnation of classical tragedy. Shaw reviewed Wagner's book with both enthusiasm and skepticism in *The World* on November 1, 1893, and his review sheds an interesting sidelight on reading any, even an admired, author's writing:

> Like all the books which have this mind-changing property—Buckle's History of Civilization, Marx's Capital, and Ruskin's Modern Painters are the first instances that occur to me—[Wagner's famous Opera and Drama] professes to be an extraordinarily erudite criticism of contemporary institutions, and is really a work of pure imagination, in which a great mass of facts is so arranged as to reflect vividly the historical and philosophical generalizations of the author, the said generalizations being nothing more than an eminently thinkable arrangement of his own way of looking at things, having no *objectivity* at all, and owing its *subjective* validity and apparent persuasiveness to the fact that the rest of the world is coming round by mere natural growth to the author's feeling, and therefore wants "proof," historical, philosophical, moral, and so on, that it is "right" in its new view . . . [some people] will never be persuaded by Opera and Drama that opera is a flimsy sham, standing as an inevitable refuse product at the end of a historical evolution in which the rise of Christianity is but an incident. (*Music* 2, 18–19; italics mine)

Wagner looked back to Greek tragedy as the epitome of art for several reasons, *all* of which the text of *Candida* incorporates: combining several arts, retelling of mythology, extolling religious purpose, stressing on the human in their relations with the gods, and involving the whole community. As Shaw suggests, Wagner also saw the transition from the classical world to the Christian world as a decline, one that Wagnerian music-drama aimed to reverse. This opposition of classical and Christian civilizations is also of major relevance in the writing in *Candida*. Despite Wagner's best intentions in putting theory into practice, Shaw, the imperfect Wagnerite, had a certain amount of fun—already evident in the above review—in *The Perfect Wagnerite* by deconstructing *Der Ring* to show that Wagner relapsed into opera, even the despised genre of grand opera.

As for the Wagner operas themselves and their influence on *Candida*, Shaw in comparing Candida to Siegfried, the hero of *Der Ring*, describes her as: "that very immoral female, [who] is as unscrupulous as Siegfried: Morell himself sees that 'no law will bind her.' She seduces Eugene just exactly as far as it is worth her while to seduce him. She is a woman without 'character' in the conventional sense" (*Letters*, 415). Under this sexually promiscuous aspect, Candida is the female equivalent of the male philanderer of Shaw's second play, as discussed in chapter 6, who reappears as Mrs. George in *Getting Married*, discussed at the end of this chapter.

Apart from *Die Walküre* (the second of the Ring tetralogy), Wagner's most successful music-dramas were *Tristan und Isolde* and *Parsifal*, both of which Shaw threaded into the textuality of *Candida*. Chapter 5 already referred to the association Shaw himself made between *Candida* and *Parsifal* in the holograph manuscript of *How He Lied*. In *Parsifal*, drama becomes indistinguishable from ritual, as Shaw, the music critic, wrote from Bayreuth—Wagner's own festival for initiates and the only place where *Parsifal* was performed—on August 7, 1889: "The performance [of *Parsifal*] is regarded on all hands as a rite" (*Music 1*, 730). The last act of *Parsifal* is, in fact, a Wagnerian version of the Christian Good Friday service. *Candida* does not go quite as far as that. The closest to an actual service happens offstage with the Reverend Morell's political speech just prior to Act III. The play, though, is plentiful in ritualistic moments, such as Candida going behind Morell and bending over to kiss him Act II, or her bringing in the lamp in the same act, or her making Eugene give her rug, cloak, and hat in the middle of Act I. Especially telling is Eugene's gesture at the very end of Act III, just before "*he flies out into the night*": "*She takes his face in her hands; and as he divines her intention and falls on his knees, she kisses his forehead*" (*Plays*, 152). A chaste kiss follows, quite different from the one Kundry gives Parsifal in Wagner's opera.

But the ritual of *Candida* is not confined to gestures. Shaw's drama takes place in a setting presided over by a priest, with one of its main features a fireplace dominated by a reproduction of an actual altarpiece, a painting of (according to one religious tradition) the mother of god. Shaw's theater becomes his temple, a ritual space, to which the participants—both characters and spectators as initiates—return night after night, where the soul, or subjective identity, may be created and re-created in a repetition of the soul's journey to the underworld, the Imaginary, and back.

In the already-quoted review, Shaw refers to the turning point of the music-drama, when Parsifal recoils from Kundry's kiss: "That long kiss of Kundry's from which [Parsifal] learns so much is one of those pregnant simplicities which stare the world in the face for centuries and yet are never pointed out except by great men" (*Music 1*, 731). Shaw obviously intended an association be made between Parsifal's rejection of Kundry's sexual advances and Marchbanks's "*secret in the poet's heart*" as he "*flies out into the night.*" This association, although not having a direct parallel in the play, can be used to see how the text of *Parsifal* intersects with that of *Candida* (we may even note an assonance between Candida's and Kundry's names—her father calls her Candy).

Shaw started to write *Candida* on October 2, 1894 ("*A fine October morning*" (*Pleasant*, 79) are the first words in the play-text) having seen *Parsifal, twice* during the summer at Bayreuth.[9] Wagner's conception of "*der reine Tor*" (the pure fool) with its Arthurian background was fresh in Shaw's mind because not only had he recently attended the opera but also he was preparing to deliver a lecture on *Parsifal* on October 16, 1894, to none other than the Guild of Saint Matthew, organized by his Christian Socialist friend—and one model for the Reverend Morell—the Reverend Stewart Headlam.[10] Ironically Shaw's reading of *Parsifal*, which embraced (that is, went beyond) the contradictions of Wagner's apparent *volte face* in composing the anti-Dionysian ascetic Christian Arthurian *Parsifal* after the sensuous pagan Celtic *Tristan und Isolde*, may have been more Nietzschean than Nietzsche. Wagner's grafting of the Christian liturgical rite onto his opera in the context of sexual chastity turned Nietzsche, the would-be Dionysian, anti-Christian disciple of Wagner, into a strident and somewhat shrill anti-Wagnerian in such tracts as *The Case of Wagner* and *Nietzsche contra Wagner*.

Parsifal is about salvation for both the individual and civilization. As Shaw puts it in an 1894 review: "The leading poetic theme is that of the innocent greenhorn (I really cannot give a more becoming translation of *der reine Thor*) who, guided only by his instinct of compassion for suffering, finds the way of salvation" (*Music 3*, 293). Louis Crompton has already noted the *Parsifal/Candida* parallel at the point in the play when the poet feels the preacher's pain as Candida chides him, which alludes to Parsifal feeling the pain of the wound of Amfortas and thereby learning the Wagnerian lesson of "*durch Mitleid wissend*" (wisdom through pity).[11] Shaw himself confirms the allusion in a letter to Richard Mansfield, scheduled to play Eugene in a first New York production with Janet Achurch before the production fell through: "The passage where you put your hand on your heart with a sympathetic sense of the stab Morell has suffered is cribbed from Wagner's *Parsifal*" (*Letters 1*, 499). Both phrases *der reine Tor*–usually translated as "pure fool"—and durch Mitleid wissend are threaded through this opera as ritualistic refrains, textual leitmotivs, which might have suggested Shaw's rhetorical technique in *Candida* of repeating keywords, as noted by King and Morgan. Shaw, fearless in conflating conflicting myths, translates the Christian myth of the quest for the Grail into Morell's Christian Socialism in his play, while also adopting the context of the conflict between sexuality and chastity at the heart of *Parsifal*. Kundry, who tempts Parsifal with her kiss, is one of the oddest characters in drama, and she shares with Shaw's Candida a marked bifurcation as sexual temptress and maternal healer. Both Shaw's play and Wagner's music-drama are telling (at least) two stories at the same time: one about the mother, the other about the sexual temptress. We must be prepared to *read* both at the same time.[12]

Nietzsche's criticism of Wagner and, by extension, of Shaw—that the Wagner-Shaw view of chastity is a relapse into mere Christian (that is, self-hating) sexual repression—is countered in both Wagner's opera and Shaw's play. Both works present *two* different forms of chastity: the passionate chastity of Parsifal and Eugene and the sexually repressed celibacy of Klingsor (literally castrated) and Lexy Mill. Thus, Shaw had probably learned from Wagner's opera, as well as from personal experience, that chastity itself represents a need and is, therefore, a *sexual* passion separate to and competing with that of concupiscence, a need to go beyond both the Imaginary of the mother, symbolized by Candida, as well as the Law of the Father in his Oedipal struggle with Morell.[13] Whereas Marchbanks's choice of celibacy at the end allows him to escape the Imaginary relation that Candida represents for him, Morell's tragedy as a married man is to discover he has never escaped that relation—in spite of his own courageous struggle with the Law of the father (personified, of course, in Candida's father, Burgess, against whom Morell fought for the rights of the women working in Burgess's factory; Morell won the argument, but the women lost their jobs). In *The Quintessence of Ibsenism*, Shaw wrote of "that higher development of [love] which Ibsen shews us occurring in the case of Rebecca West in *Rosmersholm* is only known to most of us by the descriptions of great poets, who themselves, as their biographies prove, have often known it, not by sustained experience, but only by brief glimpses. And it is never a first-fruit of their love affairs" (*Non-Dramatic*, 226). This higher love is contrasted to:

> the reckless self-abandonment seen in the infatuation of passionate sexual desire. Everyone who becomes the object of that infatuation shrinks from it instinctively. Love loses its charm when it is not free; and whether the compulsion is that of custom and law, or of infatuation, the effect is the same: it becomes valueless. The desire to give inspires no affection unless there is also the power to withhold; and the successful wooer, in both sexes alike, is the one who can stand out for honourable conditions, and, failing them, go without. (*Non-Dramatic*, 225)

In *Parsifal*, the pure fool, Parsifal, represents the latter while, despite her own tragic self-awareness, Kundry represents the "reckless self-abandonment" of sexual infatuation. In *Candida*, Shaw's pure fool, Eugene, learns to do without, by resisting both the sexual charms and domestic comforts offered by Candida, that "sentimental prostitute," earth goddess, and "Virgin Mother" (*Terry-Shaw*, 99).

While Eugene learns of the dangers of sexual infatuation, he does not learn it as Parsifal learned it from Kundry's long kiss. Still, Shaw's use of this crucial incident in Wagner's opera tells something about his play's textuality. Parsifal escapes from Kundry's embrace with a shriek and remembers Amfortas's sexual wound (in simple Freudian terms, the fear of castration), but the analogous kiss in the play occurs not from Candida kissing Eugene, but when she kisses her husband toward the end of Act II; thus the action *displaces* the reaction of the pure fool figure of Eugene onto his antagonist, the married man Morell.

> [*She laughs, and kisses him to console him. He recoils as if stabbed, and springs up.*]
>
> MORELL. How can you bear to do that when—Oh, Candida [*with anguish in his voice*] I had rather you had plunged a grappling iron into my heart than given me that kiss.
>
> CANDIDA [*amazed*] My dear: what's the matter?
>
> MORELL [*frantically waving her off*] Don't touch me.
>
> CANDIDA. James!!! (*Plays*, 141–42)

This extreme reaction includes not only Kundry's kiss but also her characteristic laugh and Amfortas's spear (Morell's "grappling iron"). Presumably Shaw is making the point, made quite clear at the end of Act III, that Morell is an even purer fool than Eugene. The textual dynamics of the play work for not only Eugene, who acquires his soul at the end by leaving the Morell household like a god returning to his heaven, but also that other soul in hell, the husband, the married man, Shaw's other doll in this variation on Ibsen's *A Doll's House*. Candida's kiss is the opening of Morell's opportunity to acquire his own soul within his marriage, which is opened further at the end with his realization that, so far, he has been living in a fool's marriage, as if in Klingsor's pleasure garden with Prossy possibly representing the flower-maidens! Candida and Morell might not know the secret in the poet's heart at the end, but they might have come to *understand* something as to their own secrets in the chasm that has opened in their marriage by the end of the play.

From Parsifal's pity for (the pain of) Amfortas comes the wisdom that will restore the Arthurian civilization that has relapsed into a wasteland for the Knights of the Holy Grail. Eugene learns Parsifal's "durch Mitleid wissend" just a little later in Act II, when Candida, unaware of the pain she is causing her husband, continues to tease him:

CANDIDA. This comes of James teaching me to think for myself, and never to hold back out of fear of what other people may think of me. It works beautifully as long as I think the same things as he does. But now! because I have just thought something different! look at him! Just look! [*She points to Morell, greatly amused*].

Eugene looks, and instantly presses his hand on his heart, as if some pain had shot through it. He sits down on the sofa like a man witnessing a tragedy.

BURGESS [*on the hearthrug*] Well, James, you certnly haint as himpressive lookin as usu'l.

MORELL [*with a laugh which is half a sob*] I suppose not. I beg all your pardons: I was not conscious of making a fuss. [*Pulling himself together*] Well. Well, well, well, well! [*He sets to work at his papers again with resolute cheerfulness*].

CANDIDA [*going to the sofa and sitting beside Marchbanks, still in a bantering humor*] Well, Eugene: why are you so sad? Did the onions make you cry?

> *Morell cannot prevent himself from watching them.*[14]
>
> MARCHBANKS [*aside to her*] It is your cruelty. I hate cruelty. It is a horrible thing to see one person make another suffer.
>
> CANDIDA [*petting him ironically*] Poor boy! have I been cruel? Did I make it slice nasty little red onions?
>
> MARCHBANKS [*earnestly*] Oh, stop, stop: I don't mean myself. You have made him suffer frightfully. I feel his pain in my own heart. I know that it is not your fault: it is something that must happen; but don't make light of it. I shudder when you torture him and laugh.
>
> CANDIDA [*incredulously*] *I* torture James! Nonsense, Eugene: how you exaggerate! Silly! [*She looks round at Morell, who hastily resumes his writing. She goes to him and stands behind his chair, bending over him*]. Don't work any more dear. Come and talk to us.[15] (*Pleasant*, 126)

Note how, for a moment, Eugene becomes the spectator *"witnessing a tragedy,"* as Shaw makes clear that his drama—and Wagner's—reaches back to the origins of classical tragedy, in which, of course, Dionysus was the ultimate spectator of his own story witnessed by his followers, the Bacchantes, and in the theater by the initiates, the spectators. Candida's laugh again associates her with Kundry. Shaw comically reprises this episode of misunderstanding and pity in the final scene when Marchbanks feels sympathy for Morell, just after Candida has announced she has decided which of the two men to choose. Morell thinks she has chosen Marchbanks; Marchbanks knows she has chosen Morell.

> *Eugene divines her meaning at once: his face whitens like steel in a furnace.*
>
> MORELL [*bowing his head with the calm of collapse*] I accept your sentence, Candida.
>
> CANDIDA. Do you understand, Eugene?
>
> MARCHBANKS. Oh, I feel I'm lost. He cannot bear the burden.
>
> MORELL [*incredulously, raising his head and voice with comic abruptness*] Do you mean me, Candida? (*Plays*, 151)

Somewhat confusingly, if typically, given the thematic concerns of chastity and celibacy shared between *Parsifal* and *Candida*, Shaw also refers us to Wagner's other major music-drama, *Tristan und Isolde*, the opera of the conflict between the knightly code of honor and the self-abandonment of sexual infatuation. For instance, Tristan's *knowing* the cup offered him to drink is poisoned in Act I is similar to Morell's *knowing* Candida has chosen Marchbanks at the end of Act III: in both cases their knowledge was courageously borne, but wrong (unknown to both Tristan and Isolde, the death draught had been changed to a love draught). Again, Shaw as dramatist displays a critic's percipience by *displacing* moments of Wagner's music-drama onto different characters and different scenes. Here, at the end of Act III of *Candida*, Marchbanks goes out into the night (that is, to accept death), and, in metaphorical terms through this reference to Act I of *Tristan und Isolde*, so also does Morell.

In a rare direct comment on the textuality and intertextuality of his writing, Shaw on March 8, 1920, recommended to some school students, who were trying to puzzle out the meaning of the end of *Candida* that they should embark on "a course of the poets on the subject of the Night. Begin with something simple, like Act V of *The Merchant of Venice*, and then work on, not forgetting Byron's "She Walks in Beauty Like the Night" until you finish up with Wagner's *Tristan and Isolde*, where you will find the complete repudiation of the day and acceptance of the night as the true realm of the poet." In a very early theater review (unpublished at the time, April 7, 1880), Shaw had described how the night scene in *The Merchant of Venice*, together with the scene of Bassanio's choice, were written to satisfy the Elizabethan demand for poetry in the playhouse; they were "not merely poetically conceived episodes, but pieces of poetry intentionally offered to the public as such . . . [both] are unsurpassed in fiction" (*Drama 1*, 6). By drawing on this textual poetic tradition, Shaw was aiming at a similar poetic effect at the end of *Candida*; the poetry, therefore, in Shaw's text lies in the implications of such allusions, in the textuality of the play itself, rather than in the much criticized juvenile gushings of his young poet.[16]

Of course, *Tristan* supplies for Shaw's pre-Raphaelite drama what *Parsifal* lacks, a model of a classic tale of courtly love involving a knight's wooing of his lord's lady—taken to the extreme situation of sexual completion. Technically Isolde is not married to King Mark, but in terms of the knightly code of honor, Tristan, who has been sent to bring back Isolde so that she may be married to Mark, is as seriously in breach of that code as if they were already married. And Wagner is in breach of the conventions of the art of courtly love by having Tristan and Isolde enjoy sexual congress. Yet in Wagner, the night, "*das Wunderreich der Nacht*" (the wondrous realm of night), is death, representing a sexual union beyond carnal need—for even in *Tristan und Isolde* there is an ascetic aspect to the love story. Above all, it connotes a rejection of the Imaginary of everyday life such as the vision of domestic heaven (or hell depending on point of view) that Candida offers Eugene in Shaw's play. Whereas Eugene, who reminds Candida that "in a hundred years, we shall be the same age" (*Plays*, 152), goes out into the night alone, Tristan asks Isolde if she will follow him to "the sacred realm of night from which my mother sent me forth," which he later describes as "the boundless realm of endless night, and there we know one thing only: endless godlike all forgetting!" (Wagner, *Tristan and Isolde*, 78, 81) Whereas Isolde sings her transfiguration aria over Tristan's dead body, Candida (in her Proserpine aspect) prefers to remain in the domestic hell of her happy marriage. And Eugene's going out into the night is both a form of death and a rebirth following the experience of death that was his journey to the underworld and back and that we have witnessed in the day's events that constitute the drama of *Candida*.

In this quasi-Ibsenite domestic drama of late nineteenth-century naturalism that inverts, at least, *A Doll's House* (which itself inverted the formal schema of the French well-made play), Shaw introduces his own highly complex formal apparatus of textuality, a Symbolic where both characters and situations become highly mutable in terms of referentiality. In applying one text to another, Shaw is not performing a simple mapping operation, neither from situation to situation nor from character to character. Morell as well as Marchbanks share aspects of both Tristan and Parsifal. Candida is both Demeter and Persephone, both Kundry and the Virgin Mother, just as Kundry is both self-denying caregiver and sexual temptress.

A final allusion to *Tristan and Isolde* comes at the end of Act II of *Candida*, and this does refer to the end of Act II of Wagner's opera. After Tristan, resigned to death, asked Isolde to follow him to the wondrous realm of the night and she agreed, "*Tristan bends slowly over her and kisses her gently on the forehead.*" This ritual gesture instigates the catastrophic end of the act when Tristan is mortally wounded. In *Candida*, Morell for the first time takes the initiative from Candida, and, with a gesture worthy of King Mark in Wagner's opera accompanied by a textual emphasis on the key word *understand*, he tells her to remain behind with Marchbanks when he goes out with the others to give his speech to the Guild of Saint Matthew.

CANDIDA [*Greatly troubled*] I cant understand—

MORELL [*taking her tenderly in her arms and kissing her on the forehead*] Ah, I thought it was *I* who couldn't understand, dear. (*Plays*, 144)

Classical Mysteries as Drama

Renaissance painting is contrasted in the text with pre-Raphaelite painting, and the medieval world is contrasted with its own depiction in nineteenth-century pre-Raphaelitism, but the whole Christian tradition is contrasted, as in Wagner, with the classical world and its mythology. The latter's place in the textual design of *Candida* is now considered. Both parts of the title *Candida: A Mystery* allude to Demeter (Ceres), the Goddess of the Corn, the White Goddess (later made famous by Robert Graves as the basis of his theory of poetry) in whose honor the most famous festivities of the ancient world were held, the Eleusinian Mysteries.[17] At the heart of the Eleusinian Mysteries and the myths associated with Demeter is the conquest of death, an understandable association in relation to the goddess of fertility. Demeter's story is often twinned with that of her daughter, Persephone, also known as Proserpine, Queen of the Underworld. In acknowledging the cyclical rhythm of death and life as manifested in the seasons, the myth of Proserpine proposes that the idea of death can be conquered. The visual symbol of this in the ancient mysteries seems to have been the manifestation of an ear of corn grown from the *white* seed sown in the ground during the winter.

As in the myth itself, Candida displays aspects of both the mythological mother and daughter. In terms of classical mythology, Mrs. James Morell née Burgess incarnates the white goddess, the triple goddess—Demeter, Proserpine, and the crone—and perhaps also Hera, the goddess of the hearth. Frazer's *The Golden Bough* was the most obvious source for Shaw's information about mythology, although the goddess of fertility and her troubled daughter were much in the air when Shaw wrote his play. The German scholar J. J. Bachofen had put forward the theory of the mother goddess as far back as 1866. The same year, the pre-Raphaelite poet Swinburne published his poem "Hymn to Proserpine," using the persona of a Roman looking back on the old religion after the conversion of the Empire to Christianity. Pater's essay on "Demeter and Proserpine" appeared in 1876 (republished in book form in 1895). And Tennyson wrote his Demeter and Proserpine poem in 1889. Like other mythological or classical names Shaw later used for his characters—including Lesbia, Hypatia, and Lilith—Proserpine, as the independent daughter, was an inspiration to feminists and had become a symbol for the New Woman in the 1890s. In fact, Shaw had *already* portrayed this aspect of the Demeter/Persephone dyad in the mother and daughter figures of Kitty and Vivie Warren in *Mrs Warren's Profession*; indeed, the relation between the myth of Demeter and Proserpine and the play-text is more oblique in *Candida* than in *Mrs Warren's Profession*. In *Candida* the New Woman is Morell's typist, just as not the wealthy Tanner, but his chauffeur Henry Straker, represents the New Man in *Man and Superman*. Both the New Man and the New Woman represented a whole new class of independent men and women making their ways in the world at the end of the nineteenth century, people for whom Shaw's plays seem to have provided great inspiration.

Demeter nursing the child Demophoon, in her attempts to make him immortal, might have contributed to the relation between Candida and Eugene. As the Homeric *Hymn to Demeter* puts it, Demophoon "grew like a god, not nourished on mortal food but anointed by Demeter with ambrosia just as though sprung from the gods, and she breathed sweetness upon him as she held him to her bosom. At night she would hide him in the might of the fire, like a brand" (Morford and Lenardon, *Mythology*, 223–24). The fire-place (fire is an attribute of Demeter) is an important part of the play's set design, especially at the beginning of Act III, when Marchbanks reads her his poems in front of the fire. The Homeric myth's Triptolemus, sometimes conflated with Demophoon, serves as another model for Marchbanks: "Triptolemus, who also appears in the concluding lines of the *Hymn*, is generally depicted as the messenger of Demeter when she restored fertility to the ground. He is the one who taught and spread her arts of agriculture. . . . He is sometimes merged in identity with the infant Demophoon . . . in Plato, Triptolemus is a judge of the dead" (Morford and Lenardon, *Mythology*, 230–31).

Candida and Prossy, who is one of the play's three subsidiary characters, are unlikely shadows of each other. Unlike in the myth and unlike Candida herself, who incarnates aspects of both Demeter and Persephone, Prossy is quite separate from the Demeter character. By making her second name "Garnett" (etymologically related to pomegranate, the seeds of which Persephone ate in the underworld), the text reinforces the link to the myth of Demeter and her daughter. The symbolism of the Demeter/

Proserpine dyad is made more general by a certain animosity between the two, as in Prossy's exasperation at the men's infatuation with Candida (despite her claims to *understand* Candida better than any of the men) and Candida ensuring her husband does not have a good-looking secretary by dismissing Prossy's prettier predecessors. Prossy is secretly in love with Morell. Psychologically, her living death is the result of this undeclared and unrequited passion—"Prossy's complaint," as Candida bitchily calls it in the text. Socially, as an enterprising independent young woman at the end of the nineteenth century, Prossy has gone into the labor marketplace, perhaps displaying some attributes of the virgin huntress Artemis, and ends up duly exploited by her employer, a point made quite clear to the audience, albeit in humorous fashion. Morell makes his secretary do both the work she is paid for and, by playing on her sexual susceptibility, the unpaid domestic chore of helping him wash the dishes. This enlarges on the thesis of *Mrs Warren's Profession*: poverty causes women who sell their labor in the market place to be inevitably exploited. This, though, is a notable intrusion on the duties of the goddess of the hearth, Hera, who in one aspect Candida must also incarnate. Shaw's Prossy, with connotations of prissiness and prosaic-ness (in terms of writing, prose to Marchbanks's poetry) as well as prostitution (temple prostitute), is not beautiful.

In their triple aspect consisting of mother, daughter, and the crone or hag as companion of Persephone in the underworld, they were known as the triple goddess. Although the play has only two onstage female characters, the hag is incarnated in the text by the third (offstage) woman of the household: the aptly named Maria, the Morells' kitchen servant and another ironic *condensation* of the classical and Christian worlds in the contrast of the ever-young virgin with the hag. Candida, whom the holograph manuscript describes as "A true Virgin Mother," points to Maria's haglike aspect after sending Eugene to the kitchen to chop onions: "He will make an excellent cook if he can only get over his dread of Maria" (*Plays*, 140). The final scene cleverly raises this third aspect of Demeter as the hag or crone when Candida herself asks Marchbanks to write a poem on the two sentences: "When I am thirty, she will be forty-five. When I am sixty, she will be seventy-five" (*Plays*, 152). Hecate conveniently fulfills this role in the Demeter myth, although she is also associated in triple aspect with the moon goddess, Selene, and the (virgin) goddess of the earth, Artemis, the huntress, who is often depicted carrying a torch signifying birth, life, and fertility. The text emphasizes this aspect of Candida by having her prosaically clean the lamps (offstage) to the poet's aesthetic horror. The knowing playwright's irony is operative here in showing the poet's practical ignorance of the mythic origins of his vocation, just as we saw the neophyte playwright Fanny was ignorant of the traditions of drama. Candida pointedly makes an entrance bearing a lamp: "*Candida comes in well aproned, with a reading lamp trimmed, filled, and ready for lighting*" (*Plays*, 138). Her apron, no doubt, adds ritual significance to the scene. The triple aspect of the goddess is associated with the seasons: the mother with the time when the earth is plentiful (summer-harvest time); the hag when the land is wasted (winter), the wasteland—a common trope, as we have seen, from Chaucer through Wagner to Eliot; and the daughter with the time of new promise (spring).

An identification of Morell with Hades quickly gives rise to so many ramifications that it would be difficult to follow them all here. Except in his domestic role as Candida's husband, Morell seems an unlikely contender as lord of the Underworld. Another character in the play better fits that description: Morell's aptly named father-in-law and Candida's father, Burgess. From the point of view of the socialist knights-errant, Shaw and Morell, Burgess is certainly a bourgeois capitalist devil. *Plays Unpleasant* had already shown the dependency of the wealthy owners of capital in modern industrialized societies on maintaining poverty by rack-renting and prostitution. Even today, these plays have shock-value for bourgeois audiences, along with a continuing relevance for a critical reading of the social and economic dynamics of capitalist societies. Yet despite Shaw's sympathy, Morell is complicit in Burgess's wasteland, hell, or underworld of bourgeois capitalism. As Proserpine is his employee under the capitalist system personified by Burgess, Morell himself can, for a moment, be taken as the lord of the Underworld to whom Proserpine is in thrall.

Writing *Candida* seems to have served reflexively as Shaw's own initiation into the mysteries of drama and the rituals of the theater, his acknowledgment of Dionysus and his relations to Demeter. But Shaw's *Mystery* provides his reader with a textual *Gesamtkunstwerk* for *understanding*. In this textual *Gesamtkunstwerk*, Morell may also be identified, like Marchbanks, with Dionysus, thus opening up more, quite unsuspected avenues of meaning. The Eleusinian Mysteries in honor of Demeter were associated with those of Dionysus, in whose honor were held the religious festivals for initiates that caused Greek drama to develop; Margery Morgan has already made the link between the play and the Eleusinian and Dionysian mysteries, perhaps the most crucial mythological classical reference in the play. In the play-text, the two are disjunctively associated in the hilarious scene in Act III, when four characters come back after Morell's lecture as intoxicated Bacchants (Bacchus and Dionysus are one and the same). Especially is Prossy drunk! The intoxication is caused by *both* Morell's rhetoric *and* Burgess's champagne (thus equating the two), much as "Dionysos" Undershaft gets Adolphus Cusins drunk in *Major Barbara*. But Candida, reflecting her temperate Demeter aspect, pointedly offers the returning intoxicated revelers only nonalcoholic lemonade. Nevertheless, the Eleusinian Mysteries and those of Dionysus are textually conflated so that for the spectator-initiate in Shaw's theater they represent a marriage between Dionysus-Pluto/Morell and Demeter-Proserpine/Candida, between inspiration and fertility in Shaw's own, and Dionysus-Marchbanks's, work of symbolic textual poetic creation.

Getting Married and the Stage Entrance

The Mysteries of the classical world supply the play-texts of both *Candida* and *Getting Married* with a myth of origins. This self-referential textual evocation of the origins of drama is associated with initiation in *Candida*, with the theme of the poet finding his vocation as artist in a Symbolic, his identity beyond the Imaginary of the narrative diegesis. Just as Marchbanks leaves the Imaginary of the Morell household, so does the spectator leave the Imaginary of the theater at the end of the play, although whether her subjectivity has been transformed depends on individual experience. In this sense, *Candida* can be read as an autobiographical text of initiation into Shaw's own art. The aspects of mythology and religious ritual in the drama of identity that is *Candida* receive different emphases in the later play. In *Getting Married*, the sacred marriage between the hierophant and the Priestess of Demeter performed as part of the Eleusinian Mysteries, which raises the question of social identity in marriage, is brought to the fore.

With its better-known companion play, *Misalliance*, which also observes the classical unities, *Getting Married: A Disquisitory Play* comes in the wake of the hilarious if grim comedy subtitled *The Doctor's Dilemma: A Tragedy* and tends to be overshadowed in terms of both production and criticism by the Heaven and Hell trilogy of plays of *Man and Superman*, *John Bull's Other Island*, and *Major Barbara*. However, *Getting Married*, read as a key work in the Shaw canon, draws on and incorporates much of the drama of *Candida*, again with powerful autobiographical resonances. Exceptionally in Shaw's work, *Getting Married* is prefaced by a technical note explaining it as "a return to unity of time and place as observed in the ancient Greek Drama." Shaw neglects to mention the obvious by unstated notion that *Candida* was the only one of his early plays, or indeed any of his longer plays up to this time, to exemplify the classical unities. Although the action there is not continuous as in *Getting Married* or *Misalliance*, the unities of classical drama (as codified in seventeenth-century French tragedy) only require the action to take place within a twenty-four hour period, which *Candida*, beginning in the morning and ending late at night, quite significantly does.

Getting Married, like many Shaw plays—including *Candida*, which begins self-reflexively with Morell *reading* letters and Prossy *writing* (typing) letters—emphasizes *writing* and *reading* at the outset, although more covertly. The action takes place in the Bishop of Chelsea's palace (a priest's house like Morell's parsonage), more precisely, its fine Norman kitchen (suggestive perhaps of the association of food with religion in both the classical mysteries and Christian liturgy) used as a living room, on the day of his sixth daughter's wedding. Various members of the family and others gather for the wedding for quite a while before the bishop himself appears; by this time the audience knows that he has been all the while (offstage) in his study *writing* a treatise on the history of marriage—not dissimilar, perhaps, to Shaw's own treatise on marriage supplied as preface to the play. At the same time, his daughter (also offstage) has been *reading* a pamphlet as to why women should not marry and his future son-in-law has been *reading* "Belfort Bax's essays on Men's Wrongs" (*Plays*, 561). These offstage readings instigate the action of the play by prompting the prospective bride and groom to decide against "getting married." Onstage, to complement this offstage reading, the play begins with the Bishop's wife *reading The Times* (in respect of which we might note that the large old pendulum clock specified in the stage directions has stopped working, thus providing a timeless setting for Shaw's "disquisitory play").

A lack of structural coherence, a major complaint against his earlier plays, was even more noticeable in *Getting Married*. However, a cursory breakdown of the play shows a very deliberate structure, whether the continuous action is divided into two or three distinct parts; Shaw, however, was adamant that the divisions did not represent acts. If divided in two, the second part (in terms of printed pages) is slightly longer.[18] The first part consists of a slow buildup of entrances of almost all the characters. Shaw saves the remaining three, including the grandest entrance of all, for the second part. Perhaps in no other play of Shaw's is the old theatrical convention (that is, ritual action) of the stage entrance as important as in *Getting Married*, emphasized by the Norman stairwell through which most characters make these entrances. Beginning with two characters onstage, the first half culminates with successive entrances until nine people are assembled onstage at the same time. There they remain for the play's longest and most sustained scene, which lasts nearly twice as long as any other up to that point. Then, Boxer, the Army general seemingly addressing the audience in the theater, announces a possible break with the words: "In the name of common sense and sanity, let us get back to real life" (*Plays*, 566). Immediately in the text, but after the interval for the benefit of the audience, the second part begins with a second entrance for Bill, this time in his alderman's robes, bringing the number of characters onstage up to ten. They remain at that number until twenty pages into the second half when we get the most impressive of all the entrances made by Mrs. George, the Lady Mayoress and Bill's sister-in-law, immediately preceded by her Beadle who announces her arrival. He carries a mace, symbol of her civic office and—with its phallic ritual connotation—of the promiscuous sexuality that Mrs. George embodies within the poetic structure of the play. Having brought the number of characters onstage up to twelve (it may have been a concession on Shaw's part to the superstition notoriously prevalent among the thespian community never to have the full cast of thirteen onstage at any one time), they are then whittled down in an inverse pattern to the first half. Shaw himself suggested a breakdown if two intervals are required, but in either case emphasis is placed on the entrances to such a great degree that the ritual of the stage entrance becomes the drama. In the case of two breaks, the entrances most emphasized are those of Mrs. George (this play's incarnation of the Goddess, as well as of Britannia—Saint George is the patron saint of England—in this very English play) and of St. John Hotchkiss, on whom the drama will increasingly focus and between whom occurs a marriage as analogue of the Sacred Marriage of the Eleusinian Mysteries. Once Mrs. George, certainly the *dea ex machina* of this play, has made her entrance, there is a sudden subsidence of activity. The stage is cleared for a series of scenes involving between two and four characters until toward the end a sort of coda occurs with a rapid accumulation of ten people onstage before quickly dwindling to a mere lone character onstage at the curtain. Ironically in a play about marriage, the belligerent celibate, Soames returns us reflexively to the *writing* with which the play began: "*Soames resumes his writing tranquilly*" (*Plays*, 589).

Original productions of Shaw's plays were frequently criticized because viewers thought that his characters were either versions of himself or, at the very least, his mouthpieces. As one of the great creators of character in dramatic literature, Shaw, in a letter of March 16, 1930, to Lady Rhondda, who had written a series of articles on women in his plays, revealed his relation as author to his characters in terms familiar to poststructuralism:

> In dealing with fictitious characters you must always bear in mind that the author is not the Creator, but only a poor devil faking up simulacra to give an illusion of life to the stage. You can always safely tell him that he does not understand women, because he does not understand even his own little self, and cannot write his own history without being immediately convicted by some prosaic investigator of being all wrong about it. (*Letters 4*, 179)

In this play especially Shaw uses entrances, clothes, names, and social rituals to contribute to the subjectivity of his characters. Whether Shaw's characters were all mouthpieces or simulacra, *Getting Married* turns out to be one of the more autobiographical of Shaw play-texts; in surprising ways he has left traces of his own subjectivity in the text. Toward the end of the play, Hotchkiss—described on his first appearance as *"a very smart young gentleman of twenty-nine or thereabouts, correct in dress to the last thread of his collar, but too much preoccupied with his ideas to be embarrassed by any concern as to his appearance"* (*Plays*, 559)—reveals that his "own pet name in the bosom of my family is Sonny" (*Plays*, 586). "Sonny" is what Shaw's family called him during his miserable childhood in Dublin, a city the Irish writer hated as much as the name of the patron saint of England. And to whom is this intimate detail revealed? None other than Mrs. George! Names are seldom accidental in Shaw's plays, and here the writer makes play with two of his own. His immediate family never called him Bernard. They used George after he became too old for Sonny, although he hated it so much that he never used it on the spine of any of his books as an inscription of authorship. Don't George me! he protested, possibly thinking of the old rhyme: "Georjy porjy pudding and pie kissed the girls and made them cry; when the boys came out to play Georjy Porjy ran away." The critics of the first production would hardly have had the benefit of this biographical knowledge; Henderson's first official biography was not published until 1911, three years after the play was written. Yet, when readers realize that Shaw, as writer, has given this fairly unpleasant character (a close relation of the philanderer, Charteris) his own name, then both the play and its structure, particularly that of the second half, may be better understood.

Structurally, the musical form the play most closely resembles is the baroque *concerto grosso*, where attention alternates between the full band and a small concerted group of individual instruments. Two-thirds of the way through the play, the trio of voices involving Mrs. George, Hotchkiss, and the Bishop come to predominate the discourse. This structural balance is difficult to comprehend without taking into account the autobiographical importance of "Sonny" Hotchkiss ("kissed the girls and made them cry!"), Mrs. George's name, and the Bishop's appearance and demeanor, for the stage directions make it clear that the latter is also modeled on G.B.S.: "*He is still a slim active man . . . (young) by temperament . . . He has a delicate skin, fine hands, a salient nose with chin to match, a short beard which accentuates his sharp chin by jutting forward, clever humorous eyes, not without a glint of mischief in them, ready bright speech, and the ways of a successful man who is always interested in himself and generally rather pleased with himself*" (*Plays*, 555).

The climax of *Getting Married*, the mystery, even if not immediately understood as such, becomes a ritualistic event as Mrs. George goes into a trance and Dionysianically loses her individuality, her principium individuationis, in order to speak for all women. As Nietzsche puts it in *The Birth of Tragedy*: "Dionysian art . . . cries to us with its true, undissembled voice: 'Be as I am! Amid the ceaseless flux of phenomena I am the eternally creative primordial mother, eternally impelling to existence, eternally finding satisfaction in this change of phenomena'" (Nietzsche, *Tragedy*, 104). Shaw's stage, a temple of prophetic utterance, becomes a ritual space associated with the classical world already alluded to in *Candida*. Even more than in *Candida*, spectators are present at a fertility rite, symbolized by the mace-carrying Beadle corresponding to the hierophant of the Eleusinian Mysteries. The hierophant was the priest who showed the sacred objects (the Hiera) associated with Demeter (Collins, when he showed the wedding-cake at the beginning of the play, fills this function). The initiate of the mysteries, corresponding to Hotchkiss, as a stand-in for Shaw's audience, was the *mystes*. The hierophant delivered the mystic utterances of the Oracle, and in the play Mrs. George, in her ecstasy, incarnates the Priestess of Demeter. As Morford and Lenardon put it: "Others insist upon an enactment of the holy marriage in connection with the ceremonies, imagining not a spiritual but a literal sexual union between the hierophant and the Priestess of Demeter" (Morford and Lenardon, *My-*

thology, 235). Immediately after Mrs. George's trance, Cecil and Edith enter to announce that they have just been married. The text highlights the sexual element with a visual reference in its description of Cecil, who throws himself into a chair *"and thrusts his hands into his pockets, like Hogarth's rake, without waiting for Edith to sit down"* (*Plays*, 584).

The end of *Getting Married* suggests that a sexual union outside marriage, between Hotchkiss, the initiate as Hierophant, and the promiscuous Mrs. George, as Priestess of Demeter, will take place—an ironic conclusion in a play about marriage.[19] Unlike the end of *Candida*, when the man walks out on the married couple, the younger man in *Getting Married* is going to walk in on a married couple, on Mrs George and her husband.[20] In a typical Shavian displacement (often obscure to the reader-spectator), this sacred marriage that is not a marriage (as a complement to the pact of assignation between the Bishop and Mrs. George to meet in heaven) between Hotchkiss and Mrs. George, rather than the one between Edith and Cecil that is the ostensible subject of the play's disquisition, becomes Shaw's main dramatic concern. Shaw's theater, his "factory of thought," becomes a (textual) temple for "a cult as eternal and sacred as any professed religion in the world" (*Prefaces*, 779). The stage is turned into a ritualistic space for reenacting the Eleusinian Mysteries associated with the celebrations of Bacchus in classical drama.

The final and, perhaps, grandest entrance is unseen, although the text prepares us for it; the Beadle has been sent off to get the wedding guests all assembled in the Hall before she makes her entrance there. This entrance is, in fact, Mrs. George's stage exit with Hotchkiss, as she leaves the stage to the exact same words from the Beadle that we heard when she first appeared. The sense of ritual, so obvious in the stage entrances, also helps explain the semiotic importance of dress in the play, notably in terms of institutional robes, official costumes, or costumes specific to the particular ritual event whereby the individual assumes, affirms, or transforms a social identity. The same applies to the extraordinary play on names. The design of the fabric of this Shaw play-text, in which entrances, costumes, and names are stitched into the text, along with many disparate threads of mythology, history, drama, and religion, comes to resemble a philosophy of signification and textuality as deconstruction—a philosophy that emerged long after this play was written.

Costumes, Ritual, and Signification

The play begins, as it will continue, by emphasizing sartorial codes: the greengrocer Bill Collins is in evening dress although the stage directions indicate it is *"a fine morning,"* while the Bishop's wife and lady of the house, Mrs. Bridgenorth, *"is dressed as for some festivity"* (*Plays*, 546–47); the characters in the play and the audience in the theater are all celebrating the imminent wedding. The Bishop's brother, General Boxer Bridgenorth, *"enters resplendent in full-dress uniform, with many medals and orders"* (*Plays*, 547), after which Collins carries the wedding cake onstage and off as a type of epiphany of the sacred objects—a purely ritual manifestation for the benefit of the spectators as no-one onstage refers to it, except that Collins seems to think seeing it causes the General to run off suddenly. The General's uniform introduces a new theme in the code of costume, a signification of the wearer's place or standing and role in society. Subjective identity is subsumed into the (national) social order, as happens also after birth, when people get named, and with marriage (before giving birth), when women are traditionally renamed. The resplendently attired general, on discovering the greengrocer to be an alderman, insists that he change out of his evening dress into his civic robes, thus setting up the beginning of the second part of the play, when Collins enters in his imposing alderman's gown. As the general says: "I attach importance to this as an affirmation of solidarity in the service of the community. The Bishop's apron, my uniform, your robes: the Church, the Army, and the Municipality" (*Plays*, 552). The bishop is no doubt wearing his bishop's apron when he appears later; Shaw does not otherwise specify this in the stage directions. The bride-to-be, rather than being dressed-up for her first entrance, is dressed-down *"in dressing-jacket and petticoat"* (*Plays*, 562). As a sartorial question mark, her appearance expresses semiotically the question of social subjective identity at the kernel of the play: in terms of the narrative, will she marry? The bride's wedding dress, the one costume most appropriate to a play set during a wedding day, is never shown in a play that emphasizes clothes. This irony is compounded when, in the midst of discussing whether the proposed bride and bridegroom will marry, Edith and Cecil, unbeknownst to both the other characters in the play and the audience, sneak out and get married in the empty church, which has been deserted by the wedding guests who have given up all hope of a wedding taking place that day. These wedding guests function as a stand-in for the audience inasmuch as they warn that the meaning of the play might be easily missed—as with the offstage reading and writing at the beginning of the play. Where or when what should be the thematic object of the spectator's attention is actually taking place is not always obvious within the Symbolic of Shaw's play-text. Offstage or on, the serious joke for the moment is that the bishop's cathedral has become the theater, while the theater has become a church. The couple are married by a curate who had remained behind in the deserted church, while the bride is given away by the Lady Mayoress's beadle, thus prompting the general's remark of satisfaction: "I'm glad it was done by somebody in a public uniform" (*Plays*, 584). And while the satisfaction of seeing the wedding dress is withheld from the audience, as the wedding guests were deprived of witnessing the marriage, Edith will be dressed appropriately as her mother makes plain towards the end:

> MRS BRIDGENORTH: We have to dress Edith. Come, Lesbia: come, Leo: we must all help. Now, Edith. [*Lesbia, Leo, and Edith go out through the tower*]. Collins: we shall want you when Miss Edith's dressed to look over her veil and things and see that theyre all right. (*Plays*, 586)

All the other guests are dressed for the wedding except possibly Reggie, the bishop's elder soon-to-be-divorced brother, who has not been invited but turns up anyway. The three remaining characters all have their own special costumes. Anthony Soames, a rather severe high church Anglo-Catholic is the bishop's chaplain, who "*comes in in cassock and biretta [and] salutes the company by blessing them with two fingers*" (*Plays*, 569)—a purely ritualistic gesture to signify that the heart of the mystery is being approached. Mrs. George, preceded by her beadle—or rather his voice before he appears himself in person with the phallic mace—then make their spectacular entrances in their official robes. The architectural setting through which they enter, described in the stage directions as "*an entrance to a vaulted circular chamber with a winding stair leading up through a tower to the upper floors of the palace*" (*Plays*, 546), itself has *both* phallic *and* omphallic connotations:

> THE VOICE OF THE BEADLE. By your leave there, gentlemen. Make way for the Mayoress. Way for the worshipful the Mayoress, my lords and gentlemen. [*He comes in through the tower, in cocked hat and gold-braided overcoat, bearing the borough mace, and posts himself at the entrance*]. By your leave, gentlemen, way for the worshipful the Mayoress.

> Mrs. George is every inch a Mayoress in point of stylish dressing; and she does it very well indeed. (Plays, 574)

The insistent *play* on costumes, derived perhaps from Carlyle's *Sartor Resartus*, both highlights and deconstructs their social significance. The emphasis on clothes as signifiers, involving dressing and undressing, mimics Shaw's technique as playwright and functions as part of the thematic of subjective identity: How is identity socially constructed? How can it be assumed? How may it be transformed? How may it differ at any given time? Identity is not fixed. In *Getting Married*, the emphases on costumes and entrances contribute strongly to the sense of ritual, whether wedding or drama, to reinforce a transmutation of social identity. Thematically in the context of marriage they help to signify the integration of the individual into her or his society, a meshing of the individual with the social that parallels the experience of the spectator in the theater. The social construction—the creation and re-creation—of subjectivity is shown as a symbolic act, event, or encounter.

Naming and the Masks of Dionysus

Similar perhaps to the different masks of Dionysus in classical tragedy, the play on naming in *Getting Married*—with different names piling up for the individual characters—is obviously very much part of the design of this construction of subjective identity. Names tend to reinforce logocentrism by reinforcing an identity between signifier and signified; two names for each individual, doubly articulated, where each is drawn from a different signifying system (for example, a lexicon of saints for a Christian name and a system of paternal property for a surname) provides one of the most powerful mechanisms for locking the subject into the social structure, into an ideological Imaginary. Even single names are doubly articulated, being always composed of at least two letters or phonemes. Yet a name as signifier of social differences is always an aporia that indicates singularity, individuality, and unique identity while always being socially and kinship based, always someone else's name—"In the name of the father," as Lacan put it. *Village Wooing*, with its unnamed characters designated as A and Z, is the exception within the Shaw text to prove the rule; it exemplifies the play, constructive and deconstructive, on naming, which is as pervasive throughout the Shaw play-texts as the emphasis on writing and reading, and nowhere more so than in *Getting Married*. As with costumes, the names in this play can be itemized.

Bill Collins, the greengrocer alderman who doubles as events manager for the bishop's family, has the same name, character type, and function (a combination of master of ceremonies cum stage manager) as the waiter, William, in Shaw's comedy about comedy, *You Never Can Tell*. Both Williams are stand-ins for the figure of the playwright, sharing their name with Shakespeare, who served Shaw as the symbol for all playwrights and the writer in general. In the earlier play Dolly explains she renamed Walter as William because he reminded her of the bust of Shakespeare at Stratford! Shaw underlines this identification by association—and his own textual relation to his famous predecessor—in *Getting Married* by giving Bill's offstage brother his own first name, George. Such play with a name hints at the many-sided complexity and scope of this text.

Anthony Soames, the bishop's curate, is a lawyer whose role is closely related to that of Lexy in *Candida*. He has something of the sexually repressed anchorite about him, derived most likely from that staple subject of Western Christian representational art, "The Temptations of Saint Anthony," as depicted so gruesomely by Bosch and Breughel. The name Soames is etymologically derived from *soma*, the body, which makes sense in relation to the primarily physical and sexual temptations to which that early Christian hermit, Saint Anthony, was subject. Those temptations resulted in hallucinatory fantasies represented here by Mrs. George's trance and her promiscuity that Soames associates with the temptations of the devil.

Shaw gives Mrs. George more names than anyone else; this is fitting for the most mythic character in the play. One of the oddest features, though, is that she is called by her husband's first name, George (also, of course, the first name of the playwright). Her husband's patronymic is Collins, and her married name is Mrs. George Collins. Apart from the autobiographical connection with Shaw himself and the point that in marriage a woman often assumes a new identity in relation to her spouse, there might be something in the name itself, which, although he hated it as his own, persuaded him to use it. *Getting Married* is probably the first state-of-England play, a genre inaugurated by Shaw that he pursued in such late plays as *Heartbreak House* and *On the Rocks*. Saint George, the patron saint of England, assumes importance because not only is England the country to which all the social symbolism in the play refers but also Mrs. George personifies herself a latter-day Britannia. Ge (or Gaea or Gaia) was an original earth goddess, who preceded even Demeter, and "orge" can be transposed to "urge" extending in meaning from the sexual to the demiurge of Plato's *Timaeus*. On the autobiographical level, George was Shaw's own first name as well as the first name of his father and of Vandeleur Lee, his mother's music partner and, possibly, Shaw's own biological father, as Rosset and O'Donovan suggest. Mrs. George's husband is a coal merchant, and in a web of Shavian associations the research of John O'Donovan discovered that Vandeleur Lee's parents were coal merchants rather than the country gentry to which he later laid claim.[21] There is no evidence that Shaw knew this, but in another play rife with autobiographical associations involving Lee and his mother, *Pygmalion*, one of the major characters, Doolittle, happens to be a coal man. Mrs. George's husband's occupation, however, makes thematic sense in mythological terms: fire is an attribute of Demeter, and Shaw uses it comically here as an objective correlative of the relationship between Mrs. George and Hotchkiss, the marriage celebrated in front of and for the audience in the play. Perhaps Mrs. George is even a long-delayed tribute to Shaw's first mistress, the widowed Mrs. Jenny Patterson, to whom he lost his virginity at the age of twenty-nine. Hotchkiss, "*of twenty-nine or thereabouts*," is the only character in the play whose age is specified, though presumably, if his name is anything to consider, he has been rather more sexually precocious than Shaw himself.

With Shavian irony to the fore, the name Mrs. George uses in love letters to the Archbishop is "Incognita Appassionata" (*Plays*, 557). And her other names are revealed in a short passage with Hotchkiss (where Polly may refer to her polyandrous disposition or simply her many-sidedness):

> MRS GEORGE. My name is Zenobia Alexandrina. You may call me Polly for short.
>
> HOTCHKISS. Your name is Ashtoreth-Durga—there is no name yet invented malign enough for you! (*Plays*, 576)

All this play of naming and identity is then turned on its head in the great set-piece of Mrs. George's trance, during which the principium individuationis is overcome: "I've been myself. I've not been afraid of myself. And at last I have escaped from myself, and am become a voice for them that are afraid to speak, and a cry for the hearts that break in silence" (*Plays*, 582). In rhetorical diction similar to that of Lilith at the end of *Methuselah*, she becomes a voice of prophecy, of Woman in general: "When you loved me I gave you the whole sun and stars to play with. I gave you eternity in a single moment . . . A moment only; but was it not enough?" The

Bishop's questions—"Do you remember who I am, and who you are?"—provoke a complete disjunction between the enunciation and the enunciator. She does not reply directly, but, ironically echoing Prossy's infatuation with the Reverend Morell, Mrs. George refers to the mystical marriage between the Bishop and herself many years previously, which had given meaning to her own life: "When you spoke to my soul years ago from your pulpit, you opened the doors of my salvation to me; and now they stand open for ever. It was enough. I have asked you for nothing since: I ask you for nothing now. I have lived: it is enough" (*Plays*, 583).[22]

When Mrs. George comes out of the trance, she explains to the bishop: "You may believe every word I said: I cant remember it now; but it was something that was just bursting to be said; and so it laid hold of me and said itself. Thats how it is, you see" (*Plays*, 583). This loss of personal identity depicts Shaw's frequent reflection on his own process of playwrighting and the impersonal nature of writing in general, which brings him close to a poststructuralist understanding of the "death of the author." His subjectivity as writer is annihilated whereby, linguistically, the subject-object relation becomes a verb, the present participle: writing.[23]

Hotchkiss's first name is St. John (pronounced Sinjon), a reference perhaps to the beginning of Saint John's gospel that is so important in the Shaw text: "In the beginning was the Word." The Word, in shifting meaning from signified to signifier, designates a vision of life as text without individual author, except in the sense of the phrase "the word of God"—a very Barthesian notion, but drawing on an ancient tradition; Mrs. George's "something that was just bursting to be said" is such an example.

The bishop, the third member of the trio dominating the action late in the play, is another Shavian self-portrait. He has been given two names, even before he appears onstage. The opening stage directions read that "*the present occupant* [of the Bishop's palace is] *A. Chelsea, unofficially Alfred Bridgenorth*" (*Plays*, 546). As with costume, the bishop's name has become one with his social function, and, being a bishop of a cathedral, is necessarily metonymically associated with a place, Chelsea, his seat—the location of the bishop's chair.

The Author as Guest in His Text

Constituting the central triangle of the play, Hotchkiss, Mrs. George, and the bishop can all be read as textual versions of Shaw as writer, and, through them, Shaw returns in his text as a Barthesian guest. Shaw in a letter to William Faversham of October 6, 1916, about the casting of Soames and Lesbia suggests the importance of these celibate characters as other autobiographical shadows or supplements:

> I forgot to urge . . . the great importance of casting Father Anthony and Lesbia, as they balance Hotchkiss and Mrs George in such a way that the least attempt to play them low down as a comic monk and an old maid would utterly destroy the atmosphere necessary for their two contrasted opposites. You need a tragic player of Irvingesque intensity for Anthony. (Laurence, *Shaw: An Exhibit*, item 338)

Lesbia echoes several opinions of Shaw as writer of the treatise on marriage that is the preface to the play. And Anthony Soames figures the writing of the play onstage during the whole last part of the play after Mrs. George's trance. This playing with characters and their identities and mixing them with aspects of his own, indeed constructing his own identity from the characters in his writing rather than the other way round, turns *Getting Married* into one of the more autobiographical of Shaw's plays. Above all the construction suggests that subjectivity within the Shaw playtexts as the relation of the individual and the social has something kaleidoscopic about it, rather than being unitary in any sense. The reflection of the writing subject's different personae, those shadowy supplements of the "paper-*I*," noted in chapter 3, may be read as the music of his writing or in the shifting metonymy of the signifiers within the text (see chapter 1). At the same time as the reader-spectator's identity receives another turn of the kaleidoscope in its ritual encounter with the Shaw text in the theater, manifold aspects of identity appear to the reader-spectator-initiate to form the shadowy identity of the author Bernard Shaw. As with a kaleidoscope, this formation of textual identity is quite likely to change from one moment to the next, a mutability that applies to the identities of not only the characters and their author but also the reader and spectator. In both *Candida* and *Getting Married*, many characters can incarnate one (material) identity, just as different actors (the hierophants in Shaw's temple) can play the same role, and equally each individual identity may comprise many different aspects. The bishop expresses this multiplicity, just before Mrs. George emerges from her trance, in the ritualistic incantory passage involving also Hotchkiss and Soames:

SOAMES. My lord: is this possession by the devil?

THE BISHOP. Or the ecstasy of a saint?

> HOTCHKISS. Or the convulsion of the pythoness on the tripod?
>
> THE BISHOP. May not the three be one?

Then, as she wakes from her trance, Hotchkiss echoes this attribution of multiple subjectivity:

> MRS GEORGE. I don't understand. I am a woman: a human creature like yourselves. Will you not take me as I am?
>
> SOAMES. Yes; but shall we take you and burn you?
>
> THE BISHOP. Or take you and canonize you?
>
> HOTCHKISS [*gaily*] Or take you as a matter of course . . . May I suggest that you shall be Anthony's devil and the Bishop's saint and my adored Polly? (*Plays*, 583)

Poststructuralism holds that what is signified in/by language is never an absolute, unitary link with a signifier. Rather, meaning—the mystery of understanding and *not* understanding as knowledge—is always a linguistic, social, cultural, literary, artistic, signifying process of similarities and differences, a playing of differing and deferring, a relation of active verbs between subject, other subjects, and the world as object(s) that Shaw labeled Creative Evolution, and Derrida referred to with his terms "signifiance" and "différance" as writing, inscripted traces of differences. As *play*, Shavian drama is a perpetual ritualistic and textual creation and recreation of identity, of subjectivity, of what in metaphysical terms might be called the staging of the transmutation of the soul. As has been shown, the (re)created identity may point to Shaw's own as author, but only as a textual question mark. The focus is on the spectator-initiate of the drama, who is asked to read/understand the symbolic place in the ritual event, which is impossible. The Dionysian experience produces a shattered subject. The only person the subject never sees is herself or himself, a self only apprehended by those shadows, the different masks of Dionysus, reflected back at her/him in such experiences.

Both *Candida* and *Getting Married* in their autobiographical aspects may thus be seen as relating to the entire corpus of his dramatic texts. In writing *Getting Married* as a drama on drama, on marriage as initiation and rite, Shaw drew extensively both in terms of method and thematic on his previous drama on marriage and dramatic origins, *Candida*. There, he confidently announced his assumption of the mantle of artist by having his poet forswear marriage. In the later play, Hotchkiss embraces what

Marchbanks had rejected. Significantly, St. John Hotchkiss, a former military man, lover, and snob is not a poet or writer, but he is, possibly, the secret or other self as shadow that Shaw as a boy dreamed of becoming. Sonny Shaw, the older Shaw informed us, was a snob who day-dreamed of military adventures and erotic adventures with beautiful women.[24] When Shaw wrote *Candida*, he was a bachelor carrying on affairs with several women. When he wrote *Getting Married*, he was married; but the relation with his wife, so we are informed, was chaste.[25]

8   The Image and the Word

> *Imagination is the beginning of creation.*
> *You imagine what you desire; you will what you imagine;*
> *and at last you create what you will.*
>
> The Serpent in Act I of *Back to Methuselah: Part I: In the Beginning* (1921)

The Chronological Myth

Anthony Burgess called Shaw "the one writer we know who synthesizes two centuries" (Burgess, *One Man's Chorus*, 176–79).[1] That the Shaw text is one of the most ambitiously written of the previous two centuries should now be clear, although its range tends to be put in the shade by opposing authorial strategies of self-promotion and self-effacement. Not for him, as Shaw himself put it, the modest cough of the minor poet, although the authority of the writer is always called into question, always deconstructed—often by calling attention to it. Shaw called *Back to Methuselah* his magnum opus, and yet on its publication he called for "younger [writing] hands" (*Prefaces*, 546) to supersede it.[2] This chapter sets out a case as to why this strangely overlooked text should be read as occupying a paradigmatic position within the larger Shaw text, as a poetically structured theory of imagination.[3] In terms of causality, materialist science insists on the past determining the present; imagination in Shaw's chronological myth, however, allows the future to enter into that equation. The play-cycle forms a dramatized inquiry from within a literary tradition inherited from Blake and Coleridge into the tricky—in all senses—workings of the human imagination, and one intimately bound up with an awareness of death. The science of metabiology, to use the term Shaw coined for the purpose in the work's subtitle, "A Metabiological Pentateuch," that the preface in particular seems to be calling for is nothing less than a science of the imagination, a new metaphysics of human consciousness, a myth of how the Imaginary works in the Symbolic—and beyond. It raises the general problematic of metaphor in language: the relation between the Image and the Word.

As outlined in chapter 4, Shaw sets up a relation between this science of the imagination and the nineteenth-century science of biology in terms of the concept of death, and he critiques the ideological basis of modern science as being more caught up in a metaphysical Imaginary than the science of imagination as metaphysics of consciousness that he advocates in *The Infidel Half Century*. But care must be taken not to fall into a reductionist trap by equating a biological theory of evolution (Creative Evolution) with the ideological critique of Natural Selection (in the preface), or with a phenomenology of imagination (in the play), or, for that matter, with a metaphysical basis for a science of natural history as put forward by Bergson in his *l'Évolution créatrice* (1907), or with the critical reading proposed here. All five approaches to the subject-object problem, however, can be put into relation with each other by Shaw's text.

What Northrop Frye in *The Great Code* calls "the neglected theory of 'polysemous' meaning" can be applied to this extended text. Frye quotes the author of *The Divine Comedy*, a great precursor of Shaw's work, who, in his turn, quotes the verse from the Psalms (114:1–2): "When Israel came out of Egypt, and the house of Jacob from a people of strange speech, Judaea became his sanctification, Israel his power." Dante then elaborates four levels of meaning:

> For if we inspect the letter alone the departure of the children of Israel from Egypt in the time of Moses is presented to us; if the allegory, our redemption wrought by Christ; if the moral sense, the conversion of the soul from the grief and misery of sin to the state of grace is presented to us; if the anagogical, the departure of the holy soul from the slavery of this corruption to the liberty of eternal glory is presented to us.

Each of these four levels of allegory, as itemized by Dante—the literal, the primary allegory, the moral, the anagogic—had express relevance to his *Divina Commedia* and can be seen as equally applicable to Shaw's *Methuselah*. As Frye says,

> polysemous meaning is a feature of all deeply serious writing, and the Bible is the model for serious writing. . . . For Dante "polysemous" does not really imply different meanings, suggesting that the chosen meaning of a given passage is purely relative, nor is there any question of a superimposed series of different contexts of understanding, where we move from one level to the next like grades in a school. What is implied is a single process growing in subtlety and

comprehensiveness, not different senses, but different intensities or wider contexts of a continuous sense, unfolding like a plant out of a seed. (Frye, *Code*, 220)

Frye returns here to the organic metaphor, liable, like any other, to deconstruction, so favored by Shaw in his own descriptions of the process of his writing.

Back to Methuselah, which is certainly "deeply serious writing" that draws on the Bible as model, can be read as a multilevel allegory where the old promise of longer life and man's victory over death is to be read as a hope that his imaginative capacity can be expanded at one level, while on another it offers a rewriting of history. It proposes an alternative utopian allegory as a contrast to the manifold effects that the publication of Darwin's book *On the Origin of Species* had on late nineteenth-century intellectual, cultural, social, economic, political, and military history in Europe and North America during what he calls "the infidel half century" that ended in the catastrophe of the Great War. Shaw's critique of religion and science, as put forward in *On the Prospects of Christianity* and *The Infidel Half Century*, convinced him that any feasible religion for a modern civilization must be scientifically credible, and his textual supplement to this critique, the play-cycle *Back to Methuselah* to be discussed here, can be read at once as rewriting *both* the Bible *and* Darwin's book in another form of discourse. This double rewriting is signaled in the text by the heretical brothers of religion and science, Franklyn and Conrad Barnabas in *Part II: The Gospel of the Brothers Barnabas*—the original title, stressing the fraternal aspect, had been "The Adelphians" (*Letters 3*, 547).[4]

Back to Methuselah is *the* chronological myth of the linguistic predicament (the subject-predicate structure of sentence grammar), to adapt a phrase used in chapter 1 to describe Creative Evolution in general. Shaw, as a didactic artist who built up with great care this imaginative construction, the play-cycle *Back to Methuselah* as a theatrical Imaginary, had also to deconstruct the text by showing both its limits and how it may lead the reader's imagination beyond the text in a transition from the Imaginary to the Symbolic. The experience of the reading or spectating of the play as text must continue to work on, in, and as the imagination of its spectators and readers, outside those temples of the Imaginary and Symbolic, the theater and the library respectively, in both their future (re)writing and practical action. Imagination and the language through which it works in writing, the working of the Symbolic within the Imaginary, eventually loses its basis in metaphor to acquire a greater perception and acceptance of the Real. *Methuselah* as a text emerges out of the Western Platonic philosophy of Logos. However, that is only half the story; a key feature of Shavian dialectic is that Platonic dialectic and what is called deconstruction are also fraternally related and interwoven throughout the text. For Shaw all artistic endeavor is in some sense writing, that is, rewriting as the inscription of new differences. Imagination must disappear, become absent, and leave traces only in subsequent texts, other writings from other hands. As the preface concludes: "It is my hope that a hundred apter and more elegant parables by younger hands will soon leave mine as far behind as the religious pictures of the fifteenth century left behind the first attempts of the early Christians at iconography" (*Prefaces*, 546).

Back to Methuselah, in effect a great dramatic poem by a writer who considered himself a dramatic poet, is crucially concerned with that aspect of imagination expressed by the metaphorical basis of language, the Image in the Word. As Franklyn Barnabas suggests in *Part II*, "the poem is our real clue to biological science" (*Plays*, 885), and a poem is above all writing, a linguistic artifact, a text of the imagination available to multiple critical readings. "Find me a word for the story that Lilith imagined and told you in your silent language," asks Eve in *Part I*. "A poem" (*Plays*, 859), answers the Serpent. Lilith, the first mother and ancient Semitic demon known in legend as Adam's first wife, had, like Pygmalion and Persephone, a certain attraction for the pre-Raphaelite artists with whose work Shaw was familiar. She is the presiding imaginative principle casting her shadow over the text of the chronological myth, *Back to Methuselah*.

Death, Imagination, and Writing

More imagination is needed to confront such problems of civilization as modern warfare, only too evident in the years from 1914 to 1918. The parable of prolonging the human life span is to be taken allegorically as a measure of enlarging the capacity of human imagination and consciousness in its fullest sense to include practical action. This allegory of creative imagination traces a movement from the Imaginary to the Symbolic, where it becomes, first, a highly developed capacity for reading multifarious cultural and social texts; second, it facilitates a capacity to rewrite texts, to write new texts; and, third, it provides a Symbolic frame or "mental fabric," from within which the subject can act with, what Shaw calls, conscience in the world. In *Part I*, Eve describes to Adam those purveyors of the imagination, her imaginative and artistic sons who are so helplessly incapable of dealing with the material necessities of mundane life, yet in whom she places her hope:

> Some of them will neither dig nor fight. They are more useless than either of you: they are weaklings and cowards: they are vain; yet they are dirty and will not take the trouble to cut their hair. They borrow and never pay; but one gives them what they want, because they tell beautiful lies in beautiful words. They can remember their dreams. They can dream without sleeping. They have not will enough to create instead of dreaming; but the serpent said that every dream could be willed into creation by those strong enough to believe in it. (*Plays*, 867–68)

Like Lacan, Shaw sees the lie as a necessary attribute of language. Without the lie, language could not become detached from the Imaginary, and thus the Symbolic, which involves intersubjectivity, could not be articulated. But he is also as alive to the limits of imagination as is Lacan to those of the Imaginary. Shaw is as concerned with language, the Word, Lacan's Symbolic, as he is with imagination and the Image. Lacan's Symbolic could not exist without the Imaginary, no matter how unreliable it is, and neither could Shaw's creative imagination, the realistic imagination, exist without language. Indeed to language and imagination, conscience, which gives the lie to the lie, can be added as the third moment of Shaw's dynamic model proposed in the play. These find their equivalent in not only Lacan's realms of the Imaginary, Symbolic, and Real but also the philosophical tradition, as in Kant's distinctions between a priori intuition, pure reason, and practical reason (action).

The realization of the full implications of death, only possible in language, becomes the spur to imagination in the context of the play. The interpretation of the theatrical allegory proposed here is that expected human life span be taken as a measure of the capacity of creative imagination; death is the spur to living longer. The very first image of the entire play-cycle is *a vision of a vision* of death, where the spectator in the theater *stares* at Adam *staring* in consternation at the dead body of a fawn. "What is the matter with its *eyes*?" says Eve.[5] They slowly realize that the fawn is not asleep, that it will not wake up, that it is dead (a new word), and that what happened to the fawn could happen to them. They find the physical corruption of the dead fawn putrid and disgusting, just as Eve later finds the secret of physical sex disgusting because of the proximity of the genital and excremental areas. Thus Saint Paul's pathological twin fears of death and sex, on which Shaw commented in *On the Prospects of Christianity*, are here associated.[6] Part of the poetic or structural method in this text is to connect these similar reactions of disgust; the metaphorical association between sex and death is telling where both lead to new life. Adam dumps the carcass of the fawn in the river, a metonymic association of death and water alluding to the symbolism implicit in the Christian rite of baptism. This symbol of rebirth is burlesqued in *Part III*, when the archbishop explains that he repeatedly had to fake his death by drowning. In the new consciousness of their own mortality, Adam and Eve decide, with the help of the Serpent, the rational principle, to set the duration of human life at one thousand years, which, in terms of the allegory, is more imagination than anyone could ever want. However, the rot sets in with their sons, Cain and Abel, who, building on their parents' invention of death, invent (animal) killing and (human) murder so that by historical time, life spans have been reduced to three score and ten, with human imaginative capacities reduced accordingly.

Chapter 4 touched on the associations between Eve learning the secret of sex at the end of *Part I*, Act I, her desire for "something else," which she calls *manna*, at the end of Act II, and Franklyn Barnabas *writing* his "Gospel of the Brothers Barnabas," which also happens to be the title of the play we are reading or spectating, at the beginning of *Part II*. These associations are all linked to what Derrida called writing as *supplement*. Writing figures often in the Shaw text, and an anti-Platonic thread in *Methuselah* can be found in this *writing* as a possibility of "something else," of dissemination. Franklyn's writing in his book-lined study figures the writing of the text we are reading/spectating. His scientist brother, Conrad, has already published a biological treatise incorporating the same ideas, each text a shadow, a supplement of the other. Conrad's book is *read* by the parlormaid ("Me and cook/had a *look*/at your book!" he declaims after she tells him), which, along with Haslam *reading* Franklyn's book, sets the rest of the drama of extending human life span in motion. Savvy Barnabas, Franklyn's daughter, a reincarnation of Eve, and Haslam's future wife, reads neither book, as the text pointedly makes clear—she does not become a longliver.

Eve's desire for "something else" is again echoed at the very end of the play-cycle, in the Epilogue to *Part V* when Lilith, the personification of imagination, expresses her hopes for the future and uses "beyond" as her very last word: "And for what may be beyond, the eyesight of Lilith is too short. It is enough that there is a beyond. [*She vanishes*]" (*Plays*, 962).

Lilith's vanishing leaves the stage in darkness; this represents the end of the metaphors of light and vision and presents an analogue of the vision of death with which the play began. The eyesight of the spectator is shut off. The word *beyond* in one of its senses is, of course, a synonym for death. Imagination can do no more after this metaphorical death, after this death of metaphor, but this time it extends *beyond* (beyond the Imaginary and the Symbolic toward the Real), as a spur to the imaginative capacities of its audience, if they have grasped its multiple implications. "Imagination dead imagine," which Shaw's compatriot Samuel Beckett used as the title for one of his shorter prose writings, would have been apt for *Back to Methuselah*.

Throughout the text, the following (many in the logocentric Platonic tradition that Derrida calls heliocentric) are repeatedly used as metaphors associated with imagination: eyes, vision, images, mirrors, telescopes, dreams, sleep, sculpture, art, stories, poetry, death, water, rebirth. In addition, drawing from the geologist Lyell and naturalist Charles Darwin, various geological, botanical, and lepidopteral metaphors are littered throughout the play to indicate levels, varieties, and stages of human life, all the deaths and rebirths that must be experienced in the evolutionary myth as part of the development of creative imagination both in a cultural textual tradition of writing and in an individual. *Back to Methuselah* is a drama of perpetually deferring metonymy of these metaphors as signifiers.

In *The Perfect Wagnerite*, Shaw described Loki in Wagner's *Der Ring* as "Logic and Imagination without living Will" (*Music 3*, 444), which is incarnated by the Serpent in Shaw's drama of *Part I: In the Beginning*, as well as by the writer, Bernard Shaw. The Serpent is a variation of Hegel's principle of negation, the principle of reason: "I tell you I am very subtle. When you and Adam talk, I hear you say 'why?' Always 'why?' You see things, and you say 'why?' But I *dream* things that never were; and I say 'why not'?" (*Plays*, 857) The Serpent, who learned to speak from listening to the purely nominative language of Adam and Eve, as a child learns to speak from its parents, constantly invents new words to account for their rapidly dawning awareness of experience, their eating of the tree of knowledge as a transition to the Symbolic. Thus, Eve learned from the Serpent the new word *dead* to describe what happened to the fawn.

The Serpent explains to Eve how Lilith, the first mother, created Adam and herself: "She *saw death* as you saw it when the fawn fell, and she knew then that she must find out how to renew herself. She *imagined* it as a marvelous story of something that never happened to a Lilith that never was" (*Plays*, 858). At this point the Serpent speaks the lines that propel this dramatic metaphor through the end of the play-cycle: "*Imagination* is the beginning of creation. You imagine what you desire; you will what you imagine; and at last you create what you will." Note, however, that for Shaw imagination is the beginning of creation, not desire, which is logically anterior. Desire without imagination cannot create. In Lacanian terms, desire, by leaving fissures or gaps in the Symbolic, can be traced in language and makes language possible by incessantly trying and never succeeding to articulate the effects of desire in the Imaginary. Action/creation can only take place in the Real.

The four moments of the dynamic of creative imagination thus are desire, imagination, will, and creation. The Serpent describes this process with the term "to conceive," the word that means "both the beginning in imagination and the end in creation." Lilith's marvelous story is "a poem." Imagination is, thus, intimately linked to writing, to language, to narrative, and to poetry. Lilith's story as poem emerged from the "silent language" (Derrida's archê-writing), the silent signifying of Lilith and the Serpent to Adam and Eve's spoken language, to their new capacity for understanding their experience following the death of the fawn and the Serpent's capacity for creating new words to match their dawning consciousness. If the auto-genetic female/mother Lilith-Serpent dyad serves as a stand-in for the writer, then Adam and Eve and their generations of descendants serve as stand-ins for the reader. The writers, the brothers Barnabas, in *Part II* and the sculptors, Martellus and Arjillax (as opposed to the scientist, Pygmalion) in *Part V,* continue this thread.

Imagination: Romantic and Realistic

Franklyn Barnabas, the evangelical former clergyman and religious writer of *Part II,* dreams of longevity. The scientific writing of his biologist brother Conrad reinforces Franklyn's dream, and together their writing constitutes "The Gospel of the Brothers Barnabas." Unlike *The Revolutionist's Handbook*, its text is known only indirectly through Shaw's play and preface, except for those very words we see Franklyn *writing* at the beginning of the play. As he tells Conrad—and note the stage directions, as well as how the play *begins* with the *end* of a sentence: "The very last words I wrote when you interrupted me were "at least three centuries." [*He snatches up the manuscript, and points to it*]. Here it is: [*reading*] "the term of human life must be extended to at least three centuries" (*Plays*, 869).

The writers Franklyn and Conrad, like Eve's visionary children, can dream their Imaginary dream, but they cannot will it into existence. The brothers' readers, the silly rector and the socially inferior parlormaid—both specific farcical types with a long theatrical history behind them—have other, unconscious reasons for prolonging their lives, for expanding their imaginative capacities, for understanding their places in Lacan's Symbolic and within the terms of Shaw's fantasy. At the end of *Part II*, the politicians reveal that their own sons had been killed in the war, as had Franklyn's, but nobody mentions the dead young men, forgotten by all except the silly clergyman: "*I* didnt forget, because I'm of military age; and if I hadnt been a parson I'd have had to go out and be killed too. To me the awful thing about their political incompetence was that they had to kill their own sons" (*Plays*, 891). In *Part III* the transfigured parlormaid, the Domestic Minister Mrs. Lutestring, relates how she used alcohol to stave off suicide: "You people nowadays can have no *conception* of the dread of poverty that hung over us then, or of the utter tiredness of forty years' unending overwork" (*Plays*, 904).

To grasp the implications of death requires imagination, which, like many concepts important to the Shaw text, has something double-edged about it. The preface to *Misalliance*, "On Parents and Children" (1910), made this clear by distinguishing romantic from realistic imagination, a Platonic distinction between the world of appearance and the world of reality, or between Lacan's Imaginary and Symbolic, carried over into *Methuselah*:

> It is necessary to clear up the confusion caused by our use of the word imagination to denote two very different powers of mind. One is the power to imagine things as they are not: this I call the romantic imagination. The other is the power *to imagine things as they are without actually sensing them*; and this I call the realistic imagination. Take for example marriage and war. One man has a vision of perpetual bliss with a domestic angel at home, and of flashing sabres, thundering guns, victorious cavalry charges, and routed enemies in the field. That is romantic imagination; and the mischief it does is incalculable. The wise man knows that imagination is not only a means of pleasing himself with romances and fairy tales and fools' paradises, but also a means of *foreseeing* and being prepared for realities as yet

unexperienced, and of testing the possibility and desirability of serious Utopias. (*Prefaces*, 103)

In Act II of *The Tragedy of an Elderly Gentleman*, Napoleon claims to have this rare gift of realistic imagination. The oracle wonders if that means he has no imagination, to which he replies in a deconstruction of the metaphor of vision in language, "I mean that I have the only imagination worth having: the power of imagining things as they are, even when I cannot see them" (*Plays*, 928). But Napoleon's tragedy is that in social terms his realistic imagination is confused with the romantic imagination of others, especially with that of his own followers. Most shortlivers, members of modern Western societies, suffer from romantic imagination, whereas, up to a point, the play champions realistic imagination. The politicians of *Part II* and, most tragically, the Elderly Gentleman in *Part IV* all suffer from romantic imagination. The Elderly Gentleman's tragedy results from his travels to the land of the Oracles and longlivers, where his romantic imagination becomes mixed up with realistic imagination in a language of "dead thought," which is why he dies after exposure to the longlivers, possessors of realistic imagination par excellence. "Dead thought" may be considered as a language whose metaphorical basis (that perpetual metonymy of signifiers) has congealed into fixed signifier-signified (Imaginary) relations, as opposed to the workings of Lacan's Symbolic or Derrida's différance. In spite of his antipathy to Plato, Derrida's deconstruction of Platonism can be read as a rewriting of Platonism, in which an archê-writing (traces of deferring differences) replaces the Platonic world of fixed ideas: writing that denotes an absence by a presence, by differing, rather than asserting a Platonic identity between the thought or spoken word and the thing, the Idea and the Real, the signifier and the signified. Interestingly Shaw's realistic imagination (not unlike Plato's Real) is based on this Derridean notion of deferring, of seeing what is *not* there.

Cain, a romantic militaristic dreamer and would-be Superman visiting his now old parents in Act II of *In the Beginning*, is a typical example of the destructive consequences of romantic imagination. "Stay with the woman who will give you children: I will go to the woman who will give me *dreams*," Cain announces to his father, Adam. But he also is a poet, and for his dream to become a reality he wants his mother, Eve, "to create more men and more women, that they may in turn create more men. I have *imagined a glorious poem* of many men. . . . I will divide them into two great hosts. . . . And each host shall try to kill the other host. Think of that! all those multitudes of men fighting, fighting, killing, killing! . . . That will be life indeed: life lived to the very marrow: burning overwhelming life" (*Plays*, 863).

Eve angrily responds to Cain's romantic dreams of military glory: "You cannot taste life without making it bitter and boiling hot: you cannot love Lua until her face is *painted*. . . . You can feel nothing but a torment, and believe nothing but a lie. You will not raise your head to look at all the miracles of life that surround you" (*Plays*, 864). Here is Shaw's Swiftean version of the Imaginary misrecognition of identity. Eve places her hope in those of her children who are dreamers, the poets, the liars—lying, like dreaming and imagination, being distinctly double-edged. The possibility of the lie and difference in language enables subjects to escape an otherwise certain determinism by the Imaginary; intersubjectivity allows subjects to transpose Imaginary relations with Lacan's shadowy "specular others" to articulating their relation to the big Other within the Symbolic (or unconscious). Articulatable language dissociates the signifier from a signified, unlike the strictly nominative "language of the bees" described with some humor by Lacan. Those professional liars, Eve's and Shaw's poets such as William Blake, can probably best discover the Imaginary worms at the heart of the Symbolic roses, while Cain is caught in the lie of his own Imaginary.

But Cain, whose flights of imagination led him to invent murder and dream of military glory, flings the accusation back in their faces: "Who invented death?" And his parents have to admit their guilt, a failure of imaginations that could not bear the thought of a life of more than a thousand years. Shaw, who as dramatist declared all his characters right from their own points of view, would say as much for the romantically imaginative and homicidal Cain.

There is a theme of the Voice in *In the Beginning*: the voice as supplement (rather than identical to thought), as Lacan's Symbolic Other and Imaginary others, God and the Devil—Good and Evil. In Act I, Adam and Eve discuss their different experiences of the voice(s):

ADAM. There is a voice in the garden that tells me things.

EVE. The garden is full of voices sometimes. They put all sorts of things into my head.

ADAM. To me there is only one voice. It is very low; but it is so near that it is like a whisper from within myself. There is no mistaking it for any voice of the birds or beasts, or for your voice.

> EVE. It is strange that I should hear voices from all sides and you only one from within. But I have some thoughts that come from within me and not from the voices. The thought that we must not cease to be comes from within.
>
> ADAM [*despairingly*] But we *shall* cease to be. We shall fall like the fawn and be broken. (*Plays*, 856)

In the difference between Adam and Eve, what is being offered is *not* a phonocentric identity of the Voice and the Word. In Act II, Cain adds his own experience:

> CAIN. Hearken to me, old fool. I have never in my soul listened willingly when you have told me of the Voice that whispers to you. There must be two Voices: one that gulls and despises you, and another that trusts and respects me. I call yours the Devil. Mine I call the Voice of God.
>
> ADAM. Mine is the Voice of Life: yours the Voice of Death.
>
> CAIN. Be it so. For it whispers to me that death is not really death: it is the gate of another life: a life infinitely splendid and intense; a life of the soul above. (*Plays*, 866)

Cain's and Adam's inner Voice (like the Protestant "inner Light") might correspond to different experiences of Lacan's Imaginary other, whereas Eve's voices (the Lacanian Other, the intersubjectivity that allows for the Symbolic) in the Garden are plural. And Eve is careful not to confuse her voices with her own thoughts. Cain's "Death is not really death" is an Imaginary claim that can be symbolically true, as most religions would proclaim. And the tension between these claims on behalf of Life and Death in the Imaginary and the Symbolic becomes a recurring theme throughout the play-cycle. The confusion of the metaphor for the reality, an Imaginary conflation of metaphor and reality in identity, is both the gravest defect of the romantic imagination that can be attributed to the nature of language itself, as well as the greatest quality of the language of poetry (poetic discourse). And language, as the Symbolic, does allow other ways of relating to the Real.

In *Part II*, Burge, a satirical caricature of wartime Prime Minister Lloyd George, boasts of "a certain power of spiritual *vision* because I have practiced as a solicitor. A solicitor has to advise families. He has to show them how to provide for their daughters after their deaths" (*Plays*, 890). Although this is a burlesque variation of Cain's "gateway to another life, splendid and intense," Shaw is making a serious point about death as a gateway to a life of the imagination. In this second part, the two politicians, both of whom served as prime minister during the most catastrophic war in history, condemn each other by pointing out each other's deficiencies. Burge, in a devastating critique of someone caught in the Imaginary, condemns Lubin, the Asquith caricature, as having no conscience, significantly using a mirror metaphor to do so: "[your mind is like] *a looking glass*. You are very clear and smooth and lucid as to what is standing in front of you. But you have no foresight and no hindsight. You have no continuity; and a man without continuity can have neither conscience nor honour from one day to another" (*Plays*, 884).

Conscience, like human time, can exist only in the Symbolic. Shaw had used this same metaphor of the Imaginary, explicitly in the context of *writing*, in a letter to his German translator, Siegfried Trebitsch (January 7, 1903). Pointing out deficiencies in Trebitsch's translations, he called him a *Spiegelmann*:

> What is a Spiegelmann? A *mirrorman*. A Looking Glass man. What is a Looking Glass? A thing that reflects what is before it with exquisite fidelity, but that has neither Rücksicht [hindsight] nor Vorsicht [foresight], neither memory nor hope, neither reason nor conscience. And that is just what you are as a translator. You translate a sentence beautifully, but you do not remember the last sentence, do not foresee the next sentence, and when you finish the play it goes out of your head just as your head vanishes from your mirror when you have finished shaving. (*Shaw-Trebitsch*, 32)

The Spiegelmann is, of course, the man caught in his Imaginary, and Shaw writes as a writer writing to a rewriter about writing. Much later in his life (1941), he wrote a preface to a book called *The Miraculous Birth of Language* by Richard Albert Wilson. There Wilson describes how language, in the evolutionary sense, gave man the capacity to exist in a Kantian space-time continuum in which logos as logic functions like perspective and shadows in visual representation. But already in 1903 Shaw's understanding of language was more complex than this, and the writing process he describes above (as a nonlogical or heterogeneous time and space constituted by differences as opposed to an atemporal spatial image), in which meaning is deferred elsewhere, can be seen as analogous to Derrida's concept of différance. It points up again the difference between the Lacanian Imaginary and the Symbolic. Shaw had provided another humorous metaphor for the Imaginary man in *On the Prospects of Christianity*: "the world is full of . . . Adams and Smiths and men in the street and average sensual men and economic men and womanly women and what not, all of them imaginary Atlases carrying imaginary worlds on their insubstantial shoulders" (*Prefaces*, 589).

But (realistic) imagination, which is required to understand the world in language, the Symbolic, is *not* homologous to the world as we see it, the Imaginary. A leap beyond imagination is required to understand how language constitutes the subject at those places in the Symbolic weave of entry and re-entry ("In the Name of the Father," the Oedipus Complex, a religious conversion, marriage, drama) and exit (death).

As a counterblast to Burge, who has already boasted of his own visionary (imaginative) capacity, Lubin angrily, and with some condescension, accuses him of having "mere energy without intellect and without knowledge. Your mind is not a trained mind" (*Plays*, 884). As Shaw indicated in the prefaces to *Misalliance* and *Heartbreak House*, imagination as expressed in action must be informed by both knowledge and a critical philosophy, by reason and conscience. In *Part IV*, the Elderly Gentleman makes a point about how imagination can be distorted by knowledge if acquired without conscience, if it remains locked in the Imaginary, and which makes play with size in a fashion similar to Swift's *Gulliver's Travels*:

> I maintain that it is dangerous to shew too much to people who do not know what they are looking at. I think that a man who is sane as long as he looks at the world through his own eyes is very likely to become a dangerous madman if he takes to looking at the world through *telescopes and microscopes*. The moment men made telescopes, their belief perished . . . they could no longer believe in their deity, because they had always thought of him as living in the sky. . . . Whatever the scientific people may say, imagination without microscopes was kindly and often courageous, because it worked on things of which it had real knowledge. But imagination with microscopes, working on a terrifying spectacle of millions of grotesque creatures of whose nature it had no knowledge, became a cruel terror-stricken, persecuting delirium. (*Plays*, 920)

Shaw's evident horror of the cruelty involved in so-called scientific experiments cannot be exaggerated.[7] What he found most reprehensible was the scientists' uncritical assumption of the role of priest with ritual torturing and sacrifice of animals in another violent consequence, as with war, of social, religious, and educational systems that inculcate imagination without conscience, where the Imaginary is out of phase, as it were, with the Symbolic, where it has become ideological. It bears repeating that for Shaw as for Lacan, there is *not* in fact a chronological movement from the Imaginary to the Symbolic. They are two aspects of the same relation, two moments of the same dynamic, which is why *Methuselah* is described here as a chronological myth.

Sexual Imagination

Within the Imaginary, the area of greatest confusion for romantic imagination is where the desire for beauty and the desire for sex become confused, which leads to a loss of what Shaw calls self-control, the possession of which is the greatest evolutionary virtue. In *Part I*, Eve disparaged Cain's relation with his wife, Lua, by calling him a "poor slave of a painted face and a bundle of skunk's fur." Cain, lost in his Imaginary relation with Lua, literally cannot see the signifier in the "painted face," the writing that is Lua, and misreads that other signifier, "the skunks fur."[8] The symptomatic confusion of Cain in relation to beauty and sex, however, can also be productive. This was the point of the deleted scene in *Part II* between Immenso Champernoon and Mrs. Etteen, subsequently published in *The Domesticity of Franklyn Barnabas*. Mrs. Etteen, the incarnation of beauty, of Goethe's *das ewig Weibliche*, figures here as the teleological function of beauty as proposed in Kant's *Critique of Judgment*, as opposed to mere sexual attraction—a distinction Plato also makes in *The Symposium*. But when Immenso, the Catholic philosopher modeled on G. K. Chesterton, accuses Mrs. Etteen of seducing other women's husbands, she declares: "don't you see that this sex attraction, though it is so useful for keeping the world peopled, has nothing to do with beauty: that it *blinds* us to ugliness instead of *opening our eyes* to beauty." And when Immenso speaks of the Church, Mrs. Etteen replies:

> When you talk of the Church, you are talking of a pack of common men calling themselves clergymen and priests, and trying to persuade us that they are demigods by wearing ugly black clothes. Michelangelo did not paint for them: he painted for me, and for people like you and me. We are the spectators for whom he painted: we are the Church which drew out his gifts. It was for us that Bach and Beethoven composed, that Phidias and Rodin made statues, that the poets sang and the philosophers became seers. . . . politicians and

priests . . . organized as States and Churches and dressed up to seem the thing they are not . . . pretend *to see* events with *glass eyes*, and to hear the music of the spheres with ass's ears. (*Plays 5*, 681)

Those who are not caught in the Imaginary or the ideological can read the "writing" of Bach and Michelangelo. Mrs. Etteen's beauty functions platonically as something other than sexual magnetism. She represents the possibility of the Higher Love that Shaw as critic found represented in Ibsen's Rebecca West and which his poet, Marchbanks, ultimately found in Candida. In relation to the gospel of the brothers Barnabas, Mrs. Etteen explains by echoing Goethe's das ewig Weibliche: "[Conrad, the scientist] had the skeleton of the great faith; but it was Franklyn who put the flesh on it. And it was I, the woman, who made that flesh for him out of my own" (*Plays 5*, 682).

The narrative function of Mrs. Etteen was replaced in Shaw's symbolic drama in *Part V*, as will be seen below, by art critic and apostle of beauty Ecrasia (*Ekasia* is Imagination as it functions in terms of the Platonic dialectic in *Republic*, and which, like love in *Symposium*, can lead beyond the worlds of sense and appearance to knowledge of reality and truth). Aspects of this theme are retained in *Part II*: for instance, the warmonger politician Lubin, when reintroduced to Conrad, cannot remember having met him because his "pretty niece engaged all my powers of *vision*" (*Plays*, 877).

Imagination's capacity for romantic distortion is expressed comically in *Part III* with the president's infatuation with the minister of health, "a handsome negress"; the president protests that his relations with her are purely "telephonic, gramophonic, photophonic, and, may I say, platonic" (*Plays*, 905). Again, ironically in terms of Derrida's criticism of Platonism, Shaw by associating intersubjectivity with various forms of inscription or writing, with present material signifiers or traces denoting an absent ideal signified (like the apparatuses in view in Act II of *Pygmalion* that facilitated the repetition of the voice as simulacra), turns his declared Platonism against itself.

By showing a sex affair between two people who have never met in the flesh, Shaw makes this serious point comically. In spite of this, it remains an affair of the romantic imagination, of the Imaginary, conducted through that exemplary modern technology of the image, which—borrowing from Christian Metz—we can call "the Imaginary signifier": television.[9] Shaw should, perhaps, be given more credit for his emphasis on the importance of imagination in human sexuality. Within the dialectic of the play, this can be either bad (romantic imagination caught in the Imaginary) or good (realistic imagination): bad, if imagination without conscience does not lead to self-control; but good, if it means that imaginative capacity of reading the signifiers that constitute the Symbolic. In this one respect only is the president contrasted favorably with his Chinese chief secretary, Confucius. A reincarnation of the Serpent, "Illustrious Sage-&-Onions," as the president calls him, reacts to the white president's infatuation with the black minister of health with a show of disgust similar to Eve's reaction when she learned the secret of sex from the Serpent: "For me a woman who is not *yellow* does not exist, save as an official" (*Plays*, 895). Caught in his own cultural Imaginary, Confucius's color prejudice as a comic inversion of white racism is a symptom of inadequate imagination. The president mentions favorably "a very interesting book by the librarian of the Biological Society suggesting that the future of the world lies with the Mulatto," to which Mrs. Lutestring, the "Eve" of a new race of longlivers, says to the new "Adam," the archbishop: "Mr Archbishop: if the white race is to be saved, our destiny is apparent" (*Plays*, 907). Here care must be taken to read the play. More than anywhere else in the play-cycle, Shaw points to racism as a major symptom of the imaginative deficiency of the shortlivers, particularly the British Islanders. Yet it seems that the archbishop and Mrs. Lutestring are going off to found a new race of long-lived superpersons that might be a white supremacist's dream! This theme is picked up again in *Part IV* as a satire on (or a rewriting of) the history of European colonization. Anticipating the recent interest in postcolonial studies, the big political question of the day for the longlivers is whether they should colonize the rest of the world or remain isolated, a race apart: "the general opinion among the colonizers is in favor of beginning in a country where the people are of a different color from us; so that we can make short work without any risk of mistakes." The white longlivers, showing symptoms of a racial "compulsion to repeat," propose first to colonize North America, where the short-lived natives of 3000 A.D. were once themselves, for the most part, white European colonists but are now the red "characteristic of their climate." Yet, as the longliver says, "We are not particular about our pigmentation" (*Plays*, 932). Shaw held that for any large society to work and be socially cohesive, a "psychological homogeneity" and a "common (cultural) language," which is usually described as a religion, is necessary.[10] Mrs. Lutestring and the archbishop set out to save European civilization, that so-called Christian civilization to which Shaw belonged (or in which he was inscribed). Having gone most disastrously wrong in the modern world, that Christian civilization most required salvation. Shaw's critique of Christianity in practice in *On the Prospects of Christianity* was that Christianity in terms of Christ's social teaching had never been tried, yet a modern civilization required such practice. In setting the action of *Part IV* in Ireland, he deliberately invokes, as he had with the character of Keegan in *John Bull's Other Island*, the myth of the Island of Saints and Scholars during the Dark Ages (sixth to tenth centuries) where the values of Christian civilization were preserved and whose missionary (colonizing) activity rechristianized the European continent.[11] Shaw describes elsewhere the irrational pride he took in his native land, and possibly (as a reversal of the previous seven hundred years of colonial history in Ireland) he also had in mind his own role as a latter-day colonial Irish missionary to his adopted country of England, as well as to the rest of the world![12]

The meeting after two hundred and fifty years in *Part III: The Thing Happens*, when the archbishop, the silly clergyman of *Part II*, is introduced to the formidable Mrs. Lutestring, the parlormaid of the earlier play, provides a more poetic example of the vagaries of romantic imagination than the relationship between the president and the minister of health. In a strange anticipation of their destiny as the Adam and Eve of a new race of longlivers, and as an ironic echo of Cain's "gate to another life," they remember their first meeting:

> THE ARCHBISHOP. This *vision* of a door opening to me, and a woman's face welcoming me, must be a reminiscence of something that really happened; though I see it now as an angel opening the door of heaven.
>
> MRS LUTESTRING. Or a parlormaid opening the door of the house of the young woman you were in love with?
>
> THE ARCHBISHOP [*making a wry face*] Is that the reality? How these things grow in our *imagination*. (Plays, 903)

What makes this so wonderful, in this most satirical of the five plays, are the reverberations set up, as a thread of différance, which extend throughout the play-cycle, from Adam and Eve, through Haslam and Savvy, the Archbishop and Mrs. Lutestring, and beyond. The thing happens: opening a door to Heaven, to the Other, in an encounter that is both a repetition and a sign of the future. It tells us something about imaginative truth:

imagination may distort reality, but it can also illuminate the significance of such prosaic realities as opening a door for someone or the everyday duties of an early twentieth-century parlormaid. Here, again, is that sense of democracy (the potential of each subject for that "completeness of activity" (*Non-Dramatic*, 359) in relating to the world, as described in *The Sanity of Art*) that pervades both the playwrighting and political writing.

Part V, with the creation of the automata, Ozymandias and Cleopatra-Semiramis, is Shaw's most extreme satire on romantic imagination as an ideology of determinism. These apparently splendid examples of humanity, exemplars of the Manly Man and the Womanly Woman, whose equivalents today might be a couple of leading Hollywood stars, react only to stimuli, but because they completely lack realistic imagination and that "highly developed vital sense" of self-control, of which it is a function, they know only violence as a way of responding, when their romantic illusions are destroyed and their vanity is pricked. They are the victims of self-interest and self-conceit; their narcissism in their Imaginary egos results, of course, in the failure to develop (creative) realistic imagination. As the He-Ancient puts it, "These things are mere automata: they cannot help *shrinking from death at any cost.* You see they have no self-control, and are merely shuddering through a series of reflexes" (*Plays*, 954).

At the end of *Part V*, this theme of sex and imagination makes its final appearance in the last line of the play proper before the epilogue. Shaw returns here to romantic imagination, but as an imagination of hope similar to the archbishop's *vision* of the parlormaid. Ecrasia, the art lover and critic who had declared "the difference between a beautiful nose and an ugly one is of supreme importance," on finding no one to spend the night with, exclaims: "Must I spend the night alone? After all, I can *imagine* a lover nobler than any of you" (*Plays*, 961). She is left alone with her imagination to dream dreams, as a reincarnation of the serpent and one of those children in whom Eve put her faith for a better world.

Ancillary to this theme of beauty, sex, and its confusion with the romantic imagination is the more prosaic reality of the social implications of procreation. When Lilith renewed herself, she divided herself in two, into Adam and Eve, so that they could share the burden of procreation between them. In fact, Lilith left a preponderance of the physical burden on the woman whom she made in her own image. And, whereas man was supposed to have been kept in woman's "power through his desire" (*Plays*, 858), the reverse happened with Cain, the first murderer, the modern military macho man, the false superman—as Eve says to him: "Superman!

You are no superman; you are anti-man" (*Plays*, 864). He boasts: "When I have slain the boar at the risk of my life, I will throw it to my woman to cook, and give her a morsel of it for her pains. She shall have no other food; and that will make her my slave. . . . Man shall be the master of Woman" (*Plays*, 864).

This turn in the destiny of men, following Adam and Eve's expulsion from the Garden of Eden to develop into the earliest of prehistorical farming civilizations in Mesopotamia, creates a physiological and social imbalance, which, within the play's scheme of themes, will be rectified by longer life. Just as the problems of government and social organization have to be solved, if the imaginative capacity of either women or men can flourish, so also must the physiological differences that lead to essentialist or Imaginary notions of gender, of Man and Woman, be overcome. As the allegory of long life indicating expanded creative imagination progresses through the play-cycle, the burden of childbearing is incrementally lifted from women.[13] By *Part V*, women do not give birth any more; gestation has become oviparous. And once the unequal burden of childbearing has been lifted, any necessity for this aspect of romantic imagination disappears, to the dismay of the children, who look forward with horror to their "old age," when they outgrow romantic love after the age of four.

The Gaze: From Image to Word

A development of the metaphor of looking, of the gaze that Shaw elaborated from his analogy between the physical eye and the mind's eye (so crucial to the relation between the subject and the world where epistemology becomes ontology), is another aspect of imagination that can be traced through the play. Looking is merely reactive at first, as Adam and Eve stare at the dead fawn or when Eve admires the Serpent's new hood. When we meet the first longlivers in *Part III*, a change starts to take place. To convince President Burge-Lubin that she is indeed two hundred and seventy-four years of age, Mrs. Lutestring "*turns her face gravely towards him*" and tells him to "*look again*." He looks "*at her bravely until the smile fades from his face, and he suddenly covers his eyes with his hands.*" The activity of looking has seemingly changed from being a passively reactive to a proactive process. Shaw makes a point that has since become a commonplace in the psychology of perception. As he puts it in his 1944 postscript to *Methuselah* in speaking about visual perception, "Attention is the first symptom of thought" (*Methuselah* [1945], 297). The image becomes the word, becomes thought, becomes Symbolic. Rather than being passive, perception and thought are proactive, what Husserl following Brentano calls "intentional," to varying degrees. It also may be seen as an interesting variant on Lacan's theory of the dynamic of the gaze: desire as it operates through our gaze desiring the gaze of the other desiring us.[14] Famously in Lacan's theory there is a gap or lack set up at the mirror stage when the undifferentiated image is split into a (misrecognized) self and a (m)other, between desire and the possibility of its fulfillment. In several encounters of the latter parts of the play-cycle, this gap becomes an unbridgeable gulf.

One example of this proactive power of looking comes in the confrontation in *Part IV*, Act II, between Napoleon (General Aufsteig, Emperor of Turania) and the Oracle, a longliver in her second century.[15] Although he has the strongest "mesmeric" field she has ever encountered in a shortliver, when she uncovers her eyes he staggers, covers his eyes, and shrieks "Help! I am dying" (*Plays*, 927). In a moment of symbolic farce, the warmongering Napoleon dies and is reborn as a coward. He goes off to gibber impotently at the statue of Sir John Falstaff, the discoverer of the precept that "cowardice was a great patriotic virtue" (*Plays*, 930).

A second example comes at the end of *Part IV*, as the Elderly Gentleman realizes his position is analogous to Gulliver's when he learnt he must leave the land of the Houyhnhnms: "That the certain prospect of an unnatural death was the least of my evils: for, supposing I should escape with life by some strange adventure, how could I think with temper of passing my days among Yahoos, and relapsing into my old corruptions, for want of examples to lead and keep me within the paths of virtue" (Swift, *Gulliver's Travels*, 329).

For Yahoos read shortlivers. The Elderly Gentleman puts it this way: "They have gone back to lie about your answer. I cannot go with them. I cannot live among people to whom nothing is real. I have become incapable of it through my stay here" (*Plays*, 937). Lying, like imagination, is double-edged: beneficial in art, dangerous in politics. The politicians' lie of *Part IV* shows them caught in the Imaginary, whereas the Elderly Gentleman's refusal to lie is his first recognition of how he had been caught in that Imaginary. His subsequent death, the death of his Imaginary, is its Symbolic tragic realization. When the Oracle tells him he will die of discouragement if he stays, he asserts, "It is the meaning of life, not of death, that makes banishment so terrible to me"—life as significance, as the Symbolic. The Oracle, according to the stage directions "*looks steadily into his face. He stiffens; a little convulsion shakes him; he falls dead*" (*Plays*,

937). Shaw, thus, in the order he presents the unofficial encounters of the Oracle with Napoleon and the Elderly Gentleman, reverses Hegel's adage that history repeats itself: first as tragedy; second as farce.

As always, the reader must not confuse Shaw's own metaphor or allegory with the reality that he is proposing. In the symbolic farce that is the Elderly Gentleman's tragedy the text illustrates the anthropological phenomenon of the intimidation of a technologically inferior civilization by an encounter with a superior one; for example, the culture of so-called primitive peoples crumbled from within on first contact with Europeans, without even requiring a full colonial apparatus. By coming into contact with longlivers, the shortlivers simply choose to die from what is called in the text "discouragement," a form of existential despair tantamount to death: "He simply dies. He wants to. He is out of *countenance*" (*Plays*, 925).

However, because imagination has positive as well as negative aspects, proactive vision can ennoble as well as discourage; this happens in *Part V* in a *reprise* of the Elderly Gentleman's final encounter with the Oracle, when the Ancients confront the automata made by the infants Martellus, the sculptor, and Pygmalion, the scientist. These manufactured twentieth-century-type humans have no self-control, and they are so terrified of the Ancients that, after killing their creator, Pygmalion, each in the grip of fear-induced self-interest immediately suggests that the other be killed. The Ancients with Solomonic wisdom ask them: "One of you is to be destroyed. Which of you shall it be?" According to the stage directions, the Ancients take the automata by one hand and place the other on their heads, and, after a slight convulsion, during which their "*eyes are fixed*" on the Ancients, the automata make their answer. Released from their stimulus/reaction determinism, the automata are capable of making an imaginative leap beyond their own self-interest toward intersubjectivity. Although similar to the Oracle's encounter with the Elderly Gentleman, the result of the Ancients' action has put "a little more life into them." Ozymandias suggests that he be killed and Cleopatra-Semiramis spared, while she asks that they both be killed: "How could either of us live without the other?" (*Plays*, 954). Whereas in *Part IV* the Oracle shows pity to the shortliver, in this scene the imaginations of the shortlivers (for that is what the automata are) are enhanced. By going beyond self-interest and the Imaginary, they embrace pity and death in their metaphorical entry into the intersubjectivity of the Symbolic.

Yet again Shaw was prescient. Far from blind to the role played by either Natural Selection in evolution or behaviorism in our mental lives, he stresses how human beings are prisoners of ingrained behavioral habits, where even the Ancients of *Part V* are tied to bodies with their inevitable "compulsion to repeat." Nevertheless behaviorism as a determinist theory banishes "mind from the human animal," to paraphrase Samuel Butler's adage, so frequently quoted by Shaw, of Darwin having banished mind from the universe. Only the exercise of realistic imagination as an understanding of the Symbolic, of self-control as "a highly developed vital sense, dominating and regulating the mere appetites," can break such behavioral patterns. The Ancients speak of this above all when wanting to escape the tyranny of their bodies that tie even them to the Imaginary.

If a conception of death or the poet's lies or the serpent's principle of negation ("why not?") can act as a spur to imaginative capacity, then the much more difficult ability to conceive of what is called life becomes the greatest challenge to imagination. This we can gather from the Ancient's response to the children's taunt of their living a miserable life: "Infant: one moment of the ecstasy of life as we live it would strike you dead" (*Plays*, 939). Beyond defective or romantic imagination and critical or realistic imagination lies a more important aspect to imagination, creative imagination, with implications in terms of epistemology, ontology, and practical action. The Serpent announced this type of imagination in the first play: "imagination is the beginning of creation," which becomes the principal theme of the final play, *As Far as Thought Can Reach*. The Infants (idealized types of shortlivers) exercise their imaginations in an Imaginary of love, art, science, and nature. All are found wanting: "Art is the magic *mirror* you make to reflect your invisible dreams in visible pictures. You use a glass mirror to see your face: you use works of art to see your soul. But we who are older use neither glass mirrors nor works of art. We have a direct sense of life" (*Plays*, 957).

The Ancients, having become *blind* to this Imaginary, can *read* the Symbolic, a writing that constitutes their world, their life, directly, thus entering into what Lacan might call a true relationship with the Real. This Symbolic is represented by their interest in mathematics, a language beyond that of metaphor and the image.

Shaw distinguishes two metaphorical antitheses involving the concept of life: life/matter and life/death. The first, life/matter, refers to perceptions in the spatial-temporal world (the Imaginary), and the second, life/death, refers to the imaginative capacity irrespective of space and time (the Symbolic) analogous to Kant's division between understanding and reason, between Plato's world of appearances and world of ideas, or between logocentrism and différance. *Part V* shows the Infants in full celebration of the life/matter antithesis, the world of the senses. It opens with the infants dancing, when an Ancient sleepwalking "with his *eyes closed*" (*Plays*, 638) appears lost in intense thought (*dreaming*) and interrupts the festivities. More and more the Ancients—like the Serpent who dreamed of "things that never were"—aspire to a liberation from the world of the senses toward a world of thought, whereby language, the Symbolic, would lose its metaphoric basis in a movement from Image to Word.

Deconstruction of Imagination: Language beyond Metaphor

Without appreciating the tendency toward the Symbolic, beyond a language fixed to the Imaginary, the text of *Back to Methuselah*, with its emphasis on the neo-Platonic metaphors of light and vision on which the Image depends, might seem to subscribe to the philosophy of the logos. To Derrida and deconstructionists, for whom thought is a special case of writing, of the Word, rather than the reverse, such photological logocentrism is anathema. Most interesting about this text is its anticipation of deconstruction's objections to logocentrism and its tracings of these doubts, which are scattered through the play-cycle. For example, Lilith devises her poem of creation before the creation of spoken language in a silent language, which might correspond to Derrida's concept of archê-writing. Most notably, in dealing with the metaphorical nature of language and imagination, the limits of the theory of imagination, carefully built up through the play-cycle, are recognized. As with the limitations Lacan recognizes in the Imaginary, the problem lies in the concept of imagination itself, which Shaw deconstructs, as it were, before the fact. Imagination requires an ability to imagine, to make images in the mind, or to understand in images as in a Kantian space-time continuum. This is accompanied by an ability to think symbolically, to use language (Kantian "pure reason," or the Ancients' thought without words), but both the Shaw text and Lacan recognize that they, the Image and the Word, are *not* homologous. At its limits, the imaginative capacity in language becomes redundant, when, by escaping the entanglements, the playing with the shadows of the Imaginary in what Lacan calls "the zone of shadow" (*Seminar II*, 204), the subject goes beyond language, the Symbolic, to enter a relation with the Real. Imagination is replaced with "a direct sense of life," as the She-Ancient puts it. The image loses its meaning in language, in the Word in the same way as Lilith, the imaginative principle, foresees her own legend losing its meaning. "Dead thought," when signifiers become fixed to signifieds, is what the longlivers of *Part IV* call the language that, like one of the Serpent's shed skins, is testimony to ancient struggles with the Imaginary. However, this does not mean that language is sterile. Rather, as a process of différance, this loss of meaning is part of a dynamic of creative imagination, which leads it beyond itself.

Ironically, by means of this deconstruction of imagination, this final part of the play-cycle proposes a Platonic ascent. By taking the eye out of the metaphor of "the mind's eye," and Image out of the concept of imagination, by stripping metaphor from language (the Word), Shaw is left with Platonic thought ("as far as thought can reach") contemplating reality—the ultimate identification of signifier with signified. But in the Shaw text this can never be an absolute or a final, being more a process, like Derridean dissemination, than an ideal Real. This process began in a small way in *Part III*, where some words, such as "parlormaid" and "landlord," had lost their meaning. It became a major theme in *Part IV*, by which time one great difference between the longlivers and the shortlivers lay in their uses of metaphor. After the Elderly Gentleman, a reincarnation of a true Macauley-ite nineteenth-century liberal, delivers a highly metaphorical description of human progress, Zoo explodes with laughter:

> ZOO. Oh, Daddy, Daddy, Daddy, you are a funny little man, with your torches and your coral insects and bees and acorns and stones and mountains.
>
> THE ELDERLY GENTLEMAN. Metaphors, madam. Metaphors, merely.
>
> ZOO. Images, images, images. I was talking about men, not about images. (*Plays*, 921)

In *Part V* these primarily metaphoric visual attributes of language, its imaginative side, are superseded in a Platonic ascent from the senses to pure thought, the world of ideas. Imagination in art is a metaphor for imagination in life; the Ancients leave art behind them when they leave their childhood. That is the point of the Ancients' parable of the rag doll, a Shavian version of Hegelian/Lacanian intersubjectivity within the context of the Imaginary. How the child's love for its rag doll, its imaginary ascription of life to the doll as an Imaginary other, is transferred in adulthood to new dolls, more Imaginary others, as replacements for it. As a desire for images and stories (art) so realistic that it can never be satisfied, the Infants seek to re-create reality (the Imaginary) itself: they create the automata (their own living dolls). Desire is desire of the desire of the other, according to Lacan, which might explain why Shaw calls his scientist creator or dollmaker in *Part V* Pygmalion, after Ovid's sculptor, who created a statue who would love him in return. However, this cannot be done, for finally we realize that our doll is not returning the favor, as it were, which Lacan says is what desire always demands. Turning to nature, friends, and lovers becomes ultimately equally dissatisfying. Eventually "it leads to the truth that you can create nothing but yourself" (*Plays*, 957)— the ego of Lacan's Imaginary. As the She-Ancient says, "It was to myself I turned as to the final reality. Here, and here alone, I could shape and create" (*Plays*, 958). Yet she found that she had made herself a slave of a slave in her search for bodily perfection, which included making "myself into all sorts of fantastic monsters. I walked upon a dozen legs: I worked with twenty hands and a hundred fingers: I looked to the four quarters of the compass with eight eyes out of four heads." Her body had become an automaton, "the last doll to be discarded" (*Plays*, 957). The Ancients discovered what was the first and ultimate Imaginary relation (or shadow): identification with their bodies over which they seemed to have such control. In fact, as subjects, they were only enslaved automatons, and as the slave becomes the master when the master cannot live without him in Hegelian fashion, they were only slaves of a slave: the body. Like the Elderly Gentleman, they look forward to another death of the Imaginary. As another variation on Cain's dream, they complain of the Imaginary dualism associated with Descartes in Western philosophy: "Whilst we are tied to this tyrannous body we are subject to its death and our destiny is not achieved . . . our destiny to be immortal. . . . The day will come when there will be no people, only thought. And that will be life eternal" (*Plays*, 958). They seek eternal life as death, as true Lacanian nonsubjects without language, or as Derrida's signifiance, "the perpetual metonymy of signifiers," as différance.

The infants, living in the Arcadia of pastoral literary tradition, reprise this discussion of aging, death, and beyond. Ecrasia, the art lover and critic, exclaims, "No limbs, no contours, no exquisite lines and elegant shapes, no worship of beautiful bodies, no poetic embraces in which cultivated lovers pretend that their caressing hands are wandering over celestial hills and enchanted valleys." Acis, the nature lover, interrupts her disgustedly: "What an inhuman mind you have, Ecrasia! Why dont you fall in love with someone? Love is a simple thing and a deep thing: it is an act of life and not an illusion. Art is all illusion." To which the sculptor, Arjillax, replies: "That is false. The statue comes to life always." But his master, Martellus, feels that "nothing remains beautiful and interesting except thought, because the thought is the life" (*Plays*, 959). And again Shaw's "thought" here should be considered as langue rather than parole (Saussure's distinction), language as distinct from speech, the Word as the Symbolic or signifiance.

Creative imagination, then, may be interpreted as a desire to emerge from the shadows of the Imaginary (the material world, which exists in space and time) within language. But Shaw's structural vision, his chronological myth, has historical implications related, perhaps, to Yeats's concept of the gyres. As with Nietzsche, history is circular; civilization advances and retreats; there appears to be no progress, no evolution, which is why the Fabian utopia of *Part III* is false: extant social problems have been solved, but duration of human life (that is, imaginative capacity) has been circumscribed. The He- and She-Ancients of *Part V* reincarnate ("metempsychosis," as Confucius calls it in *Part III*) Adam and Eve of *Part I*, Act II, just as the Archbishop and Mrs. Lutestring reincarnate the Adam and Eve of *Part I*, Act I. However, there is a difference. Whereas Adam and Eve were incapable of bearing the burden of immortality, the Ancients are not only capable but indeed want to surpass it. The difference lies in their capacity for creative imagination, which began with the entry of Adam and Eve into the realm of the Symbolic, the Word, by *staring* at the dead fawn thereby beginning their journey of différance beyond the (logic of the) Image. So, while history might be seen as circular, it can also be spiral-like as men develop a greater capacity for imagination in the Symbolic, and in which at any moment they may enter into an encounter with the Real (Aristotle's *tuche*—as opposed to *automaton*—as understood by Lacan), like Napoleon in *Man of Destiny* or when Caesar crossed the Rubicon.

As always, the cosmological and historical allegory of this aspiration toward a "direct sense of life" applies to *both* a lifetime *and* a moment of a single individual, the spectator-reader as subject. The last word, an end that is no end, on this is left to the creative principle herself, Lilith, who "in the beginning" saw death as Adam and Eve saw it and decided to split herself in two, to become différance. She now looks forward to her name as signifier becoming detached from its signified:

I shall see the slave set free and the enemy reconciled, the whirlpool become all life and no matter. And because these infants that call themselves ancients are reaching out towards that, I will have patience with them still; though I know well that when they attain it they shall become one with me and supersede me, and Lilith will be only a legend and a lay that has lost its meaning. (*Plays*, 962)

The Ancients strive to become one with the creative imagination (Lilith) and to go beyond even that, though as an instance of Derridean différance we can notice a curious circular aporia in the text. Lilith splits herself in two to become Adam and Eve, and as we and all the shortlivers and longlivers and the Ancients are all descendants of Adam and Eve, the Ancients are striving to become and supersede in time what they already are outside of time. This aporia, as a deconstruction of beginnings and origins, best expresses how the play functions as a chronological myth of a linguistic predicament that places more emphasis than elsewhere in the Shaw text on the metaphorical nature of language, as well, of course, as on its subject-object structure. Shaw, the writer, looks forward to the time when his legend of Lilith may be superseded, when the metaphorical aspect of his imaginative effort in creating this dramatic poem of Lilith and her descendants loses its meaning, as her name is detached from her legend, her poem, her narrative, as the signifier is detached from the signified. A new level of reality is reached with language, that Symbolic fabric, renewing itself like the Serpent shedding its old skin to reveal a new one, a new text as part of a new cultural fabric.

Et in Arcadia ego

The title *Back to Methuselah* is an ironic adaptation of Rousseau's slogan, "back to nature." The Rousseauist association is echoed in Savvy's name—"short for savage" (*Plays*, 871)—in *Part II* and is further picked up and mocked in the formal textual parody of the genre of pastoral that is *Part V: As Far As Thought Can Reach*. In a typical pastoral, the young shepherds and nymphs of Arcadia are completely preoccupied with such bucolic activities as making love and hunting, or making music and dancing. *As Far As Thought Can Reach* begins with flute players fluting and young people dancing, and, as the stage directions put it: *"They move with perfect balance and grace, racing through a figure like a farandole. They neither romp or hug in our manner. At the first full close they clap their hands to stop the musicians, who recommence with a saraband"* (*Plays*, 938).

A saraband is a slow, solemn dance, mournful even, compared to the spirited farandole. Thus the text in musical terms announces a dichotomy that epitomizes the genre of the pastoral. Invariably death (*Et in Arcadia ego*) irrupts into the pastoral idyll to throw the young people into a state of disorder not to be resolved until the local god, or a priest of the god, comes along.[16] Shaw's text is amazingly faithful to these genre conventions, and with some irony the He-Ancient refers to himself as a shepherd, which is also a strongly Christian metaphor; the Judeo-Christian Bible, of course, draws strongly on pastoral associations. In fact, most of the names Shaw uses are associated with pastorals: Strephon, Martellus, Chloe, Amaryllis—all names, incidentally, to be found in Swift's notorious scatological antipastorals.

For some reason, rather than trace such play with genre intertextuality, critics of the play-cycle, lost like *The Philanderer's* theater critic in their own Imaginary shadows that they label art, became incensed with Shaw's attack, as they saw it, on art. The text throughout *Back to Methuselah*, with great dramatic and, indeed, poetic ingenuity, portrays onstage many life experiences including birth, childhood, marriage, and death. *Part V* shows the processes of children maturing into adults, displaced onto young adults trying to stave off old age, and of people in old age preparing to die, displaced onto unimaginably old Ancients who can only die by an inevitable accident. These displacements work as double articulation or as analogy to express the workings of the Imaginary within the Symbolic. The critics of the original productions of the play-cycle reacted with hostility and disgust to the portrayal of these existential realities of youth and romance and old age and death, and surely Shaw appreciated this irony; these reactions replicated those of the young people reacting to the old people in the play and of Eve to the mechanics of sex. But there is method in the madness of the text. Death, a constant in conventions of the pastoral, is also the originating (non-) metaphor for Shaw's play-cycle. Death as a concept provided a basis for a general phenomenological inquiry into imagination, into metaphor and language, the Image and the Word, the Imaginary and the Symbolic, in a drama that presents to the audience an extended vision of death, which phrase is itself a deconstruction as, like the lie, it can only pertain to the Symbolic, to language.[17] The pastoral textual conventions Shaw evokes, if seen in the light of the classical sources, can be thought of as Ovid superimposed on the *Eclogues* of

Virgil—with Ovid's sculptor Pygmalion the name most relevant to the Shaw text. Critics have noted another poet and his use of language who is frequently alluded to in Shaw's play *Pygmalion*: John Milton, whose Satan, from *Paradise Lost*, infects aspects of Shaw's Henry Higgins.[18] *Paradise Lost* is a rewriting of Genesis, and *Back to Methuselah: Part I* is a rewriting of both Genesis and *Paradise Lost*. In all three, death and sex rear their ugly heads in the pastoral setting of Eden as irruptions of Lacan's Real. The similarity of Milton's biblical pastoral to the conventions of the pastoral set in Arcadia is obvious. Thus this thread of Bible-Milton-Pastoral intertextuality is another link between *Methuselah: Part I* and *Part V*.

Shaw's reference to *the fourth century B.C.* in the opening stage directions suggests, of course, Plato. Milton had been much influenced by the neo-Platonism of Italian Renaissance pastorals during his travels in Italy, and he would have viewed his rewriting of what went on in Eden in terms of those Arcadian and pastoral conventions. William Blake, a great admirer of Milton, was also in this line of neo-Platonism, and his influence has been traced in the Shaw text before now.[19] A neo-Platonism, referred to earlier, is also evident in the title of *Part I, In the Beginning*, which uses the first words of not only *Genesis* but also the Gospel of St. John, "In the beginning was the Word." Shaw writes in the postscript that "the Thought was what the Greeks meant by the Word [Logos]," and Thought is incorporated into the seemingly immodest title of *Part V: As Far as Thought Can Reach*. However, as the title itself is an aporia that suggests both the limits of Platonism as well as its apotheosis, it might be a case yet again in the Shaw text of both/and, with a refusal to favor one side of a logocentric binary opposition over the other.[20]

Allegory of Imagination: Textuality and the Critical Reader

An integral part of the thematic of imagination and language, the Image and the Word, in the play-cycle is the interaction between the play and its audience. Shaw, a self-confessed didactic writer, was concerned about how this allegorical text would be read. Modernist critics like Eliot, Pound, and Yeats failed to appreciate that Shaw's didacticism in his text does not insist on any one particular reading or any one textual interpretation of his writing. The reverse is the case. Yet G.B.S. would do anything, stand on his proverbial, acronymical, textual, metaphorical head if necessary, to attract the reader's attention to his tub-thumping booth. Shaw never claimed an author's authority over his texts, and readers have to read them by supplying their own level of interest, range of knowledge, and investment in or commitment to the text. The allegory of imagination can be read on many levels: social, historical, psychological, philosophical, poetic, and theatrical. It demands a creative act of critical reading. Shaw knew that, as he wrote in a letter to Sasha Kropotkin-Lebedeff in November 1920, "as far as the theatre is concerned [it is] all quite impossible except for a very thoughtful and advanced audience" (*Letters 3*, 701). In the theater, the play-cycle can work on the spectator analogously to the way the Great War had worked on him in prompting its writing, or the way the realization of death by Adam and Eve at the beginning of the drama prompted the working of imagination in language and history. *Back to Methuselah*, written as a self-reflexive text, can be appreciated in an act of critical reading that is itself the result of the working of imagination, with imagination begetting imagination.

After writing his finest example of character-based drama in *Heartbreak House*, Shaw decided against using that mode as the dramatic form for the play-cycle when he redrafted *Part II* of *Methuselah*. So, while Captain Shotover's seventh degree of concentration is transmuted into the Barnabas brothers' gospel of longevity, he preferred to elaborate a multi-part fable in the manner of the medieval mystery plays to the extent of beginning his myth with such familiar biblical characters as Eve, Adam, and Cain. This time Shaw was not interested solely in evoking a critical response by means of a drama of feelings and ideas, as his dramaturgy had been for the most part up to this stage. *Methuselah*, in breaking away from character-based drama as well as from any notion of the Aristotelian unities, suggests to the spectator-reader a turning away from the Imaginary.[21] Not, of course, that *Back to Methuselah* is totally devoid of Imaginary fascinations—it is full of them. But *Back to Methuselah* seeks to fascinate the imagination to make it think, as Brecht in his own way (often with fable or parable) later did with his audience. If the thematic of creative imagination pervades the play-text, it applies also outside of it, where a development in human imagination might be educed in a way analogous to the proactive power of vision of the longlivers in the play. His next play, *Saint Joan*, reverted to character-based drama; Joan became the very incarnation of Shaw's gospel of creative imagination, of the Word made flesh, although its dream epilogue became notorious for offending the sensibilities of those who held the classical unities dear.[22] The plays of the 1930s such as *Too True to Be Good* and *The Simpleton of the Unexpected Isles* continued the formal experiments initiated with *Back to Methuselah*.

To understand the novel dramaturgy of this play-text of the imagination, three other aspects, already touched on, of the textuality and intertextuality of the text apart from allegory should be noted. First, Shaw developed a technique of symbolic farce quite different from the forms of drama he had heretofore made his own: the problem play, the play of ideas, and the disquisitory play. Shaw had already experimented with different forms in such works as *Fanny's First Play* and some of the shorter plays. And *Back to Methuselah*, which veered away from the tragic undertones of *Heartbreak House*, retained aspects of that play's symbolic comedy with the Elderly Gentleman's butterfly dance in *Part IV*, or with the poetic bathos of "Me and cook had a look at your book" (*Plays*, 872) in *Part II*, or with the echo of the Peasants' Revolt in Cain's "When Adam delved and Eve span, where was then the gentleman?" (*Plays*, 868) in *Part I*. This symbolic farce also operates by using the same actors to depict similar character types in different contexts throughout the play-cycle. This technique of dramatic reincarnation or metempsychosis enabled Shaw to expand the conceptual possibilities of his drama and to undermine traditional ideas on identity—as well as cut production costs for his epic drama. In a letter to Lawrence Langner he identified some possible doublings and character types:

> Adam, Conrad, The Accountant General, the Envoy (unsympathetic character actor)
>
> Eve, Mrs Lutestring, the Oracle, the She-Ancient (dignified leading lady)
>
> Cain, Burge, Burge-Lubin, Napoleon, Ozymandias (Brilliant swagger and geniality)
>
> Lubin, Confucius, Elderly Gentleman, Pygmalion (Must have a gentle and very distinct voice)
>
> Savvy, Zoo, The Newly Born
>
> Franklyn, The He-Ancient. (*Letters 3*, 727)

A second aspect of technique is Shaw's weaving of recurrent concepts thematically throughout the work, much as Wagner did with musical motifs (*Leitmotiven*) in his music-dramas. Again *Heartbreak House* and *Back to Methuselah* are, albeit in differing ways, supreme examples of how Shavian drama operates as music. In *Methuselah* concepts such as rationality, laughter, language, metaphor, vision, image, imagination, love, art, wisdom, conscience, creativity, civilization, militarism, good government, empire, history, science, geology, biology, religion, evolution, immortality, death, sex, and even the importance of good manners are all worked into the dense textual texture. These themes are introduced in different contexts, recur in others, undergo development and variation, and are often inverted: "I don't think it will come to a Socratic dialogue pure and simple. . . . To the end I may have to disregard the boredom of the spectator who has not mastered all the motifs, as Wagner had to do" (*Letters 3*, 575).

This is significant because not only does Shaw refer to Wagner's system of Leitmotiven but Shaw also associates the system with the dialogue form of Platonic philosophy. However, Shaw is adamant that he is writing a drama, not simply a philosophical dialogue. The logic of the development of his themes is musical-dramatic, rather than strictly philosophic, and the end lies in the encounter between text and audience or reader and "beyond," not in an ideal Real or Truth or Good or Beautiful.

Allusion presents a third intertextual aspect of *Back to Methuselah*'s technique: the play constantly alludes, in both form and content, to people, history, books, texts, and genres external to it. "The father of history," to give one instance, is referred to in *Part IV* as "Thucyderodotus Macollybuckle." Shaw's comment, written to H. G. Wells when he was working on *Methuselah* is telling: "Classical literature is nine-tenths allusion." Thus the text is not unlike Joyce's *Ulysses*, published the following year, which Shaw had been reading during the composition of *Methuselah* "in its serial form" (*Letters 3*, 719) in the *Little Review* (1918–1920), as he informed Sylvia Beach.[23] Later allusions were made in the opposite direction; for instance, Martha Black offers a persuasive account of how *Back to Methuselah* casts a large shadow over Joyce's *Finnegans Wake*.[24]

In its cosmological comprehensiveness, *Back to Methuselah* can be seen to allude to a wide range of textual models, of which the Bible is the most obvious. But Shaw drew on other epoch-making texts: Plato's *Republic*, Augustine's *City of God*, Dante's *The Divine Comedy*, Milton's *Paradise Lost*, Swift's *Gulliver's Travels*, Blake's *Jerusalem*, Shelley's *Prometheus Unbound*, Goethe's *Faust*, Nietzsche's *Also sprach Zarathustra*, Darwin's *On the Origin of Species*, Wagner's *Der Ring des Nibelungen*, and, perhaps, Hegel's *Phenomenology of Mind*.

The allusiveness to the Bible, as the most obvious example, appears immediately in the titles. "Pentateuch" in the subtitle refers to Genesis:

"In the beginning" as the title of the first play refers to both Genesis (Old Testament) and Saint John's Gospel (New Testament); "Gospel" and "Barnabas" in the title of the second play refer to the Gospels and the Acts of the Apostles in the New Testament (where Barnabas is Paul's companion on his missionary journeys). "The Thing Happens" possibly refers to the Annunciation. "The Elderly Gentleman" is an amalgam of Moses, who sees the Promised Land, but does not enter it, and Job. For a drama that looks forward so much, the Rousseauist main title, *Back to Methuselah*, ironically insists on going backward by implying the cyclical aspect of history implicit in the play and with Methuselah—the longest lived character in the Bible at 969 years-old (Genesis: 5–27)—suggesting the prophetic aspect of Shaw's work. However, Shaw's nature is more the symbol-laden Garden of Eden rather than Rousseau's Imaginary nature. The He-Ancient offers a devastating critique of the Romantic view of the beauty of nature in its original state in *Part V*: "Mere metaphor . . . the mountains are corpses" (*Plays*, 958). Rousseau is described in the play as "a sort of Deist" (*Plays*, 887), where Deism is a kind of clockwork Christianity typical of the Enlightenment, a mechanistic view of the world inimical to Shaw's.[25] It may not be entirely a coincidence that part 2 of Derrida's *Of Grammatology* is a commentary on a text by Rousseau. Certainly Shaw has a much more complex view of origins, ideals, and goals than Rousseau. But, perhaps, as with Derrida, who found Rousseau worth deconstructing because his text actually supplied so much of the deconstruction itself, Shaw found more in Rousseau than something to criticize.

This textual and conceptual allusiveness is a part of the text's cultural context, which, along with the other aspects of technique, becomes an integral part of its dialectic. *Back to Methuselah*, as a text among texts, becomes a model of intertextuality. It reflects and can only proceed out of the Westernized Judeo-Hellenic-Christian cultural tradition, the "mental fabric" of which it is a part—or, rather, with which it is interwoven. Appreciation of that language, that cultural writing as Word, must be part of the spectator's or reader's response to the drama of the Image. In loose Hegelian terms, the spectator-reader is invited to make a synthesis from her experience of the play (antithesis) in the light of her own historical experience and knowledge (thesis).

The allusions, themes, and motifs that recur in the play are all concepts or ideas, differing signifiers. But Shaw did not have to anticipate Derrida; his dialectic develops, more or less, after Plato and Hegel, by using concepts such as creative imagination, desire, thought, language, knowledge, reason, conscience, will, vision, curiosity, hope, and dream. This play of ideas is its dramatic form, a Shavian dialectic, which, as in Plato and Hegel, has a double nature. The play of concepts, the development of ideas, involves experience, the experience of a subject interacting with both the world (object) and others in the world: intersubjectivity. *Methuselah* is not only a rewriting of Plato's *Republic*, as has been often commented on, but *Part V* in particular is a rewriting of *Symposium*, a highly influential text in the neo-Platonic tradition stemming from Plotinus and Augustine and Scotus Eriugena, to the Renaissance neo-Platonists and on to the English poets Milton, Blake, and Shelley (who translated it). In *Symposium*, the experience of sexual desire leads toward, or gives way to, a Platonic or spiritual desire for beauty, which ultimately may lead to that bête noir of Derrida's, truth. In *Heartbreak House*, heartbreak in love leads to the beginning of wisdom. In *Back to Methuselah* both these intimately related existential experiences of desire and heartbreak are present, but they are subsidiary to those of death and imagination, that is, the concept of death in language and the imaginative experience of death in life. Death thus becomes the catalyst for developing the creative imagination as dialectically developed in the play, which involves the Imaginary, the Symbolic, and the Real. Although all allegory as a series of correspondences must be arbitrary to some extent, this aspect of death in the dramatic design makes the allegory linking human life span with creative imagination, or the increase of life expectancy with heightened imaginative activity, not as arbitrary as it might otherwise appear.

Creative Imagination

The personification of the Word "in the beginning" is Lilith, the principle of Creative Imagination, as Shaw makes quite clear in the conversation between Eve and the Serpent in Act I. The Serpent tells Eve that Lilith created Adam and herself. "How did Lilith work this miracle?" asks Eve. "She imagined it" (*Plays*, 858), answers the Serpent. Lilith is the creative principle behind the play itself, behind Shaw's writing of it, while within the narrative of the play, Prometheus-like, she creates Adam and Eve. Yet, as an ultimate act of deferral, Lilith is not actually present "in the beginning." Her existence is inferred as a "something else" through the characters and their drama and from the fact of that text/drama as a work of imagination. She appears only at the play's end that is not really an end.

As a drama of imagination with characters drawn from the realm of the fantastic, neither fully particularized as in traditional realist drama, nor as abstract as in an economics treatise, Shaw's warning in *The Perfect Wagnerite*—against the assumption that the giants and gods of Wagner's drama *Der Ring* were superhuman—should be heeded: "The danger is that you will jump to the conclusion that the gods, at least, are a higher order than the human order. On the contrary the world is waiting for man to redeem it from the lame and cramped government of the gods" (*Music 3*, 445).

Thus, in *Back to Methuselah* the longlivers and the Ancients, as well as Lilith and the biblical characters, the writers and politicians, the military men and oracles, the shortlivers, infants, and automata, are symbolic components of the drama of life, of subjectivity in its encounter with the world, as incomplete moments in the drama of becoming more fully human, as traces in a writing of différance. Again Shaw writes in *The Perfect Wagnerite*: "Unless the spectator recognizes in it an image of the life he is himself fighting his way through, it must needs appear to him a monstrous development of the Christmas pantomimes" (*Music 3*, 421). This dialectical play-text of creative imagination acts as a catalyst on the imagination of the spectator-reader who re-creates the text, but here that technique, a metaphorical "pulling oneself up by the bootstraps," is at the same time its thematic. Readers can read the text as the paradigmatic simulacrum of the Shaw text in general, although such textual understanding can never be simple or preordained. If in that encounter the reader responds with her or his own leap of imagination, then an understanding or sympathy of the playing with ideas (the signifiance in the text) might arise as a shadow of Shaw's own critical and textual response to World War I. Encouraging creative imagination in its spectator-readers, not just as a question of understanding themes and techniques, means that the textual *play* takes place in the context of the readers' own experiences. These imaginative encounters and readings provoke further writings and texts like Joyce's *Finnegans Wake* and Clarke's and Kubrick's *2001: A Space Odyssey*, two of the more significant twentieth-century texts to replay the drama of the Image and the Word, in both of which traces can be found of *Methuselah*. In the end, and in spite of the Ancients' disparagement of art, *Back to Methuselah*, as a drama of imagination, remains a highly ambitious, complex, artistic, textual, theatrical experiment, which also seeks to go beyond imagination, beyond the Image, and even beyond the Word. As an epic construction with its own deconstruction, it supplies evidence to justify Shaw's supplementary contention that *Back to Methuselah: A Metabiological Pentateuch* "is a world classic or it is nothing" (*Methuselah* [1945], 300).

Post Scriptum

> *The meaning of [my plays] lies in what had preceded them and in what follows them. The beginning of one of my plays takes place exactly where an unwritten play ended. And the ending of my written play concludes where another play begins. It is the two unwritten plays [the critics] should consider.*
>
> Bernard Shaw as quoted by Paul Green in *Dramatic Heritage*

This volume, this stage for a play of disparate Shaw shadows—image/word, imagination/thought, ideal/real, romance/critique, artist/philosopher, Imaginary/Symbolic, pleasure/jouissance, logocentrism/deconstruction, speech/writing, Apollonian/Dionysian, painting/music, dream/intoxication, principium individuationis/vivisection, philosophy/comedy, ghost/machine, life/death, religion/science, subject/object, signifier/signified, absence/presence, shadow/thing, reading/writing—is now full. The writing is finished, although the text, casting its own shadow(s), may continue elsewhere in other volumes; its meaning lies beyond this text.

The argument presented here has suggested that the writings of poststructuralism are useful for reading the writing and plays of Bernard Shaw. We have not asserted that Shaw is a poststructuralist, nor have we attempted to argue about the validity—one way or the other—of the philosophies of Barthes, Lacan, Derrida, or Shaw. Whether Shaw's insistence on the thematic of writing in the play-texts has the theoretical importance that Derrida ascribes to writing, is a reasonable question to ask. At the very least, a discussion of Derrida's grammatology has allowed us to raise this question and to ask why the Shaw text always seems to refer reflexively to writing: writing as a process of subjectivity, as a shadow of the world where the world is itself a shadow of writing. What has interested us has been how the Shaw text—including the Shaw play-texts—opens itself to this poststructuralist reading. The value of such an attempt lies in making legible what may have been previously misread in the Shaw text or rendering more complex what has heretofore been read too simplistically. Chiefly this concerns its humanism and metaphysics in the context of the subject-object relation. And yet these also present the greatest challenges for a poststructuralist reading. Shaw, one of the best-known advocates of phonetic writing, may be suspected of metaphysics given Derrida's definition of logocentrism as "the metaphysics of phonetic writing" (Derrida, *Grammatology*, 3).

This study has proposed that the metaphysics Shaw argues is necessary would be a new metaphysics to replace what he called the "old fashioned metaphysics of Bacon and Locke." We have also hinted that Shaw's understanding of humanism was quite different from that of Enlightenment rationalists and could be likened more to Heidegger's phenomenology of Dasein (human existence)—a concept that stemmed from a deconstruction of the old metaphysics as derived from the Greeks, but which, according to Derrida, itself became a new metaphysics.[1] And, undoubtedly, Shaw's new metaphysics would be liable to a similar deconstruction. However metaphysics as a Symbolic, a beyond of the pleasure principle, with its own pleasures (as Shaw explained, there are higher passions as well as lower ones), is a need, like hunger and sex, that we will always have with us. As long as it is accompanied by a critique or deconstruction such as supplied by Kant, Nietzsche, Shaw, Heidegger, or Derrida, their texts will be prevented from congealing into the old metaphysics that Derrida labeled logocentrism—whatever the authorial intentions.

As subjects, we are written in a play of signification by différance and constituted by the Symbolic—the book of the world. In either case we are dealing with language and meaning based on differences. Shaw's metaphysics of consciousness is one of imagination, of language and writing, of rewriting and reading and rereading, which in his plays—his dramatic poetry—becomes a site for the conflict between the Image and the Word, between the Imaginary and the Symbolic. The Shaw text was rudely inserted into Western discourse at the end of the nineteenth century, critical of the century that was ending and prophetic of the new one. At the beginning of a newer one, the Shaw text is not dead yet. Imagine.

In the end—if we need to write of ends and beginnings—Plato, Kant, Marx, Shaw, and Lacan were concerned with how the subject acts in encountering the Real, whether called right action, practical action, *praxis*, true speech ("joining the subject to another subject, on the other side of the wall of language, [as] the final relation of the subject to a genuine Other," (Lacan, *Seminar II*, 246)), or what I have described on Shaw's behalf as passionately informed action. The sea-faring inventor Captain Shotover offered a prescription in *Heartbreak House*: "Navigation. Learn it and live; or leave it and be damned." But, typically, Shaw never specified it himself. He comes closest in the famous declaration in the Epistle Dedicatory when the artist-philosopher identifies himself with the purpose of the world as he understands it: "This is the true joy in life, the being used for a purpose recognized by yourself as a mighty one; the being thoroughly worn out before you are thrown on the scrap heap" (*Prefaces*, 163). This remains the beyond of his text and of his theater for the reader-spectator.

Given that Shaw situates his drama as a (textual) Symbolic between the (stage) Imaginary and an (unknowable) Real, and bearing in mind the reading of Shaw's writing proposed by this study, let us close with Shaw's own reading of his writing, his 1894 essay "A Dramatic Realist to His Critics." In it he opposes logocentrism, the Imaginary of stage life, to real life, the Lacanian Real insofar as Shaw asserts that "no sort of consistency is discoverable in it . . . and, as a whole, it is unthinkable," but is, nevertheless, "credible, stimulating, suggestive, various, [and] free from creeds and systems." He goes on:

> It does not concern me that, according to certain ethical systems, all human beings fall into classes labelled liar, coward, thief, and so on. I am myself, according to these systems, a liar, a coward, a thief, and a sensualist; and it is my deliberate, cheerful, and entirely self-respecting intention to continue to the end of my life deceiving people, avoiding danger, making my bargains [irrespective of] abstract justice, and indulging all my appetites, whenever circumstances commend such actions to my judgement. . . . As a realist dramatist, therefore, it is my business to get outside these systems. (*Non-Dramatic*, 325)

In contrast to the man who prefers Imaginary shadows, "stage monsters—walking catalogues of the systemised virtues—to his own species," Shaw declares: "The fact is, though I am willing and anxious to see the human race improved, if possible, still I find that, with reasonably sound specimens, the more intimately I know people the better I like them" (*Non-Dramatic*, 326).

And like Derrida foreswearing origins, he acknowledges that he is not an original dramatist and that for the Symbolic of his theater, rather than the more usual course of taking it from the Imaginary of other dramas, he has:

> plundered ... everyone ... who had anything that was good to steal. I created nothing; I invented nothing; I imagined nothing; I perverted nothing; I simply discovered drama in real life. I now plead strongly for a theatre to supply the want of this sort of drama. I declare that I am tired to utter disgust of imaginary life, imaginary law, imaginary ethics, science, peace, war, love, virtue, villainy, and imaginary everything else, both on the stage and off it. I demand respect, interest, affection for human nature as it is, and life as we must live it even when we have bettered it and ourselves to the utmost. (*Non-Dramatic*, 338)

Notes

Preface

1. Ohmann's *Shaw: The Style and the Man* was an early literary study to incorporate into its analysis the influence of structural linguistics, from which structuralism and poststructuralism derive. This path has hardly been further explored in Shaw studies, although Dietrich's pioneering article "Deconstruction as Devil's Advocacy: a Shavian Alternative" should be acknowledged, as should Reynolds's study *Pygmalion's Wordplay*.

2. Dates given in the main body of the text generally indicate when the work was written. These dates are drawn from several sources including Laurence's *Bernard Shaw: A Bibliography*, *SHAW 20: Bibliographical Shaw*, edited by Laurence and Crawford, *The Cambridge Companion to Bernard Shaw*, edited by Innes, and Morgan's *File on Shaw*. In the case of Shaw's plays, some were published before production and some a considerable time after. For example, the given dates, 1903 and 1921 for the long gestating works, *Man and Superman* and *Back to Methuselah*, respectively, are publication dates, while the date given for *Major Barbara* is 1905, although it was not published until 1907.

3. Neo-Platonism is understood here as that tradition that begins with Plotinus and Porphyry and continues with Augustine, Eriugena, through the Renaissance neo-Platonists, and up to the English poets Milton, Blake, and Shelley.

4. Throughout this study the terms "Imaginary," "Symbolic," and "Real" are capitalized to denote their Lacanian association.

Chapter 1. Reading Writing: Going Behind the Scenes of the Text

1. C.E.M. Joad attempted a systematic exposition of Shaw's philosophy in *Matter, Life and Value*.

2. See Morgan, *Playground*, 100, who, in turn, refers to McDowell "Heaven, Hell and turn-of-the-century London," 245–68.

3. Shaw wrote to Charles Charrington on December 26, 1903, reprinted in *Letters 2*, 85–86, that he had also been reading a verse adaptation of Molière's play by Thomas Corneille, the less famous brother of Pierre Corneille.

4. See *Prefaces*, 864 and 666.

5. See *Methuselah* (1945), lxxxvi.

6. See Lévi-Strauss, "Overture to *le Cru et le Cuit* (*The Raw and the Cooked*)," reprinted in Ehrmann, *Structuralism*, 52–55, and Barthes, "From Work to Text," in Barthes, *Image-Music-Text*, 162–63.

7. See Shaw's "Shakespeare: A Standard Text," in *Times Literary Supplement*, March 17, 1921: "the notation at my disposal cannot convey the play as it should really exist: that is, in its oral delivery. I have to write melodies without bars, without indications of pitch, pace, or timbre, and without modulation, leaving the actor or producer to divine the proper treatment of what is essentially word-music" (*Drama 4*, 1369).

8. Among many others, I consulted the following that give an overview of the field from the advent of Structuralism in the 1960s to the Postmodernism of the 1990s: Ehrmann, *Structuralism*, Hawkes, *Structuralism and Semiotics*, Sturrock, *Structuralism and Since*, Norris, *Deconstruction* and *Derrida*, Devaney, *'Since At Least Plato. . .' and Other Postmodernist Myths*, and Powell, *Postmodernism for Beginners*. Kearney's *Dialogues with Contemporary Continental Thinkers* is also useful in this regard.

9. See *Books 2*, 328–29.

10. See preface to *Major Barbara*: "I first heard the name of Nietzsche from a German mathematician, Miss Borchardt, who had read my Quintessence of Ibsenism, and told me that she saw what I had been reading: namely, Nietzsche's Jenseits von Gut und Böse [*Beyond Good and Evil*]. Which I protest I had never seen, and could not have read with any comfort, for want of the necessary German, if I had seen it" (*Prefaces*, 117). He reviewed the first volume of a projected Collected Works of Nietzsche in English in 1896.

11. See Albert, "Reflections on Shaw and Psychoanalysis," 194.

12. For more on Lacan and the question of "woman," see Lacan, *Feminine Sexuality*, edited by Mitchell and Rose.

13. See Kristeva, *The Kristeva Reader*, 111, for a translation of selections of Kristeva's *La Révolution du Langage Poétique* (Paris: Seuil, 1974).

14. We may also note Berst's comment about the characters in *Man and Superman*: "Each character is not unitary, or a mere collection of masks, but a complex tension of forces and façades, within which lies the individual personality" (Berst, *Drama*, 126).

15. "'A chaos of clear opinions'—this is the latest summary of Shaw's work" (Bentley, *Shaw*, xv), and "Chesterton says of Shaw, as Faguet said earlier of Voltaire, that his work is 'a chaos of clear ideas'" (Watson, *Shavian Guide*, 30).

16. Shaw rather subtly criticizes Marx and Engels for declaring their allegiance to Hegel's dialectic, while, in fact, remaining stuck with "the old-fashioned metaphysics of Bacon and Locke . . . the crudely positive Lockian theory . . . in the absolute Lockian manner" (*Books 2*, 142).

17. These quotations are culled from Reynolds's *Pygmalion's Wordplay*.

Chapter 2. The Critic: The Writer's Shadow

1. See *Music 3*, 106.

2. Edwin Wilson in his introduction to Shaw's criticism on Shakespeare, *Shaw on Shakespeare*, gives examples that echo Shaw's statement that "Shakespeare's power lies in his enormous command of "word-music" (*On Shakespeare,* 26). For example, "When we come to those unrivalled grandiose passages in which Shakespear turns on the full organ, we want to hear the sixteen-foot pipes booming, or, failing that . . . the ennobled tone, and the tempo suddenly steadied with the majesty of deeper purpose. You have, too, those moments when the verse, instead of opening up the depths of sound, rises to its most brilliant clangor, and the lines ring like a thousand trumpets" (*On Shakespeare,* 19). Wilson explains: "It was Shaw's contention that the magic of Shakespeare's language owes more to the music of the verse, the sheer sound of words, than to its meaning or even its imagery" (*On Shakespeare,* 18).

3. See passage beginning "Pray, amiable sir or madam, what is the thing you call yourself?" in "How to Become a Man of Genius," reprinted in *Non-Dramatic,* 341 ff.

4. See Laurence, *Shaw: An Exhibit,* item 192.

5. Ibsen referred to Shaw as a "social-democratic moral philosopher" (Wisenthal, *Shaw and Ibsen,* 15), when rebutting the implication in a newspaper article that he had been critical of either Shaw's lecture or Shaw's interpretation.

6. See Derrida, *Writing and Difference,* 302, n. 8.

7. See Barthes, *Pleasure,* 66.

8. That Shaw associated the word *neurasthenia* with Nordau (and possibly Freud) can be seen in his newspaper controversy in 1911 with Ernest Newman on Hugo von Hofmannsthal's and Richard Strauss's *Elektra*: "psychopathic or neurasthenic, or whatever the appropriate scientific slang may be, and descant generally on the degeneracy of the age in the manner of Dr Nordau" (*Music 3,* 602).

9. The term was first introduced by Joan Riviere in a 1929 article, "Womanliness as Masquerade," and later picked up by Lacan. See Lacan, *Feminine Sexuality,* 43, 53, 74, 84–85.

10. Shaw, in *The Quintessence,* commented on the linguistic ambiguities of such words as *idealist* and *realist* (*Non-Dramatic,* 221–22). Here please note that the Shavian Realist does not correspond to the Lacanian Real, but to the Lacanian Symbolic.

Chapter 3. Authorial Identity: Promethean Strategies of a Pantomime Ostrich

1. I am indebted to Jean Reynolds for allowing me to read her unpublished dissertation, "Immodest Proposals: The Performer in Shaw's Prose," which has areas of interest in common with this chapter.

2. Derrida writes: "a new concept of writing [which] can be called *gram* or *différance* . . . the *a* of *différance* refers to the generative movement in the play of differences." See Derrida, *Positions,* 26–27.

3. Biographies include Henderson (1911), Harris (1931), Henderson (1932), Pearson (1942 and supplementary volume 1963), St John Ervine (1956), Henderson (1956), Rosset (1964), and Holroyd (5 vols., 1988–1992). Margot Peters (1980) and

Sally Peters (1996) deal with particular aspects of the life rather than attempting a full-scale biography.

4. See Harris, *Bernard Shaw*, 3, and also W. R. Titterton's recollection as quoted in Gibbs, *Interviews*, 63–65, for first-hand descriptions of Shaw's platform manner.

5. See the preface to *Ellen Terry and Bernard Shaw: A Correspondence* in *Prefaces*, 780–81.

6. Both these early works were published posthumously: *My Dear Dorothea* in 1956, and *Passion Play* in *Plays 7* in 1974.

7. See the studies of Dietrich (1969, 1996), Carpenter, and Sally Peters. The titles of their books indicate the iconoclastic and aspirational aspects of the young writer, Bernard Shaw.

8. See Tompkins's *To a Young Actress* and *Shaw and Molly Tompkins*.

9. Shaw positively denied having homosexual inclinations while positively asserting his sexual attraction toward the opposite sex in a letter of June 24, 1930, to the extremely frank sexual autobiographer Frank Harris and also on April 15, 1932, to his friend Nancy Astor, whose son was imprisoned for homosexual acts, in *Letters 4*, 190–93, 284–86.

10. See O'Donovan, *Charlatan Genius*, 36–38.

11. In fact, although Shaw called Lee an agnostic, he did associate him with Roman Catholicism, as is clear from a letter to St John Ervine (to which O'Donovan probably did not have access) on October 31, 1942, in *Letters 4*, 645.

12. Shaw's perhaps disingenuous account is in a letter to Frank Harris on June 20, 1930, in *Letters 4*, 188.

13. See Shaw's letter to Harris on June 20, 1930: "As to your question whether Lee's move to London and my mother's were simultaneous, they could not have been. Lee had to make his position in London before he could provide the musical setting for my mother and sister" (Harris, *Shaw*, 43). See also O'Donovan, *Charlatan Genius*, 78, and Rosset, *Shaw of Dublin*, 238–48.

14. See "The Playwright and the Pirate: Bernard Shaw and Frank Harris" in Weintraub, *Shaw's People*, 160. Shaw was mostly rewriting Harris's ghostwriter, Frank Scully, rather than Harris's own writing.

15. See Wisenthal, *Shaw and Ibsen*, 18.

16. The character of John Tanner in *Man and Superman* was partly based on the Marxist leader of the Social-Democratic Federation, H. M. Hyndman, with whom Shaw had a contentious relationship. The germ of the play, begun in May 1900, was possibly an extraordinary letter of Shaw's to Hyndman on April 28, 1900, which lays out the Blakean-Nietzschean antimoralism of the play, in what Shaw calls an "apologia pro mia vita" (*Letters 2*, 160–63).

17. On the question of the liver injections, which caused something of a stir in the press at the time, Shaw sent a rejoinder on June 28, 1938, to Frank Wyatt of the London Vegetarian Society, reprinted in *Letters 4*, 501–2. See also the letter to his old antivivisection friend, Henry S. Salt, of August 29, 1938, in *Letters 4*, 506–7.

18. See preface to *Ellen Terry and Bernard Shaw: A Correspondence*: "Let those who

may complain that it was all on paper remember that only on paper has humanity yet achieved glory, beauty, truth, knowledge, virtue, and abiding love" (*Prefaces*, 795).

19. When W. B. Yeats first read *John Bull's Other Island*, he wrote to Shaw on October 5, 1904: "I thought in reading the first act that you had forgotten Ireland, but I found in the other acts that it is the only subject on which you are entirely serious. . . . You have said things in this play which are entirely true about Ireland, things which nobody has ever said before, and these are the very things that are most part of the action. It astonishes me that you should have been so long in London and yet have remembered so much" (*Letters 2*, 453).

20. This Irish theme of the returning exile is used later by Joyce in his play *Exiles*, which Shaw recommended for production to the Stage Society in 1916 and then went to see when eventually produced by them in 1926; see Weintraub, *Shaw's People*, 128–29. Joyce possibly picked up something of the bitter melancholy of Larry Doyle for his exile, Richard Rowan, as well as for Stephen Dedalus in both *A Portrait of the Artist as a Young Man* and *Ulysses*, all of which Shaw had read and appreciated. See *Letters 3*, 766.

21. Shaw may have known the translations of Plato and Plotinus and other works by Thomas Taylor, a friend of Blake's, who was chiefly responsible for making accessible neo-Platonic writings in English. Shaw certainly knew of Plotinus, as he writes of him and his student Porphyry in an 1887 lecture, "Utopias," published in *SHAW 17*. Most relevantly to *John Bull's Other Island*, Shaw had the two neo-Platonists and this lecture in mind in relation to the ideas of heaven in the play. "Utopias" discusses two visions of Heaven: one, Shaw's own dream of heaven as a child, which is transposed to Broadbent in the play; the other, of "the only people who can really fix their conception of Heaven without foreseeing infinite emptiness and boredom, have been those mystics who, like Porph[y]ry and Plotinus, aspired to an endless ecstasy of contemplation" (*SHAW 17*, 67), is associated with Keegan when we first see him in Act II "*in a trance of intense melancholy, looking over the hills as if by mere intensity of gaze he could pierce the glories of the sunset and see into the streets of heaven*" (*Plays*, 416). We might note further that the neo-Platonism derived from Plotinus links also into Don Juan's dream of contemplation in *Don Juan in Hell*, as well as that of the Ancients in *As Far As Thought Can Reach*.

22. That Shaw knew of Dürer's engraving *Melencolia I* is clear from a letter on March 15, 1927, of Charlotte Shaw to T. E. Lawrence: "[G.B.S.] wants one like Dürer's Melancholia for his Socialism book" (Dunbar, *Mrs. G.B.S.*, 280).

23. Although there is no evidence that Shaw knew of the ninth-century Irish philosopher at the court of Charles the Bald in Paris, Johannes Scotus Eriugena—whom Jorge Luis Borges compared to Shaw in "A Note for (towards) Bernard Shaw" in Borges, *Labyrinths*, 249–50—he would be the most likely and appropriate exemplar of the wandering Irish religious scholar, mystic, and heretic, represented by Peter Keegan in *John Bull's Other Island*. Eriugena was perhaps the best-known neo-Platonist between Augustine and the Renaissance. His philosophy can be seen as an exposition of the doctrine of the Blessed Trinity, most famously associated in Ireland with Saint Patrick and the shamrock, and attributed to Keegan in the play. The similarities between Shaw's thought and Eriugena's, in particular his heresies on predestination, evil, and God as an

unknowable goal, are astonishing. Eriugena's teaching on predestination was condemned as heretical by two Church councils during his lifetime, and his major work, *De Divisione Naturae* (*On the Division of Nature*), was condemned at the Council of Sens (1225), when Pope Honorius III ordered it to be burnt.

Chapter 4. The Spoken/Written Subject: The Machine in the Ghost

1. The most recent defense of Shaw's views in relation to religion and science is Stuart Baker's *Bernard Shaw's Remarkable Religion* (2002). Jacques Barzun's *Darwin, Marx, Wagner* (1941) highlights the problems with Darwinian evolutionary theory in line with Shaw's critique.

2. See Shaw's letter "Shaw Explains His Religion" in *The Freethinker,* November 1, 1908, reprinted in *Agitations,* 117.

3. Shaw writes in the preface (1941) to Richard A. Wilson's *The Miraculous Birth of Language*: "Obviously a playwright working on the Shakespearean plane in the great laboratory of the world with its uncontrived conditions, its innumerable untampered-with animals (mostly human) under observation, and its recorded history as I am, must be a biologist" (13).

4. Derrida's paper is usually translated "Freud and the Scene of Writing," but the word *stage,* which is the meaning the French word *scène* has in the body of the text of the essay, seems more appropriate in relation to a playwright like Shaw. For a similar reason I prefer to translate Derrida's "*Le facteur de la vérité*" as "The Postman of Truth," rather than the more usual "The Purveyor of Truth."

5. A study group of which he had been a leading light in the 1880s "blossomed into the British Economic Association" (*Autobiography 2,* 137). In a letter on January 1, 1935, to Shaw, Maynard Keynes announced in 1935 that he was at work on his *General Theory;* see Skidelsky, *Keynes,* 520–21.

6. For an account of the chronology that led to the writing of *Back to Methuselah* and *The Infidel Half Century,* see my article "*Back to Methuselah*: an Exercise of Imagination" in *SHAW 17.* The rest of that essay is incorporated into chapter 8 of this book.

7. Shaw heavily revised and shortened *The Infidel Half Century* in the 1945 Oxford World Classics edition of *Back to Methuselah.* The version referred to here, therefore, is basically the original 1921 version to be found in the omnibus edition of *Prefaces.* References to the postscript are to *Methuselah* (1945).

8. Darwin's own approach can be seen in a letter to S. P. Woodward of March 6, 1860: "The fair way to view the argument of my book, I think, is to look at Natural Selection as a mere hypothesis . . . & then to judge whether the mere hypothesis explains a large body of facts in Geographical Distribution, Geological Succession, & and more especially in Classification, Homology, Embryology, Rudimentary Organs. The hypothesis to me does seem to explain several independent large classes of facts; & this being so, I view the hypothesis as a theory having a high degree of probability" (Darwin, "Letter to S. P. Woodward").

9. Darwin himself was not opposed to the notion of the inheritance of acquired characteristics, but Weismann insisted on their incompatibility with the theory of natu-

ral selection. Succeeding developments in genetics have generally reinforced Weismann's view although, somewhat ironically, Stephen Jay Gould has suggested that the inheritance of acquired characteristics is not even essential to Lamarck's theory.

10. *The Infidel Half-Century* suggests that Shaw had read, at least, the English translations of Weismann's *The Germ-Plasm: A Theory of Heredity* (1893, reprinted 1974) and *The Evolution Theory* (1904).

11. Warren Sylvester Smith's *Bishop of Everywhere* provides a good introduction to the development of Shaw's thinking on evolutionary theology. Part 2 of Smith's book presents an excellent comparison between Shaw's thinking and that of Teilhard de Chardin in *The Phenomenon of Man*, with which it has much in common, as well as commenting on Shaw's neo-Darwinian antagonist, Julian Huxley, direct descendent of Darwin's great champion, T. H. ("Bulldog") Huxley. See *Shaw-Wells*, 141–53, for information on this controversy, which ranged Shaw on one side, and Huxley, H. G. Wells, and his son ("Gyp") G. P. Wells (who had collaborated on *The Science of Life*) on the other.

12. Shaw writes in *The Quintessence of Ibsenism*: "It is as well to warn those who fancy that Schopenhauerism is one and indivisible, that acceptance of its metaphysics by no means involves endorsement of its philosophy" (*Non-Dramatic*, 214).

13. The best account of Shaw's understanding of Hegel, possibly gleaned from his fellow socialist, music critic, and writer on philosophy, Belfort Bax, are the chapters "Hegel and the Shavian Dialectic" and "A Priest of Hegelian Mysteries" in Whitman, *Shaw and the Play of Ideas*, 119–66.

14. Shortly before writing the *Methuselah* preface in 1920, Shaw delivered a lecture subsequently published as "Foundation Oration," in which he puts the problem in terms of the contrast between the medical scientists of the day and Mrs. Baker Eddy's Christian Science: "You will find that there will be two [medical] schools; there will be a school of persons who will regard the human body, the living organism, as presenting to them a purely chemical problem, and a purely mechanical problem; and, on the other hand, you will have people who will regard the human body as presenting to them a vital problem, and, indeed, one may say an almost inscrutable vital problem, a finally inscrutable vital problem. . . . Of course, it is a return to the old medical school, who used to call themselves vitalists. Their opponents, the mechanical and chemical school [have] been outraging and slaughtering the human race for the last fifty years . . . but . . . when [the old vitalism] is reintroduced at last on a higher plane by, let us say, Scott Haldane, you will find nothing will exasperate him more than to tell him he is a vitalist" (*Platform and Pulpit*, 145ff).

15. The "science wars" followed some time after the publication of Kuhn's *The Structure of Scientific Revolutions* in 1962. In large part these are directed against the poststructuralist writings that form the background to this book with those of Lacan and Derrida as key targets. By interpreting deconstruction as a denial of the possibility of truth in discourse, scientists naturally see it as an attack on the truth claims of their own discourse. However, the "wars" have also occurred within the scientific community itself centered on the problematic of truth and science.

16. Lacan writes: "*Wiederholungszwang*—which we will translate as *compulsion de répétition* [compulsion to repeat] rather than *automatisme de répétition*" (Lacan, *Seminar II*, 64); and: "The beyond of the pleasure principle is expressed by the word *Wiederholungszwang*. This is incorrectly translated in French by *automatisme de répétition* and I think I can give you a better rendition with the notion of *insistence* [*insistance*], repetitive insistence, significant insistence. This function is at the very root of language in so far as a world is a universe subjected to language" (Lacan, *Seminar II*, 206).

17. Trebitsch was a nonpracticing Jew. His Jewish origins did not take any prominence in his life, it seems, until the rise to power of the Nazis in the 1930s. Like Freud, he would eventually have to flee Vienna after the *Anschluss* in 1938. However, according to Hamann's *Hitler's Vienna* (230–31), his half-brother, Arthur Trebitsch, at first was a practicing Jew but later turned into an archetypal self-hating Jew. Arthur published anti-Semitic literature and even sued Siegfried for criticizing in print one of his books. His writings, like Houston Chamberlain's, became a source for the anti-Semitic theories of the young Adolf Hitler living in Vienna. Trebitsch seems never to have informed Shaw of this brother and his activities.

18. See my article, to be published in *SHAW 24*, which examines the connections between *Jitta's Atonement* and Freud and psychoanalysis.

19. Albert's article "Reflections on Shaw and Psychoanalysis" gives a good account of some of the links between Freud and Shaw.

20. Samuel Butler's most famous books were *Erewhon* (1872) and *The Way of All Flesh* (1873–1884, published posthumously in 1903). Shaw was instrumental in getting Butler's last book published, *Erewhon Revisited* (1901). His books on evolutionary theory include *Luck, or Cunning?* (1887), which Shaw reviewed in the Pall Mall Gazette on May 31, 1887 (reprinted in *Books 1*, 277–79).

21. Freud acknowledges this debt to Butler's *Unconscious Memory*, and, indirectly through it, his debt to the Viennese Erwald Herring, whose 1870 lecture to The Imperial Academy of Sciences in Vienna, "*Über das Gedächtnis als eine allgemeine Funktion der organisierten Materie*" ("On Memory as a Universal Function of Organized Matter"), Butler had translated in his book. Freud in his turn translated into German the section on Butler from Israel Lévine's *The Unconscious* (London, 1923). See Appendix A of Freud, *The Unconscious*, 211.

22. *The Infidel Half Century* refers to Blake as "the most religious of our great poets" (*Prefaces*, 533).

23. The naive Haslam in Shaw's play-cycle is a parody of Wagner's Superman, Siegfried, in *Der Ring*.

24. Freud writes: "Our views have from the very first been *dualistic*, and today they are even more definitely dualistic than before—now that we describe the opposition as being, not between ego-instincts and sexual instincts but between life instincts and death instincts" (Freud, *Beyond*, 326).

25. For Althusser, the different Ideological State Apparatuses, which prescribe the different discourses in society, are so efficient in constituting the subject that a singular

superstructure or ideology like religion is no longer necessary; see Althusser's essay "Ideology and Ideological State Apparatuses" in *Lenin and Philosophy*, 121–73. Lacan, for his part, emphasized that the subject, although a fiction, represents something: "there is absolutely no question of the negation of the subject. What is in question is the dependence of the subject . . . specifically at the level of the return to Freud, the dependence of the subject in relation to something truly elementary, which we have tried to bring out with the term 'signifier'" (Forrester, *Seductions*, 381).

26. Forrester points out that for Lacan, desire in the Symbolic denotes a place of lack, which is always the other's desire: "the true realm of psychoanalytic action is the world of desire, which is created by language (the Symbolic) transforming need (the Real; biological demand in the Imaginary) into desire in answer to the unsatisfiable demands of the (m)other" (Forrester, *Seductions*, 110).

27. Shaw explained: "All thinking is wishful . . . we cannot think unless our wishes or fears or cupidities or curiosities create what we call attention. I have known this since my childhood, when somebody shewed me that if I held up my two forefingers in a line from my eyes, I could see two of the nearest when I looked at the farthest, or vice versa, because I had on my two retinas two separate images of everything in sight except the thing I wanted to see. Yet I was conscious of them only when I coordinated them" (*Methuselah* [1945], 296).

28. Freud's *Beyond the Pleasure Principle*, 331, has a footnote on Plato's discussion of love in the *Symposium*. It links Plato's myth of the creation of humans as the division of an original being into two to the myth in the Upanishads ("where the origin of the world from the Atman (the Self or Ego) is described"), and also to Sumerian, Babylonian and Hebrew myths, which is the provenance of the myth of Lilith as she appears in *Back to Methuselah*. Shaw might himself have had *all* of these in mind. Plato is constantly alluded to in the play; the deleted scenes published as *The Domesticity of Franklyn Barnabas* in *Short Stories, Scraps, and Shavings* refer to the Upanishads; and Lilith, who splits herself in two, is the controlling and *originating* creative principle in *Methuselah* who puts in an appearance at the *end* of the play. When *Back to Methuselah* was first published, Ernest Jones, who was in the middle of translating *Beyond the Pleasure Principle*, made the connection between the two works in a letter to Freud on September 6, 1921: "It may interest you to know that Bernard Shaw has just written an epic play in which he attempts to deal with the origin of death and also with Plato's idea of the origin of sex in connection with Lilith." Interestingly he goes on to voice a fear that Freud could be labeled a Creative Evolutionist: "I have just refused an article for the *Journal*, in which the attempt is made to identify your *Anschauung* with that of Bergson. I remarked that it needed to be completed by an indication of the gulf between you. In general, I fear that your Life Instinct [*libido*] in the *Jenseits* [*Beyond the Pleasure Principle*] will lead to your being claimed an adherent of self-creation evolution and vitalism; it will be said that you have found out the error of materialistic determinism" (Freud and Jones, *Correspondence*, 439).

29. See Forrester, *Seductions*, 365–66n150, on death, and also Freud's dictum "*Vor allem beginnt er die Kur mit einer solchen Wiederholung*" (above all, the patient will *begin*

his treatment with a *repetition*), in the article "Remembering, repeating and working through" (1914), SE XII, 150.

30. See Muller and Richardson, *Purloined Poe,* 323–34. See also chapter 4 in Bertolini, *Playwrighting,* 77–96, which treats of *The Doctor's Dilemma* as a Doppelgänger play and links it with the doubling theme of *The Devil's Disciple.* Lacan writes: "the ego's fate, by its very nature, is to always find its reflection confronting it, which dispossess it of all it wishes to attain. This sort of shadow, which is simultaneously rival, master, sometime slave, keeps it at a distance from what is fundamentally at stake, namely the recognition of desire" (Lacan, *Seminar II,* 266).

31. Forrester writes: "From Hegel, Lacan takes . . . the necessarily intersubjective character of all human cognitive . . . states. . . . From . . . Lévi-Strauss he takes the assumption that exchange relations, of women, of words, of . . . "gifts"—with the mirroring obligation they bring with them—are primary in human relations" (Forrester, *Seductions,* 138).

32. Borges writes: "Can an author create characters superior to himself? I would say No and in that negation include both the intellectual and the moral. . . . It is on this opinion that I base my conviction of Shaw's pre-eminence. . . . Lavinia, Blanco Posnet, Keegan, Shotover, Richard Dudgeon and, above all, Julius Caesar, surpass any character imagined by the art of our time. If we think of [Valery's] Monsieur Teste alongside them or Nietzsche's Zarathustra, we can perceive with astonishment and even outrage the primacy of Shaw" (Borges, *Labyrinths,* 249–50).

33. What Lacan says in the preface to the English language version of *Four Fundamental Concepts* is worth bearing in mind and can be applied to the Shaw text: "All I can do is tell the truth. No, that isn't so—I have missed it. There is no truth that, in passing through awareness, does not lie. But one runs after it all the same" (Lacan, *Fundamental Concepts,* vii).

34. For Derrida's uncharacteristic unease with Lacan see especially the extremely long footnote in *Positions,* 107–13, as well as the translator's preface to *Of Grammatology,* lxii–lxiii, and Johnson's "The Frame of Reference" and Peraldi's "A Note on Time in 'The Purloined Letter'" in Muller and Richardson, *Purloined Poe,* 219, 227, 338. Derrida has continued his engagement with Lacan in later essays.

35. See Gallop, "The American Other," in Muller and Richardson, *Purloined Poe,* 280.

36. Freud, in a fascinating digression explains why his theories might undermine what is called here Kant's logocentric understanding of space-time: "we are today in a position to embark on a discussion of the Kantian theorem that time and space are "necessary forms of thought." We have learned that unconscious mental events are in themselves "timeless." This means in the first place that they are not ordered temporally, that time does not change them in any way and that the idea of time cannot be applied to them. These negative characteristics can only be clearly understood if a comparison is made with *conscious* mental processes. However, our abstract idea of time seems to be wholly derived from the method of working of the system *Pcpt.-Cs.* [perception-consciousness] and to correspond to a perception on its own part of that method of

working. This mode of functioning may perhaps constitute another way of providing a shield against stimuli" (Freud, *Beyond*, 300). Freud describes in these last two sentences what Derrida calls archê-writing, where the world writes, as it were, by leaving traces of differences on the perceptual organs of the body.

37. Although clockwork time can be identified with Kant's a priori understanding of space and time, it could be argued that Kant's recognition of logical antinomies works as a deconstruction of logocentrism long before Derrida. By citing Kant, Derrida seems to acknowledge this.

38. Derrida has said in an interview: "We are still *in* metaphysics in the special sense that we are *in* a determinate language. Consequently the ideas that we might be able to get outside of metaphysics has always struck me as naive" (Kearney, *Dialogues*, 111).

Chapter 5. A Writing Machine

1. Derrida points to the etymology of text in words like textile, tissue, texture, which become the basis for more suitable metaphors of weaving and threads etc. than photological or phonological metaphors, as for instance: "This interweaving, this textile, is the *text* produced only in the transformation of another text" (Derrida, *Positions*, 26). (This book might have been called Shaw Threads rather than Shaw Shadows.)

2. The debate with Archer can be followed in *Letters 1–3* right up to the time of Archer's death in 1924. Shaw inserted Walkley twice into the Shaw text: as the dedicatee of the Epistle Dedicatory to *Man and Superman*, as discussed in chapter 1, and as the critic "Trotter" in *Fanny's First Play*, as discussed in chapter 6. Despite their differences Shaw was on the best of personal terms with both critics: Archer was one of his best friends; and, according to Shaw's preface, Walkley himself helped with Trotter's makeup for the first production of *Fanny's First Play*; see Dukore, *Shaw's Theater*, 196–205. See also Pharand, *Bernard Shaw and the French*, 49–69, for a closer look at Shaw and the French theater.

3. Shaw was fond of contrasting his organic method of writing with the clockwork methods of the plot constructors. Paul de Man's *Blindness and Insight* has deconstructed that particular metaphor of artistic creation in relation to the Romantics who so heavily influenced Shaw. I bypass this particular debate, although not without noting that critics like Meisel, Dukore, and Bertolini all point to constructivist methods in Shaw's dramaturgy, in spite of his protestations to the contrary. As in so much else, the formula "both/and" might well apply here.

4. See Shaw's review "Sardoodledom" from Saturday Review, June 1, 1895, reprinted in *Drama 2*, 353–59.

5. For instance, T. S. Eliot insisted that people need to "be made to understand that the potent ju-ju of the Life Force is a gross superstition," in "Shaw, Robertson, and the Maid in *The Criterion 4* (April 1926), reprinted in Weintraub, *Joan Fifty Years After*, 92–93.

6. Godard featured the cover of Derrida's *De la Grammatologie* in his film *Le Gai Savoir* (1968), the year after it was first published.

7. Shaw removed this revealing reference to Sardou in later editions of the play.

8. See Berst, "*The Man of Destiny*: Shaw, Napoleon, and the Theater of Life" in *SHAW 7*.

9. See Forrester, *Seductions*, 208 ff.

10. Shaw would have known *The Aeneid* through Dryden's translation, from the first lines of which he drew for the title *Arms and the Man*. Shaw paid for the publication in 1926 of Henry Salt's translation of The Story of Dido and Aeneas from The Fourth Book of Virgil's *Aeneid*, although he confessed he "could not read [Virgil] through" (*Autobiography 1*, 126).

11. The play was first produced in New York on September 26, 1904. It was published in English in 1907, along with *John Bull's Other Island* and *Major Barbara*.

12. *Candida* received its first private London performance in 1900, given by the Stage Society, while its first public performances opened at the Court Theatre on April 26, 1904. *Man and Superman* was published in 1903 but not produced until 1905.

13. See Patrick White "Chaucer: *Franklin's Tale* as analogue for *Candida*" in *SHAW 12*. Shaw himself links that Arthurian tale *Parsifal* with *Candida* and *How He Lied to Her Husband* in the holograph manuscript, but not in the published edition, of *How He Lied*. In the manuscript, the poet and the lady discuss whether they should go out to see *Candida* or *Parsifal* at the theater that evening; see *Candida: Holograph*, 204–5.

14. Although in his economics writing Shaw laments his inadequacy in algebra, he always retained an interest in numbers as can be seen with the fun he has with logarithms in *In Good King Charles's Golden Days*, as well as in his advocacy of the duodecimal system for common usage; see *Agitations*, 125–27.

Chapter 6. The Playwright and the Critics

1. Shaw wrote to Richard Mansfield on February 27, 1895: "Cuthbertson is a caricature of Clement Scott" (*Letters 1*, 488).

2. Shaw best describes the early part of the Ibsen boom and his activities in it in a letter to Charles Charrington of March 30, 1891, reprinted in *Letters 1*, 286–91. Wisenthal's sober retelling of Shaw's involvement in *Shaw and Ibsen* rebuts Michael Egan's attempt in his Introduction to *Ibsen: The Critical Heritage* to downplay Shaw's role in the Ibsen controversy of the early 1890s. Wisenthal's critique can also be applied to Simon Williams's more recent article, "Ibsen and the Theatre 1877–1900" in *The Cambridge Guide to Ibsen*, edited by McFarlane, 167–89, which inexplicably gives an account of the Ibsen boom in London in the early 1890s without reference to Shaw. While the Ibsen boom in London would have happened without Shaw, its effects on Shaw and how he reacted to it, particularly on the Ibsen/Fabian audience, had enormous consequences. Shavian theater grew from it, leading to the Shaw boom in the first decade of the new century in association with Granville Barker, as well as with other dramatists of the New Drama, and from that grew twentieth-century British theater. And in politics, *The Quintessence* became something of a manifesto for feminism and socialism.

3. On August 17, 1890, Shaw wrote and told Archer, who was going to meet Ibsen in Munich, to explain to the Norwegian dramatist the part Shaw had *not* read aloud to Archer before the lecture. Archer's input as translator of Ibsen was necessary to Shaw's knowledge of the plays as not all had been translated into English at that time. Archer himself wrote in November 1891: "Your treatment of *Brand* and *Peer Gynt* [in *The Quintessence*] fills me with envious awe. I have read and re-read these poems . . . you, on the other hand have never read them at all, but have merely picked up a vague second-hand knowledge of their outlines; yet you have penetrated their mystery (I speak in all seriousness) much more thoroughly than I have" (Wisenthal, *Shaw and Ibsen,* 25).

4. Shaw had persuaded Farr to produce *Rosmersholm,* because the New Woman of that play, Rebecca West, finally attains a higher love quite different from the ideal of romantic love. Such a higher love has no place in *The Philanderer* and would not appear in a Shaw play until *Candida,* a twin play in some respects to *The Philanderer* with the character of Candida as the philanderer's female counterpart (which might account for Beatrice Webb's disapproval). Farr produced *Arms and the Man* in 1894, which can be called Shaw's first "success" on the London stage. The 1891 production of *Widowers' Houses* had been more of a *succès du scandale,* and neither of the other *Unpleasant* plays had been produced.

5. The leading article was not in fact by Scott, as Shaw later acknowledged.

6. In this respect Cuthbertson/Scott is more like Count O'Dowda in *Fanny's First Play* than the critic Trotter who is modeled on A. B. Walkley. See also the text of Shaw's lecture of 1889 "Acting, by one who does not believe in it; or the place of the stage in the fool's paradise of art," reprinted in *Drama 1,* 92.

7. A third (type of) woman is thrown into this mix: the degendered or masculine woman, in the person of Sylvia, the sister of the Womanly Woman—although the lesbian implications, like in the later *Getting Married* (discussed as another "autobiographical" play in chapter 7), are not fully brought out. Sylvia wears a trousers outfit (with detachable skirt!), insists on being addressed as if she were a man, and smokes. All these were highly coded signifiers of masculinity in 1893. And the comment by her father that she is of "a different nature" could be seen as censor-induced code for lesbianism. Among Shaw's closest friends at this time were Edward Carpenter and Kate Salt, both homosexual; it is unlikely this circumspection was due to self-censorship on Shaw's part. Although Sylvia is presented as being impervious to a relation with a man and above the romantic intrigues of the "womanly woman," nowhere is it suggested that a relation with a woman might be a possible alternative. Shaw seems to have taken both her name and Julia's from Shakespeare's *Two Gentlemen of Verona,* though there Julia is the cross-dresser. Shaw's point might have more to do with Julia, who puts on her "Woman"-liness, just as Sylvia puts on her "Man"-ly clothes, or as Shakespeare's Julia does hers.

8. When Archer on January 22, 1900, solicited a play of Shaw's for The New Century Theatre to put on with Elizabeth Robins in a leading role, he cautioned Shaw in block capitals in a postscript "N.B. NO PHILANDERERS NEED APPLY!" (*Letters 2,* 136).

9. Shaw wrote in an appendix to *Widowers' Houses*: "it is impossible for any fictionist, dramatic or other, to make true pictures of modern society without some knowledge of the economic anatomy of it" (*Prefaces,* 708).

10. Vivisection is also an aspect of the myth of Dionysus, the god in whose honor classical drama was performed and who the philanderer incarnates to some extent. Whether Shaw had this association in mind, as he certainly had in later plays (see in chapter 7), is not certain. He might, though, have read Frazer's *The Golden Bough,* which had begun to be issued in 1890.

11. A deleted section of the play in the holograph manuscript was to emphasize that strange bifurcation whereby an animal vivisector can be naturally affectionate toward animals; see Julius Novick's introduction to the Garland facsimile edition: "the dog Dr. Paramore was too tenderhearted to vivisect" (*The Philanderer: Holograph,* xxii).

12. In the early 1930s, Shaw responded favorably to the suggestion of his Polish translator, Floryan Sobieniowski, that the Ibsen Club of Act Two should become the Bernard Shaw Club: "You have solved the problem . . . how to bring The Philanderer up to date and make it intelligible to people who have never heard of Ibsen" (Laurence, *Bernard Shaw: An Exhibit,* item 204).

13. See Mander and Mitchenson, *Theatrical Companion,* 326. In the section of their book listing the longest first runs of Shaw's plays, they apparently give the wrong figure: "the longest original run of a Shaw play is that of Fanny's First Play at the Little Theatre (transferred to the Kingsway Theatre), 1911–1912 (266 [*sic*] performances)." The play had opened on April 19, 1911, and transferred to the Kingsway on January 1, 1912. As Shaw later explained to his French translator, Augustin Hamon, on December 3, 1925, he had arranged that everyone concerned get extra money "on the 500th night of Fanny's First Play during its first run" (*Letters 3,* 922). So we may presume that the figure given in Mander and Mitchenson, 143, of "622" performances is, in fact, the correct one, and that the "266" is a misprint. This part of the chapter derives from my article "Ruskin and *Fanny's First Play,*" which first appeared in *SHAW 15.*

14. Eric Bentley, Martin Meisel, Margery Morgan, and John Bertolini are exemplary critics in this regard.

15. See Jeremy Bernstein's article, "The Life and Times of Fanny Burney."

16. Shaw was appalled when he learned that the first production of *Fanny's First Play* in Germany had been announced as a play by him. He remonstrated with his German translator, Siegfried Trebitsch, on October 23, 1911: "it was announced as a play by me. Why did you let them do such a silly thing? The whole prologue & epilogue become absurd if the authorship is announced. Also the announcement makes people expect a big & serious play instead of a trifle—'a little play for a little theatre'" (*Shaw-Trebitsch,* 158). Shaw did not formally acknowledge authorship until *Fanny's First Play* was published in 1914. See also Mander and Mitchenson, *Theatrical Companion,* 143.

17. We only note here Derrida's similar interest in the "supplementary" logic of the frame, *parergon* (literally "beyond the work"), see "Translator's Preface" to *Of Grammatology:* "*Parergon,* a latecomer among these nicknames, is both a frame and a supplementary 'addition'" (Derrida, *Grammatology,* lxxii).

18. See *Letters 1*, 464–67.
19. See Barthes, *Elements of Semiology*, 25–27.
20. See Morgan, *Playground*, 187–99.
21. See Adams, *Bernard Shaw and the Aesthetes*, a book highly relevant to this chapter, although it is somewhat surprising that she does not discuss *Fanny's First Play*.
22. This lecture was delivered at the Ruskin Centenary Exhibition, held at the Royal Academy of Arts, London, November 21, 1919, reprinted in *Platform and Pulpit*.
23. Perhaps most comic was Shaw's dispute in 1922 with Ezra Pound over whether he would subscribe to a special edition of James Joyce's *Ulysses* or not. Shaw actually places the squabble in the context of Wilde and Whistler. Shaw also reveals that he had already read most of *Ulysses* in the *Little Review*, and Joyce's *A Portrait of the Artist as a Young Man*, as well as advocating *Exiles* for performance by the Stage Society. He further insisted, making a moral, aesthetic, and economic point with typically perverse Shavian generosity: "Five pounds be blowed! You can sell this postcard for ten" (*Letters 3*, 763–67). Beach in her memoir, *Shakespeare and Company*, 51–53, reports that Joyce greatly enjoyed this postcard of a reproduction of Ribera's "The Dead Christ" showing the grieving Marys over the dead body of Christ in the tomb (reproduced in Weintraub, *Shaw's People*, 132), with Shaw's annotation: "Miss Shakespear consoling James Joyce, who has fainted on hearing the refusal of his countryman to subscribe for Ulysses. Isn't it like him?" Shaw picked up, perhaps, the martyr symbolism implicit in Joyce's alter ego, Stephen Dedalus.
24. In *Savage Mind* Lévi-Strauss writes: "It seems not untrue to say that some modes of classing, arbitrarily isolated under the title of totemism are universally employed: among ourselves this 'totemism' has merely been humanized. Everything takes place as if in our civilization every individual's own personality were his totem: it is the signifier of his signified being" (Lévi-Strauss, *Savage Mind*, 217). And, like Lacan's Imaginary "ego," Lévi-Strauss continues, "All classification proceeds by pairs of contrasts: classification only ceases when it is no longer possible to establish oppositions" (Lévi-Strauss, *Savage Mind*, 214).
25. According to Dan H. Laurence, Shaw began writing the inner play in Ireland on August 13, 1910 and continued it on a voyage to the Caribbean. Laurence adds, "The Induction and Epilogue were afterthoughts, composed in February and March 1911" (Laurence, *Shaw: An Exhibit*, Item 362).
26. See *Letters 2*, 902–12, for two letters to Arthur W. Pinero in March, in which Shaw reports Cannan's remark and where he details debates in the Dramatists Club that may have contributed to the writing of *Fanny's First Play*. Shaw seems to have felt that the Club was not taking the New Drama and its dramatists associated with the Royal Court Theatre as seriously as he thought they ought.
27. Shaw, typically, adopted the persona of Flawner Bannel (*sic*) when he wrote a letter to *Play Pictorial* in January 1912 to celebrate the success of the play, reprinted in Mander and Mitchenson, *Theatrical Companion*, 143–44.
28. Shaw makes this identification clear in the rhyming prologue to be used if the inner play is performed without the framing play; the actress who plays Margaret speaks the prologue as Fanny.

29. See Morgan, *Playground*, 94–95.

30. Even in Barbara Fisher's excellent article "*Fanny's First Play*: A Critical Potboiler."

31. In *Practical Criticism*, I. A. Richards presented thirteen unsigned poems and asked his reader to criticize them before opening the accompanying identification. Paul Ricoeur's textual hermeneutics in relation to metaphor was influenced to some degree by Richards, see Ricoeur, *Hermeneutics and the Human Sciences*, 12, 170.

32. Act III of *Fanny's First Play* was originally to be two acts, and the joint between the two parts is *not* perfect, as was discovered during rehearsals for a production this writer directed in Dublin.

33. I am grateful to the late Fred Crawford for not only this suggestion, but also, and more especially, for his initial encouragement of my first attempts at critical writing on Shaw.

34. The binary opposition metaphor of construction/generation parallels that of mechanical/organic, and both permeate the Shaw text.

35. See Barthes, *Image-Music-Text*, 148.

Chapter 7. Mystery and Ritual: Theater and Textuality

1. In "The Trembling of the Veil" (1922), reprinted in *The Autobiography of William Butler Yeats,* Yeats wrote: "we all hated him with the left side of our heads, while admiring him immensely with the right side. . . . At that time he was an obscure man, known only for a witty speaker at street corners and in Park demonstrations. He had, with an assumed truculence and fury, cold logic, an invariable gentleness, an unruffled courtesy" (Yeats, *Autobiography*, 90). Yeats interestingly does not identify Shaw by name in this paragraph, as he does in the well-known passages on the first production of *Arms and the Man,* perhaps because his own animosity is made so obvious, especially in the last sentence: "I can even remember sitting behind D———[i.e., Shaw] and saying some rude thing or other over his shoulder" (Yeats, *Autobiography,* 91).

2. Two of the most relevant of the many writings on *Candida* are: Walter King's highly astute "The Rhetoric of *Candida*," which reads the play "as a kind of passacaglia and fugue dependent for ultimate thematic unity and development upon the iteration of a few key words: "fool," "mad," "love," and "happiness," with all of them subsumed in the word *understand* (Stanton, *Casebook*, 249); and Margery Morgan's chapter on the play in *The Shavian Playground*, where, following on from King, she adds more keywords to his list: "'lie' and 'truth,' 'shy,' dumb,' 'secret' contribute similarly to the verbal patterning," and is highly suggestive when referring to the play as "a game of words, a patterned fabric rather than a transparent medium of communication. Words may conceal more than they reveal" (Morgan, *Playground,* 68).

3. See Morgan, *Playground,* 70n1. According to *Webster's*: "candid \Can*did\ (k[a^]n"d[i^]d), a. [F. candide (cf. It. candido), L. candidus white, fr. cand[=e]re to be of a glowing white; akin to accend[e^]re, incend[e^]re, to set on fire, Skr. chand to shine. Cf. Candle, Incense.] 1. White. [Obs.]" (*Webster's Revised Unabridged Dictionary*, 1996, 98).

4. Mystery: middle English misterie, from Latin mystrium, from Greek mustrion, secret rite, from musts, an initiate, from mein, to close the eyes, initiate. See *American Heritage Dictionary of the English Language* (4th ed.) Houghton Mifflin Company, 2000. In the archaic sense "mystery" means a trade, or guild, or occupation, hence the Mystery plays presented by the trade guilds on the Mysteries of the life of Christ [Middle English misterie, service, craft, from Medieval Latin misterium, craft-guild, from Late Latin, alteration of Latin ministerium, occupation, from minister, assistant, servant. See mei-2 in Indo-European Roots.] See *American Heritage Dictionary*. Cardullo in "The Mystery of *Candida*" gives an interpretation of the play in the context of the medieval mystery plays.

5. See also *Letters 1*, 502.

6. See *Autobiography 1*, 158–59.

7. See Raine's chapter on Blake's use of the Demeter and Proserpine legend, "The Myth of the Kore" in *Blake and Antiquity*, which might also suggest some neo-Platonic influences on Shaw.

8. Richard Dietrich informs me that Marchbanks was also the name of a London street near where the Yeats family lived in their early years in London. And Yeats, the Irish fin-de-siècle Romantic poet who Shaw knew from meetings at the home of William Morris, is a likely model for the poet in Shaw's play.

9. In later editions, Shaw changed the beginning to: "A fine morning in October 1894" (*Plays*, 123).

10. See Weintraub, ed., *Diaries 2*, 1044–45.

11. See Crompton, *Shaw the Dramatist*, 39.

12. The Freudian implications of this play, written at a time when Freud was developing psychoanalysis (*Studies on Hysteria* was published in 1895), should not go unnoted. In a letter to Fliess in 1898, Freud describes psychoanalysis in a way applicable to the thematic of this play: "In all analyses, one therefore hears the same story twice: once as a fantasy about the mother; the second time as a real memory of the maid." See Forrester, *Seductions*, 50.

13. See the section titled "Inconsistency of the Sex Instinct" in *On the Prospects of Christianity*, the preface to *Androcles and the Lion*, where Shaw argues for two components of the sex instinct: "concupiscence and chastity" (*Prefaces*, 584).

14. This stage direction in the original 1898 edition of *Plays Pleasant and Unpleasant* is omitted in later editions; see *Plays*, 142.

15. Again, later editions omit the reference to Morell in the last stage direction, as well as to Candida's ritual-like action in standing behind him and bending over him; see *Plays*, 142.

16. Apparently Shaw himself considered the young poet's gushings as "real poetry." See footnote in *Bernard Shaw: A Chronicle*, 104, reprinted in Stanton, ed., *Casebook*, 193.

17. See note 3 above. Candida shares the connotations of whiteness with those of other Shaw heroines like Blanche Sartorius and Ann Whitefield.

18. Shaw himself allowed for the play to be divided into three parts, as indicated in

a letter of February 2, 1927, to his French translator, Augustin Hamon: "When two breaks are made in the performance of Getting Married, the first occurs at the end of the scene between the three Bridgenorth brothers; and the play is resumed with the first entrance of Hotchkiss. The second is made at the entry of Mrs George, who appears at the door. The curtain then descends; and when it rises the stage is exactly as before.... But the play must not be described as in three acts" (*Letters 4*, 38). Shaw had written along the same lines to Siegfried Trebitsch in a letter of January 15, 1909; see *Shaw-Trebitsch*, 141–43. This division also stresses the importance of the stage entrance in the text and marks out two of its characters, both of whom can be identified with Shaw himself, for special emphasis. Rosset, for different reasons than those offered here, suggests that *Getting Married* is Shaw's "major autobiographical contribution entombed within a play" (Rosset, *Shaw of Dublin*, 302).

19. According to Morgan, *Playground,* 180n1, a double wedding was originally intended for *Getting Married.* Shaw retained part of that concept in this second "marriage" between Mrs. George and Hotchkiss in addition to the marriage between Edith and Cecil, the ostensible subject of the play.

20. Shaw need have looked no further than Lee walking into this parents' marriage or himself walking into May Morris's marriage as models for this turn of events.

21. John O'Donovan discovered: "the directories list Robert Lee [Lee's father] as a coal-merchant, which in the circumstances may be construed as Dublinese for a small-time coalman" (O'Donovan, *Charlatan Genius,* 41). See also Rosset, *Shaw of Dublin*, 35–38.

22. Shaw wrote of a "Mystical Betrothal" (*Autobiography 1,* 166–69) that took place between May Morris and himself.

23. In his next play, *Misalliance,* Hypatia expresses her desire "to be an active verb" (*Plays,* 618).

24. See "Who I am, and What I Think," reprinted in *Non-Dramatic,* 451.

25. The indications are that Charlotte, forty-one when they married on June 1, 1898, did not want the marriage to include full sexual intercourse that might lead to childbearing. Shaw obviously went along with this decision, and no evidence indicates he was unhappy complying.

Chapter 8. The Image and The Word

1. This chapter is extensively reworked from an article, which first appeared in *SHAW 17* as "*Back to Methuselah: An Exercise of Imagination.*" That essay was itself an expanded version of a paper, "Shaw: *Back to Methuselah* and Creative Imagination," read at the Bernard Shaw Summer School held at the Dublin Institute of Technology in June 1991. The present chapter does not necessarily supersede the original article; rather, it can be read as an alternative version. Indispensable and illuminating guides to the labyrinthine construct of the intertextual imagination that is *Back to Methuselah* are found in Bertolini, *The Playwrighting Self of Bernard Shaw,* Meisel, *Shaw and the Nineteenth-Century Theater,* Morgan, *The Shavian Playground,* and the article by Valli Rao, "*Back to Methuselah*: a Blakean Interpretation," as well as several articles by Harry

Geduld, notably "Shaw's Philosophy and Cosmology," "The Lineage of Lilith," "Sources and Influences of Shaw's Pentateuch," "Shaw's Philosophy as Expounded in Back to Methuselah," and "Place and Treatment of Persons in *Back to Methuselah*"; Daniel Leary's "*Too True to be Good* and Shaw's Romantic Synthesis: A Religion for Our Times" has also been useful.

2. *Back to Methuselah* was published on June 23, 1921, in England by Constable. Its publication was apparently an important cultural event: note, for instance, the comment from composer Michael Tippet: "I can remember the excitement when Back to Methuselah was first published" (Tippet, *Moving into Aquarius,* 10). The entire play-cycle was first performed in New York by the Theater Guild starting in February 1922 and in England at the Birmingham Repertory Theater in October 1923. Shaw made minor revisions in the Collected Works Limited Edition (1930–1932), the Standard Edition (1931–1950), and, in April 1939, for the Penguin paperback. In July 1939, a special collectors' edition appeared with woodcut illustrations by John Farleigh and supervised by Shaw. The most thorough revision was in 1945 for the 500th volume of Oxford University Press's series of The World's Classics, in which Shaw considerably cut and revised the text of both preface and play-cycle, as well as supplying an entirely new "Post Script: After Twenty Five Years." As in earlier chapters, my references are to the 1965 omnibus editions of *Plays* and *Prefaces* and to the 1945 edition for the postscript. This play needs a variorum edition more, perhaps, than any other; see explanation in Geduld, "The Textual Problem in Shaw."

3. For instance, Wisenthal in *The Marriage of Contraries* places his chapter on *Back to Methuselah* last, out of chronological order, so that what he calls "its relative artistic failure" can point up the success of the other middle plays in his previous chapters—including *Saint Joan*, written after *Methuselah*. Bertolini, in *The Playwrighting Self of Bernard Shaw*, squeezes what he has to say on *Methuselah* into a chapter on *Saint Joan*, but he does so to show that the later play can be seen as an addendum to Shaw's thematic of imagination in *Methuselah*. Berst's major survey bypasses it altogether, but not without comment: "My selection omits *Back to Methuselah*, a fascinating monster which may warrant a book in itself" (Berst, *Drama,* xx). These examples demonstrate the critical sidelining of this major work even in three of the most insightful studies of the Shaw play-texts.

4. Adelphia is defined as a "brotherhood" in *Webster's Revised Unabridged Dictionary*, 1996, 1998. It might also be noted that Shaw lived in Adelphi Terrace in London after his marriage. Saint Barnabas was associated with Saint Paul in his evangelical journeys, which, Shaw claimed in *On the Prospects of Christianity,* became the actual foundation of the Christian church rather than the teachings of Jesus Christ. The theory of natural selection had been proposed simultaneously by *both* Alfred Russel Wallace and Charles Darwin; their joint paper resulted when Darwin realized that Wallace intended to publish first.

5. By italicizing certain words in quotations in this chapter, I intend to emphasize the visual metaphors connected with the concept of imagination.

6. As Geoffrey Hartman points out, this idea was also "phrased memorably both by

Augustine and Yeats, 'For love has built his mansion in/The place of excrement'" (Ehrmann, *Structuralism,* 153). See Shaw's letters to St John Ervine for his fullest exposition on this point (*Letters 4,* 95–98).

7. See preface to *London Music in 1888–90* for Shaw's views on Pavlov (*Prefaces,* 860–61).

8. The text mentions other mammals: squirrel, rabbit, stoat, ermine, sable, blue fox, and so on.

9. Metz's Lacanian inquiry into film, *The Imaginary Signifier,* used this term to describe the "cinematic apparatus."

10. See Shaw's letter to H. G. Wells on July 7, 1921 (in response to Wells's response to the publication of *Methuselah*): "Psychological Homogeneity is indispensable to political combination. The conditions, as far as I could work them out, were (a) a common language (one in which marriage, justice, honor etc. meant the same thing, whether you used the French, German or English dialects) and (b) intermarriage without any sense of miscegenation. You might get a Teutonic Protestant League, a Latin Catholic League, a Yellow League, a Black League, and a Brown League to come to an agreement about so obvious and universally noxious [a] thing as war and even about unsectarian super-Christianity; but if you attempted such a complete amalgamation as is implied in the World State you would get Babel. You may get something practically homogenous from the Urals to the Rockies, but not from the Rockies to Japan by the Atlantic route" (*Shaw-Wells,* 107).

11. He would also have had in mind the even older Irish myth of *Tír na nÓg,* the Land of Eternal Youth, or "the Land of the Ever-living Ones," in the retelling by his friend Augusta Gregory in *Gods and Fighting Men.* In yet another connection that links *Methuselah* and *Finnegans Wake,* as discussed in Black's *Shaw and Joyce,* Joyce's book is a retelling of the legend of Finn MacChumhail (McCool), the subject of Lady Gregory's book. The location of *Back to Methuselah: Part IV,* Burrin Pier, is set very close to Coole, where Lady Gregory, with whom the Shaws stayed several times early in the century, lived in the west of Ireland. Lady Gregory records in her journal that Shaw read *Part I* to her, on March 3, 1919, during a visit she paid to the Shaws at Ayot St. Lawrence. On May 27, 1921, just before publication, he again read *Part I* in Dublin for a fund-raising venture at the Abbey Theatre. See Gregory, *Journals,* 204, 66–67, and also *Shaw-Gregory,* 143.

12. In a letter to Clara M. Kennedy of September 27, 1947, Shaw wrote: "I am myself a missionary" (*Letters 4,* 803).

13. In a letter to Horace Plunkett (August 3, 1917) Shaw wrote of the "Intellectual imagination" (*Letters 3,* 494), in contrast to the romantic imagination he usually associated with Irish nationalism.

14. See chapters 6 to 9, "Of the Gaze as *Objet Petit a*" in Lacan's *Four Fundamental Concepts,* 65–119.

15. In German, *aufsteigen* (to rise).

16. A motif in Renaissance pastoral painting, see the chapter "Et in Arcadia ego: On

the Conception of Transience in Poussin and Watteau," in Panowsky, *Meaning in the Visual Arts*.

17. "I have no 'view' of death" (*Letters 4*, 849), Shaw wrote on May 9, 1949, to Daniel G. Day, a year before he died, a comment that suggests that death did not have metaphorical attributes for him.

18. See Silver, *Darker Side*, 220.

19. See Fiske's article, the first to take seriously the connection between Shaw and Blake, "Bernard Shaw and William Blake." See also Rao's article "*Back to Methuselah*: a Blakean Interpretation" referred to in chapter 8, note 1. Kaye in *Nineteenth Century*, 119–27, discusses Shaw's relation to Blake, in particular the depiction of Lilith as the good serpent in Blake's engraving of *The Laocoön*—an astonishing combination of the Image and the Word that could serve as an illustration for this chapter.

20. Just as Derrida said that deconstruction must use the language of metaphysics against itself, the Shaw text reiterates that the *logic* of an argument can become a *reductio ad absurdum*. For examples, see the essays "A Dramatic Realist to his Critics" and "A Degenerate's View of Nordau" in *Non-Dramatic*, 325, 371.

21. Shaw's understanding of playwrighting as organic development is rather more similar than dissimilar to Aristotle's prescriptions in *Poetics* than Shaw's polemics might have us believe.

22. See Bertolini, *Playwrighting*, 144.

23. Shaw wrote to Sylvia Beach on June 11, 1921, that *Ulysses* was "a revolting record of a disgusting phase of civilisation," but that "at last somebody has felt deeply enough about it to face the horror of writing it all down and using his literary genius to force people to face it." To other people it might be "art," and he was aware it had "other qualities," "but to me it is all hideously real" (*Letters 3*, 719). It is even possible that Shaw's play on the word *metempsychoses*: "Met—Emp—Sy–Good Lord!" (*Plays 5*, 456), shadows its recurrent use in *Ulysses* where, to give one instance, it becomes "met him pike hoses" (Joyce, *Ulysses*, 149).

24. See Black, *Shaw and Joyce: The Last Word in Stolentelling*, especially the long chapter on *Finnegans Wake*. The earlier chapters of her book persuasively suggest how Shaw provided a role-model for the young Joyce, which, Black suggests, Joyce went to some trouble to obscure.

25. That European intellectual history is so intertextually interwoven can be realized from Part 2 of Derrida's own magnum opus, *Of Grammatology*, being a commentary on one of Rousseau's texts, *On the Origin of Languages*.

Post Scriptum

1. See the section "Reading Us" in Derrida's essay "The Ends of Man" (1968) reprinted in Derrida, *The Margins of Philosophy*, 109–136.

Bibliography

SHAW: The Annual of Bernard Shaw Studies, Vols. 1–24. Edited by Stanley Weintraub (1981–1990), Fred D. Crawford (1990–1999), and Gale K. Larson (1999–). Bibliography compiled by John R. Pfeiffer. University Park: Pennsylvania State University Press, 1980–2004. Volumes of *SHAW* on specific topics are listed under the names of their guest editors in this bibliography.

Works by Bernard Shaw.

Note: Except where otherwise indicated, the writer has worked from the omnibus editions *The Complete Plays of Bernard Shaw* (London: Paul Hamlyn, 1965), and *The Complete Prefaces of Bernard Shaw* (London: Paul Hamlyn, 1965). These editions are not as heavily revised as the "definitive" versions in *The Bodley Head Bernard Shaw: Collected Plays with their Prefaces*, edited by Dan H. Laurence (1970–1974).

An Unsocial Socialist by George Bernard Shaw (1883). London: Swan Sonnenschein, 1887. Reprinted in *Non-Dramatic Writings*.

Fabian Essays in Socialism. G. Bernard Shaw, Sydney Oliver, Sidney Webb, Annie Besant, William Clarke, Graham Wallas, and Hubert Bland. Edited by G. Bernard Shaw. London: The Fabian Society, 1889.

The Quintessence of Ibsenism: by G. Bernard Shaw. London: Walter Scott, 1891. This first edition is reprinted in *Non-Dramatic Writings* (1965). [Later editions with additions and revisions can be found in *Drama 1 & 4* and *Shaw and Ibsen*, edited by Wisenthal.]

"A Dramatic Realist to his Critics," *The New Review*, London, July 1894. Reprinted in *Non-Dramatic Writings* (1965), 323–40.

"How to Become a Man of Genius," *Town Topics*, New York, December 6, 1894. Reprinted in *Non-Dramatic Writings* (1965), 341–46.

"A Degenerate's View of Nordau," open letter to editor Benjamin R. Tucker, *Liberty*, 1895. Reprinted in *Non-Dramatic Writings* (1965), 347–77. [Later revised and printed under the title of *The Sanity of Art: An Exposure of the Current Nonsense about Artists being Degenerate* (1908), and further revised when printed in Vol. 19 of the Collected Edition (1930), along with *The Quintessence of Ibsenism* and *The Perfect Wagnerite*, under the title *Major Critical Essays*.]

"On Going to Church," *The Savoy*, London, January 1896. Reprinted in *Non-Dramatic Writings* (1965), 378–90.

"The Illusions of Socialism," *The Home Journal*, New York, October 21 and 28, 1896. Also in *Forecasts of the Coming Century*, 1897, edited by Edward Carpenter. Reprinted in *Non-Dramatic Writings* (1965), 427–32.

Plays Pleasant and Unpleasant by Bernard Shaw. 2 vols. London: Grant Richards, 1898.

"Tolstoy on Art," *Daily Chronicle*, London, September 10, 1898. Reprinted in *Non-Dramatic Writings* (1965), 446–55.

The Perfect Wagnerite: A Commentary on The Ring of the Niblungs. By Bernard Shaw. London: Grant Richards, 1898.

Love Among the Artists (1881). Chicago: Herbert S. Stone, 1900.

"Who I Am, and What I Think," replies to a questionnaire by editor Frank Harris, in *The Candid Friend*, London, May 11 and 18, 1901. Reprinted in *Non-Dramatic Writings* (1965), 446–55.

Dramatic Opinions and Essays with an Apology by Bernard Shaw, containing as well A Word on the Dramatic Opinions and Essays of Bernard Shaw by James Huneker. 2 vols. New York: Brentano's, 1909.

"On Parents and Children" (1912–1914). Preface to *Misalliance*. Reprinted in *Prefaces* (1965), 45–105.

On the Prospects of Christianity (1916). Preface to *Androcles and the Lion*. Reprinted in *Prefaces* (1965), 547–603.

The Infidel Half Century (1921). Preface to *Back to Methuselah*. Reprinted in *Prefaces* (1965), 501–546.

Immaturity (1879). London: Constable, 1930.

Pen Portraits and Reviews. London: Constable, 1931.

Ellen Terry and Bernard Shaw: A Correspondence, edited by Christopher St. John. London: Constable, 1931.

The Adventures of the Black Girl in Her Search for God. London: Constable, 1932. [Subsequently entitled *The Black Girl in Search of God*, republished by Penguin Books in 1946.]

"The Domesticity of Franklyn Barnabas." In *Short Stories, Scraps and Shavings*. London: Constable, 1932.

London Music in 1888–89 as heard by Corno di Bassetto (later known as Bernard Shaw). London, Constable, 1937.

Back to Methuselah: A Metabiological Pentateuch. Harmondsworth: Penguin Books, 1939.

Back to Methuselah: A Metabiological Pentateuch. With wood-cut illustrations by John Farleigh. New York: Limited Editions Club, 1939.

Back to Methuselah: A Metabiological Pentateuch. Rev. ed. with a postscript. The World's Classics, edited by Humphrey Milford. London: Oxford University Press, 1945.

Sixteen Self Sketches. London: Constable, 1949.

Bernard Shaw: A Chronicle, compiled by R. F. Rattray. Luton: Leagrave Press, 1951.

My Dear Dorothea: A Practical System of Moral Education for Females. 1878b. With a note by Stephen Winsten. New York: Phoenix House, 1956.

To a Young Actress: Letters to Molly Tompkins 1921–1949, edited and with an introduction by Peter Tompkins. London: Constable, 1960.

Platform and Pulpit, edited by Dan H. Laurence. New York: Hill and Wang, 1961.

The Complete Plays of Bernard Shaw. London: Paul Hamlyn, 1965.

The Complete Prefaces of Bernard Shaw. London: Paul Hamlyn, 1965.

Collected Letters: 1874–1897, edited by Dan H. Laurence. London: Max Reinhardt, 1965.

Selected Non-Dramatic Writings of Bernard Shaw, edited by Dan H. Laurence. Boston: Houghton Mifflin, 1965.

Shaw on Shakespeare, edited by Edwin Wilson. 1961. Harmondsworth: Penguin Books, The Penguin Shakespeare Library, 1969.

Bernard Shaw: An Autobiography 1856–1898, edited by Stanley Weintraub. London: Max Reinhardt, 1969.

Bernard Shaw: An Autobiography 1898–1950, edited by Stanley Weintraub. London: Max Reinhardt, 1970.

Collected Letters: 1898–1910, edited by Dan H. Laurence. London: Max Reinhardt, 1972.

Collected Plays and their Prefaces: Volume 5, edited by Dan H. Laurence. The Bodley Head Bernard Shaw. London: Max Reinhardt, 1972.

Collected Plays and their Prefaces: Volume 7, edited by Dan H. Laurence. The Bodley Head Bernard Shaw. London: Max Reinhardt, 1974.

Candida & How He Lied to Her Husband: Facsimiles of the Holograph Manuscripts, edited by Dan H. Laurence, with an introduction by J. Percy Smith. New York and London: Garland, 1981.

The Philanderer: Facsimiles of the Holograph Manuscripts, edited by Dan H. Laurence, with an introduction by Julius Novick. New York: Garland, 1981.

Shaw's Music: The Complete Musical Criticism of Bernard Shaw Volume 1 1876–1890, edited by Dan H. Laurence. 1981. 2d rev. ed. The Bodley Head Bernard Shaw. London: Max Reinhardt, 1989.

Shaw's Music: The Complete Musical Criticism of Bernard Shaw Volume 2 1890–1893, edited by Dan H. Laurence. 1981. 2d rev. ed. The Bodley Head Bernard Shaw. London: Max Reinhardt, 1989.

Shaw's Music: The Complete Musical Criticism of Bernard Shaw Volume 3 1893–1950, edited by Dan H. Laurence. 1981. 2d rev. ed. The Bodley Head Bernard Shaw. London: Max Reinhardt, 1989.

Agitations: Letters to the Press (1875–1950), edited by Dan H. Laurence and James Rambeau. New York: Ungar, 1985.

Collected Letters: 1911–1925 Vol. 3, edited by Dan H. Laurence. London: Max Reinhardt, 1985.

Bernard Shaw: The Diaries 1885–1897, with Earlier and Later Fragments from 1875–

1917, edited by Stanley Weintraub. 2 vols. University Park: Pennsylvania State University Press, 1986.
Bernard Shaw's Letters to Siegfried Trebitsch, edited by Samuel A. Weiss. Stanford: Stanford University Press, 1986.
Collected Letters: 1926–1950 Vol. 4, edited by Dan H. Laurence. London: Max Reinhardt, 1988.
Bernard Shaw on the London Art Scene, edited with an introduction by Stanley Weintraub. University Park: Pennsylvania State University Press, 1989.
Bernard Shaw's Book Reviews: originally published in The Pall Mall Gazette 1885–1888, edited by Brian Tyson. University Park: Pennsylvania State University Press, 1991.
Bernard Shaw: The Drama Observed Volume I 1880–1895, edited with an introduction by Bernard F. Dukore. University Park: Pennsylvania State University Press, 1993.
Bernard Shaw: The Drama Observed Volume II 1895–1897, edited with an introduction by Bernard F. Dukore. University Park: Pennsylvania State University Press, 1993.
Bernard Shaw: The Drama Observed Volume III 1897–1911, edited with an introduction by Bernard F. Dukore. University Park: Pennsylvania State University Press, 1993.
Bernard Shaw: The Drama Observed Volume IV 1911–1950, edited with an introduction by Bernard F. Dukore. University Park: Pennsylvania State University Press, 1993.
Shaw, Lady Gregory and the Abbey: A Correspondence and a Record, edited by Dan H. Laurence and Nicholas Grene. Gerrards Cross: Colin Smyth, 1993.
Bernard Shaw and H. G. Wells: Correspondence, edited by J. Percy Smith. Toronto: University of Toronto Press, 1995.
Bernard Shaw's Book Reviews: Volume Two 1884–1950, edited by Brian Tyson. University Park: Pennsylvania State University Press, 1996.

Works by other writers

Adams, Elsie B. *Bernard Shaw and the Aesthetes.* Columbus: Ohio State University Press, 1971.
Albert, Sidney P. "Reflections on Shaw and Psychoanalysis." *Modern Drama* 14, no. 2 (September 1971): 169–94.
Althusser, Louis. "Ideology and Ideological State Apparatuses" (*La Pensée,* 1970). In *Lenin and Philosophy and Other Essays,* translated by Ben Brewster. London: New Left Books, 1971. 127–86.
———. *Lenin and Philosophy and Other Essays,* translated by Ben Brewster. London: New Left Books, 1971.
Aristotle. *Poetics* in *Aristotle's Poetics: A Translation and Commentary for Students of Literature,* translated by Leon Golden. Tallahassee: Florida State University Press, 1981.
Arnold, Matthew. *Culture and Anarchy: An Essay in Political and Social Criticism.* London: Smith, Elder, & Co., 1869.

Augustine (Saint). *The City of God* (*De Civitate Dei*). London: Griffith, Farran, Okeden & Welsh, 1890.

Baker, Stuart. *Bernard Shaw's Remarkable Religion: A Faith that Fits the Facts*. Gainesville: University Press of Florida, 2002.

Barker, Harley Granville. *The Madras House: a comedy in four acts*. 1908. London: Sidgwick & Jackson, 1911.

Barry, Peter. *Beginning Theory: An Introduction to Literary and Cultural Theory*. Manchester: Manchester University Press, 1995.

Barthes, Roland. *Mythologies* (*Mythologies*, 1957), translated by Annette Lavers. New York: Farrar Straus & Giroux, 1972.

———. *Elements of Semiology* (*Eléments de sémiologie*, 1964), translated by Annette Lavers and Colin Smith. New York: Hill and Wang, 1968.

———. "Introduction to the Structural Analysis of Narratives" ("*Introduction à l'analyse structurale des récits,*" Communications 8, 1966), In *Image-Music-Text*, essays selected and translated by Stephen Heath. London: Fontana, 1977, 79–124.

———. "The Death of the Author" ("*La mort de l'auteur,*" Mantéia V, 1968). In *Image-Music-Text*, essays selected and translated by Stephen Heath. London: Fontana, 1977, 142–48.

———. "From Work to Text" ("*De l'oeuvre au texte,*" Revue d'esthétique 3, 1971). In *Image-Music-Text*, essays selected and translated by Stephen Heath. London: Fontana, 1977, 155–65.

———. *The Pleasure of the Text* (*Le Plaisir du texte*, Éditions du Seuil, 1975), translated by Richard Miller. New York: Hill and Wang, 1975.

———. *Image-Music-Text*. Essays selected and translated by Stephen Heath. London: Fontana, 1977.

———. *The Grain of the Voice: Interviews 1962–1980*, translated by Linda Coverdale. Berkeley: University of California Press, 1991.

Barzun, Jacques. *Darwin, Marx, Wagner: Critique of a Heritage*. Rev. 2d ed. New York: Doubleday Anchor Books, 1958.

Beach, Sylvia. *Shakespeare and Company*. New York: Harcourt Brace, 1959.

Beckett, Samuel. *Imagination Dead Imagine*. London: Calder & Boyars, 1965.

Bentley, Eric. *Bernard Shaw*. 1947, 2d Brit. ed. London: Methuen, 1967.

Bergson, Henri. *Creative Evolution* (*l'Évolution créatrice*, 1907), authorized translation by Arthur Mitchell. London: Macmillan, 1911.

Bernstein, Jeremy. "The Life and Times of Fanny Burney." *New Criterion* (November 1999).

Berst, Charles. *Bernard Shaw and the Art of Drama*. Urbana: University of Illinois Press, 1973.

———, ed. *SHAW 1: Shaw and Religion*. University Park: Pennsylvania State University Press, 1981.

———. "The Action of Shaw's Settings and Props." *SHAW 3* (1983): 41–65.

———. "*The Man of Destiny*: Shaw, Napoleon, and the Theater of Life." *SHAW 7* (1987): 85–118.

Bertolini, John A. *The Playwrighting Self of Bernard Shaw*. Carbondale: Southern Illinois University Press, 1991.

Black, Martha Fodaski. *Shaw and Joyce: The Last Word in Stolentelling*. Gainesville: University Press of Florida, 1995.

Blake, William. *Jerusalem: The Emanation of the Giant Albion*, Vol. 1 of the Illuminated Books. Introduction and Notes by Morton D. Paley. Princeton, N.J.: Williams Blake Trust and Princeton University Press, 1998.

Borges, Jorge Luis. *Labyrinths: Selected Stories and Other Writings*. Harmondsworth: Penguin Books, 1979.

Buckingham (George Villiers, Duke of). *The Rehearsal*. 1671. Oxford: Shakespeare Head Press, 1914.

Bunyan, John. *The Pilgrims Progress from This World to That Which is to Come; Delivered Under the Similitude of a Dream* (1678). With a Memoir of the Author by George Cheever, D.D. London: David Bogue, 1850.

Bürch, Noel. *To the Distant Observer: Form and Meaning in Japanese Cinema*. Berkeley: University of California Press, 1979.

Burgess, Anthony. *One Man's Chorus*. New York: Carroll & Graff, 1998.

Burney, Fanny. *Evelina, or, The History of a Young Lady's Entrance Into the World*. 1778. Illustrated by Hugh Thomson. London: Macmillan, 1903.

Burton, Robert. *Anatomy of Melancholy: What It Is With All The Kinds, Causes, Symptoms, Prognostics And Several Cures Of It. In Three Partitions With Their Several Sections, Members & Subsections, Philosophically, Medically, Historically Opened & Cut Up By Democritus Junior*. 1621. London: William Tegg and Co., 1857.

Butler, Samuel. *Erewhon or Over the Range*. London: Trübner & Co., 1872.

———. *The Way of All Flesh*. 1873. London: Grant Richards, 1903.

———. *Luck, or Cunning, as the means of Organic Modification? An Attempt to throw additional light upon the late Mr. Charles Darwin's Theory of Evolution*. London: Trübner & Co., 1887.

———. *Erewhon Revisited*. London: Grant Richards, 1901.

Cardullo, Bert. "The Mystery of *Candida*." SHAW 6 (1986): 91–100.

Carlyle, Thomas. *Sartor Resartus: The Life and Opinions of Herr Teufelsdröckh*. 1831. London: Chapman & Hall, 1871.

Carpenter, Charles A. *Bernard Shaw and the Art of Destroying Ideals: The Early Plays*. Madison: University of Wisconsin Press, 1969.

Chaucer, Geoffrey. *The Canterbury Tales* in *The Works of Geoffrey Chaucer—a Facsimile of the William Morris Kelmscott Chaucer*. Cleveland, Ohio: World Publishing, 1958.

Chesterton, G. K. *George Bernard Shaw* (1909), new edition with additional chapter. 1935. London: Guild Books, 1949.

Crompton, Louis. *Shaw the Dramatist*. Lincoln: University of Nebraska Press, 1969.

Dante, Alighieri. *The Divine Comedy: Inferno, Purgatorio, and Paradiso*. 3 vols. (*Divina Commedia*, 1321), translated by Allen Mandelbaum, illustrated by Barry Moser. Berkeley: University of California Press/BOMC, 1995.

Darwin, Charles. *On the Origin of Species by means of Natural Selection, or the Preservation of favored Races in the Struggle for Life*. London: John Murray, 1859.

———. "Letter to S. P. Woodward, 6 March, 1860," reprinted in exhibition brochure *Charles Darwin: An Exhibition February 25–June 24, 2001*. Pasadena: The Huntington Library, 2001.

Darwin, Erasmus. *The Botanic Garden; a Poem, in Two Parts. Part I containing The Economy of Vegetation. Part II. The Loves of Plants. With Philosophical Notes*. London: J. Johnson, 1791.

Derrida, Jacques. "Force and Signification" ("Force et signification") *Critique* (June–July 1963): 193–94. Reprinted in *Writing and Difference (L'écriture et la différence*, 1967), translated with an introduction and additional notes by Alan Bass. London: Routledge & Kegan Paul, 1978.

———. "Freud and the Scene of Writing" ("Freud et la scène de l'écriture," *Tel Quel* 26 (summer 1966). Reprinted in *Writing and Difference (L'écriture et la différence*, 1967), translated with an introduction and additional notes by Alan Bass. London: Routledge & Kegan Paul, 1978.

———. "Structure, Sign, and Play in the Discourse of the Human Sciences" ("La structure, le signe et le jeu dans le discours des sciences humaines"). Lecture delivered at The Johns Hopkins University, Baltimore, October 21, 1966. Reprinted in *Writing and Difference (L'écriture et la différence*, 1967), translated with an introduction and additional notes by Alan Bass. London: Routledge & Kegan Paul, 1978.

———. *Speech and Phenomena and Other essays on Husserl's Theory of Signs* (*La Voix et le Phénomène: introduction au problème du signe dans la phénoménologie de Husserl*, Presses Universitaires de France, 1967), translated with an introduction by David B. Allison. Evanston, Ill.: Northwestern University Press, 1973.

———. *Of Grammatology* (*De la Grammatologie*, Les Editions de Minuit, 1967), translated by Gayatri Chakravorty Spivak. Baltimore, Md.: Johns Hopkins University Press, 1976.

———. *Writing and Difference* (*L'écriture et la différence*, 1967). Translated with an introduction and additional notes by Alan Bass. London: Routledge & Kegan Paul, 1978.

———. "Differance" (*La Différance*, Bulletin de la Société française de la philosophie 62, no. 3 [July–September 1968]: 73–101). In *Speech and Phenomena and Other essays on Husserl's Theory of Signs* (*La Voix et le Phénomène: introduction au problème du signe dans la phénoménologie de Husserl*, Presses Universitaires de France, 1967), translated with an introduction by David B. Allison. Evanston, Ill.: Northwestern University Press, 1973.

———. *Positions* (*Positions*, Les Editions de Minuit, 1972), translated and annotated by Alan Bass. Chicago: University of Chicago Press, 1981.

———. *Margins of Philosophy* (*Marges de la philosophie*, Les Editions de Minuit, 1972), translated with notes by Alan Bass. Chicago: The University of Chicago Press, 1981.

———. "The Purveyor of Truth" (*Le facteur de la vérité*, 1975). Abridged English version in *The Purloined Poe: Lacan, Derrida, and Psychoanalytic Reading*, edited by John P. Muller and William J. Richardson. Baltimore: Johns Hopkins University Press, 1988, 173–212.

Devaney, M. J. *'Since At Least Plato. . .' and Other Postmodernist Myths.* New York: St. Martin's Press, 1997.

Dietrich, Richard. F. *Portrait of the Artist as a Young Superman: A Study of Shaw's Novels.* Gainesville: University of Florida Press, 1969.

———. "Shavian Psychology." *SHAW* 4 (1984): 149–71.

———. "Deconstruction as Devil's Advocacy: a Shavian Alternative." *Modern Drama* 29, no. 3 (September 1986): 431–51.

———. *Bernard Shaw's Novels: Portraits of the Artist as Man and Superman.* Gainesville: University Press of Florida, 1996.

Dukore, Bernard F. *Shaw's Theater,* includes reprint of *Bernard Shaw, Director.* 1971. Gainesville: University Press of Florida, 2000.

Dunbar, Janet. *Mrs. G.B.S.: A Biographical Portrait of Charlotte Shaw.* London: Harrap, 1963.

Egan, Michael, ed. *Ibsen: The Critical Heritage.* London: Routledge and Kegan Paul, 1972.

Ehrmann, Jacques, ed. *Structuralism* (reprint of Yale French Studies, 1966). New York: Doubleday Anchor, 1970.

Ellis, Havelock. *Man and Woman: A Study of Human Secondary Sexual Characters.* London: Walter Scott, 1894.

———. *Studies in the Psychology of Sex.* 7 vols. (1897–1928). New York: Random House, 1936.

Eriugena, Johannes Scotus. *Periphyseon: De Divisione Naturae (On the division of Nature)*, edited by I. P. Sheldon-Williams. Dublin: Dublin Institute for Advanced Studies (Scriptores Latini Hiberniae), 1968, 1972, 1981.

Ervine, St. John. *Bernard Shaw.* London: Constable, 1956.

Fabricant, Carole. *Swift's Landscape.* Baltimore, Md.: Johns Hopkins University Press, 1982.

Fisher, Barbara. "*Fanny's First Play:* A Critical Potboiler." *SHAW* 7 (1987): 187–205.

Fiske, Irving. "Bernard Shaw and William Blake" in *G. B. Shaw: Twentieth Century Views,* edited by R. J. Kaufmann, 57–75.

Forrester, John. *The Seductions of Psychoanalysis: Freud, Lacan and Derrida.* London: Cambridge University Press, 1990.

Frazer, James. *The Golden Bough: A Study in Magic and Religion.* Abridged version (1922), originally published in 12 volumes (1890–1915). Ware: Wordsworth Reference, 1993.

Freud, Sigmund. "Project for a Scientific Psychology" (1894). SE [*The Standard Edition of the Complete Psychological Works of Sigmund Freud,* 24 vols., edited by James Strachey in collaboration with Anna Freud, assisted by Alix Strachey and Alan

Tyson (subsequently abbreviated to SE). London: The Hogarth Press and the Institute of Psycho-Analysis, 1953–74.] 1: 295–387.

———. *The Interpretation of Dreams.* 1900. SE 4 and 5.

———. "On the Two Principles of Mental Functioning." 1911. SE 12. Reprinted in Freud, *On Metapsychology,* 29–44.

———. *The Unconscious.* 1915. SE 14. Reprinted in Freud, *On Metapsychology,* 159–222.

———. *Beyond the Pleasure Principle.* 1920. SE 18. Reprinted in Freud, *On Metapsychology,* 269–338.

———. "A Note upon the 'Mystic Writing-Pad.'" 1925. SE 19. Reprinted in *On Metapsychology,* by Sigmund Freud. The Penguin Freud Library Vol. 11. Harmondsworth: Penguin Books, 1984, 427–34.

———. *On Metapsychology.* The Penguin Freud Library Vol. 11. Harmondsworth: Penguin Books, 1984.

Freud, Sigmund, and Ernest Jones. *The Complete Correspondence of Sigmund Freud and Ernest Jones, 1908–1939,* edited by R. Andrew Paskaukas. Cambridge, Mass.: Harvard University Press, 1993.

Frye, Northrop. *The Great Code: The Bible and Literature.* New York: Harcourt Brace Jovanovich, 1981, 1982.

Gahan, Peter. "Ruskin and Form in *Fanny's First Play.*" *SHAW* 15 (1995): 85–103.

———. "*Back to Methuselah*: an Exercise of Imagination." *SHAW* 17 (1997): 216–38.

Gallop, Jane. "The American Other." In *The Purloined Poe: Lacan, Derrida, and Psychoanalytic Reading,* edited by John P. Muller and William J. Richardson. Baltimore: Johns Hopkins University Press, 1988: 268–82.

Geduld, Harry. "Shaw's Philosophy and Cosmology." *California Shavian* 1 (May–June 1960).

———. "The Textual Problem in Shaw." *Shaw Review* 5 (May 1962): 54–60.

———. "The Lineage of Lilith." *Shaw Review* 7 (May 1964): 58–61.

———. "Sources and Influences of Shaw's Pentateuch." *California Shavian* 5 (May–June 1964): 1–10.

———. "Shaw's Philosophy as Expounded in Back to Methuselah." *California Shavian* 5 (Sept.–Oct. 1964): 11–19.

———. "Place and Treatment of Persons in *Back to Methuselah.*" *California Shavian* 5 (Nov.–Dec. 1964): 1–12.

Gibbs, A. M. *Shaw: Interviews and Recollections.* Iowa City: University of Iowa Press, 1990.

Goethe, Johann W. von. *Faust: A Tragedy* (1773–1831), translated by Lewis Filmore. London: William Smith/George Routledge, 1841.

Graves, Robert. *The White Goddess.* 1948. Amended and enlarged ed. New York: Farrar Strauss and Giroux, Noonday Press, 1966.

Gregory, Lady Augusta. *Lady Gregory's Journals 1916–1930,* edited by Lennox Robinson. New York: Macmillan, 1947.

———. *Gods and Fighting Men: The Story of the Tuatha De Danaan and of the Fianna of Ireland, Arranged and Put Into English By Lady Gregory* (1904). Gerrards Cross: Colin Smythe, 1987.

Hamann, Brigitte. *Hitler's Vienna: A Dictator's Apprenticeship*, translated by Thomas Thornton. New York: Oxford University Press, 1999.

Harris, Frank. *Bernard Shaw: an unauthorized biography based on firsthand information. With a postscript by Mr. Shaw*. London: Victor Gollancz, 1931.

Hartman, Geoffrey. "Structuralism: the Anglo-American adventure." In *Structuralism* (1966), edited by Ehrmann. Reprint of Yale French Studies, 1966. New York: Doubleday Anchor, 1970: 137–57.

Hawkes, Terrence. *Structuralism and Semiotics*. London: Methuen, 1977.

Hegel, Georg W. F. *Phenomenology of Mind (Phänomenologie des Geistes*, 1807). 2 vols. London: George Allen, 1910.

Heidegger, Martin. *Being and Time (Sein und Zeit*, Halle, 1927), translated by John Macquarrie and Edward Robinson. Evanston: 1962.

Henderson, Archibald. *G. B. Shaw: His Life and Works—A Critical Biography*. London: Hurst and Blackett, 1911.

———. *Bernard Shaw: Playboy and Prophet*. New York: Appleton, 1932.

———. *George Bernard Shaw: Man of the Century*. New York: Appleton-Century-Crofts, 1956.

Hesse, Hermann. *The Glass Bead Game (Das Glasperlenspiel*, 1943), translated by Richard and Clara Winston. New York: Holt, Rinehart and Winston, 1969.

Holroyd, Michael. *Bernard Shaw*. 5 vols. London: Chatto and Windus, 1988–92.

Homer. *The Odyssey*, translated by S. H. Butcher and A.(Andrew) Lang. London: Macmillan, 1879.

Homeric *Hymn to Demeter*. In *Classical Mythology*, edited by Mark P. O. Morford and Robert J. Lenardon. 1971, 2d ed. New York: Longman, 1977, 218–30.

Hooper, Judith. *Of Moths and Men—An Evolutionary Tale: The Untold Story of Science and the Peppered Moth*. New York: W. W. Norton and Company, 2002.

Husserl, Edmund. *Ideas: General Introduction to Phenomenology*, translated by W. R. Boyce Gibson. London: George Allen & Unwin, 1931.

———. *Cartesian Meditations*. Originally published in French in 1931, translated by J. Peiffer and E. Lévinas. (*Cartesianische Meditationen und Pariser Vorträge*, The Hague, 1950), translated by Dorion Cairns. The Hague: Martinus Nijhof, 1970.

Ibsen, Henrik. *Peer Gynt, A Doll's House, Rosmersholm, Ghosts, Hedda Gabler* in *The Works of Henrik Ibsen*. 13 vols. Introduction by William Archer. New York: Charles Scribner & Sons, 1911–12.

Innes, Christopher, ed. *The Cambridge Companion to George Bernard Shaw*. Cambridge: Cambridge University Press, 1998.

Jenkins, Stephen. *Fritz Lang: The Image and the Look*. London: British Film Institute, 1981.

Joad, C.E.M. *Matter, Life and Value*. London: Oxford University Press, 1929.

Johnson, Barbara. "The frame of reference: Poe, Lacan, Derrida." In *The Purloined Poe: Lacan, Derrida, and Psychoanalytic Reading*, edited by John P. Muller and William J. Richardson. Baltimore: Johns Hopkins University Press, 1988, 213–51.

Jones, Ernest. "The Oedipus Complex as an explanation of Hamlet's Mystery: A Study in Motive." *American Journal of Psychology* 21 (January 1910): 72–113.

Jones, Ernest, and Sigmund Freud. *The Complete Correspondence of Sigmund Freud and Ernest Jones, 1908–1939*, edited by R. Andrew Paskaukas. Cambridge, Mass.: Harvard University Press, 1993.

Joyce, James. *Ulysses: The Corrected Text*. New York: Random House, 1986.

———. *The Essential James Joyce: A Portrait of the Artist as a Young Man; Exiles—a play in 3 acts; Dubliners; etc.*, edited by Harry Levin. Harmondsworth: Penguin Books, 1972.

Kant, Immanuel. *Critique of Judgment* (*Kritik der Urteilskraft*, 1790), translated by J. H. Bernard. London: Macmillan, 1914.

Kaufmann, R. J., ed. *Twentieth Century Views: G. B. Shaw*. Englewood Cliffs, N.J.: Prentice-Hall, 1965.

Kaye, J. B. *Bernard Shaw and the Nineteenth Century Tradition*. Norman: University of Oklahoma Press, 1958.

Kearney, Richard. *Dialogues with Contemporary Continental Thinkers: The Phenomenological Heritage*. Manchester: Manchester University Press, 1984.

King, Walter N. "The Rhetoric of *Candida*." *Modern Drama* 2, 2 (September 1959): 71–83. Reprinted in *A Casebook on Candida*, edited by Stephen S. Stanton. New York: Crowell, 1962, 243–57.

Koestler, Arthur. *The Case of the Midwife Toad*. New York: Random House, 1971.

Kristeva, Julia. *The Kristeva Reader*, edited by Toril Moi. New York: University of Columbia Press, 1986.

Kuhn, Thomas H. *The Structure of Scientific Revolutions*. Chicago: University of Chicago Press, 1962.

Lacan, Jacques. "The Function and Field of Speech and Language in Psychoanalysis" (*Fonction et champ de la parole et du langage en psychanalyse*) *La Psychanalyse* 1 (1956): 81–166. Reprinted in *Écrits: A Selection*, by Jacques Lacan, from original publication in French (*Éditions du Seuil*, 1966), translated by Alan Sheridan. New York: Norton, 1977, 30–113.

———. *The Seminar of Jacques Lacan: Book I, Freud's Papers on Technique, 1953–1954*, translated with notes by John Forrester, edited by Jacques-Alain Miller. Cambridge: Cambridge University Press, 1988.

———. *The Seminar of Jacques Lacan: Book II, The Ego in Freud's Theory and in the Technique of Analysis 1954–1955*, translated by Sylvana Tomaselli, with notes by John Forrester, edited by Jacques-Alain Miller. Cambridge: Cambridge University Press, 1988.

———. "Seminar on *The Purloined Letter*" (*La Psychanalyse* 2, 1956), translated by Jeffrey Mehlman in *French Freud: Structural Studies in Psychoanalysis*, Yale French

Studies 48 (1972): 39–72. Reprinted in *The Purloined Poe: Lacan, Derrida, and Psychoanalytic Reading*, edited by John P. Muller and William J. Richardson. Baltimore: Johns Hopkins University Press, 1988, 28–54.

———. *Écrits: A Selection*, from original publication in French (*Éditions du Seuil*, 1966), translated by Alan Sheridan. New York: Norton, 1977.

———. *The Four Fundamental Concepts of Psycho-Analysis* (1973), translation of Séminaire XI (1964) by Alan Sheridan (Hogarth, 1977), edited by Jacques-Alain Miller. Harmondsworth: Penguin Books, 1979.

———. *Feminine Sexuality: Jacques Lacan and the école freudienne*, edited by Juliet Mitchell and Jacqueline Rose, translated by Jacqueline Rose. New York: Norton Pantheon, 1985.

Laurence, Dan H. *Shaw: An Exhibit*. Austin: Humanities Research Center, The University of Texas at Austin, 1977.

———. *Bernard Shaw: A Bibliography*. 2 vols. Oxford: Oxford University Press, 1983.

Laurence, Dan H., and Fred D. Crawford, eds. *SHAW 20: Bibliographical Shaw*. University Park: Pennsylvania State University Press, 2000.

Leary, Daniel. "*Too True to be Good* and Shaw's Romantic Synthesis: A Religion for Our Times." *SHAW 1* (1981): 183–203.

———, ed. *SHAW 3: Shaw's Plays in Performance*. University Park: Pennsylvania State University Press, 1983.

Lévine, Israel. *The Unconscious: an introduction to Freudian psychology*. London: Leonard Parsons, 1923.

Lévi-Strauss, Claude. *Introduction à l'oeuvre de Marcel Mauss* (*Introduction to the Work of Marcel Mauss*). In Marcel Mauss, *Sociologie et anthropologie*. Paris: Presses Universitaires de France, 1950.

———. "Overture to *le Cru et le Cuit* (*The Raw and the Cooked*)," translated by Joseph H. McMahon. In *Structuralism*, edited by Jacques Ehrmann. Reprint of Yale French Studies, 1966. New York: Doubleday Anchor, 1970: 52–55.

———. *The Raw and the Cooked: Introduction to a Science of Mythology, 1* (*Le Cru et le cuit, Mythologiques,* Librairie Plon 1964), translated by John and Doreen Weightman. New York: Harper and Row, 1964.

———. *The Savage Mind* (*La Pensée sauvage*, Librairie Plon 1962). London: Weidenfeld and Nicholson, 1966.

Lyotard, Jean-François. "Answering the Question: What is Postmodernism?" (1979), translated by Régis Durand. Published as an appendix to *The Postmodern Condition: A Report on Knowledge*, by Jean-François Lyotard (Volume 10 of Theory and History of Literature series), translated by Geoff Bennington and Brian Massumi. Minneapolis: University of Minnesota Press, 1984.

———. *The Postmodern Condition: A Report on Knowledge* (Volume 10 of Theory and History of Literature series), translated by Geoff Bennington and Brian Massumi. Minneapolis: University of Minnesota Press, 1984.

de Man, Paul. *Blindness and Insight: Essays in the Rhetoric of Contemporary Criticism.* 1971. 2d ed. London: Methuen, 1983.

Mander, Raymond, and Joe Mitchenson. *Theatrical Companion to Shaw: A Pictorial Record of the First Performances of the Plays of Bernard Shaw.* Introduction by Barry Jackson. New York: Pitman, 1955.
Marx, Karl. *Capital: A Critique of Political Economy* (*Das Kapital: Kritik der Politischen Ökonomie*, 1867). 3 vols. Reprint of the 1887 English edition, translated from the third German edition by Samuel Moore and Edward Aveling and edited by Frederick Engels. London: Swan Sonnenschein & Co Ltd, 1901.
McDowell, F.P.W. "Heaven, Hell and turn-of-the-century London: Reflections upon Shaw's *Man and Superman.*" *Drama Survey* 2 (1963): 245–68.
McFarlane, James, ed. *The Cambridge Guide to Ibsen.* Cambridge: Cambridge University Press, 1994.
Meisel, Martin. *Shaw and the Nineteenth Century Theater.* Princeton: Princeton University Press, 1963.
Metz, Christian. *The Imaginary Signifier: Psychoanalysis and the Cinema* (*Le signifiant imaginaire, psychanalyse et cinéma*, 1977), translated by Celia Britton, Annwyl Williams, Ben Brewster, and Alfred Guzzetti. Bloomington: Indiana University Press, 1982.
Milton, John. *Paradise Lost.* Illustrated by Gustave Dore. London: Cassell and Company, 1894.
Mitchenson, Joe, and Raymond Mander. *Theatrical Companion to Shaw: A Pictorial Record of the First Performances of the Plays of Bernard Shaw.* Introduction by Barry Jackson. New York: Pitman, 1955.
Molière. *Don Juan* (*Le festin de pierre*, 1665). Oxford: Oxford University Press, 1998.
Morford, Mark P. O., and Robert J. Lenardon. *Classical Mythology.* 1971. 2d ed. New York: Longman, 1977.
Morgan, Margery. *The Shavian Playground.* London: Methuen, 1972.
———. *File On Shaw.* London: Methuen, 1989.
Muller, John P., and William J. Richardson, eds. *The Purloined Poe: Lacan, Derrida, and Psychoanalytic Reading.* Baltimore: Johns Hopkins University Press, 1988.
Nietzsche, Friedrich. *The Birth of Tragedy, Out of the Spirit of Music* (*Die Geburt der Tragödie aus dem Geiste der Musik*) (1872). [Reissued in 1886 as *The Birth of Tragedy, Or: Hellenism and Pessimism* (*Die Geburt der Tragödie, Oder: Griechentum und Pessimismus*).] In *The Birth of Tragedy and The Case against Wagner*, translated with commentary by Walter Kaufmann. New York: Vintage Books, 1967.
———. *Beyond Good and Evil: Prelude to a Philosophy of the Future* (*Jenseits von Gut und Böse: Vorspiel einer Philosophie der Zukunft*, 1886). Translated with commentary by Walter Kaufmann. New York: Vintage Books, 1966.
———. *Thus Spoke Zarathustra: A Book for All and None* (*Also sprach Zarathustra: Ein Buch für Alle und Keinen*, 1883–85), translated by Walter Kaufmann. New York: Viking Press, 1966.
———. *The Case of Wagner* (*Der Fall Wagner*, 1888). In *The Birth of Tragedy and The Case against Wagner*, translated with commentary by Walter Kaufmann. New York: Vintage Books, 1967.

———. *Nietzsche contra Wagner* (1895) in *The Case of Wagner, Nietzsche Contra Wagner, The Twilight of the Idols, The Antichrist.* London: T. Fisher Unwin, 1899.
Nordau, Max. *Degeneration* (*Entartung*, 1893), translated from the second edition of the German. London: William Heinemann, 1895.
Norris, Christopher. *Deconstruction: Theory and Practice.* Rev. ed. London: Routledge, 1996.
———. *Derrida.* Cambridge, Mass.: Harvard University Press, 1987.
O'Donovan, John. *Shaw and the Charlatan Genius: A Memoir.* Dublin: Dolmen, 1965.
Ohmann, Richard M. *Shaw: The Style and the Man.* Middletown, Conn.: Wesleyan University Press, 1962.
Ovid. *Ovid's Metamorphoses. In Fifteen Books.* Translated into English Verse under the direction of Sir Samuel Garth by John Dryden, Alexander Pope, Joseph Addison, William Congreve and Other Eminent Hands (1717). Verona, Italy: Limited Editions Club, 1958.
Panowsky, Erwin. *Meaning in the Visual Arts.* New York: Doubleday, 1955.
Pearson, Hesketh. *G.B.S.: A Full Length Portrait* (English title: *Bernard Shaw: His Life & Personality*). New York: Harpers, 1942.
———. *G.B.S.: A Postscript.* New York: Harpers, 1950.
Peraldi, François. "A Note on Time in *The Purloined Letter*." In *The Purloined Poe: Lacan, Derrida, and Psychoanalytic Reading,* edited by John P. Muller and William J. Richardson. Baltimore: Johns Hopkins University Press, 1988, 335–42.
Peters, Margot. *Bernard Shaw and the Actresses.* New York: Doubleday, 1980.
Peters, Sally. *Bernard Shaw: The Ascent of the Superman.* New Haven: Yale University Press, 1996.
Pharand, Michel W. *Bernard Shaw and the French.* Gainesville: University Press of Florida, 2000.
Plato. *Phaedrus* in *Lysis, or Friendship, the Symposium, Phaedrus,* translated with introductory analysis by Benjamin Jowett. New York: Limited Editions Club, 1968.
———. *Republic,* translated with introduction, analysis, marginal analysis, and index by Benjamin Jowett. 3d ed. Oxford: Clarendon Press, 1888.
———. *Symposium* in *Lysis, or Friendship, the Symposium, Phaedrus,* translated with introductory analysis by Benjamin Jowett. New York: Limited Editions Club, 1968.
———. *Timaeus* in *The Dialogues of Plato, Vol. 3: Philebus Cratylus, Timaeus, Critias,* translated by Benjamin Jowett. London: Sphere Books, 1970.
Poe, Edgar Allan. "The Purloined Letter" (1844). In *The Purloined Poe: Lacan, Derrida, and Psychoanalytic Reading,* edited by John P. Muller and William J. Richardson. Baltimore: Johns Hopkins University Press, 1988, 213–51.
Powell, James N. *Postmodernism for Beginners.* New York: Writers and Readers, 1998.
Raine, Kathleen. *Blake and Tradition.* Princeton: Princeton University Press, 1981.
———. *Blake and Antiquity* (A Shorter Version of *Blake and Tradition*): *The A. W. Mellon Lectures in the Fine Arts, 1962, The National Gallery of Art, Washington, D.C.* London: Routledge, 1979.
Rao, Valli. "Back to Methuselah: a Blakean Interpretation." *SHAW 1* (1981): 141–81.

Reynolds, Jean. "Immodest Proposals: The Performer in Shaw's Prose." Ph.D. diss., University of South Florida, 1988.
———. *Pygmalion's Wordplay: The Postmodern Shaw*. Gainesville: University Press of Florida, 1999.
Richards, I. A. *Practical Criticism*. New York: Harcourt Brace, 1929.
Richardson, William, and John P. Muller. *The Purloined Poe: Lacan, Derrida, and Psychoanalytic Reading*. Baltimore, Md.: Johns Hopkins University Press, 1988.
Ricoeur, Paul. *Hermeneutics and the Human Sciences*, edited and translated by John B. Thompson. Cambridge: Cambridge University Press; Paris: Editions de la Maison des Sciences de l'Homme, 1981.
Riviere, Joan. "Womanliness as Masquerade," *International Journal of Psychoanlysis* 10(1929): 303–13. Reprinted in *Psychoanalysis and Female Sexuality*, edited by Hendrik M. Ruitenbeek. New Haven: College and University Press Services, 1996.
Rosset, Benjamin C. *Shaw of Dublin: The Formative Years*. University Park: Pennsylvania State University Press, 1964.
Ruskin, John. *Modern Painters*. 5 vols. London: Smith, Elder & Co., 1843–1860.
———. *The Stones of Venice*. Illustrated by John Ruskin. London: Smith, Elder & Co. 1851.
———. *Sesame and Lilies*: Two Lectures Delivered at Manchester in 1864; 1. Of kings' Treasuries, 2. Of queens' Gardens. London: Smith, Elder & Co. 1865.
———. *Ruskin On Music*, edited by A. M. Wakefield. Orpington: George Allen, 1894.
Russell, Bertrand. "George Bernard Shaw." *Virginia Quarterly Review* 27 (1951): 2–3.
Sarolea, Charles. "Has Mr. Shaw Understood Joan of Arc?" *English Review* 43 (1926): 175–82.
de Saussure, Ferdinand. *Course in General Linguistics* (*Cours de linguistique générale*, 1915), edited by Charles Bally and Albert Sechehaye in collaboration with Albert Reidlinger, and translated by Wade Baskin. New York: Philosophical Library, 1959.
Schopenhauer, Arthur. *The World as Will and Representation* (*Die Welt als Wille und Vorstellung*, 1819), translated by E.F.J. Payne. New York: Dover Publications, 1958.
Shakespeare, William. *The Two Gentlemen of Verona, The Merchant of Venice, Romeo and Juliet, A Midsummer Night's Dream, Hamlet, Othello*.
Shelley, Percy Bysshe. *Prometheus Unbound*. London: C. and J. Ollier, 1820.
Sheridan, Richard Brinsley. *The Critic Or a Tragedy Rehearsed*. A Dramatic Piece in Three Acts. London: T. Becket, 1781.
Silver, Arnold. *Bernard Shaw: The Darker Side*. Stanford: Stanford University Press, 1982.
Skidelsky, Robert. *John Maynard Keynes: Economist Savior*. Harmondsworth: Penguin Books, 1992.
Smith, Warren Sylvester. *Bishop of Everywhere: Bernard Shaw and the Life Force*. University Park: Pennsylvania State University Press, 1982.
Stanton, Stephen S., ed. *A Casebook on Candida*. New York: Crowell, 1962.
Sturrock, John, ed. *Structuralism and Since: From Lévi-Strauss to Derrida*. Oxford: Oxford University Press, 1979.

Swift, Jonathan. *Gulliver's Travels.* Harmondsworth: Penguin Books, 1967.
Taylor, Thomas. *A Dissertation on the Eleusinian and Bacchic Mysteries.* Amsterdam (London): J. Weitstein, 1790.
Teilhard de Chardin, Pierre. *The Phenomenon of Man (le Phénomène humain).* Introduction by Julian Huxley. London: Collins, 1955.
Tippet, Michael. *Moving into Aquarius.* London: Paladin, 1974.
Tolstoy, Leo. *What is art?,* translated by Aylmer Maude. London: Brotherhood, 1898.
Tompkins, Peter, ed. *To a Young Actress: Letters to Molly Tompkins 1921–1949.* London: Constable, 1960.
———. *Shaw and Molly Tompkins: In Their Own Words.* New York: Clarkson B. Potter, Inc., 1961.
Trebitsch, Siegfried. *Frau Gittas Sühne.* Berlin: Fischer, 1920.
Turco Jr., Alfred, ed. *SHAW 7: The Neglected Plays.* University Park: Pennsylvania State University Press, 1987.
Valency, Maurice J. *The Cart and the Trumpet: the Plays of Bernard Shaw.* New York: Oxford University Press, 1973.
Virgil. *Aeneid,* translated by John Dryden. Introduction By Robert Fitzgerald. New York: Collier/Macmillan, 1965.
———. *The Eclogues of Virgil.* Bilingual edition, translated by David Ferry. New York: Farrar, Straus & Giroux, 2000.
Voltaire. *Candide. The Complete Romances of Voltaire.* New York: Walter J. Black, 1927.
Wagner, Richard. *Opera and Drama (Oper und Drama,* 1852), Vol. 2 of *Richard Wagner's Prose Works,* translated by William Ashton Ellis. London: Kegan Paul, 1893.
———. *Tristan and Isolde (Tristan und Isolde,* 1859), translated by Andrew Porter (Opera Guides in association with English National Opera, Series Editor: Nicholas John). London: Calder, 1981.
Watson, Barbara Bellow. *A Shavian Guide to the Intelligent Woman.* London: Chatto and Windus, 1964.
Weintraub, Stanley, ed. *Saint Joan Fifty Years After, 1923/23–1973/74.* Baton Rouge: Louisiana State University Press, 1973.
———. *Shaw's People: Victoria to Churchill.* University Park: Pennsylvania State University Press, 1996.
Weismann, August. *The Germ-Plasm: A Theory of Heredity,* translated by W. Newton Parker and Harriet Ronnfeldt. London: Walter Scott, 1893.
———. *The Evolution Theory.* 1st English ed., 2 vols., translated by J. Arthur and Margaret Thompson. London: Edward Arnold, 1904.
Wells, H. G. *The Science of Life.* Written with Julian Huxley and G. P. Wells. London: Cassell, 1931.
White, Patrick. "Chaucer: *Franklin's Tale* as analogue for *Candida.*" *SHAW* 12 (1992): 213–28.
Whitman, Robert F. *Shaw and the Play of Ideas.* Ithaca, N.Y.: Cornell University Press, 1977.

Wilson, Colin. *The Outsider*. London: Gollancz, 1956.
Wilson, Richard A. *The Miraculous Birth of Language*. Preface by Bernard Shaw. London: Guild Books, 1941.
Wisenthal, J. L. *The Marriage of Contraries: Bernard Shaw's Middle Plays*. Cambridge, Mass.: Harvard University Press, 1974.
———, ed., with introductory essay. *Shaw and Ibsen: Bernard Shaw's The Quintessence of Ibsenism and Related Writings*. Toronto: University of Toronto Press, 1979.
Wolf, Milton T., ed. *SHAW 17: Shaw and Science Fiction*. University Park: Pennsylvania State University Press, 1997.
Yates, Frances A. *The Occult Philosophy in the Elizabethan Age*. London: Routledge and Kegan Paul, 1979.
Yeats, William Butler. *The Autobiography of William Butler Yeats*. London: Macmillan, 1944.

Index

Adams, Elsie: *Bernard Shaw and the Aesthetes,* 283n21
Albert, Sidney: "Reflections on Shaw and Psychoanalysis," 270n11, 276n19
Althusser, Louis, 4, 5, 18, 33, 44, 54, 57, 100, 112, 276n25; "Ideology and Ideological State Apparatuses," 277n25
Aquinas, Thomas, 101, 102
Archer, Charles, 157
Archer, William, 22, 46, 47, 64, 76, 157, 158, 161, 178, 279n2, 281nn3, 8
Aristophanes, xviii
Aristotle, 9, 66, 101, 113, 116, 136, 143, 166, 179, 181, 186, 254; *Poetics,* 136, 187, 289n21
Arnold, Matthew, xx, 44, 45, 57, 78; *Culture and Anarchy,* 56
Artaud, Antonin, xvi, 164
Augustine (Saint), 102, 262, 269n3, 273n23, 288n6; *De Civitate Dei (City of God),* 260
Aveling, Edward, 157

Bach, Johann Sebastian, 14, 242, 243
Bachofen, Johann Jacob, 209
Bacon, Francis, 32, 265, 270n16
Baker, Stuart: *Bernard Shaw's Remarkable Religion,* 274n1
Barker, Harley Granville, 123, 148, 178, 186, 280; *Madras House,* 173, 177
Barry, Peter: *Beginning Theory,* 181, 182
Barthes, Roland, xiv, 5, 13, 15, 18, 21–23, 31, 37, 39, 45, 48–53, 59, 60, 71, 83, 127, 151, 155, 163, 166, 173, 188, 190, 264; "Death of the Author," 22, 168, 184; *Elements of Semiology,* 21, 283n19; "From Work to Text," 22, 70, 270n6; *Grain of the Voice,* 49, 55, 57; *Image-Music-Text,* 8, 17, 22, 23, 70, 168, 169, 184, 270n6, 284n35; "Introduction to a Structural Analysis of Narratives," 21; *Mythologies,* 21; *Pleasure of the Text,* 14, 22, 40, 48–51, 53, 271n7
Barzun, Jacques: *Darwin, Marx, Wagner,* 274n1
Baughan, Edward A., 178
Bax, Ernest Belfort, 46, 214, 275n13
Beardsley, Aubrey, 174
Beckett, Samuel, xvi, 234
Beethoven, Ludwig van, 47, 77–79, 242; *Creatures of Prometheus* (ballet), 78; *Eroica* (symphony), 78
Bentley, Eric, xx, 8, 9, 26, 77, 270n15, 282n14
Benveniste, Emile, 18, 21
Bergson, Henri, 9, 10, 28, 29, 91, 99–102, 125, 127, 229, 277n28
Bernstein, Jeremy: "Life and Times of Fanny Burney," 282n15
Berkeley, George, 115, 137
Berst, Charles, xix, xx, 142, 270n14; "*The Man of Destiny*: Shaw, Napoleon, and the Theater of Life," 280n8; *Shaw and the Art of Drama,* 287n3
Bertolini, John, xix, xx, 64, 79, 155, 279n3, 282n14; *Playwrighting Self of Bernard Shaw,* 79, 155, 278n30, 286n1, 287n3, 289n22
Black, Martha Fodaski: *Shaw and Joyce: The Last Word in Stolentelling,* xvii, 260, 288n11, 289n24

Blake, William, 39, 72, 87, 107, 196, 197, 228, 238, 257, 262, 269n3, 273n21, 276n22, 285n7, 289n10; *Jerusalem,* 35, 83, 260; *Laocoön,* 289n19
Borges, Jorge Luis, 121, 278n32; "Note for (towards) Bernard Shaw," 273n23
Bosch, Hieronymus, 222
Boswell, James, 23, 71
Botticelli, Sandro, 195
Brandes, Georg, 53
Brecht, Bertolt, xvi, 13, 121, 139, 164, 258
Brentano, Franz, 113, 248
Breughel, Pieter, 222
Brieux, Eugène, 178
Buckingham (George Villers, Duke of): *Rehearsal,* 167, 186
Bunyan, John, 29, 62; *Pilgrim's Progress,* 64
Bürch, Noel: *To the Distant Observer,* xx
Burgess, Anthony: *One Man's Chorus,* 228
Burne-Jones, Edward (Sir), 194
Burney, Charles, 168
Burney, Fanny, 167, 282n15; *Evelina,* 168; *Whitlings,* 168
Burton, Robert: *Anatomy of Melancholy,* 85
Butler, Samuel, 17, 91, 96, 102, 107, 250, 276n20
Byron, George Gordon (Lord), 62, 171, 181, 182; "She Walks in Beauty Like the Night," 207
Byron, Henry James, 182; *Our Boys,* 181

Cannan, Gilbert, 178, 283n26
Carlyle, Thomas, 44, 45; *Sartor Resartus,* 173, 221
Carpenter, Charles, xx, 64, 272; *Bernard Shaw and the Art of Destroying Ideals,* 12
Carpenter, Edward, 17, 281n7
Chamberlain, Houston, 276n17
Chaucer, Geoffrey, 193, 198, 200, 212; *Canterbury Tales,* 192; *Franklin's Tale,* 150, 192, 280n13
Chekhov, Anton, 7, 123, 178
Chesterton, Gilbert Keith, 34, 242, 270n15
Coleridge, Samuel Taylor, 228
Conrad, Joseph, xvi
Corneille, Pierre, 142, 269n3

Corneille, Thomas, 269n3
Crébillon, Prosper, 120; *Atrée et Thyeste,* 118
Crompton, Louis, xx, 202, 285n11

Dante Alighieri, 41, 88, 194; *Divina Commedia (Divine Comedy),* 152, 229, 260
Darwin, Charles, 17, 29, 94–96, 102, 196, 234, 250, 274nn8–9, 275n11, 287n4; *On the Origin of Species,* 91, 131, 230, 260
Darwin, Erasmus, 95, 196; *Botanic Garden,* 196
Derrida, Jacques, xiv, xv, 4–6, 11, 13, 15, 16, 18, 19, 21–33, 35, 39, 50, 57, 60, 81, 91–93, 102, 103, 108, 111, 122–30, 136, 137, 143, 151, 154, 155, 187, 226, 233–35, 237, 240, 243, 251, 253, 262, 264–66, 270n8, 275n15, 279nn36–38, 289n20; "Force and Signification," 28; "Freud and the Stage of Writing," 92, 93, 124, 125, 274n4; "Postman of Truth," 92, 93, 116, 120, 122, 274n4; "Structure, Sign, and Play," 30; *Margins of Philosophy,* 289n1; *Of Grammatology,* 99, 129, 133, 261, 265, 278n34, 279n6, 282n17, 289n25; *Positions,* 271n2 (chap. 3), 278n34, 279n1; *Speech and Phenomena,* 28, 128; *Writing and Difference,* 26–31, 120, 124–29, 271n6
Descartes, René, xv, 92, 93, 99, 100, 113, 114, 115, 127, 137, 185, 253
Dickens, Charles, 39, 62, 64, 136
Dietrich, Richard, xix, xx, 57, 64, 78, 79, 272n7, 285n8; "Deconstruction as Devil's Advocacy: a Shavian Alternative," 269n1
Dukore, Bernard: *Shaw's Theater,* 178, 279n3
Dürer, Albrecht: *Melencolia,* 84, 85, 273n22; *Saint Jerome,* 85

Egan, Michael: Introduction to *Ibsen: The Critical Heritage,* 280n2
Eliot, George (Marian Evans Cross), 39, 63
Eliot, T. S., 123, 138, 156, 193, 212, 257; "Shaw, Robertson, and the Maid," 279n5
Ellis, Havelock, 17; *Man and Woman,* 9; *Studies in the Psychology of Sex,* 9, 104
Engels, Frederick, 270n16
Epstein, Jacob (Sir), 73

Eriugena, Johannes Scotus, 262, 269n3, 273n23; *De Divisione Naturae* (*On the Division of Nature*), 274n23
Ervine, St. John, 69, 271n3, 288n6
Eschenbach, Wolfram von: *Parzifal,* 193
Euripides, 104, 123

Fabricant, Carole: *Swift's Landscape,* xx
Farleigh, John, 62, 287n2
Fichte, Johann Gottlieb, 113
Fisher, Barbara: "*Fanny's First Play*: A Critical Potboiler," 284n30
Fiske, Irving: "Bernard Shaw and William Blake," 289n19
Forrester, John: *Seductions of Psychoanalysis,* 113, 277nn26,29, 278n31, 280n9, 285n12
Foucault, Michel, 15, 18, 44
Frazer, James (Sir), 196; *Golden Bough,* 192, 198, 209, 282n10
Freud, Sigmund, xv, 12, 15–17, 20, 53, 57, 96, 99, 102–8, 110–19, 123–29, 131, 271n8, 274n4, 276nn17–19, 276n21, 277n29, 278n36, 285n12; "Note upon the 'Mystic Writing-Pad,'" 92, 124, 126, 127; "Two Principles of Mental Functioning," 92, 103, 104; *Beyond the Pleasure Principle,* xv, 92, 93, 102–7, 110, 111, 116, 124, 128, 276n24, 277n28, 279n36; *Interpretation of Dreams,* 19, 104, 106, 124; *Project for a Scientific Psychology,* 92
Frye, Northrop: *Great Code,* 229, 230

Gahan, Peter: "*Back to Methuselah*: An Exercise of Imagination," 286n1; "Ruskin and *Fanny's First Play,*" 282n13
Gallop, Jane: "American Other," 278n35
Galsworthy, John, xvi, 178
Galton, Francis, 95, 194
Geduld, Harry, 287n1
Genette, Gérard, 18
Gilbert, W. S., 74, 79, 104, 181
Giotto, 29
Godard, Jean-Luc, 139, 279n6
Goethe, Johann Wolfgang von, 7, 9, 39, 41, 66, 71, 78, 242, 243; *Faust,* 10, 260
Goldsmith, Oliver, 123

Gould, Stephen Jay, 275n9
Gounod, Charles: *Faust* (opera), 10
Graves, Robert, 209
Green, Paul: *Dramatic Heritage,* 264
Gregory, Augusta (Lady): *Gods and Fighting Men,* 288n11

Hamann, Brigitte: *Hitler's Vienna,* 276n17
Hamon, Augustin, 29, 282n13, 286n18
Händel, Georg Friedrich, 29
Hankin, St. John (Edward Charles), 178
Hardy, Thomas, xvi
Harris, Frank, xvii, 23, 47, 61, 69, 70, 72, 73, 77, 271n3, 272nn13–14; *Bernard Shaw,* 272n4
Hartman, Geoffrey, 287n6
Hauptmann, Gerhart, 178
Hegel, Georg W. F., xvii, 7, 30, 101, 108, 119, 166, 234, 249, 252, 253, 260–62, 270n16, 275n13, 278n31; *Phenomenology of Mind,* 107, 260
Heidegger, Martin, 29, 100, 101, 108, 124, 129, 162, 265; *Being and Time,* xv
Helmholtz, Hermann von, 40
Henderson, Archibald, 68, 69, 72, 216, 271n3; *Man of the Century,* 23
Hesse, Hermann: *Glass-Bead Game,* 191
Hofmannsthal, Hugo von, 104, 271n8
Hogarth, William, 39, 62, 218
Holbein, Hans, 195
Holroyd, Michael, xix, 66, 69, 271n3
Homer, 147, 152; *Hymn to Demeter,* 210
Hooper, Judith: *Of Moths and Men,* 98
Hume, David, 115
Husserl, Edmund, 99, 100, 101, 113, 126, 185, 248
Huxley, Julian (Sir), 275n11
Huxley, T. E., 275n11

Ibsen, Henrik, 22, 41, 46–48, 54–56, 79, 90, 123, 157–59, 164–166, 178, 243, 271n5, 280n2, 282n12; *Brand,* 281n3; *Doll's House,* 157, 158, 192, 205, 208; *Ghosts,* 48, 54, 56, 158, 162, 179; *Hedda Gabler,* 158; *Peer Gynt,* 281n3; *Rosmersholm,* 158, 160, 203, 281n4

Jakobson, Roman, 18, 20, 151
Jenkins, Stephen: *Fritz Lang: The Image and the Look*, xiii
Joad, C.E.M.: *Matter, Life and Value*, 269n1
John, Augustus, 72
Johnson, Barbara, 122; "Frame of Reference," 278n34
Johnson, Samuel, 23, 71, 168
Jones, Ernest, 104, 105, 123, 162, 194, 277n28
Jones, Henry Arthur, 191
Joyce, James, xvi, xvii, 85, 138; *Exiles*, 273n20, 283n23; *Finnegans Wake*, 260, 263, 288n11, 289n24; *Portrait of the Artist as a Young Man*, 273n20, 283n23; *Ulysses*, 86, 260, 273n20, 283n23, 289n23

Kant, Immanuel, xiv, 4, 9, 100, 101, 112, 126, 137, 171, 176, 232, 240, 250, 251, 265, 278n36, 279n37; *Critique of Judgment*, 242
Kaye, J. B.: *Bernard Shaw and the Nineteenth Century*, 289n19
Kearney, Richard, xx; *Dialogues with Contemporary Continental Thinkers*, 185, 270n8, 279n38
Keats, John, xvii, 61; *Grecian Urn*, 196
Keynes, Maynard, 274n5
Kipling, Rudyard, xvi
Koestler, Arthur: *Case of the Midwife Toad*, 98
Kristeva, Julia, 21, 71, 270n13
Kubrick, Stanley: *2001: A Space Odyssey*, 263; *Eyes Wide Shut*, 194
Kuhn, Thomas: *Structure of Scientific Revolutions*, 275n15

Lacan, Jacques, xiv, xv, xvi, xvii, 4, 5, 13, 15, 18–21, 31–34, 36, 54–57, 61, 68, 71, 91–93, 99, 102, 103, 107–24, 127, 136, 140, 144, 150, 154, 184, 221, 232, 236–39, 242, 248, 250–54, 257, 264, 270n12, 271n9, 275n15, 277n26, 278nn31,34, 283n24, 288n9; "Function and Field of Speech and Language in Psychoanalysis," 115, 116; "Seminar on 'The Purloined Letter,'" 92, 116–23, 147; *Écrits*, 115, 117; *Four Fundamental Concepts of Psychoanalysis*, 143, 278n33, 288n14; *Seminar I*, 113; *Seminar II*, 1, 37, 92, 96, 107, 111, 112, 116, 120, 124, 251, 265, 276n16, 278n30
Lamarck, Jean-Baptiste, 9, 91, 96, 107, 275n9
La Rochefoucauld, François, 11
Laurence, Dan H., xix, xx, 84, 269n2; *Shaw: An Exhibit*, 225, 271n4, 282n12, 283n25
Lawrence, T. E., 273n22
Leary, Daniel: "*Too True to be Good* and Shaw's Romantic Synthesis: A Religion for Our Times," 287n1
Leavis, F. R., 181
Leibniz, Gottfried, 33
Leonardo da Vinci, 4
Lessing, Gotthold Ephraim, 172
Lever, Charles, 62
Lévi-Strauss, Claude, 14, 18, 19, 21, 31, 57, 119, 138, 150, 151, 270n6, 278n31; "Introduction to the Work of Marcel Mauss," 30; *Savage Mind*, 283n24
Liszt, Franz, 47
Locke, John, 32, 265, 270n16
Lyell, Charles (Sir), 94, 109, 234
Lyotard, Jean-François, 44; "What is Postmodernism?" 15

Malthus, Thomas, 94
Man, Paul de: *Blindness and Insight*, 279n3
Mander, Raymond, and Joe Mitchenson: *Theatrical Companion*, 282n13, 283n27
Marx, Karl, 15, 17, 57, 77, 94, 100, 158, 265, 270n16; *Das Kapital*, 16, 157, 200
McDowell, F.P.W.: "Heaven, Hell and turn-of-the-century London," 269n2
Meisel, Martin, xx, 279n3, 282n14; *Shaw and the Nineteenth-Century Theatre*, 286n1
Metz, Christian, 243; *Imaginary Signifier*, xx, 288n9
Michelangelo Buonaroti, 44, 62, 63, 79, 242, 243
Mill, J. S., 159, 203
Milton, John, xix, 262, 269n3; *Paradise Lost*, 257, 260
Molière (Jean-Baptiste Poquelin), 123; *Le Festin de Pierre*, 10
Morford, Mark, and Richard Lenardon, 217; *Classical Mythology*, 210

Morgan, Margery, xix, xx, 194, 203, 212, 269n2, 282n14; *Shavian Playground,* xx, 25, 177, 269n2, 283n20, 284n29, 284nn2–3, 286n19, 286n1

Morris, William, 52, 192, 194, 195, 285n8

Mozart, Wolfgang Amadeus, 14, 80, 167, 176; *Die Zauberflöte,* 173; *Don Giovanni* (da Ponte), 10, 11, 78, 173

Muller, John, and William Richardson, eds.: *Purloined Poe,* 116, 147, 278nn30,38

Murray, Gilbert, 104, 178

Newton, Isaac (Sir), 107, 119, 127, 137

Nietzsche, Friedrich, xv, 9, 15–17, 22, 48, 91, 92, 101, 108, 202, 203, 254, 265; *Also sprach Zarathustra,* 10, 260, 278n32; *Beyond Good and Evil,* 270n10; *Birth of Tragedy,* 16, 78, 198, 199, 217

Nordau, Max, 53, 57, 271n8; *Degeneration,* 51, 54, 194

Novik, Julius, 160

O'Bolger, Demetrius, 69

O'Casey, Sean, 123

O'Donovan, John, xix, 65, 223; *Shaw and the Charlatan Genius,* 272nn10,12, 286n21

Ohmann, Richard: *Shaw: The Style and the Man,* 269n1

Oken, Lorenz, 99

Ovid, 194, 253, 256, 257

Panowsky, Erwin: *Meaning in the Visual Arts,* 289n16

Pater, Walter, 138, 174, 209

Pavlov, Ivan, 102, 288n7

Pearson, Hesketh, 68, 271n3

Peraldi, François: "Note on Time in 'The Purloined Letter,'" 278n34

Peters, Margot, xx, 271n3

Peters, Sally, xix, xx, 64, 78, 79, 272n3; *Ascent of the Superman,* 65

Pharand, Michel: *Bernard Shaw and the French,* 279n2

Phidias, 242

Picasso, Pablo, 138

Pinero, Arthur (Sir), 123, 162, 186, 283n26

Pirandello, Luigi, 123

Plato, xv, 3–6, 9, 23, 24, 71, 98, 101, 107, 115, 129, 180, 196, 210, 237, 250, 257, 260–62, 265, 273n21; *Phaedrus,* 130; *Republic,* 3, 112, 130, 243, 260, 262; *Symposium,* 130, 242, 243, 262, 277n28; *Timaeus,* 223

Plotinus, 196, 262, 269n3, 273n21

Poe, Edgar Allan, 140, 143; "Purloined Letter," 92, 93, 116–23, 136, 147, 148

Porphyry, 269n3, 273n21

Pound, Ezra, 138, 257, 283n23

Poussin, Nicolas, 289n16

Proust, Marcel, 44

Rao, Valli: "*Back to Methuselah*—a Blakean Interpretation," 286n1

Raphael (Raffaelo Sanzio), 195

Rembrandt van Rijn: *Anatomy Lesson of Dr. Nicolaes Tulp,* 50, 164

Reynolds, Jean, xix, 271n1; *Pygmalion's Wordplay,* 269n1, 270n17

Ribera, José de: "Dead Christ," 283n23

Ricardo, David, 94

Richards, I. A., 182, 284; *Practical Criticism,* 181, 284n21

Ricoeur, Paul, 15, 18, 31, 170, 184, 185; *Hermeneutics and the Human Sciences,* 284n31

Riviere, Joan: "Womanliness as a Masquerade," 271n9

Rodin, Auguste, 73, 242

Rosset, Benjamin, 65, 223, 271n3; *Shaw of Dublin,* 272n13, 286n18, 286n21

Rossetti, Dante Gabriel, 194, 195

Rousseau, Jean-Jacques, xviii, 255, 261, 289n25

Ruskin, John, 40, 44, 45, 87, 157, 170–77, 179, 180, 194, 283n22; *Modern Painters,* 167, 200; *On Music,* 172; *Sesame and Lilies,* 173, *Stones of Venice,* 167, 171–76

Russell, Bertrand, 12, 81, 151

Salt, Henry, 280

Sardou, Victorien, 136, 139–141, 143, 160, 280; *Fedora,* 140; *Madame Sans-Gêne,* 139

Sarolea, Charles: "Has Mr. Shaw Understood," 23

Sartre, Jean Paul, 55
Saussure, Ferdinand de, 19, 113, 151, 170, 254; *Cours de Linguistique Générale,* 18, 180
Schnitzler, Arthur, 104
Schopenhauer, Arthur, 9, 17, 39, 55, 76, 91, 98, 99, 101, 106, 107, 115
Scott, Clement, 54, 56, 57, 157–59, 161, 179, 280, 281
Scott, Walter, 62, 74, 137
Scribe, Eugène (Augustin), 136, 160
Shakespeare, William, 6, 36, 37, 42, 51, 62, 64, 67, 70, 121, 123, 153, 177, 180, 184, 186, 222, 270, 271n2; *Hamlet,* 41, 86, 105, 162; *Merchant of Venice,* 207; *Othello,* 105, 148; *Two Gentlemen of Verona,* 281n7
Shaw, Bernard: "Author's Apology" (preface to *Dramatic Opinions*), 37; "Degenerate's View of Nordau" (*Sanity of Art*), 38, 44, 51, 53, 194, 289n20; "Dramatic Realist to His Critics," 266; "Economic Basis of Socialism," 155; "How to Become a Man of Genius," 10, 66, 125, 271; "Illusions of Socialism," 9, 124; "On Parents and Children" (preface to *Misalliance*), 236; "Religion of the Pianoforte," 38, 47, 48, 51, 52, 166; *Androcles and the Lion,* 85; *Arms and the Man,* 47, 67, 280n10, 281n4, 284n1; *Back to Methuselah,* xiv, xv, xvi, xxi, 5, 8, 11, 19, 26, 31, 44, 60, 68, 84, 91, 92, 95, 98, 102–4, 106–10, 113, 124, 128, 130, 131, 223, 228–36, 242, 247, 251, 255–63, 269n2, 270n5, 275n14, 286n1, 289n19; *Infidel Half Century,* xv, 91–103, 106, 107, 110, 129, 135, 229, 230, 274n7, 275n10, 276n22; *In the Beginning* (Part I), 31, 91, 92, 108, 109, 115, 128–30, 228, 231, 233, 234, 237, 238, 242, 254, 257, 259, 288n11; *Gospel of the Brothers Barnabas* (Part II), 84, 85, 108, 109, 130, 230, 231, 233, 235–37, 239, 242, 243, 245, 255, 258, 259; *Domesticity of Franklyn Barnabas* (draft for Part II), 242, 277n28; *The Thing Happens* (Part III), 131, 233, 236, 243, 245, 247, 252, 254; *Tragedy of an Elderly Gentleman* (Part IV), 5, 19, 35, 44, 114, 237, 241, 244, 245, 248, 249, 252, 259, 260, 288n11; *As Far As Thought Can Reach* (Part V), 24, 107, 110, 113, 114, 130, 131, 233, 235, 243, 246, 247, 249–57, 261, 262, 273n21; "Postscript: After Twenty-five Years," 8, 102, 106, 113, 247, 274n7, 287n2; *Black Girl in Search of God,* 8, 11, 62, 99, 101, 169; *Candida,* xvi, 82, 148, 149, 150, 158, 166, 189–214, 217, 218, 222, 225–27, 243, 280nn12–13, 281n4, 284nn2–3, 285n4; *Captain Brassbound's Conversion,* 80; *Cymbeline Refinished,* 42; *Dark Lady of the Sonnets,* 42; *Devil's Disciple,* 80, 116, 278; dialogue on truth (in preface to *On the Rocks*), 8, 24, 25; *Doctor's Dilemma,* 60, 116, 213, 278n30; *Dramatic Opinions,* 37; *Fabian Essays* (ed.), 46, 155; *Fanny's First Play,* xvi, 43, 45, 142, 157, 161, 166–88, 259, 279n2, 281n6, 282n13, 16, 283n19, 21, 284n32; *Farfetched Fables,* 24; *Getting Married,* xvi, 14, 128, 173, 189, 190, 192, 193, 197, 201, 213–27, 281n7, 286n18; *Great Catherine,* 13; *Heartbreak House,* xx, 7, 23, 84, 222, 241, 258, 259, 262, 266; *How He Lied to Her Husband,* xv, 139, 147–53, 189, 192, 201, 280; *Immaturity,* 64, 68, 82, 89, 90; *In Good King Charles's Golden Days,* 280n14; *Irrational Knot,* 20; *Jitta's Atonement* (Trebitsch), 104, 276n18; *John Bull's Other Island,* xv, 8, 44, 76, 83–85, 87, 189, 213, 245, 273n19, 21, 280n11; *London Music in 1888–90,* 288n7; *Love Among the Artists,* 47, 79, 80; *Major Barbara,* 16, 17, 76, 79–81, 83, 84, 128, 213, 269n2, 270n10, 280n11; *Man and Superman,* xiv, xv, 8–11, 15, 23, 25, 27, 44, 50, 51, 60, 76, 80, 83, 86, 100, 103, 106, 148, 155, 159, 210, 213, 269n2, 270n14, 272n16, 280n12; "Epistle Dedicatory," 9, 10, 17, 29, 35, 39, 52, 106, 111, 161, 174, 179, 266, 279n2; *Don Juan in Hell,* 10, 11, 27, 197, 273n21; *Revolutionist's Handbook and Pocket Companion* by John Tanner, M.I.R.C., 11, 35, 107, 235; "Maxims for Revolutionists," 11; *Man of Destiny,* xv, 67, 80, 117, 139–49, 153, 171, 254, 280n8; *Misalliance,* 173, 213, 214, 236, 241, 286n23; *Mrs Warren's Profession,* 13, 17,

210, 211; *My Dear Dorothea*, 63, 272n6; *O'Flaherty V. C.*, 123; *On the Prospects of Christianity* (preface to *Androcles and the Lion*), 35, 99, 100, 112, 230, 233, 241, 245, 285n13, 287n4; *On the Rocks*, 8, 24, 36, 222; *Passion Play*, 63, 272n6; *Pen Portraits and Reviews*, 34, 59, 116, 120, 121; *Perfect Wagnerite*, 16, 41, 77–79, 175, 200, 234, 263; *Philanderer*, xvi, 13, 17, 41, 43, 50, 54, 57, 80, 84, 145, 157–66, 178, 179, 194, 256, 281n8, 282nn11–12; *Platform and Pulpit*, 275, 283n20; *Plays Pleasant and Unpleasant*, 13, 40, 75, 76, 141, 149, 164, 192, 195, 212, 281n4, 285n14; preface to *Ellen Terry and Bernard Shaw: A Correspondence*, 68, 272n5; preface to *The Miraculous Birth of Language* by R. A. Wilson, 8, 63, 99, 124, 127, 274n3; *Press Cuttings*, 138; *Pygmalion*, 177, 189, 194, 223, 231, 235, 243, 249, 253, 257; *Quintessence of Ibsenism*, 16, 21, 22, 38, 41, 47, 54, 57, 78, 79, 138, 157, 158, 159, 165, 166, 203, 270–71n10, 275n12, 280n2, 281n3; *Saint Joan*, 7, 23, 82, 152, 258, 287n3; *Shakes Vs Shav*, 42; *Short Stories, Scraps, and Shavings*, 277n28; *Simpleton of the Unexpected Isles*, 152, 258; *Six of Calais*, 123; *Sixteen Self Sketches*, 65, 68, 105; *Three Plays for Puritans*, 21, 41, 81, 179; *Too True to be Good*, 25, 26, 130, 258, 287n1; *Unsocial Socialist*, 16, 39, 46, 80; *Village Wooing*, xv, 117, 135, 139, 143, 151, 152, 154, 167, 221; *Widowers' Houses*, 13, 17, 45–48, 54, 158, 179, 281n5, 282n9; *You Never Can Tell*, 80, 178, 180, 222

Shelley, Percy Bysshe, 62, 63, 77–79, 171, 262, 269; *Prometheus Unbound*, 77, 79, 260

Sheridan, Richard Brinsley, 123, 168; *Critic*, 167

Silver, Arnold: *Bernard Shaw: The Darker Side*, 289n18

Smith, Warren Sylvester: *Bishop of Everywhere*, 275n11

Snow, C. P., 102

Sobieniowski, Floryan, 282n12

Socrates, xviii, 23, 71

Spencer, Herbert, 96

Spinoza, Baruch, 7

Spivak, Gayatri, 99; "Translator's Preface" to *Of Grammatology*, 282n17

Stanford, Charles Villiers, 43

Strauss, Richard: *Elektra* (von Hofmannsthal), 271n8

Strindberg, August, 123, 178

Sudermann, Hermann, 178

Sullivan, Arthur (Sir), 181; *Ivanhoe*, 74, 75

Swift, Jonathan, xx, 67, 87, 238, 256; *Gulliver's Travels*, 137, 241, 248, 260

Swinburne, Algernon, 194, 209

Taylor, Harriet, 159

Taylor, Thomas, 273n21; *On The Eleusinian and Bacchic Mysteries*, 196

Teilhard de Chardin, Pierre: *The Phenomenon of Man*, 275n11

Tennyson, Alfred (Lord), 209

Tippet, Michael: *Moving into Aquarius*, 287n2

Titian (Tiziano Vecellio), 72; *Assumption*, 195, 197

Tolstoy, Leo, 123, 178; *What is Art?*, 52

Tompkins, Peter: *Shaw and Molly Tompkins*, 272n8

Trebitsch, Siegfried, 132, 170, 193, 240, 276n17, 282n16, 286n18; *Frau Gittas Sühne*, 104

Turner, William, 39, 62, 171

Vasari, Giorgio, 44, 62

Velasquez, Diego de Silva y, 72

Virgil, 145, 257; *Aeneid*, 145, 280n10; *Eclogues*, 256

Voltaire (François-Marie Arouet), xviii, 7, 13, 55, 194, 270n15

Wagner, Richard, 14, 17, 39, 41, 47, 79, 171, 172, 191, 199–209, 212, 259; *Der Ring des Nibelungen*, 42, 77, 199–201, 234, 260, 263; *Die Walküre*, 175, 201; *Siegfried*, 78, 109, 201, 276n23; *Opera as Drama*, 192, 199, 200; *Parsifal*, 149, 193, 199–208, 280n13; *Tristan und Isolde*, 199, 201, 202, 206, 207, 208

Walkley, Arthur Bingham, 11, 136, 161, 179, 279n2, 281n6

Wallace, Alfred Russel, 95, 287n4
Watteau, Antoine, 141, 142, 289n16
Weintraub, Stanley, xx, 279n5, 285n10; *Shaw's People*, 272n14, 273n20, 283n23
Weismann, August, 91, 97, 102, 106–8, 274n9; *Evolution Theory*, 275n10; *Germ-Plasm: A Theory of Heredity*, 275n10
Wells, H. G., xvi, xvii, 35, 60, 260, 275n11, 288n10
Whistler, James McNeil, 172, 174, 176, 283n23
White, Patrick: "Chaucer: *Franklin's Tale* as analogue for *Candida*," 280n13
Whitehead, Alfred North, 100, 101, 151
Wilde, Oscar, 23, 123, 174, 283n23
Williams, Simon: "Ibsen and the Theatre 1877–1900," 280n2

Wilson, Colin: *The Outsider*, xix
Wilson, Edwin, 271n2
Wilson, Richard, 8; *Miraculous Birth of Language*, 240
Wisenthal, Jonathan, xx; *Marriage of Contraries*, 287n3; *Shaw and Ibsen*, 26, 271n5, 272n18, 280n2, 281n3
Wittgenstein, Ludwig, 151
Wollstonecraft, Mary, 159

Yates, Frances: *Occult Philosophy in the Elizabethan Age*, 85
Yeats, William Butler, 60, 138, 190, 254, 257, 273n19, 285n8, 288n6; "Trembling of the Veil," 284n1

Zola, Emile, 138, 161

Peter Gahan, a philosophy graduate from Trinity College, Dublin, has written several articles and reviews on Shaw, which were published in *SHAW: The Annual of Bernard Shaw Studies* by Pennsylvania State University Press. He lives in Los Angeles and works in the film industry.

The Florida Bernard Shaw Series
This series was made possible by a generous grant from the David and Rachel Howie Foundation.
Edited by R. F. Dietrich

Pygmalion's Wordplay: The Postmodern Shaw, by Jean Reynolds (1999)
Shaw's Theater, by Bernard F. Dukore (2000)
Bernard Shaw and the French, by Michel W. Pharand (2001)
The Matter with Ireland, second edition, edited by Dan H. Laurence and David H. Greene (2001)
Bernard Shaw's Remarkable Religion: A Faith That Fits the Facts, by Stuart E. Baker (2002)
Bernard Shaw's The Black Girl in Search of God: *The Story Behind the Story*, by Leon Hugo (2003)
Shaw Shadows: Rereading the Texts of Bernard Shaw, by Peter Gahan (2004)